THE SCOTTISH QUESTION

The Scottish Question

JAMES MITCHELL

OXFORD

UNIVERSITY PRESS

Great Clarendon Street, Oxford, OX2 6DP,
United Kingdom

Oxford University Press is a department of the University of Oxford.
It furthers the University's objective of excellence in research, scholarship,
and education by publishing worldwide. Oxford is a registered trade mark of
Oxford University Press in the UK and in certain other countries

First Edition published in 2014
Impression: 1

Published in the United States of America by Oxford University Press
198 Madison Avenue, New York, NY 10016, United States of America

British Library Cataloguing in Publication Data
Data available

Library of Congress Control Number: 2014933776

ISBN 978–0–19–968865–4

Printed and bound by
CPI Group (UK) Ltd, Croydon, CR0 4YY

Preface

This book began life as a short background to the 2014 Scottish independence referendum. But over time, it grew in size and ambition, aided by the award of an ESRC Fellowship and work completed for the Society of Local Authority Chief Executives (SOLACE) in Scotland. The former allowed me to spend more time in the archives and complete new research but mostly to revisit earlier work that I had completed over the last three decades. The latter work involved an examination of the background to the current system of local government and institutional arrangements across a wide range of public bodies.

I am very grateful to both the ESRC and SOLACE for supporting this work. I am also grateful to many colleagues who have commented on earlier drafts of chapters, answered questions, and pointed me towards where I might find answers. These include: Richard Finlay, Colin Kidd, Bob Purdie, Alan Riach, Paula Somerville, and John Young. Many others have in different ways contributed to my better understanding of the matters discussed through their published work and often conversations on matters discussed in this book. I would heartily thank all of the following for their assistance at some stage over many years in the production of this book: Lynn Bennie, Christopher Harvie, Gerry Hassan, David Heald, Rob Johns, David Judge, Michael Keating, Neil McGarvey, Iain McLean, Colin Mair, Brendan O'Hara, Richard Rose, and Cliff Williamson.

I am very grateful to Jo North for her meticulous and prompt editing of the submitted draft and to Oxford University Press for encouragement and support.

Finally, I must thank my family—Laura, Euan, and Kirsty—who have become accustomed to my absence, whether in my study at home often working late into the night or away in archives and elsewhere engaged in understanding the various facets of the Scottish Question. Laura remains by far the most important intellectual influence on my work, offering incisive criticism, identifying weaknesses, and suggesting themes and frameworks I would not otherwise have been aware of. Euan and Kirsty have grown up with parents discussing the Scottish Question amongst many other matters and are now increasingly keen to offer their own fresh perspectives on these old issues. While this and future generations will almost certainly have to grapple with the issues discussed in these pages, the backdrop and specific forms this ever mutating question will pose to be addressed is far from certain. This book is for them.

JM

Contents

1

Introduction: The Scottish Question

INTRODUCTION

In the conclusion to a book published over half a century ago, J. M. Reid, a leading Scottish journalist, suggested that Scotland was 'very unusual'—'a country which is, at least in some sense, a nation, but in no sense a State. Can anything so anomalous continue to exist in this modern world?' Reid had raised an important question. Could a Scottish nation continue to exist in an established state in which people felt an almost unquestioned loyalty to that state? This was a period when there was considerable scholarly work on 'nation-building', constructing identification with and uniting previously disparate communities, in newly independent states. These states had emerged from the process of decolonization and it was widely recognized that there was an absence of identification by the citizens with the new states. Nation-building was assumed to have been achieved in long-established, and some not so long-established, states. There was an unstated assumption that established states were homogeneous, even uniform, in their citizens' and decision-makers' political behaviour. When diversity was acknowledged, it was seen as peripheral in every sense. Reid's comments reflected the common frustration of those committed to maintaining Scottish culture and identity at this time. His concerns were mirrored, but less sympathetically, in the scholarly community where local cultures and identities were viewed as antediluvian throwbacks in advanced liberal democracies standing in the way of progress.

The United Kingdom was commonly thought to have dealt with such problems with the resolution of the Irish Question. Successive UK governments were aware of Scotland's 'anomalous' position though this was rarely a matter of any consequence. Scotland was a special case, occasionally a minor irritant in requiring special attention but in no sense a threat to the integrity of the state. There had been brief moments when the Scottish dimension, for lack of a better term, proved troublesome but it never reached the salience or persistence that the Irish Question achieved in the nineteenth and early twentieth centuries. Scotland's position within the union was largely a matter that concerned Scots, hardly impinging on people living in other parts of the UK or even, for the most part, those in power. If there was awareness that Scotland's position was 'anomalous' then it was accepted if barely understood. If there was a Scottish Question, then it had been answered.

A dramatic change occurred within a decade of the publication of Reid's book. What had appeared to be a problem in new states seemed to afflict a number of well-established states. The assertion of identity and demands for autonomy now came to be seen as more than an irritant. If any events brought about this change then it was the election of a Welsh Nationalist to Parliament in 1966 and then a Scottish Nationalist the following year. The heightened awareness of Scottish, and Welsh, dimensions following years of assuming that the state was one and indivisible led to exaggerated fears and reactions. As would become common over the following half century, interpretations of the threat to the state's integrity would wax and wane with each rise and fall in demands for more autonomy. Sober assessments of the complex relationship between Scottish national identity, everyday politics, and Scotland's constitutional status were often lost in interpretations reflecting the 'Manichean nationalism', in Colin Kidd's terms, of elements in both Scottish and British nationalisms.

The historiography of Scottish nationalism has tended to view the past through the prism of the latest political development as if the current strength in support for independence or the Scottish National Party (SNP) was the latest development in an ineluctable and inevitable process. Even when this is avoided, the focus on the 'national movement' has obscured the wider context. There was nothing inevitable about the establishment of the Scottish Parliament but equally there is nothing inevitable about the integrity of the UK. Debate today needs to be set in historical context taking account of political, social, and economic developments. Most of all, it requires an appreciation of what is referred in this book to as the 'Scottish Question' and how this has changed over time. In *When was Wales?*, the Welsh historian Gwyn Williams posed a question that is as relevant, but rarely asked, about Scotland in the modern era. The questions arising from the history of Wales—that is, whether, the extent, and the manner, in which Wales existed as a recognized entity and by whom—can be asked about Scotland. Welsh history was more turbulent and may have been less certain and more dislocated than the history of Scotland. But the nature of what was distinctly Scottish has been equally uncertain, changing, and difficult to predict.

It can be no coincidence that the rise of political nationalism in Scotland in the 1960s happened around the same time as similar developments elsewhere. A sense of Scottish identity was not new but how it was articulated changed. Anthony Smith has described national identity as chameleon-like, taking its colour from its context and capable of endless manipulation only to be understood in each specific instance. And each specific instance should not be read as each specific nationalism because each specific nationalism changes according to its context. Manipulation may be too strong a term as each specific instance at each specific point in time will be affected by conscious effort but also, and this has been most evident in twentieth-century Scotland, by other factors. Major processes of change familiar to students of politics, society, and the economy have affected Scotland's position in the UK and perceptions thereof. Understanding nationalism requires first an appreciation of context and then how nationalists respond to this context.

Interest in what was happening and had been going on below the level of the state (or the metropolitan centre, which was and is still often confused with the state-level) increased whenever peripheries asserted themselves. The idea that the UK was one and indivisible was challenged in the 1960s, but more importantly there was greater understanding of life beyond the centre and that the lives of citizens could not be understood by a focus on the study of the political centre, the contemporary social science equivalent of studying the Great Men of History. This was a development acknowledged well beyond the UK. Robert Dahl, a leading democratic theorist, acknowledged that it was remiss to ignore subordinate levels of government and social organizations in considering processes of democratization. Appreciation of politics beyond the centre grew but it was a partial awakening and commentators tended to fall asleep as soon as the perceived threat receded only to be rudely awakened at each revival of peripheral assertion. Our capacity to be blinded by the highs and lows of politics and to ignore the living, vital everyday is astounding. A focus on punctuations at the expense of the general narrative is a mistake. But punctuations are important if only in highlighting, if exaggerating, a development.

WHAT IS THE SCOTTISH QUESTION?

In the nineteenth century, there was a tendency to describe complex and seemingly intractable problems as 'Questions'. Hence, there were the Irish Question, the Schleswig-Holstein Question, and the Eastern Question. The Irish Question was an amalgam of nationalism, religion, and constitutional and everyday public policy concerns. Dealing successfully with this mix required sensitivity that was all too often absent. Potent myths and misunderstandings were thrown into the mix leaving an impression that the Irish Question was intractable. Prime Minister Palmerston reportedly said that only three people ever understood the Schleswig-Holstein Question: one was dead, another mad, and himself, but he had forgotten all about it. The Eastern Question concerned the implications of the collapse of the Ottoman Empire: less a single question than a series of challenges. In each case, the 'Question' was more a conundrum—intricate, changeable, evading simple solution, and as chameleon-like as nationalism. Another feature of these 'Questions' was that the issues involved were always present but only became 'Questions' when they approached, or were thought to have approached, crisis point.

The Scottish Question today shares these characteristics. There is little agreement on what the question is, far less its answer. It has involved a shifting mix of linked issues. These have included questions of national identity; Scotland's constitutional status and structures of government; party politics; and everyday public policy concerns. It is hardly surprising that there is so little agreement on the Scottish Question given the wide range of issues. Politics is about agendas and defining issues. Determining what is on the agenda, what is important and needs to be addressed will always be contested. The emergence of the Scottish Question and battles over its definition reflect the politics of Scotland's political agenda.

Any attempt to understand the Scottish Question, therefore, needs to start by acknowledging that what might have been termed the 'Scottish Question' at the start of the twentieth century may not be what is meant by it today. The Question has mutated over time and continues to change. Indeed, there was no 'Scottish Question' at the start of the twentieth century, at least not in the sense of a highly contested issue attracting public, media, and decision-makers' attention to the extent that we see today. But the issues addressed under this broad heading have arisen persistently though without the same level of intensity. What has changed has been the nature of the mix and degree of salience. Issues and concerns at the forefront of public debates today would have been unrecognizable a century ago except in the most attenuated form. Few people argued for a Scottish Parliament in the first half of the twentieth century and those who did were on the fringe of Scottish politics. Scotland's constitutional status, at least in the sense understood today, was simply not an issue. But the seeds were planted during the late nineteenth and early twentieth centuries that would allow for the emergence of demand for a Scottish Parliament. The argument made here is that these seeds were planted and nurtured inadvertently by successive governments in London.

There has never been a single Scottish Question except in the broadest sense of how Scotland relates to the rest of the UK and the question of how Scotland should be governed. Any Scottish Question has been a concern for Scots, almost exclusively, rather than for people throughout the UK until very recently, including those in power. Yet how a state maintains its territorial integrity, governs, and caters for its diverse parts are of importance in all states, other than micro states. Before considering the components of the question, there are a number of key ideas that need to be outlined in order to clear away some misconceptions.

WHAT IS A STATE? WHAT IS A NATION?

All states and nations are artificial. State boundaries are not fixed in perpetuity as the history of the UK, as much as any other modern state, testifies. It is worth recalling Edmund Burke's comments in his speech on conciliation with America in 1775. Burke warned against action that might rupture the relationship between England and America, maintaining that this was a single nation 'in the close affection which grows from common names, from kindred blood, from similar privileges, and equal protection. These are ties which, though light as air, are as strong as links of iron.' England and America shared the 'sacred temple consecrated to our common faith' in liberty. For Burke and many others at that time, war between England and America was a civil war, a war within the family. Within a few years, America had become independent and would see itself as a separate nation and the notion that there was a common nation of Anglo-America was as fanciful to Americans as to English people. The American War of Independence might have been called a British Civil War had the outcome been different, just as what is referred to as the American Civil War would likely be known by a very different name, perhaps another War of Independence, had it not ended in favour of the union.

The idea of Scotland as a nation is equally contingent. Scottish nationalists who see some unbroken line reaching back to Bannockburn and the Declaration of Arbroath, as Alex Salmond has done, make the same mistake as British nationalists who reach back to Runnymede in 1215, as Gordon Brown has done. It is intriguing that both Alex Salmond and Gordon Brown are both history graduates, perhaps displaying greater skills as politicians than as historians in making such claims. Humankind may have a primordial need to live in and associate closely with communities but these communities have never been fixed and rarely exclusive over time. Identification with modern nations came very late in history and identification with states tended to come after the state had been formed. What is of particular interest is the relationship between states and nations. Despite the Anglo-Scottish Union, Scots still refer to the 'Wars of Independence' of the thirteenth and fourteenth centuries, testifying to the enduring belief that Scotland remains a nation and that these earlier battles were not part of a civil war.

Statesmen commonly refer to the ancient nature of their states. Leaders of movements of aspirant states do the same. Sometimes some sacred text or supreme being will be invoked to sanctify the state or nation. Traditions are invented to justify and sustain political communities, to lend them legitimacy in the eyes of the people. The power of this attachment is most evident in the fact that people are willing to die and kill for their country (whether an existing state or an aspirant state). Looked at from outside these appeals appear irrational but from within go unchallenged. Europeans scoff at the American worship of the 'stars and stripes' while Americans are bemused by old Europe. We are better at identifying 'irrational' behaviour in others than in ourselves. Scottish nationalists often view British nationalism as artificial. The language of states and nations has not always served us well in making sense of the UK. There has been a marked reluctance to admit the existence of any national identity or at least state nationalism in the UK as a whole. The assumption is all too often made that nationalism is something to be found in the peripheries: Scottish, Welsh, and Irish nationalisms. From this perspective, nationalism's antonym is unionism but unionism is just another nationalism. The extent to which and circumstances under which these compete or complement each other have changed over time.

States and nations are conceptually different though often conflated. Indeed, we commonly refer to 'nation-states' as if this kind of entity is common when there are few, if any, states with boundaries coterminous with nations. The German sociologist Max Weber defined a state as a 'human community that (successfully) claims the *monopoly of the legitimate use of physical force* within a given territory'. Weber's emphasis on violence should not be taken to mean that states are necessarily violent institutions, only that no other organization, institution, or individual has the right to enforce laws, rules, and policies on citizens. Other definitions of states identify key characteristics. These include a defined territory, having institutions capable of making decisions that are binding on people within the territory. It is assumed that states have some degree of cohesion but may be organized in a variety of ways, some permitting considerable autonomy to levels of government within the state while others are highly centralized. But a common characteristic in any definition is the existence of a central authority. As Robert Dahl stated in the aforementioned book, states differ in the extent to which they 'furnish opportunities for contestation and participation in the processes not only of the national government but of various subordinate governmental and social organizations as well'. All states require a degree of loyalty from their citizens otherwise enforcing laws requires the ultimate sanction referred to in Weber's definition. The extent to which this is compatible with other loyalties remains a matter of investigation rather than definition.

In the sense that all states require some degree of loyalty from their citizens, states will seek to become nations. Indeed, a state will set out to foster a sense of belonging and loyalty from its people whether consciously or not. Without this a state will lack authority and require force to conduct its business. Paying taxes is never popular but most people acknowledge the right of the state to extract taxes. The greatest demand any state will place upon its people, the ultimate test of loyalty, is to fight, kill, and die for it. But even when a state is able to extract taxes and a willingness to die for it, thus exhibiting powerful signs of being a nation, there may be other nations within or lying across its borders. States are mostly multi-national though there is a remarkable tendency to ignore this in the conflation of states and nations. As a growing number of new states emerged in the post-Imperial world and then in another wave of state creation after the collapse of Communism in the 1990s, it became clear that creating a state was not the same as creating a sense of nationhood. The sense of belonging which had largely been taken for granted in European states in the early 1960s was absent within these new states. Establishing the familiar three branches of government institutions—legislature, executive, and judiciary—and other paraphernalia of a modern state was not enough. A sense of belonging was essential. Something similar had been captured in Massimo d'Azeglio's 1861 comment, 'We have made Italy. Now we must make Italians.' But once established, there is a tendency to assume unquestioningly the loyalty of people living within a state's borders. Indeed, so strong is this assumption that it genuinely perplexes those who owe loyalty to a state when others within its boundaries feel less attached to it. Indeed, the strength of nationalism is often most evident in the denial of its existence.

The UK is a state. Scotland is a nation. Each was manufactured by people and circumstances, not nature or God. The UK is a nation insofar as there is sufficient feeling of belonging and there has been a long history of people willing to lay down their lives in the name of the state (whether for the state or for the monarch, as the head of state). It has not always been a nation and it is an odd nation. As has often been remarked, there is no collective noun to describe the nation associated with the UK. There has been little in the way of the state consciously engaged in nation-building, at least outside war or until very recently. The strength of the sense of belonging was evident in its unquestioned integrity. Tom Nairn has long argued that the UK is akin to the Austro-Hungarian Empire, a pre-modern state that is loosely held together by loyalty to the monarchy. Nairn refers to it as 'Ukania' and the 'Anglo-British' state, implying a state with an underdeveloped sense of belonging. Yet, if correct, people within the UK have been remarkably willing to accept its authority. And that includes Scots. Only Turkey and Serbia lost a higher proportion of their adult male population in the First World War than Scotland. These figures do not speak of a lack of loyalty to the state. Compare this with the situation in Northern Ireland during the Second World War when the UK government decided that it was advisable to avoid conscripting the population in that part of the UK. There was strong support for conscription by the government of Northern Ireland but not amongst the Catholic community. Despite the SNP's strong opposition to UK involvement in the Iraq and Afghan wars, there has been no effort by Scottish nationalists to urge Scottish soldiers to withdraw from the war.

Nations, on the other hand, are self-defined collective communities. Joseph Stalin defined the nation as an 'historically constituted, stable community of people, formed on the basis of a common language, territory, economic life, and psychological make-up manifested in a common culture' and claimed that it was 'only when all these characteristics are present together that we have a nation'. Such efforts to define some objective characteristics of nations are restrictive, excluding many communities generally believed to be nations. The alternative way of defining a nation is subjective. This was captured well in Benedict Anderson's idea of an 'imagined community'. People must feel some sense of belonging, even with people they have never met, do not know or even like. This 'deep, horizontal comradeship' is imagined in the sense of being something people believe in as opposed to something that is imaginary. A nation as an imagined community is very real. There is more agreement on what a nation is not than how it can be defined. A nation is not the same as a state. The state, as we have seen, can be objectively defined and takes institutional form whereas a nation must have some subjective form.

In a lecture in 1882, Ernest Renan referred to the nation as a 'daily plebiscite', identifying an important feature of any nation. The sense of belonging to a nation was something that was not permanent and could not be taken for granted. A nation 'presupposes a past, it renews itself especially in the present by a tangible deed: the approval, the desire, clearly expressed, to continue the communal life. The nation is an everyday plebiscite.' In this sense, a national community cannot be taken for granted. This applies equally to states. History is littered with nations that have ceased to exist for a variety of reasons. States too have disappeared (and in some cases reappeared) in history. In many instances, building loyalty to the state-nation has involved destroying pre-existing nations or communities. This phenomenon has been largely absent in the case of Scotland within the UK. There were official references to North and South Britain in the sixteenth and seventeenth centuries and 'North Britain' was a term used for a period from the nineteenth into the twentieth century, though more commonly in business than amongst the public at large. The North British Railway existed for about eighty years into the 1920s. Its last vestige was the North British Hotel at the east end of Princes Street in Edinburgh, renamed the Balmoral Hotel in 1991. The extent to which references to 'North British' are to be found should not be exaggerated. There were ample references to 'Scottish' and related terms in this period. The North British Railway Company's main rival was the Caledonian Railway Company. In each case, these companies followed the familiar pattern of aggrandizement through swallowing up smaller, more local companies.

But an absence of *conscious* nation-building does not mean an absence of nation-building. All states will have the paraphernalia of nationhood and national traditions. The strength of belonging in the UK has been most evident in the lack of conscious nation-building: in the fact that the UK is simply taken for granted.

NATIONAL IDENTITY

A sense of national identity is a necessary but not sufficient condition for the development of demands for distinct institutions/policies. We do not have polls and surveys from early in the twentieth century on the extent to which people felt Scottish but there is evidence that a strong sense of Scottish identity existed. But a sense of Scottishness means very little. Indeed, there is evidence that Scotland was more distinct institutionally in the first quarter of the twentieth century than in the last quarter though awareness of Scottish identity may not have been stronger. This was captured well by Paul Scott, a former diplomat and later SNP Vice President, who remarked on the paradox that, 'Scotland of the 80s had also become more conscious of its distinctiveness and more anxious to preserve it against the pressure for global conformity [than when he was a boy in the inter-war period]; but, paradoxically, it had become markedly less distinctively Scottish in practice.' This was evident in language, with a decline in native Gaelic speakers and speakers of Scots over the course of the century but, as Scott remarked, in the latter part of the century there were 'more dictionaries, books, scholarly conferences and organisations devoted to their preservation'.

Perception is a key to this and particularly perception of the *Other*. Identities are formed in contradistinction to some Other or Others. The Other(s) can be fluid and need not be a person or people. It may be an ideology, a place, or a perception of some of these. In the case of Scottish identity it has ranged over the century to include England, the English, London, Westminster/Whitehall, and latterly, the Conservatives in power at the centre. Scotland's Other is very different from England's Other. England's Other has rarely been Scotland and more often and especially of late it has been Europe or Brussels, Germany, or some combination of these. However, in the late 1970s at the height of the devolution debate and again after the Scottish Parliament was created in 1999, Scotland became the Other for some in north-east England though this should not be exaggerated. After the SNP's electoral breakthrough in October 1974, Members of Parliament (MPs) in the north of England demanded meetings with government ministers with the strong support of the local press. *The Journal* newspaper, based in Newcastle, warned, '"North" must not be poor relation', fearing that Scotland, and to a lesser extent Wales, would be able to command more resources at the expense of the north of England. Labour MPs for the area warned that the north-east might become 'second best' in the allocation of resources. But Scotland hardly registered in the rest of England and the extent to which this elite-led identification of Scotland as the Other was felt amongst people in the north-east of England is unclear. When demand for a Scottish Assembly receded following the 1979 Scottish devolution referendum so too did this elite-informed sense of Scotland being the Geordie's Other. This discussion reminds us of a very important point. When we refer to the 'Scottish' or 'British' we are in danger of making a similar mistake to that identified earlier when we noted the mistaken equation of the metropolitan capital with the state. Nations may be collective entities but they are diverse, not unified single 'actors'.

For much of the twentieth century, some Scots worried about the fate of the nation and what it meant to be Scottish, creating a small industry of Scottish studies in the media, academe, and beyond. Confidence in an identity can be measured in inverse proportion to the output on its meaning and nature. This fear of extinction amongst nationalists was at its height in the late 1950s but was a recurring theme in late twentieth-century Scotland. By contrast, the absence of studies of Britishness signalled a sense of security rather than an absence or weakness in the sense of being British. This creates a paradox in identifying and measuring the strength of any national identity similar to seeking evidence of the existence of power. The most visible manifestation of a national identity—at least in terms of writings and discussion—can connote a weak or, at least, troubled sense of belonging whereas an undiscussed national identity may signify either its demise or else its robust strength.

IDEOLOGY OF UNION

Successive UK governments made no effort to destroy the Scottish nation or impose a sense of Britishness on people living in Scotland. Indeed, the state itself contributed to maintaining and developing a sense of Scottish national identity though rarely doing so in a conscious effort but more out of a willingness to concede to demands and respond to grievances. What we would now understand by a national identity was largely absent at the time of union. The extent to which people felt some common bond with others within Scotland is uncertain. Significant linguistic differences would have separated people in different parts of the country had they tried to communicate. But that would apply whether Scotland was independent or part of the UK. A common sense of belonging required communication. This was a key point in Anderson's understanding of a nation as an 'imagined community'. A distinct Scottish print media—'national print capitalism' in Anderson's terms—played an important part in forging a sense of community and was only emerging at the time of the union. But there already was a sense of Scottishness amongst the elites and it was these elites who both abandoned the Scottish state but fought to preserve Scottish institutions.

Scotland entered union with England in 1707 on terms permitting the preservation of important Scottish institutions. Privileged status accorded to these institutions at the start of the eighteenth century would have been insufficient for the survival of the sense of Scottish identity when these institutions lost salience in the everyday life of Scotland. What was important three centuries ago in maintaining and transmitting a sense of Scottish identity from one generation to the next would not necessarily be relevant over the course of a union described in the Treaty as existing 'forever after'. More important than the institutions themselves was an ideology of union that accepted diversity and acknowledged that the institutional form this should take would require revision over time. Unionism, as a form of nationalism, was also a daily plebiscite.

Challenges to this pluralist conception of union came from changes in society and economy rather than directly from the state. The processes of industrialization, urbanization, secularization, and development of communications and democracy—the characteristics of modernization—threatened to eradicate or at least diminish national and other sub-state identities. Modernization could lead to integration, even assimilation. Industrialization and urbanization pitted the countryside against the cities, cutting across internal national boundaries. Secularization reduced the importance of national churches which, in Scotland, meant the Church of Scotland—potentially eroding an important Scottish institution. Modern communication in the form of the expanding railway network cut across the Anglo-Scottish border. Later still, broadcasting was thought likely to have assimilationist tendencies with broadcasts beaming the same message and the same culture into the homes of people in all parts of the state. It was perhaps no surprise that some of the most celebrated and enduring references to 'North Britain' and support for British institutions relate to modern communications. But these processes did not cause assimilation and where this tendency did occur, it provoked a backlash.

The Church of Scotland's position in Scottish society, protected by the Treaty of Union, had far less impact in more secular and multi-faith times. If the Kirk had been the sole repository of Scottish national identity, then the Scottish nation would have withered into insignificance by the end of the twentieth century. The Kirk along with the educational system had become 'scaffolds, organisations within the whole', in the words of Agnes Mure Mackenzie in 1941. The first significant challenge to its authority came in 1843 caused by an ecclesiastical split—the Disruption—when around a third of its congregations broke away. The Kirk's earthly role was just as important as its spiritual function. The local parish Kirk was the basis for the provision of education and social welfare. Its role in the life of the community, providing a network of institutions as well as in propagating its values, was immense, touching the lives of almost everyone living in Scotland. But secularization and increased demands in the provision of social welfare as well as internal schisms combined to reduce the Kirk's role over time. But while many of the pressures of modernization were rapid, the Kirk's influence declined slowly.

The Kirk's annual General Assemblies attracted considerable media attention well into the latter half of the twentieth century. There is disagreement on when secularization occurred but little doubt about its occurrence and much agreement on the acceleration of decline from the late 1950s. In 1957, the Kirk had over 1.3 million members but by the end of the century this had fallen by about half. In the inter-war period, the Kirk was concerned that Scotland was being 'de-nationalized' by the twin processes of immigration and aristocratic distance. In the late 1920s, at the height of anti-Catholic sentiment in Scotland, a leading Churchman warned that Scotland was being 'Anglified on the upper strata and Irishised on its lower strata', fearing that Roman Catholicism's 'mastery' would result in Scotland losing 'one of the noblest qualities of Scottish character, her civil and religious freedom'. Scotland's Other at that point in time, at least for many members of the Kirk, was Irish Catholic immigration. This anti-immigrant sentiment infected most of Scottish society at this time. But even as the Kirk declined, it left an important legacy. In common with developments in other European countries, state institutions replaced churches. These state institutions were organized on a Scottish and local basis previously provided by the Kirk. In time, Scotland's Irish Catholic immigrant community became integrated, without losing its sense of identity, into the Scottish community. The Kirk offered a distinct institutional nexus and a sense of Scottish national distinctiveness that transferred with ease into a more secular age. It was both a manifestation and purveyor of pluralist unionism.

Formal institutions alone could not sustain a sense of national identity. Nonetheless, formal institutions played an important part in providing a framework for an enduring sense of Scottish distinctiveness. Amongst the most important was the state itself. There is an irony in the state having played such a significant part in maintaining, even encouraging, Scottish distinctiveness given that this sense of distinctiveness later became the basis for pressures undermining the state's integrity. The notion that allowing for a Scottish dimension might be incompatible with the future integrity of the state would once have been incomprehensible. There was little sense that the UK's integrity was in any real danger until very recently. There may not have been any formal constitutional provision, but that does not mean an absence of deeply embedded practices and norms. As Sidney Low commented at the turn of start of the twentieth century, 'We live under a system of tacit understandings. But the understandings themselves are not always understood.' Pluralist unionism, at least as far as Scotland was concerned, was part of the unwritten element of the UK constitution.

Michael Freeden has described nationalism as a 'thin-centred ideology'. This has been as evident, perhaps much more so, in unionism as in Scottish nationalism. Unionism spanned left and right to a far greater extent than Scottish nationalism. This proved both its strength and its weakness. It could unite Mrs Thatcher and Tony Benn in allusions to a glorious and mythical past or, rather, different understandings of the past united Mrs Thatcher and Mr Benn in their unionism. Nationalism as an ideology is reflective and as no ideology will ever completely dominate any nation, it is likely that competing ideologies will be evident in any nationalism. British nationalism has taken left- and right-wing forms simultaneously. So, too, with Scottish nationalism.

PUBLIC POLICY

The scope of policies pursued by government increased significantly over time. What the citizen living in Scotland expected from the state in the nineteenth century would change over time. This had implications for how the state was organized. The night-watchman state required limited state apparatus compared with an advanced interventionist welfare state. But who decided when to intervene and how? This was linked to democratization. An extended franchise meant many more people vying to define both the scope and content of public policy. Differences were bound to exist especially across social classes. Class was the key political cleavage around which debates on public policy and the scope of state intervention raged. But there was also a territorial dimension. Scotland was a distinct entity and services were mostly provided locally, often coordinated at a Scottish level.

Even as the scope of public policy expanded, it most often did so from a local base and from civil society. Public policy pursued by the state grew out of pre-existing institutions and bodies from below rather than superimposed from above. The transition from night-watchman to interventionist state was a gradual process in which Scottish institutions played a significant part. While there is much argument about the British or Scottish roots and nature of the National Health Service today, the reality is that public health owed its origins to highly localized institutions. David Donnison, one of the leading figures transcending the academic and practitioner worlds of public policy, recently reminded us that the 'most important policy innovations of the past—the building of the first district general hospitals and subsidised housing, the creation of comprehensive schools, the invention of foster care for children previously consigned to institutions of various kinds—all began in local government, usually in the teeth of opposition from central authorities'. Local government in turn owed its origins to the organization of the Kirk in Scotland. The policies themselves, the institutions that delivered these policies and the ethos and values that informed policy formation had strong Scottish roots that were carried through into the era of the interventionist state.

There was always a Scottish dimension to public policy. Scottish public institutions as institutions were hollow without Scottish public policies. The expanded electorate expected not only distinct Scottish institutions but also distinct public policies. Sometimes these expectations were based in beliefs that Scotland was in some vague sense 'different'; often that Scottish problems were greater. There were claims that Scottish policies ought to reflect Scottish wishes especially noting divergent policy preferences north of the border. The challenge was to concede a degree of policy divergence while maintaining unity across the state. But how much scope was there for policy divergence especially if equity, if not equality, was important across the state as a whole? This would be a major challenge that required attention in each generation. The

changing nature of society and the economy added to the changing expectations of the Scottish public, ensuring that some final resolution of the Scottish
dimension of public policy could never be found. Public policies were at the
heart of the Scottish Question especially as the reach of the state increased and
expectations grew.

PARTY POLITICS

Scotland had a distinct party system from before the extension of the
franchise but the same parties dominated Scottish politics as in Britain
as a whole. The most notable difference was the relative weakness of the
Conservatives. The Liberals dominated the nineteenth century and Labour
dominated the latter part of the twentieth century. The Conservatives did
best in Scotland when they were aligned with Liberals or when their opponents were in disarray. There were occasions when the party in government
in London was not the largest party in Scotland but this did not last over
many elections and under the old two-party system neither major party was
ever very much behind the other. There was a tendency for whichever party
was in opposition to accuse the governing party of neglecting Scotland.
Equally, each party when in government would claim to deliver generously
for Scotland. Playing the Scottish card in whichever way became a standard
part of political debate.

Opposition to a specific policy or policies was less damaging than diffuse
opposition to a government. Even opposition to a government did not mean
support for constitutional change. Successive UK governments were aware of
Scottish sensitivities. P. G. Wodehouse commented in one of his novels that,
'It is never difficult to tell the.difference between a Scotsman with a grievance
and a ray of sunshine.' Such attitudes where they may have existed were rarely
expressed in public though the irritation at having to accommodate Scottish
sensitivities is evident in many private communications over time in correspondence amongst officials and politicians now held in the public archives.
But irritation could be understandable and led to acceptance of the need to
accommodate. Lord Salisbury's weary comment that the expectations of the
Scottish people were 'approaching to Arch-angelic' needs to be understood in
the context of his appointment of the first modern Scottish Secretary.

But opposition to specific policies could turn into diffuse opposition to
a government, which could in time lead to challenges to the system of government. The perfect storm was created in the 1980s after a government was
elected that misread the Scottish public badly. Context was all-important.
Support for a Parliament became a focal point for opposition to individual

policies and an unpopular government. The Conservatives were in power over a long period of time as their support declined in Scotland. The distinct party system alone did not mobilize opposition support for a Parliament but was an important contributory factor.

SCOTLAND'S CONSTITUTIONAL STATUS

The sense of Scottishness has acquired a political dimension partly due to the willingness of Parliament and successive UK governments to acknowledge Scotland in institutional and public policy terms. The UK has simultaneously been a centralized and pluri-national state. This ambiguity has had a number of consequences. In acknowledging that Scotland was a distinct political entity, the state gave unintended credence to the case for self-government. It also required continuous attention. The Treaty of Union may have set out provisions for acknowledging that Scotland was a distinct community within the union but that could not be the last word on the matter. A key pressure in the twentieth century came from the extended franchise. Accommodating Scottish distinctiveness then had to take account of a wider public than in previous generations. There remained a need to accommodate Scottish distinctiveness but the Scots who needed to be accommodated grew in number from the small elites of the pre-modern era to the enfranchised masses. This was reflected in the shift in relative importance of the two chambers of Parliament. How the House of Commons accommodated Scottish distinctiveness became far more important. What became important in time, though without any formal constitutional foundation but with significant political implications, was the governing party's level of parliamentary support in Scotland. There was no constitutional requirement that the governing party required majorities in each component of the state but a governing party, especially when without majority support in Scotland, had to show sensitivity. The key issue was legitimacy. What would happen when a governing party lost legitimacy in a component of the state?

Whether debates on accommodating Scotland can be described as about 'Scotland's constitutional status' depends on what is meant by 'constitutional'. In its broadest sense, these were constitutional debates in that they involve how the state was constituted. Many functional definitions of constitutions focus on defining authority within states between government bodies, especially between legislatures, executives, and the judiciary and between central and sub-state levels. But which government bodies and which sub-state levels? When does administrative law become constitutional law? This book consciously evades such questions by focusing on the 'Scottish Question' rather than 'Scotland's constitutional status', recognizing

the changing nature of the Scottish Question, which has included a constitutional question by most definitions. It matters less whether the debates
have been or currently are constitutional than that they address a perennial
and changing set of questions around whether and, if so, how to accommodate Scottish distinctiveness, how Scotland relates to the rest of the UK, and
how it should be governed. These have been central issues in each generation since the time of the union though responses have differed considerably over that time.

CONCLUSION

An answer to the Irish Question eluded Gladstone, according to the authors of
1066 and All That, because whenever the Grand Old Man came close to finding a resolution, the Irish kept changing the question. That is also the nature
of the Scottish Question. It has many components and is affected by many different factors, some within the power of government but most are not. There
is no answer to the Scottish Question, only a series of responses appropriate
at each point in time. This book seeks to elaborate on that theme and to contribute to an understanding of debates today with an understanding that the
past, a highly contested past, is an essential first step to providing a response
in any generation.

2

Groundings

INTRODUCTION

This chapter will explore how diversity was respected by successive UK governments and how this changed over time. It will also consider the challenges to Scotland as a distinct entity within the UK. The central argument is that the persistence of a sense of Scottish identity and distinct Scottish institutions owed more to the ideology of union than to the obligations in the Treaty of Union. Indeed, had the sense of Scottishness been defended only by what was mentioned in the Treaty, it would have been much weaker, if not imperilled. The Treaty not only dissolved the Scots Parliament but the Scottish Privy Council was abolished in 1708 in an Act 'for rendering the Union of the two Kingdoms more entire and complete', even though the Privy Council had supposedly been protected in the Treaty of Union. A new British Privy Council took its place.

But the greatest threats to Scotland as a distinct entity did not come from direct challenges or efforts to impose a unified British identity but from changes in society, the economy, and the state. The Treaty of Union could do little to prevent these challenges. Equally, the continued existence of Scotland as a distinct entity resulted from a mixture of conscious efforts and practices to preserve Scottish institutions but more often from a combination of the convenience of maintaining or establishing distinct Scottish institutions and an ideology of union that respected, or at least accepted, diversity. These challenges and responses occurred haphazardly. Seeking to impose order on these processes is mistaken and assuming that the preservation of a sense of Scottishness was inevitable is wrong.

TERRITORIAL PLURALISM OF THE UK

The formation of states during what scholars have described as the National Revolution—when new states were created through unification and national standardization was imposed across diverse territories—involved two important developments. First, new central authorities were created that had, at least to some degree, authority across the entire state. This was initially limited but over time involved a deeper and wider penetration of the centre's authority. Second, this authority came into conflict with other pre-existing sources of authority, most notably churches and religious bodies as well as regional and local sources of authority. What was significant about the creation of the new state of Great Britain was the relaxed attitude towards pre-union institutions. Efforts to impose British-wide standards and practices were limited, not least because there was little to standardize. Indeed, to refer to a *system* of government, at least in any sense understood today, at the time of union is wrong. Equally, references to the union preserving Scotland's distinct legal and education systems raise the question as to whether anything approaching a legal or an education system then existed. Any prospect of standardization, other than creating common standards facilitating trade and commercial activity, came well after the union.

References to the protection of systems of law and education have generally been made by commentators looking back from the twentieth and twenty-first centuries. There was an absence of interacting, interrelated, interdependent, and certainly no integrated set of, laws or educational practices across Scotland at the time of union. But there were Scottish institutions, which were or might have become important means of maintaining and fostering a sense of Scottishness. Scottish legal and education systems developed *after* the union. The Treaty of Union neither prevented these systems from emerging nor brought about their materialization. Imposing strict authority across the union was not required at the time nor would it have been feasible. The Treaty made no direct reference to education other than the provision requiring professors, principals, and others in Scottish universities to declare their faith 'in all time coming', essentially meaning that university employment required membership of the Kirk. In 1853, the requirement that university professors should subscribe to the Westminster Confession was dropped for all but divinity professors. Many provisions in the Treaty were altered, negated, or ignored over the course of time and on each occasion some claim would be made that this undermined or negated the Treaty, which would, in turn, be rejected or ignored. The Treaty itself was a manifestation of flexible continuities which were more enduring than the provisions of the Treaty itself.

There was little direct communication in the form of transport links between Edinburgh and London in the century after the union. To a very large extent, London was content to let the Scots run their own affairs. It had little choice. Nonetheless, communication and trade increased and contacts and some cultural assimilation occurred especially amongst the aristocracy and merchants. But political and business elites continued to be recruited from within Scotland. It was no democracy but those with power and authority in Scotland were drawn from Scotland.

Another feature of the National Revolution across Europe had been the challenge posed to the central state authorities by the Church. But this relationship in Scotland was unusual. There was little conflict between church and state that was found in other European countries. The Kirk had supported the union, largely because union was seen as a bulwark against Catholicism. Its position symbolized the nature of the union more than any other institution in the eighteenth century: autonomous and distinctly Scottish while emphatically pro-union. Its special status in the Treaty of Union came at little cost and much gain. The reach and influence of the Kirk were huge. It was much more important in the lives of people living in Scotland than the state.

As late as the end of the nineteenth century, 80 per cent of Scots with a religious affiliation were members of one of the Presbyterian churches. This gave the Kirk formidable influence over everyday matters of Scottish life. John Knox's ideal of a school in every parish, articulated a century and half before the union, was only beginning to be realized at the dawn of the union. The Kirk provided the administrative apparatus and raised the money for education in parishes across Scotland until the state gradually intervened during the nineteenth century. The Kirk also contributed to some potent Scottish myths: the fabled *lad o'pairts*, boys able to rise above their birth status through equal access to education to achieve prominence in one of the professions. More than any other institution, the Kirk influenced the social mores and social control in Scottish society through control of poor relief, rudimentary education, and other social activities in every parish throughout Scotland. Over the course of the nineteenth century, the state took over these roles but it built on the existing structures inherited from the Kirk. The Kirk operated alongside a pattern of what would become local government. Parish councils were one of the basic units of local government until legislation passed in 1929 and had been based on the old parishes of the Kirk. The Royal Burghs had a degree of autonomy, as did Commissioners of Supply in the countryside and Justices of the Peace. These scattered bodies and individuals administered the rudiments of what eventually evolved into the system of local government and administration.

MALAGROWTHER, KILTS, AND BALMORALTY

In 1826, Sir Walter Scott published his *Letters of Malachi Malagrowther*, an attack on proposals that would have prevented Scottish banks from printing their own notes. It was not the only occasion when he strongly opposed measures which removed what made Scotland distinct. As he warned Lockhart, his nephew and biographer, there was a danger that 'little by little, whatever your wishes may be, you will destroy and undermine, until nothing of what makes Scotland shall remain'. The banking proposals followed the stock market crash and banking crisis of 1825 when around seventy English banks collapsed. A stock market boom and export-driven expansion combined with investment in infrastructure associated with urbanization and early industrialization to create conditions of lax lending. Many banks printed banknotes unchecked. Country banks and the Bank of England became the focal point of criticism and proposals emerged to prevent the former issuing banknotes. Scottish banks avoided the crisis, in part because joint stock banking, which involved several people owning a bank and sharing risk, was permitted under Scots law while not allowed in England. Institutional design, rather than national characteristics, explains why Scottish banks evaded this crisis.

Scott was financially ruined by the crisis as he had invested heavily in businesses that had collapsed. He was forced to write more novels to clear his debt, though most of his best-known novels had already been published. However, his Malagrowther letters were not concerned with his own financial troubles but the prospect that Scottish banks would be unable to issue £1 notes. The *Letters of Malachi Malagrowther* stimulated a campaign to allow the Scottish banks to continue to print their own banknotes. The fictional character Malagrowther purported to be a descendant of Sir Mungo Malagrowther, another of Scott's fictional characters. This earlier character had appeared in *The Fortunes of Nigel*, one of Scott's less well-received novels, who had suffered financial misfortune and sought to make everyone as miserable as he was. Scott's central argument was that Scots should not have to suffer because of the inadequacies of others.

In the first letter, Scott argued against uniformity of laws, as this would undermine the Scottish economy. He maintained that the measure would be in breach of the Treaty of Union. The 'equal distribution of punishment', as Scott described the proposal, was 'one which is extremely predominant at present with our Ministers—the *necessity* of uniformity in all such case'. He criticized the thinking that saw 'what an awkward thing it would be to have a Board of Excise or Customs remaining independent in the one country, solely because they had, without impeachment, discharged their duty; while the same establishment was cashiered in another, for no better reason than that it had been misused'. In the second letter Scott urged Scottish MPs and representative peers—'uniting together in their national character of the Representatives of Scotland'—to oppose all government business, essentially to engage in parliamentary disruption, in defence of Scottish banknotes. This support for parliamentary obstruction, coming before Parnell employed such tactics in the pursuit of Irish home rule, revealed his depth of feeling. The third letter pointed to difficulties in implementing uniformity. Taken together, they represented a strong articulation of the case for diversity within the union, underlined by the threat of radical action in its defence. The government was rattled and initially proposed that the scheme would not apply to Scotland for six months, extending this to six years before abandoning its application to the Scottish banks altogether. Scott's role in saving Scottish banknotes, and effectively providing free advertising for Scottish banks in everyday economic exchanges, was commemorated by subsequently having his picture and works celebrated on Scottish banknotes. The episode is important less because it was typical of campaigns in the post-union period to preserve Scottish institutions and practices. There was rarely a need to defend them. But it highlighted the ideology of union which could be appealed to whenever it was felt that Scottish institutions were under threat. It did not involve questioning the union, only asserting the rights believed to underpin it.

While there was no attempt to assimilate Scotland into the rest of the union, there was a strategy of assimilation of the Highlands, with its Jacobite and Catholic tendencies. But this strategy had more to do with the Union of Crowns than the Union of Parliaments. Jacobite loyalties were a very real threat to the monarch that could not be treated in the same way as Scottish loyalties in relation to the united Parliament. Assimilationist unionism was evident in this case in which concessions were seen as impossible. This unionism resembled attitudes towards Ireland. But by the end of the eighteenth century, a more relaxed attitude was possible and Highland societies and Highland dress were embraced by those in power. Sir Walter Scott organized King George IV's visit to Scotland in 1822 giving impetus to tartanry and Highlandism. The King was dressed in Highland garb in a synthetic merger of the Highlands and Scotland, the Gael and lowland Scot, embracing a sanitized and safe Jacobitism. It meant that the monarchy and aristocracy embraced synthetic Scottishness. These were invented traditions of the union as much as of Scottishness. Many Scottish radical politicians would be highly suspicious of kilts and tartanry well into the late twentieth century due to their association with the upper classes. There was to be no better symbol of the state's willingness to embrace diversity so long as it held out no threat than in this invention of a Scottish tradition. It was not to be the last occasion when those in power embraced Scottish symbols as gestures of support for Scottish identity.

Queen Victoria took this a stage further. Her frequent trips to Scotland were made easier by modern communication by train. She and Prince Albert sponsored a version of Highland culture and the Queen spent long periods at Balmoral on (what became known as 'Royal') Deeside, which the monarch bought in 1852. Successive monarchs have been keenly aware of Scottish identity. A fifteenth-century Act of the Scots Parliament determined that the heir apparent to the Scottish throne would hold the Dukedom of Rothesay. But the title was not used, though held by the heir, after the Union of Crowns of 1603. The preference was to use the title 'Prince of Wales'. Victoria was keenly aware of the diversity of the state and insisted that Rothesay be resurrected and used whenever the heir was in Scotland. As one of the peers of Scotland, the Duke of Rothesay was entitled to vote in elections for the representative peers of Scotland but did not participate. A Scottish Royal Standard or Lion Rampant continued to be used. The paraphernalia of monarchy incorporated Scotland and was given new life during Victoria's reign. From then onwards, the monarchy wore the kilt, both literally and metaphorically.

SCOTLAND AND THE
NIGHT-WATCHMAN STATE

The institutions associated with the night-watchman state were the police, courts, and military. Each was organized on a Scottish basis. Scots criminal law had been protected under the terms of the union. Separate Scottish legal and judicial systems were emerging at the time of union, helping to maintain the sense of separateness amongst an important element of Scottish society. Even if the details are not known, as with other artefacts of national identity, Scots would have been familiar with the idea of separate laws. Having a separate legal system had implications for more than the state. Professional organizations—the Faculty of Advocates and Society of Writers to the Signet—pre-dated the union and continued to exist thereafter. The courts were organized separately in Scotland. The Court of Session, originally a Commission of the Scots Parliament before the union, was Scotland's supreme court in criminal matters. The legal elites were recruited in Scotland maintaining a degree of separateness from their English counterparts. Scots law was more distinct in the period of the night-watchman state but there were few laws on the statute book compared with today and this distinctiveness diminished with the state's developing reach into society and economy. The office of Lord Advocate, a post which originated in the office of advocate to the monarch, continued to exist and became one of the most important public offices in Scotland after the union.

Policing had a very different meaning in the eighteenth and nineteenth centuries from that of today though in its broadest terms it referred to ensuring compliance with laws and accepted mores. It was unsystematically administered with Kirk sessions playing their part punishing minor misdemeanours, including zealously interpreted sexual misconduct, while courts would try more serious offences. Scots would be well aware of this local administration of justice from appearances of miscreants before them on the 'stool of repentance' or 'cutty stool' in the Kirk to the administration of justice in local Sheriff courts. Religion and religious institutions once more played a significant part in public life.

There was also a strong Scottish dimension to the military. While there was no special dispensation from fighting in British wars, separate Scottish regiments exemplified the willingness to accept Scotland's special place in the union. The British army came into being at the time of union by incorporating, not assimilating, Scottish regiments. Edmund Burke's incisive observation on the attachment to the subdivision, 'to love the little platoon we belong to in society' as the 'first principle (the germ as it were) of public affections' was well understood. Soldiers owing strong allegiance to Scottish regiments, with all the mythology surrounding distinctive features, played their part in a succession of British wars and the expansion of the Empire. The myths of sacrifice by fearless fighting Scots contributed to the sense of separateness while playing no part in undermining the contribution to British military causes.

The extent to which persistence of distinct Scottish institutions—the Kirk, courts, and regiments—was a deliberate policy or one which resulted from necessity at a time when the imposition of standardization would have been difficult, is unclear. This approach to governing the state would be replicated in British Imperialism, though otherwise there were few similarities. The British Empire developed a system of 'indirect' rule in the Indian subcontinent and later in Africa, notably articulated by colonial administrator Lord Lugard.

INDUSTRIAL REVOLUTION AND THE CHANGING NATURE OF THE STATE

The nineteenth century was one of rapid change including change in the nature of Scotland's status within the union. It did not, however, lead to assimilation as might have happened without the distinct Scottish basis on which state intervention occurred. Accepting that Scotland had a distinct, if undefined, position within the UK created challenges. The means of accommodating Scottish distinctiveness in one generation could become irrelevant in the next. The Industrial Revolution led to urbanization, created new industries, and produced new pressures. By 1900, a third of Scots lived in Glasgow, Edinburgh, Dundee, or Aberdeen. This had implications for the development of the sense of civic identity, strongly associated with cities, which operated alongside, rather than undermining Scottish national identity. Evidence of (particularly middle-class) pride in belonging to the city can be found in engagement with a range of institutions and initiatives. In Glasgow, for example, the Philosophical Society, Hunterian Museum, various public exhibitions, and print media suggested a lively civic culture spawned by the Industrial Revolution and urbanization.

Around one in ten Scots worked in agriculture though Scotland had been a predominantly agricultural society a century before. The expansion of coal and textiles had been followed by the growth of iron and shipbuilding. Industry became more specialized and surpluses led to a massive growth in exports. This attracted people into urban environments from the Highlands and Ireland in search of work, especially following disastrous famines, but also to growing towns often from the immediate surrounding rural areas. Glasgow became Britain's second largest city within the second decade of the nineteenth century.

The Industrial Revolution also created new tensions that would have implications for Scotland as a distinct entity. This second transformatory revolution affected the UK, including Scotland, earlier than other European states and created pressures that led to greater state intervention. Industrialization, urbanization, improved transport and communication, and increased international trade were common across Europe at this time but there were differences in scale and details. Scottish distinctiveness might have been diluted at this juncture had state intervention led to uniform responses from central government. The impact of the Industrial Revolution highlighted differences between urban and rural areas, and created new cleavages in society, with the potential to have some impact on the existing centre–periphery cleavage that had emerged from the earlier National Revolution. The experience of the Industrial Revolution meant that urban areas in Scotland, notably Glasgow and Clydeside, shared similar experiences to urban centres in the rest of Britain. Glasgow's needs were more similar to those of Liverpool than to rural areas in Scotland.

New harbours were built, trade routes opened, and trade expanded throughout Britain. The Clyde became the workshop of the Empire in the nineteenth century. Commercial shipbuilding was later augmented by passenger liners. The UK dominated world shipbuilding in the latter half of the nineteenth century making fortunes for shipbuilders and providing employment for large numbers of men. The Atlantic economy and international developments, most notably the opening of the Suez Canal in 1869, created new opportunities for Clyde built businesses. The revolution in communication was also evident within Britain with a network of railways criss-crossing the country showing no respect for internal national boundaries. The North British Locomotive Company came into being at the start of the twentieth century after the merger of three companies and created the largest locomotive manufacturing company in Europe at Springburn in Glasgow. The Clyde was an early example of what would later be called cluster development, with interconnected businesses clustering together near research institutes to take advantage of proximity and creating a virtuous cycle of economic development and growth. As Tom Devine states, it is 'easy to lapse into superlatives when describing the global impact of Glasgow's heavy industries at this time'. But the Industrial Revolution was not confined to Clydeside. Dundee was the main producer of linen in Britain in the 1830s. It also became 'Juteopolis', producing carpets and bags from jute imported from India. Textiles were produced in a number of Scottish towns. Paisley became the world's largest producer of thread.

These economic developments had major social consequences. Not only was there massive population movement into towns and cities but Scotland experienced a significant increase in its population. The Scottish population grew from about 1.5 million at the start of the nineteenth century to around 4.5 million by its end. But it had its downside. This led to over-crowding, insanitary conditions, and ill-health. Industrialization occurred with little concern for environmental regulation or health. The Industrial Revolution may have increased total wealth but it was distributed amongst Scotland's people in a grossly uneven manner. The emergence of a sense of class consciousness, struggle for trade union recognition, and agita-tion and riots in the interests of the least well off were as much a part of Scotland's history as the emergence of Glasgow as the 'second city of the Empire'. Class became the most important social cleavage in Scottish soci-ety. Agitation grew for improvements in working conditions and to address public health problems across Britain. Parliament was forced to intervene, creating new bodies of law regulating working-conditions and child labour in a series of Factory Acts. This new body of law was state-wide in its appli-cation. The extent to which this agitation had a Scottish dimension has been disputed, seen in some quarters as simply part of a wider class struggle but elsewhere as having a strong Scottish dimension. Events such as the 1820 Insurrection or Radical Uprising saw 60,000 workers striking, fusing industrial and political objectives. Three of the leaders became martyrs after being tried and sentenced to death. Debates over the interpretation of the Rising and its Scottish content have since ensued with some emphasizing support for Scottish independence amongst the rebels while others play this down. But orthodox opinion has it, as Bill Knox has stated, that the nation-alism of 1820 was 'half-hearted'. It is more often seen as part of Scottish working-class awakening. This was evident in the development of trade unionism and the foundation of the Scottish Labour Party. Home rule was one part of a crowded radical platform in nineteenth-century politics but it came nowhere near the top of the agenda. It is difficult to refer to a Scottish Question during this period, only a Scottish dimension to the Industrial Revolution and the emerging class cleavage.

NASCENT SCOTTISH GOVERNANCE

Scotland continued to be treated as a unit for political purposes after the union. The post of Secretary of State for Scotland existed for a short period but was abolished after the Jacobite Rebellion of 1745. There had been two Secretaries of State in England prior to the union—one responsible for the 'Northern Department' and the other for the 'Southern Department'—each advising the monarch. The Northern Secretary of State was responsible for the Protestant north of Europe and the Southern for the Catholic South of Europe, with each sharing responsibility for domestic affairs. The Secretary of State for Scotland was a third appointee who would have a more limited role. The Duke Roxburghe was dismissed from the post in 1725 by Sir Robert Walpole over disagreement on the malt tax and the post lapsed. The Marquess of Tweeddale served as Secretary of State for Scotland in 1742–6 in a brief revival of the office. Responsibility for Scottish affairs in London eventually fell to the Lord Advocate and the Home Office, an office created in 1782 out of the old office of Southern Department. But an unofficial position emerged with far greater authority. The 'Manager for Scotland', with considerable powers of patronage, existed until 1828. The Manager was not a formal post but grew out of the vacuum created after the demise of the Secretary of State for Scotland. Its key characteristic was a system of spoils. Key Managers in the early years post-union were the second and third Dukes of Argyll but the most famous was Henry Dundas, 1st Viscount Melville. At the end of the eighteenth century, Dundas controlled most of the Scottish seats in both Houses of Parliament as well as numerous appointees in Scotland including university chairs. He held a succession of posts including Lord Advocate and Secretary of State for War and First Lord of the Admiralty, all the while maintaining extraordinary control of Scotland. His appointment as President of the East India Company was central to the expansion of the already extensive influence Scots had in that company and part of the Empire. His real strength derived from his ability to deliver Scotland for Prime Minister Pitt the Younger. Dundas was the last person in Britain to be impeached, though he was acquitted. His impeachment had nothing to do with his Scottish activities but concerned the misappropriation of public money during his time at the Admiralty. His statue, dressed in Roman garb as was the style in the nineteenth century when it was erected, stands in the centre of St Andrew Square, Edinburgh, a short distance from the headquarters of the late twentieth-century home of the Scottish Office, an office run by a succession of Secretaries of State who were at various times compared to Dundas, the 'uncrowned King of Scotland'. The Scottish Manager system ended when Dundas's son resigned in 1827. It had been a thoroughly corrupt system but maintained Scotland as a political unit.

A limited degree of central administration and direction was provided by boards based in Edinburgh in the nineteenth century. With the exception of the Board of Manufactures, established in 1726 to assist with fisheries and 'manufactures', government and administration emerged from the bottom-up in Scotland during this century. The boards were appointed by patronage, often consisting of Edinburgh lawyers and owing their existence to the increasing role of the state during the nineteenth century. They had responsibilities for the limited but growing domestic activities of the state: poor law and public health, education, prisons, fisheries, lunacy and mental deficiency, and agriculture. To a large extent, the various boards operated as semi-judicial bodies. The result was that Scotland was administered mainly at local level with minimal control at Scottish level until late in the nineteenth century.

A Board of Supervision was set up in 1845 to provide some guidance on the administration of the poor law. It would be replaced by the Local Government Board for Scotland with a much wider role in 1894. These boards had their equivalents in England. The difference between the Scottish boards administering poor relief and those in England had much to do with the Scottish Board's lack of control over parochial boards which ensured a considerable degree of local discretion in the operation of the poor law. Much of the work of the Board was arbitrating between different parochial boards.

Boards in England came under increasing criticism during the nineteenth century. Half-way through the century, the Northcote-Trevelyan Report offered a trenchant critique of the boards and proposed what would become the basis of the modern civil service. Board staff were recruited by nepotism rather than merit. The Report made four recommendations: recruitment by merit through open competition; recruitment of 'generalists' to a unified civil service; the creation of a hierarchical structure where advancement was based on merit; and the abolition of appointment on the grounds of 'preferment, patronage or purchase'. The Civil Service Commission, overseeing this new system, was created in 1855 though it was another fifteen years before the Northcote-Trevelyan Report's main recommendations were implemented in England.

But it would be a further seventy years before these ideas were properly implemented in Scotland. The Civil Service Commission's writ did not initially run to Scotland. The Scottish boards remained largely unaffected though they were no less corrupt or inefficient. They were based far from London where there was a willingness to accept that Scotland was different and where there was a reluctance to interfere. If considered at all in London, the Scottish boards were an insignificant aberration that would fall into place in time. The boards and related bureaucracy were few and small at the start of the twentieth century but the growth in government had begun and would continue to grow over the course of the twentieth century making the board system more anomalous.

TWO UNIONS

Ireland had come into the union in 1800. As with union with Scotland, scant attention was paid as to how Ireland would be governed and many pre-union institutions continued to exist. But there were key differences between the two unions. The predominantly Catholic population was seen as the 'Other', an alien threat within the new united state. There were no provisions to protect the church of the majority of Ireland's population as there had been in Scotland. Indigenous elite recruitment in Ireland excluded its internal Other thus creating an enemy within. The Irish Question would be a recurrent problem for nineteenth-century London governments. Future Prime Minister Disraeli articulated the problem well in a speech in Parliament in 1844:

> A dense population, in extreme distress, inhabit an island where there is an Established Church, which is not their Church, and a territorial aristocracy the richest of whom live in foreign capitals. Thus you have a starving population, an absentee aristocracy, and an alien Church; and in addition the weakest executive in the world. That is the Irish Question.

Only one of these conditions prevailed at the time of the Scottish union. Scotland had a weak executive but that had mattered less at the time of the Anglo-Scottish union and though many Scottish aristocrats had come to live in 'foreign capitals' post-union this counted for little. The Highlands of Scotland also suffered famine in the nineteenth century but by that time the central authorities had embraced Highlandism and tartanry. The Highlands presented challenges but the potent issue of religion as a key political cleavage was absent. The prospect of insurrection was not part of the challenge. The famine was not perceived as a national catastrophe and never entered national mythology as it had in Ireland.

The Irish Question in the nineteenth century had three significant implications for Scotland. First, it divided the Liberal Party which dominated Scottish politics in the nineteenth century. Second, it resulted in the migration of Irish people to Scotland during the nineteenth and early twentieth centuries. Third, the dominance of Irish business at Westminster and in Cabinet meant that other business, including Scottish business, was relatively neglected, becoming a source of grievance for many Scots. The Conservatives had struggled in Scotland but the Liberal split offered an opportunity. The Conservatives aligned themselves with the Liberal Unionists, dropping the name 'Conservative' in 1912, and styling themselves the Scottish Unionist Party. This remained the party's official name until 1965. The 'Union' in Scottish Unionist Party referred to the union with Ireland, not to the Anglo-Scottish union, even after Irish secession. In 1927, Lord Balfour reflected on the themes of domestic and Imperial unity. He told his audience that he did not care whether he was called a Tory, Conservative, or Unionist and accepted all such names but preferred unionist 'because it seems to me really to embrace a large number of the things that I most passionately desire...I like Unionist partly because so much of my life was spent—and perhaps some of you will say, vainly spent—in attempting to preserve in its full sense the union with Ireland'. But unionism also meant uniting different social classes, he maintained, acknowledging the importance of the class cleavage in politics. Looking forward, he rejected the conflict in society caused by class politics. The union that received little attention in Balfour's speech was the Anglo-Scottish union. This did not mean that this last union was unimportant to Balfour or his audience, or indeed to Scots, only that it was so secure as to require no mention. Looking backwards, Balfour saw the Irish union as having been important.

The Scottish Unionists never seriously advocated the reintegration of the Irish Republic into the UK but there were deep personal, family, and political connections between Ulster and Scottish Unionists. This social union had roots that were unaffected by constitutional change. Similar tensions existed within both Scottish and Ulster traditions—between those supporting greater assimilation across the state as a whole and those wanting greater recognition of the UK's diversity—but the Ulster Unionist Party dominated Northern Ireland's politics from the establishment of the Northern Ireland Parliament to its prorogation while the Scottish Unionists declined. One legacy in Scottish electoral politics was the Unionist Party's appeal to the Protestant working class. This lasted into the 1960s. 'Playing the Orange card' kept sectarian attitudes in Scotland both alive and under some control. Leading Scottish Unionists such as Sir John Gilmour, Scottish Secretary and Home Secretary in the inter-war period, were members of the Orange Order. Gilmour resisted repatriation of Irish Catholics, which would have been illegal anyway, and discrimination in favour of Protestants in employment, adopting a less hostile attitude than coarser Orange elements. The Labour Party was a class-based party for most of the twentieth century but with a particular appeal in the Catholic community. Labour's appeal to the Catholic vote appears odd when compared with the strong association of Catholicism with parties of the right elsewhere in Europe. The explanation is simple. Labour was the immigrants' party, as parties of the left were across Europe. Religion and class operated together in the emergence and development of a distinct Scottish party system that was quite different underneath the surface from the party system in England though superficially it appeared the same.

Irish business came to prominence and took up much parliamentary time and government attention in the late nineteenth century, contributing to the sense that Scottish affairs were neglected. What has been described as the first nationalist movement in Scotland—from around the middle of the nineteenth century—was in large measure a reaction to perceived neglect of Scottish affairs but was otherwise unlike nineteenth-century Irish nationalism. Its roots lay more in Walter Scott's defence of Scottish institutions than in any demand for a Scottish Parliament. This grievance had been brewing over the course of the century, finding voice in various campaigns but without a clear focus. A National Association for the Vindication of Scottish Rights, established in 1853, complained that Ireland received more attention and better treatment than Scotland. It attracted support from a few significant Scottish public figures including Duncan McLaren, a leading Scottish Liberal often referred to as the 'Member of Scotland', and support from a number of local authorities and the Convention of Royal Burghs. At its first meeting, resolutions were passed opposing centralization, supporting increased parliamentary representation for Scotland and for the restoration of the office of Secretary of State for Scotland. It is difficult to assess the strength of support for the campaign. The *Glasgow Herald* supported it, saying that 'Any man calling himself a Scotsman should enrol in the National Association', while the *Scotsman*'s editor attacked its 'childish agitation' for a Secretary of State for Scotland. The Association fizzled out but complaints continued and eventually gained focus.

It is easy to find evidence of dissatisfaction but little that this was more than low-level discontent and even less to suggest that many of those who felt aggrieved saw Scottish home rule as the answer. There was some support for Scottish home rule but even this was supported in the context of debates on Irish home rule. The various nineteenth-century organizations identified in a number of histories of Scottish nationalism were generally responses to perceived slights and lacked focus or coherence: more parliamentary time for Scottish business; opposition to the 'brain tax' (or 'brain drain' as it would be called today) of talented Scots leaving for London; concentration of state spending on defence (one of the most important items of state expenditure in the night-watchman state) on the south coast of England; the perceived neglect of significant Scottish buildings—castles, palaces, and cathedrals; concern that Scotland's financial contribution to the Exchequer was not matched by expenditure; and a general concern at the lack of awareness of Scottish distinctiveness in London. Much of this was fuelled by a sense that Scotland was not treated as favourably as Ireland. Scots felt aggrieved that good behaviour was not rewarded while the Irish attracted more attention and money. Ireland was more Scotland's Other at this time with Scots feeling a common sense of injustice with England in appeals to London.

FOCUSING GRIEVANCES

Over time, Scottish grievances focused on the absence of a Scottish Minister in London. Cabinet government under a Prime Minister had been developing from the time of union and by the late nineteenth century had established itself as a core part of the British constitution. Walter Bagehot had described the Cabinet as the 'efficient secret' in his *English Constitution* in 1867. According to Bagehot, the Cabinet was where business was really conducted, as opposed to the symbolic 'dignified' part of the constitution. Gaining a seat where power had come to be truly situated became the focus of campaigns in the second half of the nineteenth century. At this point in time the Scottish Question came to mean how Scottish affairs should be managed and how Scottish interests should be represented at the heart of government.

By the early 1880s, there was broad agreement, if little enthusiasm on the part of successive Prime Ministers, on the case for a Scottish Secretary. But there was little agreement on what functions such an office should have beyond being some ill-defined 'Minister for Scotland'. Much public and government business was distinctly Scottish: law, the courts, education, and the emerging local administrative apparatus dealing with problems associated with industrialization and urbanization. There were ample complaints about the handling of each of these in Scotland. However, while there was near universal support for a Scottish Minister in Scotland, there was little agreement on which of these issues should be given to the Scottish Minister. Significantly, voices arguing for a Scottish Minister were often keen to prevent their sectional interests from coming under the new Scottish Office. The Educational Institute of Scotland, a significant professional voice in education, opposed the Scottish Minister having responsibility for education on the grounds that education would become marginalized within a Scottish Ministry. Various legal interests opposed law and order moving from the Home Office to a new Scottish Ministry for similar reasons. But if a new office was to be established it needed a role beyond simply representing Scottish interests. Legal interests were always likely to come out on top in any battle with representatives of education—'Schoolmasters and Professors are not as powerful as lawyers in this House', as Sir Lyon Playfair MP stated. As the *Times*, unsympathetic to a Scottish Office, maintained in 1884, demands were incoherent and undefined. But that gave the demands strength, bringing together a bundle of grievances and aspirations. After various proposals were brought before Parliament setting out different functional responsibilities for a new Scottish Minister, the Secretary for Scotland Act, 1885, was finally passed giving the new office responsibility for education and local education in Scotland.

This represented a key moment in Scottish constitutional and political history, another case of the UK embracing diversity. However, until then, this had had little direct impact at the heart of government but had involved allowing Scots to run Scottish affairs in Scotland through the Kirk, legal and judicial bodies, boards, and the array of local administrative arrangements. The new Scottish Office with its Scottish Secretary formally took Scottish distinctiveness into the heart of British central government. The legislation establishing the office had been unusual. Its progress through Parliament began under the Liberals but was completed under the Conservatives, one of the few bills to have survived the unusual circumstances of a change of governing party in 1885 without an election. Despite the campaigns for a Scottish Minister, with large public rallies and press support—the *Scotsman* campaigned vigorously for the office after early opposition—Prime Minster Salisbury struggled to find anyone willing to accept the office. His fourth choice reluctantly accepted. Salisbury's letter offering the Duke of Richmond and Gordon the office may explain his difficulties:

> What are your feelings about the Secretaryship for Scotland? The work is not very heavy—the dignity (measured by salary) is the same as your present office [President of the Board of Trade]—but measured by the expectations of the people of Scotland it is approaching to Arch-angelic. We want a big man to float it—especially as there is so much sentiment about it.

The elderly Duke of Richmond and Gordon, whose membership of the Lords came through the Richmond line and not as a representative peer of Scotland, was equally unenthusiastic. In his reply to Gladstone, he described the office as 'quite unnecessary, but the Country and Parliament think otherwise—and the office has been created, and someone must fill it'. The office would find a home in Dover House on Whitehall which looked onto Horse Guards Parade.

A number of issues still remained to be resolved including the status of the Scottish Secretary. Campaigners had wanted a Scotsman in the Cabinet with the status of Secretary of State but were given a Secretary for Scotland, a more junior title. The fourth appointee, A. J. Balfour, was its most important in its early years. Beyond the vague but important notion of standing up for Scotland, the Minister's responsibilities were unclear. Local government and education came under the Scottish Office at the outset but the boards remained separate. Law and order was the responsibility of the Lord Advocate and Home Office. Within two years, law and order was added following disturbances on Skye which were mishandled by the authorities leading Balfour, the only person to date to have held the office to go on to become Prime Minister, to take advantage and expand his office's remit in this area.

The Scottish Office was created around the time that the organization of the British system of central government was evolving with increasing state intervention around functional departments. The Scottish Office would be a territorial department in Whitehall based on functional departments. This anomaly would prove important in ensuring the continuation of a strong Scottish dimension to UK politics at a crucial period of change. The timing of its creation was important in another way too. It coincided with a major extension of the franchise. The franchise had been extended in fits over the nineteenth century. In common with the rest of Britain, Scotland was edging towards universal male enfranchisement. The growing body of voters had many identities and interests. Being Scottish, whatever form that took, would be one and the growing Scottish electorate would, as Salisbury had warned, have high expectations of the Scottish Office.

No future Prime Minister could seriously consider abolishing the Scottish Office without incurring the wrath of the Scots. The Office did not remove complaints. Within two years, the *Journal of Jurisprudence* complained that the Scottish Secretary had no power to force the government to introduce and press for legislation and left Scotland in no better place than it had been before. The very existence of the Scottish Secretary created a focal point for future grievances and claims. It was simultaneously a manifestation of the UK's willingness to accept diversity and gave credence to the idea of a distinct Scottish dimension of politics and fuelled further demands.

SIXTEEN PEERS OF SCOTLAND

The Treaty of Union provided for Scottish representation in both Houses of the united Parliament: forty-five (from 159 in the old Scots Parliament) members of the Commons and sixteen peers of Scotland (from 154 before the union). There were 168 English peers at the time of the union though England had around five times the population of Scotland hence the limited numbers of Scottish peers returned to the united Parliament. The representative peers sat for the duration of one Parliament, or a maximum of seven years, before facing a new election from amongst their number. Scottish peers would be summoned to Holyrood Palace in Edinburgh by the Lord Clerk Register, the oldest of the pre-union officers of state to survive the union, where they met in the Great Gallery. Each peer would publicly announce his votes for the sixteen peers. This strongly favoured the Court, later the Conservatives, who dominated the Scottish peers and constituted an overwhelming majority or, often enough, all representatives. Matters became complicated as members of Scottish and English aristocratic families married. Peers combined titles and claimed rights to both Scottish and English titles. Within a few years of the union, the Duke of Hamilton, a Scottish peer, became Duke of Brandon, an English title, and attempted to take his seat in the Lords in the latter capacity. English peers opposed this on the grounds that the Treaty had limited the number of Scottish peers eligible to sit in the upper house. This view held until the end of the eighteenth century. Similar arrangements followed union with Ireland when twenty-eight representative Irish peers were returned to the House of Lords. It is worth recalling that the House of Lords was a much more important chamber in the first two centuries after the union. Prime Ministers and senior ministers were often drawn from the Lords. The status of the House of Lords vis-à-vis the Commons changed over the course of the nineteenth century as the expanded franchise gave the lower House greater authority and by the early twentieth century there was less interest in members of the Lords, many of whom were inactive anyway, including the position and role of the sixteen representative peers of Scotland. As far as the aristocracy was concerned, the union involved a greater degree of assimilation over the course of two centuries, albeit while protecting titles and privileges, than most other parts of society.

The election of the representative peers of Scotland ended under the Peerage Act, 1963, which opened up membership of the Lords to all Scottish peers. It also allowed for hereditary peeresses to take up their seats. There was an attempt to allow Irish peers to sit in the Lords under the 1963 Act, though Ireland had left the union four decades before, but this was heavily defeated. The main purpose of this legislation had been to allow members of the Lords to disclaim membership of the Lords. Tony Benn had inherited the viscountcy on the death of his father but was already a member of the House of Commons and keen to pursue a career in what had become the more important chamber. Benn was the first to benefit from the 1963 Act but he was soon followed by the 14th Earl of Home. Home had been MP for Lanark in Scotland from 1931, serving as Neville Chamberlain's parliamentary private secretary, but lost his seat in 1945 with Labour's landslide victory though regained the seat in 1950. He had to abandon it on his father's death to inherit the earldom. As a newly ennobled peer, he had been made the first Minister of State at the Scottish Office in 1951 by Winston Churchill who had told Home that he had to 'Go and quell those turbulent Scots', a reference to home rule agitation in the immediate post-war period. This was a time when the leader of the Conservative Party 'emerged' from consultation amongst a 'magic circle' of party grandees. Home became party leader and Prime Minister but it was felt that he ought to have a seat in the Commons. Home resigned his seat in the Lords, under the provisions of the 1963 Act, to allow him to find a seat that allowed him to enter the Commons as Prime Minister. George Younger, a young Tory candidate, had already been chosen to fight a by-election caused by the death of a junior Scottish Office minister. Younger, himself heir to a Scottish viscountcy, stood down to make way for the Prime Minister though he went on to become MP for Ayr in 1964 and Secretary of State for Scotland from 1979–85. The 1963 by-election was unique in having an incumbent Prime Minister as a candidate but it was a rock solid Tory seat at the time and there was never much doubt that Home—now styling himself in slightly more plebeian form as Sir Alec Douglas Home—would win.

The system of electing hereditary peers would later be used in the House of Lords Act, 1999, part of the Blair government's constitutional reform programme. In a minor distraction from the main arguments, it was suggested that removing the hereditary peers from the Lords was in breach of the Treaty of Union but this was rejected as the 1963 Peerage Act had already repealed the section of the Treaty dealing with the Scottish representative peers. The government also argued that Parliament could amend the Treaty, or any other provision, under the doctrine of parliamentary sovereignty.

EXTENSIONS OF THE FRANCHISE

The Great Reform Act of 1832 fundamentally altered the franchise in England and Wales. The urban middle classes and owners of large farms got the vote; large urban conurbations were given representation and small 'rotten boroughs' were done away with. At the same time separate legislation was passed for Scotland and Ireland. It was less far-reaching in its impact than the equivalent for England and Wales. Scotland was given eight new burgh seats and the emerging urban centres were given representation. The number of constituents in the average Scottish constituency became twelve times what it had been previously. The second Reform Act in 1867 for England and Wales was followed by similar measures for Scotland and Ireland. Seven Scottish seats were created, including two university seats, and the franchise was extended in Scottish burghs to include most householders, as had happened under legislation for England and Wales. There continued to be complaints that Scotland was under-represented, as measured by population share. Agricultural workers remained disenfranchised until the third Reform Act, an Act that covered the whole of the UK. Scotland gained an additional twelve seats giving it a total of seventy-two in a Commons of 670, proportionate to its population. This meant that two-thirds of adult men could vote in England and Wales while three-fifths could vote in Scotland but no women could vote. A pattern had been established: separate and parallel but slightly different developments in Scotland as Britain moved towards universal adult enfranchisement. The share of Commons' seats became more favourable to Scotland as the franchise was extended.

Changes in the franchise contributed to greater integration of Scotland in the union over the course of the union though integration was limited by an electoral system based on members representing electors within territorially defined constituencies. In 1774, Edmund Burke famously insisted that Parliament was not a 'congress of ambassadors from different and hostile interests' but a 'deliberative assembly of one nation, with one interest, that of the whole'. But Burke soon realized that this was not how his Bristol constituents viewed matters. Constituents expected their Member to represent their interests and this could mean representing a local constituency or local national interest. Would this larger electorate think of itself in British, Scottish, or more local constituency terms? It would at various times do each of these.

Extending the franchise brought new interests into decision-making and led to more professional political parties. Pressure for change from an increasingly organized and mobilized working class, particularly living in urban areas and working in harsh conditions, contributed to a series of Acts of Parliament regulating labour and industry. Democratization and greater state intervention went hand in hand, each fuelling the other and leading to significant changes in the state, society, and economy. Whatever explanation is offered for these developments, what became clear was that on the eve of the twentieth century, changes were occurring in parallel but not uniformly across the state.

TRANSMITTING NATIONAL IDENTITY

Given the limited role of the state prior to the twentieth century, it could not hope to transmit much sense of identity, either uniformly state-wide or pluralistically. Wars, national elections, and visits by the monarch were rare and did not have much impact on the population in the early years after the union. But the basis was being laid for a developed interventionist welfare state in the twentieth century that took account of Scotland as a distinct entity. The state was less important than civil society in transmitting a sense of Scottish national identity. There was little doubt that a distinctly Scottish dimension existed in Scottish civil society though local manifestations of Scottish national institutions were most important in the lives of the Scottish people.

There was a strong sense of Scottish national identity in the 'daily plebiscite' of Scotland's demotic culture which came in a rich variety of forms, whether of 'high' or 'low' culture. Much of it may have been mauldin' and comic at the turn of the twentieth century, as Catriona MacDonald has suggested, though whether this was any different from demotic cultures elsewhere is doubtful. Scottish culture was far more than the Kailyard 'school' of Scottish fiction—including Ian MacLaren, J. M. Barrie, and S. R. Crockett—who offered a sentimental, idealized version of Scotland. There was no lack of myths and historical figures to draw upon in creating and developing a sense of national identity and there was no lack of writers and poets to reproduce these over time. Though many stories were rooted in the wars of independence in the thirteenth and fourteenth centuries they were told without an explicit contemporary political message. But beyond these, there was ample work that drew heavily on Scotland's past and contributed to a sense of community, including the work of Robert Burns and Walter Scott, and much that experimented in language styles and dialects. A thriving Scottish print media made a considerable contribution. Newspapers such as the *Scotsman* and *Glasgow Herald* were respected and authoritative. Even as communication was breaking down barriers within Britain, this form of communication transmitted a sense of Scottishness in everyday life. Indeed, as communications improved, people became more aware of their Others, thus enhancing the sense of difference.

A robust Scottish local press also ensured the survival of Scottish identity. Again, this was not done consciously but its unconscious effect contributed to regenerating a sense of Scottish identity over generations. This was not a static culture but a living, changing culture. The basis for treating Scotland as a distinct *political* community was rooted in this sense of national identity that was unrelated to politics and government. Novels, poetry, sermons in the Kirk, the press, everyday speech and communication all served to ensure living continuities against the disruptive backdrop of changes in Scotland's economy and society. The vitality of the sense of Scottishness lay in its diversity, its deep roots in Scottish society, and, as with all national identities, its malleability.

CONCLUSION

'The noblest prospect which a Scotchman ever sees', according to Samuel Johnson in his *Life of Boswell*, 'is the high road that leads him to England'. Union offered Scots opportunities previously unavailable. Scots would sit in the Parliament at Westminster and have the opportunity of attaining high office but the only Scot to become Prime Minister in the eighteenth century was the Earl of Bute, one of the sixteen elected peers of Scotland, though Dundas wielded considerable power in London as well as being Scottish Manager. However, seven Scots (or at least men who could claim some Scottish ancestry or link) became Prime Minister in the seventy-five years after 1850: Aberdeen, Gladstone, Rosebery, Balfour, Campbell Bannerman, Bonar Law, and Ramsay MacDonald—though not all would be recognizably Scots by their speech. The high road to London was only one opportunity. The Empire offered opportunities aplenty for aspiring Scots on the make. The East India Company was transformed, in Tom Devine's words, into a 'veritable Scottish fiefdom'. And, of course, indigenous elite recruitment in Scotland was permitted as a consequence of Scotland retaining many pre-union institutions, notably the Kirk and Scots law. Nowhere was this more obvious than in the military. The Scottish regiments offered opportunities, especially during the expansion of the Empire.

What should not be forgotten was how people living everyday lives identified themselves. We have no surveys or robust evidence but can assume that a strong demotic sense of Scottish identity existed, conveyed via the institutions that would be most familiar to them, rooted in the Kirk, schools, and administration of justice. The extent to which they were aware of and sensitive to challenges to Scotland as an entity, in the way that Sir Walter Scott had been, is unclear. The likelihood is that they were not but that does not mean that any challenge which focused directly on their daily lives would not have met similar resistance.

3

From Night-Watchman to Interventionist State

INTRODUCTION

The key institutions transmitting a sense of Scottish identity from one generation to the next in the era of the night-watchman state were necessarily civic institutions. The state's role was too minuscule to have much impact. Policing and the justice system were visible on the ground in Scotland and would touch the lives of many Scots. The twentieth century saw the state become more important in people's lives. In 1973, the Kilbrandon Commission on the Constitution summed up the changes well:

> The individual a hundred years ago hardly needed to know that the central government existed. His birth, marriage and death would be registered, and he might be conscious of the safeguards for his security provided by the forces of law and order and of imperial defence; but, except for the very limited provisions of the poor law and factory legislation, his welfare and progress were matters for which he alone bore the responsibility. By the turn of the century the position was not much changed. Today, however, the individual citizen submits himself to the guidance of the state at all times. His schooling is enforced; his physical well-being can be looked after in a comprehensive health service; he may be helped by government agencies to find and train for a job; he is obliged while in employment to insure against sickness, accident and unemployment; his house may be let to him by a public authority or he may be assisted in its purchase or improvement; he can avail himself of a wide range of government welfare allowances and services; and he draws a state pension in his retirement. In these and many other ways unknown to his counterpart of a century ago, he is brought into close and regular contact with government.

Increased state intervention, in its manifold forms, was often, though by no means always, mediated through Scottish institutions. These institutions grew out of civic institutions. Much state intervention that was visible and touched the lives of Scots on a daily basis had a Scottish dimension. It was not the institutions themselves that mattered but the policies pursued and implemented.

Even when policies broadly followed the same pattern across Britain there was often scope for differences of interpretation and implementation. These differences were constrained. Westminster was the formal source of authority, with its legitimacy derived from the outcome of state-wide elections, so there was no prospect of Scotland heading off in a completely different policy direction from the rest of the country.

The existence of the Scottish Office with a government minister at its head reminded others in government that Scotland was different, with special needs, and ensured that a Scottish dimension existed in the long transition from night-watchman to interventionist welfare state. Whether or not state intervention should have a Scottish dimension depended in large measure on whether a precedent of distinct Scottish policy-making existed. Another factor was the cost of pursuing a distinctly Scottish policy. Successive Scottish Secretaries were successful in making the case for additional resources for a vast array of policies, which cumulatively had consequences for the kind of society and economy that emerged in Scotland.

In this chapter, the extent and nature of state intervention will be outlined, highlighting the unintended consequences that gave rise to a political culture that measured success in terms of pork barrel politics—resources squeezed out of the Treasury—but lacked emphasis on tackling the roots of social and economic problems. But this form of politics was framed emphatically in Scottish terms. The generosity of successive UK governments in responding to the most frequently asked Scottish question of the twentieth century—can we have more?—created long-term problems. Short-term responses to a minor irritant proved politically difficult in the long term.

EDUCATION AND SOCIAL WELFARE

Other than provisions for Scottish universities, Scottish education was not directly protected under the terms of the union but was indirectly protected given the role the Kirk played in school governance. But that formal protection would potentially last only so long as the Kirk dominated the provision of education. John Knox's *Book of Discipline*, written well before the union, provided the basis for schools in every parish—an ambition that laid the foundation for the myth of universal education. Under the 'Necessity of Schools', Knox had written that every church should appoint a school master able to teach grammar and Latin 'if the town be of any reputation'. The Disruption in the Kirk in 1843 undermined its capacity to provide education but it remained an aspiration. The Free Church shared the Church of Scotland's educational ambitions and trained its own teachers and schools. *Scotland a Half Educated Nation*, a polemic written by George Lewis in 1834, attempted to puncture inflated claims. Four Royal Commissions were set up in the 1860s to inquire into education in Britain including one into Scottish education under the Duke of Argyll. The Argyll Commission described the 'extreme variation' in educational provision across Scotland, noting that there was no 'competent authority to initiate, to administer, or to superintend':

> Schools spring up where they are not required and there are no schools where they are required. The buildings may be good or they may be unsuitable. The school apparatus may be adequate, or there may not be a bench to write at or a blackboard or map throughout the length and breadth of a whole district. The teachers may be good or they may be utterly incompetent: they may be wealthy men, or they may be starving: they may be under official supervision, or the entire management of the schools may devolve upon themselves, and they may be responsible to no one. The children may attend school or they may not attend, but grow up in absolute ignorance. All these evils are due to want of organisation, and suggest the necessity of some central authority to regulate the education of the country.

Grants for education were provided by central government during the nineteenth century largely after pressure in England. It would have been impolitic to have failed to make similar provision for Scotland. An English Education Act in 1870 provided the basis for a system of elementary schools in England and Wales. Much of Scotland already offered this so the equivalent legislation for Scotland, passed two years later, took local control of education from the churches and gave it to elected school boards, established the Scotch Education Department (SED) and made schooling compulsory between the ages of 5 and 13. Thus began a very different era in the provision of education. Funding from central government increased with tight central control under the SED. Controversy had surrounded who should control the SED. Argyll had proposed a Board in Edinburgh along the lines of other Edinburgh boards but others preferred the SED to be responsible to a Committee of the Privy Council. Amongst others, the Duke of Richmond and Gordon, later to become the first Secretary for Scotland, criticized this latter idea as 'nothing but a sham' and 'simply a room in Whitehall, with the word "Scotland" painted on the door'. A temporary Board was established to appease critics but it failed to establish itself and was withdrawn in less than a decade. There was concern that the demise of the Board would mean a lack of a 'really Scotch element in the administration of the Scottish system of Education'. In response, the Chancellor of the Exchequer had insisted that 'there would be a Scotch administration, he would not say all composed of Scotchmen, but of men conversant with Scotch business'. But the Committee of the Privy Council existed in little more than name and like its English equivalent was an example of what Bagehot had described as a 'dignified' element in the constitution. The 'effective' government of education became the growing body of SED officials and the Scottish educational inspectorate. The Privy Council Committee rarely met—about two or three times a year until the 1890s and less frequently thereafter. Just before the outbreak of the First World War, SED officials and especially its secretary were accused of being autocratic, making decisions without authority. The last occasion the Committee of the Privy Council on Education in Scotland met was in 1913, having last previously met in 1899, and this was to discuss a legal case challenging the authority of SED officials to act without the authority of the Committee.

Dalziel School Board v. *The Scotch Education Department* highlighted a number of underlying developments. Dalziel School Board in Motherwell had dismissed a teacher because she had become a Catholic. The teacher had appealed to the SED, which had found in the teacher's favour and required the Board to pay her compensation. The school board argued that the decision lacked legitimacy as they had been 'decisions of the secretary or other official'. The Scottish Secretary was not involved in day-to-day matters. The state's increasing reach combined with a separate administrative system based in Scotland left education with little ministerial oversight.

The Dalziel case also highlighted the existence of sectarianism in Scotland. Across Europe, education had been at the heart of conflict between the church and the state. The privileged position of the Church of Scotland carried through to the era of state involvement in the provision, including the funding, of education. There was support for a truly non-denominational system of education but this was resisted by Presbyterian and Catholic churches. There was no Scottish equivalent of the Cowper-Temple clause in the 1870 English Education Act which prevented any 'religious catechism or religious formulary which is distinctive of any religious denomination' to be taught in schools. State provision of education went a long way towards protecting the Kirk's pervasive influence. The 1872 Act allowed for ecclesiastical bodies to transfer schools to the state. This reflected another form of sectarianism, the battles between the Presbyterian churches unable to agree amongst themselves and which had to leave provision of education to the state. The state would accept responsibility for these schools including funding them from locally raised rates, but this was not taken up by the Catholic hierarchy, which neither wanted to repudiate religious education nor to hand Catholic children over to schools to be run by Presbyterians where Catholics were in a minority.

The Catholic community argued that Catholic schools should be put on the same financial footing as others with support from local taxation. Catholic schools were voluntary, in the sense of having no local financial support though receiving some funding from central government. It was argued in a private internal SED note at the start of the twentieth century that the 1872 Act had not discriminated on grounds of religion, only that it gave the majority in local authority areas the right to decide on the provision of education and what Catholics complained about was 'really the result of the fact that they are a minority'. If Catholics were in a majority in any local area then 'they can, and do, have their own distinctive religious tenets taught at the expense of the rates'. This was disingenuous as Catholics rarely found themselves in a majority and in many instances found themselves in a hostile majority community. Pressure from the Catholic community continued. At least one deputation to see the Scottish Secretary a few years before the outbreak of the First World War included three Irish MPs along with members of the Scottish Catholic hierarchy. Scottish Catholics looked to Irish Nationalist MPs to look after their interests. Only a small proportion of nineteenth-century Irish emigrants came to Scotland but this still constituted a large number given the massive outflow of people from Ireland. The Irish in Scotland were predominantly poor and resented for undercutting local wages, especially in economically difficult times.

Towards the end of 1917, the Scottish Secretary presented a paper to the Cabinet proposing a bill to improve the education 'for all classes of the population'. It discussed how this aim might be realized for Roman Catholic schools. Catholic children, constituting around one-eighth of Scotland's school population, were deprived of opportunities available in public schools. Local authorities were under no obligation to fund Catholic schools and the state's involvement had been limited. The Act brought Catholic schools under counties, newly reconstituted local education authorities, and were resourced appropriately. Given the extent to which Scottish identity had been wrapped up in Presbyterianism, the provision of state support of Catholic education in the 1918 Act was remarkable. It would have far-reaching implications, facilitating class mobility and eventually social integration.

The 1918 Education Act also ensured generous provision for Scottish education in general. It enshrined the Goschen formula in statute. Goschen had been Chancellor of the Exchequer in the late 1880s and, aware of the increasing role of the state, sought to rationalize public finances by separating central and local finances. As part of his plans, Goschen established separate taxation accounts for England and Wales, Ireland, and Scotland into which certain 'assigned revenues'—taxes and duties—would be paid for local purposes. Rates, one form of realty tax, already contributed to local spending so Goschen decided that personalty, another form of property tax, ought also to contribute to local finances. He especially wanted to include probate duty, the tax on property after death, later known as estate duty. He could have simply allocated the amount of probate duty each component of the UK raised but Ireland would have lost out. Instead, as he explained in Parliament, he would 'give each country a share of it in proportion to the general contributions of that country to the Exchequer. On this principle, England will be entitled to 80 per cent, Scotland to 11 per cent, and Ireland to 9 per cent. This division is, if anything, a little too favourable to Ireland, as its contributions are in reality only 8.7 per cent; but I have felt obliged to give the benefit of the doubt to the poorer country.'

Goschen's attempt to separate local and Imperial taxation failed but one detail—the formula used for allocating sums to the component parts of the UK—remained. The formula was used on a number of occasions when a sum of money was allocated to England and Wales for some public policy purpose where separate Scottish arrangements existed and some equivalent sum had to be allocated to Scotland, even if the service was already funded from local rates in Scotland. It was a convenient, if rough-and-ready, means of providing Scotland with an equivalent whenever central funding was allocated to English and Welsh public services.

The main use of the formula came with the 1918 Education Act. The Treasury agreed that Scotland should receive 11/80ths—the Goschen formula when Ireland was left out of the equation—of any changes in educational expenditure for England and Wales. The Treasury was willing to accept this formula but proposed that 1911–12 should be used as the base year, rather than the SED's preference for 1913–14. On this occasion, the SED was victorious, providing Scotland with an advantage in its base year which would have year-on-year consequences. Goschen assumed totemic status and would be used—though not consistently—in other areas of public policy over the next half-century.

The formula had important consequences for twentieth-century Scotland far beyond the immediate issue of determining how much money should be allocated by the central state to education. It had path-dependent qualities. Future decisions on spending would be determined by Goschen not only because of the law, which could have been changed by a simple Act of Parliament, but because Goschen created expectations that would be difficult to resist. It was also important in a more fundamental way. Scotland was treated as a unit for determining public finances in many areas of policy.

Not all areas of state funding required separate Scottish accounts. In some matters, spending decisions were made which took no account of territorial impact. Defence spending, for example, followed previous patterns of expenditure, reflecting where defence needs had been greatest. But questions would be asked as to whether Scotland received its fair share. This had been a cause of complaints in the late nineteenth century as many Scots saw defence expenditure concentrated on the south coast of England as an anachronism, as if England was still preparing for war with France or Spain.

The simplicity of Goschen had attractions as a convenient means of determining how much Scotland should receive. As the Cabinet Secretary remarked in the late 1940s, the formula 'may not be right, but no one has been able to show that it is wrong'. But it was extremely crude and took no account of needs which could vary not only between Scotland and the rest of Britain but also by public service. The formula's totemic status meant that it would be used in negotiations and debates both within government and in public. The tendency to use Goschen in this way had preceded the 1918 Act but thereafter it became more common. Sir Henry Craik, a former civil servant head of the SED who became an MP, warned against this on a number of occasions before the First World War, maintaining that Goschen, when Chancellor of the Exchequer, had told him that it was the SED's business to 'find out where the shoe pinches' and how much is needed for each area of educational spending and then to approach the Treasury to make the case. The 'endless and tiresome comparisons of the exact proportions between England and Scotland' were 'absolutely wide of the mark', he insisted. But this became embedded as part of the Scottish Question in the twentieth century.

HOUSING

Public health emerged as an issue for governments with the twin developments of industrialization and urbanization. Pressure for action came especially from Britain's growing cities suffering from poor sanitation, overcrowding, and consequential periodic epidemics. But intervention was initially resisted. In 1885, the same year that the Scottish Office was established, a Royal Commission on the Housing of the Working Classes issued three reports: on England and Wales; Scotland; and Ireland. The Scottish report was based on interviews over four days in Edinburgh. The reports focused particularly on overcrowding and the Scottish report was effectively an appendage to the first, in recognition that housing problems, public health administration, and legislation were broadly the same. The report acknowledged the scale of problems in Scotland exceeded those elsewhere but maintained that these conditions were due 'as much to the habits of the people as to certain outside influences', by which they meant the 'large sums they spend in drink'. Attitudes changed over the next three decades. At the beginning of the twentieth century, the holder of the Adam Smith Chair in political economy at Glasgow University urged local authorities to extend their role by building houses. This 'great public emergency' was no time to 'stand out for the abstract rights of private interests'. The hidden hand had failed to provide decent houses. However, emphasis was on the local rather than central authorities. In the conclusion to a Cabinet memorandum written in 1901, Lord Balfour of Burleigh remarked that as Secretary for Scotland he had 'no initiative, and except as "confirming authority", very little power of bringing pressure to bear on local authorities'. Up to the First World War, the central state's function was largely regulatory though legislation was passed enabling local authorities to build certain low standard housing. By 1913, fewer than 4,000 Scottish families, about 1 per cent of the total, were rehoused under these schemes.

In January 1909, the Scottish Secretary's private secretary warned him that the Royal Commission on Mines, then meeting, intended to criticize

one-roomed cottages in Scottish mining villages. In a short unequivocal statement, the Commissioners condemned the 'extremely unsatisfactory' housing
conditions. The Scottish Secretary and his staff met miners' representatives
and MPs from mining districts and requested further information from the
Scottish Local Government Board and County Medical Officers in mining
areas. This was the background to the establishment of the Royal Commission
on the Housing of the Industrial Population of Scotland under Sir Henry
Ballantyne in late 1912. The outbreak of war delayed the publication of the
Commission's report until 1917. It was a very different document from that
published thirty years before, reflecting changing expectations. Emphasis was
placed on the role of the state and the need to provide 'healthy, comfortable
dwelling for every family in the land'. The Ballantyne Commission argued that
the Local Government Board should conduct a survey to find out the extent of
Scotland's housing problems but estimated that 235,990 houses were needed,
with 121,430 needed immediately, and that existing standards of accommodation had to be raised. It was noted that there were substantial variations in the
provision of housing across Scotland due to the institutional and legal framework which gave local authorities considerable autonomy. It recommended
the explicit acceptance of the state's responsibility for housing the working
classes with an obligation on local authorities to make provisions with central government powers of compulsion to ensure that local authorities should
meet this new responsibility. To this end, it recommended strengthening the
Local Government Board. Overcrowding was the most obvious example of the
difference between Scotland and England. The 1921 census showed that one
in five Scots (991,344 people) lived in overcrowded conditions compared with
under two in a hundred (631,627 persons) in England and Wales, according
to a Scottish Office memorandum of 1927. A similar report in 1937 found that
little had changed in Scotland.

   Pressure for greater state intervention in public health and housing was
common across Britain as a whole. War had made the authorities aware that
it could not expect to get 'an A1 population out of C3 homes'. As soldiers
returned from the front, politicians promised houses fit for heroes. Rent strikes,
especially on Clydeside, led to the introduction of rent restrictions in 1915.
Planning post-war reconstruction involved creating new institutions and policies. In July 1917, the Haldane Committee on the Machinery of Government
recommended that a Ministry of Health be set up while 'leaving the separate
systems already in operation in Scotland and Ireland for separate treatment'. It
made no effort to explain or justify the retention of Scottish and Irish boards
which seemed anomalous in the context of the overall report. A Ministry
of Health was established for England and Wales while a Scottish Board of
Health was set up, despite criticisms of boards by the Royal Commission on
the Civil Service which had reported at the start of the war, as well as Haldane.
Christopher Addison, the Minister for Reconstruction, met Scottish MPs to

discuss reconstruction and noted in his diary their 'intensely national' feeling. Housing became the most important responsibility of the Scottish Board, later Department, of Health. Addison became the first Minister for Health in 1919 but his department's writ did not run to Scotland. Even if the pressures for state intervention were common, a single ministry responsible for the whole of the state was unacceptable. There had to be a separate Minister for Scotland.

The 'Addison Act'—the Housing, Town Planning Etc. Act, 1919—was the first major piece of legislation recognizing the limited ability of local authorities to tackle the housing shortage. It had become clear that there would be little progress if local authorities were left responsible on their own. Over the course of the next sixty years, housing legislation was passed at regular intervals offering subsidies to assist house building. The Scottish Office and local authorities successfully made the case for increased funding for Scottish housing but rarely initiated policies which differed from those south of the border other than in the extent of application. Slum clearance was an important part of housing improvement in the inter-war period and usually involved private rented accommodation making way for public sector funded accommodation. A Scottish Office memorandum in 1927 noted that Scotland had 'scored' by receiving more than the Goschen fraction in this area of housing policy. One of the few initiatives was the establishment of the Scottish Special Housing Association in 1937. In a memorandum to the Cabinet in January 1937, Walter Elliot wrote of the 'deplorable condition of Scottish housing and comparatively slow progress' being made to address this problem. The defence programme was absorbing much of the labour needed for house building. Elliot wanted an agency separate from local authorities to construct houses by non-traditional methods. Neville Chamberlain, as Chancellor of the Exchequer, was receptive to the idea of some separate agency and suggested an arrangement similar to the North Eastern Housing Association operating in Durham and Tyneside. The provision of housing through this new agency was to be linked to employment generation. The emphasis on non-traditional house building, particularly concrete construction, was evidence of some degree of innovation in Scottish housing policy.

Over the course of the twentieth century, central government experimented with state subsidies for housing. Generous grants were offered when times permitted and would be cut back in more challenging economic circumstances. The Scottish Office argued for a separate assessment of any subsidy for Scotland, whether for rural or urban dwellings, dealing with overcrowding or special housing. A new junior Minister responsible for public health in Scotland was created under the legislation establishing the separate Scottish Board of Health in 1919. This ensured that there was a ministerial voice making the case for Scottish health. The case made was invariably the same: Scotland was different, had more severe problems, and required more support. The case for special treatment and larger Exchequer subsidies rested on the scale of Scotland's problems and, to a lesser extent, the additional costs involved in house building north of the border. The Scottish authorities—local and central—worked together in making this case. In March 1923, Walter Elliot, then Under Secretary for Scotland, outlined his approach at a meeting in the Scottish Conservative Club: 'in essence, our claim is differential treatment in favour of Scotland, and as you can well imagine the more strongly you can enable me to put this claim the better I shall be pleased'. Scottish Secretaries took up the cause in Cabinet. The view in Whitehall was that the Scottish Office was chauvinistic in calling for special treatment. On one occasion after the Cabinet agreed to more generous subsidies for Scotland, Neville Chamberlain commented in a letter to his sister that he had 'very little confidence in the Scottish Office which will always make a bungle if it is possible to do so'. But accepting that the Scots should receive extra money was easier than denying it. The Ministry of Health tended to side with the Scottish Office in the latter's demands for more favourable treatment, especially in the 1930s. It was the Treasury that tended to object.

Though the most significant growth occurred after 1945, 70 per cent of all new house building in the inter-war period had been completed by local authorities in Scotland. Scotland was not unusual in experiencing growth in public sector housing after 1945. Churchill gave Harold Macmillan the task of overseeing the 1951 Tory manifesto pledge of building 300,000 new houses per year. In Scotland, this was the responsibility of the Scottish Secretary. Scotland retained a special housing subsidy unavailable in the rest of Britain. Between 1945 and 1951, 113,825 houses were built and 239,925 were built between 1952 and 1957 (around 11 per cent of the total across Britain throughout the period). Council house building continued apace over the next two decades. The large proportion of council houses combined with low rents subsidized by local rates, provided by Labour-controlled local authorities, to create a highly unusual housing sector in Scotland.

The 1981 census showed that 54.6 per cent of Scots lived in public sector rented housing compared with 32 per cent in the rest of Britain. In Glasgow, the proportion was 63 per cent and the city council was the largest landlord in Western Europe with about 170,000 houses in its stock. Within the city, there were large areas where housing was almost exclusively owned by the council. In Bellshill, Clydebank, Coatbridge, Irvine, Livingstone, Motherwell, and Wishaw over 80 per cent of the housing was rented by tenants from local authorities. Councils set rents, decided on who was given preference in housing allocations, planned where houses would be built, controlled home improvements, and decided on housing standards within guidelines set by the Scottish Office. Standard, uniform houses were built and tenants had little choice. The quality of housing was often poor and many houses were built using materials and construction methods unsuited to the Scottish climate. Not all of it was bad, however, and some municipal housing, including that built in the 1920s, would stand the test of time and even substandard housing was often an improvement on what went before. The party political divide on housing included bitter battles over the contribution local rates should make to subsidizing rents, with wealthier and predominantly Tory-voting home owners subsidizing Labour-supporting council tenants. But low rents meant that authorities were often in no position to pay for better housing or necessary improvements. In power at Westminster, Conservatives attempted to limit these cross-subsidies but came up against strong opposition from a number of councils. This was a feature of politics in England too but the scale was different in Scotland.

Understanding the Scottish housing market is incomplete without appreciating the absence of private sector development. Private house building lagged behind that in the rest of Britain. In some areas such as Glasgow, local authorities deliberately inhibited private house building. Local authorities controlled building licences and set standards and even selling prices in the immediate post-war period though many controls were abolished in the mid-1950s. For much of the time, Scotland was a net exporter of the savings of building society funds to help build houses elsewhere in Britain.

What the family in the council house lacked in terms of choice—even the colour of the front door would often be prescribed by local authorities—they gained in cheap accommodation. A form of clientelistic politics grew up around council housing in a highly asymmetric relationship between council house tenants heavily dependent on Labour-run councils. Large council housing schemes created corrals of Labour voters, which in the two-party system that dominated Scottish politics through to the 1970s all but removed choice in voting intention or, at least, linked it fairly directly to housing tenure. Churchill had told Macmillan that success as Housing Minister would pay electoral dividends but in Scotland it had the opposite effect.

The state's involvement in housing in Scotland over the twentieth century had become greater than in any other part of Western Europe and even some parts of Communist Europe. State intervention in housing had happened piecemeal. There had been no great plan for such a massive public sector. Scotland's housing improved over the course of the century compared to what it had been but remained poor relative to the rest of Britain and other advanced liberal democracies.

HEALTH

Housing had been the key responsibility of the Scottish Board of Health established after the First World War but the establishment of the National Health

Service (NHS) after the Second World War widened the scope of health considerably. Former Prime Minister Gordon Brown often argued that, 'when we talk of the National Health Service, national means Britain'. But the situation was more complex than that. There was separate legislation to establish the NHS in Scotland. In the period before the establishment of the NHS, local authorities had provided and ran most health services including hospitals. The establishment of the NHS reduced the role of local authorities, making them more concerned with preventative matters but administratively detached from the rest of the health service. As Joseph Westwood, Scottish Secretary, explained in moving the second reading of the National Health Service (Scotland) Bill in the Commons, 'Scotland has her own legal system, her own traditions, and her own system of local government. The geographical distribution of her population is different. It is necessary, therefore, to adjust the application of general principles to suit Scotland's particular circumstances and need.' The particular circumstances and needs were listed towards the end of his speech. These included different administrative arrangements for the ambulance services which would be under the Scottish Office rather than local health authorities as in England. In addition, teaching hospitals would be taken out of the 'regional ambit'. While Scotland had 10 per cent of hospital beds, one-third of all of the UK's medical students were trained in Scotland. Endowments to hospitals would also be dealt with differently. The exceptional problems in the Highlands and Islands had been acknowledged when the Highlands and Islands Medical Service had come into being in 1913, subsumed within the Scottish Board of Health after the First World War. This Board was claimed by Westwood to have been the 'necessary pointer' for a comprehensive health service. A Committee on Scottish Health Services, the Cathcart Committee, had been set up by Scottish Secretary Sir Godfrey Collins to review health services in Scotland in the 1930s. In 1936, the Cathcart Report recommended 'linking up measures for the diagnosis and treatment of mental and nervous disorders with the corresponding measures for physical conditions'. The idea had been put forward in the annual report of the chief medical officer for Scotland in 1931. Scotland's poor health record, paralleling its poor housing, had been the cause for concern. Cathcart's main argument was that a national health policy for Scotland was necessary including health promotion and prevention, tackling poor diet, and emphasis on recreation and environmental and sanitary standards. It also warned of problems arising from an ageing population. The Clyde Basin Experiment during the Second World War had provided free medical care for war workers in the west of Scotland. The success of the scheme led to it being rolled out across Scotland. The origins of the separate legislation were clear and the degree of consensus in favour of change was strong.

The extent to which what emerged was different depends on perspective. The Scottish Office was responsible for the NHS but Cabinet collective responsibility meant that the Scottish NHS would never stray far from the path set by health ministers in England. There was nonetheless scope for differences in implementation and interpretation. What was significant was that levels of spending in Scotland *per capita* were consistently higher than in the rest of Britain. Within the broad parameters of health policy—less a policy than a heading for a vast array of policies—there was scope for divergence. There was as much scope for arguing that the NHS was a British policy as there was for arguing that it was a Scottish policy.

By the early 1950s, key health statistics highlighted what the Royal Commission on Scottish Affairs in 1954 referred to as 'disquieting features'. Infant mortality rates were 3.8 points higher in Scotland than in England, though the gap had been slowly narrowing over the course of the first half of the twentieth century. Respiratory tuberculosis was Scotland's major health problem. Scottish and English infection and mortality rates for this disease had been similar before the Second World War but by the late 1940s had worsened significantly in comparative terms. The Scottish NHS devoted considerable energy and resources to this area. By the end of 1951, 1,700 patients were on waiting lists to receive treatment for tuberculosis in hospitals but within the decade the waiting lists had been wiped out and patients received treatment immediately after diagnosis and the death rate fell from thirty-seven per 10,000 of the population to twelve by the end of the 1950s. New treatments, vigorous campaigns to detect the disease, and early detection had a direct impact but there was little doubt that underlying social conditions causing problems needed to be addressed. The Scottish NHS became a formidable institution in attending to Scotland's ill-health needs over the decades after its establishment.

FINANCIAL RELATIONS

The union has long been justified on economic grounds and the very idea of a separate Scottish economy has often been challenged. In this sense, the United Kingdom was primarily an economic union. As we have seen, regulation of banking in the nineteenth century involved taking account of Scottish distinctiveness and a Board of Manufactures had been established as far back as 1726 to help fisheries and 'manufactures'. Infrastructure was provided by local bodies in the Victorian period and consequently varied considerably across the state. The beginnings of a 'managed economy' are to be found during the mobilization of resources in the First World War and the efforts to understand and tackle depression in the inter-war period. Government intervention in the economy came falteringly and in a variety of forms: regulating economic activity and producing goods and services. There was little machinery of government designed to address specifically Scottish economic matters at central government level until well into the twentieth century and this was generally part of British-wide efforts to deal with the 'distribution of industry'.

Evidence suggests that Scotland was prosperous relative to other parts of Europe, including the rest of the UK, before the First World War. Debate on the Irish Question was once more important in providing evidence. Killing (Irish) home rule with kindness was not enough. It had to be demonstrated. From the early 1880s, the Treasury published a succession of returns setting out revenues, taxes, and population in each component of the UK. The focus was on Ireland and information was published right up to Ireland's secession but there was also interest in Scotland's position. A Royal Commission on the Financial Relations between Great Britain and Ireland which reported in the 1890s acknowledged 'errors of some magnitude' in previously published returns. An 1896 government report maintained that 'Scotland's true revenue' was £11,435,000 and her 'local expenditure' amounted to £4,143,000 with the 'balance available for Imperial charges' and that the Imperial contribution, 'with the exception of what may be spent in Scotland for military and naval purposes (probably not more than about two millions), constitutes a real "drain" upon the wealth-production of Scotland, to which there is nothing corresponding in the case of Ireland'. The financial relations returns 'died a natural death with the setting up of the new Irish Governments and which I hoped would never be revived', according to one Whitehall official in 1924. But the precedent had been established though pressure for further returns showed Scotland's relative position could more easily be resisted. Within Whitehall it was privately admitted that the figures were little better than 'guesswork' and there was no appetite in the Treasury to engaging in similar exercises for Scotland as had been necessary for Ireland.

However, pressure for information from Scotland did not disappear. In 1932, the junior Scottish Office Minister asked the Treasury for figures on Scotland's financial relations because Scottish nationalists were making a great deal of the fact that the Treasury was reluctant to supply figures. The Treasury replied that it had always been easier to separate the Irish figures and that separating the Scottish figures was 'always laborious and unsatisfactory'. Figures were supplied but the Treasury urged that they should not be used in a way that provoked 'demand for more detailed inquiry or for a return giving exhaustive information'. The return in December 1932 suggested that Scotland contributed only 5.62 per cent towards the cost of Imperial services while England and Wales provided the balance. These figures suggested that there had been a substantial decline within seven years since the last estimate of Scotland's contribution to Imperial services. Scotland's financial relations emerged during debates on the grants to distressed areas in 1933 and 1934 when the 11/80 basis was used 'causing a good deal of heartburning north of the Tweed', according to one Treasury official. In 1935, Sir Godfrey Collins, the Scottish Secretary, felt it necessary to produce a fairly comprehensive reply to demands for more information on Scotland's financial relations, including expenditure on social services, as the financial relationship between Scotland and England 'would almost certainly be a burning question in Scotland' at the next election. He wanted information to be available for candidates to 'refute critics such as the Scottish National Party'. The SNP was having an inordinate impact for a party that barely existed. In October, the government published another financial return purporting to show Scotland's contributions to and receipts from the Exchequer. Once more, the figures were challenged and once more nothing was resolved. A further return in 1936 offered a similar picture and provoked a similar reaction.

The Treasury argued that though any additional expenditure granted to Scotland might not amount to much in total UK expenditure there might be problems if the additional Scottish money had British-wide application. John Simon, Chancellor of the Exchequer, explained his view in a letter to Walter Elliot in February 1938:

> I feel quite certain that it would be impossible to apply a special stimulus to Government assistance to Scotland without arousing demands from the rest of the United Kingdom for corresponding treatment. In fact we should see the reverse of the familiar process under which England initiates a series of social schemes and Scotland demands that a proportion of the expenditure contemplated should be applied to her needs.

But while there were limits to what the Scottish Office could ask for, it was not too difficult to win more resources. The Goschen formula was not used systematically in allocating resources. It was rarely used at all for housing and health spending. However, it was used rhetorically with frequency in negotiations and debates. Members of Parliament, local authorities, interest groups, the Scottish Office and its departments, as well as the Treasury would all refer to Goschen when it suited them. The assumption was that Goschen offered some undefined and contested notion of fair shares.

THE FAILING ECONOMY

While official returns showed Scotland to be a net financial contributor to the union in the late Victorian and Edwardian periods, matters changed in the inter-war period. This reflected changes in the underlying Scottish economy. Shipbuilding peaked in 1913 and within two decades had fallen by over 90 per cent and three-quarters of its workforce was unemployed. The shipbuilding industry's response was to engage in mergers and 'anti-competitive' behaviour but to little avail. The decline in shipbuilding had serious consequences for demand for coal. Concern was expressed that the centre of economic gravity was in the south. Economic decline was matched by a culture of near despair. 'What's wrong with Scotland?' was the question posed in a series of BBC broadcasts by a number of prominent public figures in late 1929. There were a number of non-governmental initiatives in the inter-war period. A Scottish National Development Council was set up in 1931 and a Scottish Economic Council in 1936. William Power, who would later unsuccessfully contest the leadership of the SNP in 1942, had written a series of newspaper articles in 1929 outlining the economic challenges facing Scotland and had proposed a body to consider how these should be addressed. The idea was picked up by the Convention of Royal Burghs when they met in 1931. Power had suggested that the Convention of Royal Burghs, rather than central government, should take a lead in any new initiative. But when the Scottish National Development Council was set up in 1931, west of Scotland businessmen—Sir James Lithgow, Lord Weir, and Sir Steven Bilsland—were at the forefront and gave it impetus and this ensured its activities were viewed with suspicion by the trade union movement. The Council soon dropped 'National', fearing it might be associated with the home rule movement, and worked with the Scottish Office. In 1936, a Scottish Economic Committee was set up with government support. One criticism subsequently levelled against government in the 1930s was that it tended to focus on existing, struggling businesses rather than developing new industries. It was defensive and protective rather than innovative. Over time, the Scottish Economic Committee came to appreciate the need for new industries and diversification. But it was also a period when Scotland was seen across the political and economic spectrum as a distinct *economic* entity. Reports were issued feeding the idea that there was a distinct Scottish economy with its own problems requiring its own solutions. The idea of a *Scottish* response was viewed with suspicion in Whitehall while those involved in these activities in Scotland viewed Whitehall as out of touch.

These ad hoc measures were not very successful but paved the way for greater intervention after 1945. The 'Special Areas' that were designated in 1934—the first attempt at a regional policy in the UK—included much of central Scotland. Two Special Commissioners were appointed—one for England and Wales, the other for Scotland. The existence of a Scottish Commissioner was testimony to Whitehall accepting a Scottish dimension to the depression. The Scottish Commissioner was appointed by the Scottish Secretary and was expected to work with the Scottish Office rather than the Ministry of Labour as was the case with the other Commissioner. Rearmament in preparation for war helped improve economic conditions and had a much bigger impact than the Special Areas legislation. Nonetheless, one in ten of the Scottish workforce was still unemployed at the end of 1939.

The Special Areas legislation ushered in an era of planning and, crucially, raised expectations of government responsibility for economic well-being. The

1944 White Paper on employment asserted that maintaining high and stable levels of employment should be a government priority. In 1940, the (Barlow) Royal Commission on the Distribution of the Industrial Population recommended that central government should be responsible for tackling the distribution of industry. The more interventionist state that emerged from the Second World War would raise expectations that something should be done to reduce or remove disparities of wealth between classes of people but also between regions and the components of the United Kingdom.

There was a distinct Scottish dimension to this wartime activity. Tom Johnston was appointed Scottish Secretary in 1941 having been a radical home ruler earlier in his career. Churchill gave Johnston considerable autonomy. Johnston's approach was to build consensus in Scotland and lobby London with what would be presented as Scotland's national interest. He was concerned that English ministers, especially wartime Minister of Labour Ernest Bevin, were insensitive to Scottish needs and failed to consult him. He established his 'Council of State', the nearest Scotland came to having a Privy Council in two and a half centuries, consisting of all living former Scottish Secretaries. The Council met infrequently and was not very effective though it gave support to the development of hydro-electricity. In his memoirs, Johnston credited the Council with stirring up a 'new spirit of independence and hope in our national life…We were a nation once again.' This exaggeration fed into a potent post-war idea of corporate Scotland. His successors, none of whom operated in anything approaching the conditions Johnston worked in, would suffer from unfair comparisons. The Scottish Council (Development and Industry) (SCDI) was created in early 1946 through the merger of the Scottish Development Council and the Scottish Council on Industry and would be referred to in some quarters as 'Scotland's industrial parliament'. It brought together sections of business, trade unions, local authorities, and the Scottish Office and had a semi-official status. It was an extension of Johnston's wartime approach. The SCDI played a key role in encouraging inward investment to Scotland. A succession of reports and inquiries concluded that Scotland needed to diversify economically to address reliance on declining heavy industries. Between 1951 and 1959, eighteen new American firms had set up in Scotland and were expected to employ about 6,000 people when at full capacity but this led to fears that the Scottish economy was becoming a branch factory economy.

Another development, in keeping with the times, was the Clyde Valley Plan. Johnston appointed Patrick Abercrombie to draw up a plan for the development of the Glasgow city-region. Abercrombie is better known for planning Greater London during the war. His plans for Greater Glasgow extended this thinking north of the border. The Clyde Valley Plan recommended establishing 'new towns' and limiting the size of Glasgow. This would mean removing half a million Glaswegians from overcrowded tenements, with about half moved into new towns and the remainder into new housing schemes around the peripheries of the city. The peripheral schemes represented some of the worst of planning and state intervention. Soulless schemes devoid of many amenities left the impression that policy was to corral social and economic deprivation out of sight and mind of policy-makers. Depopulating urban Scotland was not quite the twentieth-century equivalent of the Highland Clearances but it had some of the same features.

New towns were created in East Kilbride, south-west of Glasgow, and Glenrothes in Fife in 1948. Cumbernauld to the east of Glasgow was created in 1955, the only one in Britain in the decade after 1951, reflecting powerful lobbying by the Scottish Office. Livingstone in West Lothian in 1962 and Irvine in Ayrshire in 1966 would be created under a new phase of new town developments. There was nothing particularly Scottish about the Clyde Valley Plan and new towns. Abercrombie's thinking was based on half a century of work in England. Comprehensive planning involved decongesting city centres, creating a green belt, moving people to the outer rings of cities and creating new garden suburbs with 'overspill'. But this thinking had significant economic, political, and social consequences not least in undermining the authority of Glasgow Corporation, the local city council. The report reiterated the need for greater diversification of industry, a point made many times before and later. Crucially, the state would have a major role.

Nationalization was at the heart of the Attlee Labour government's busy programme. The Conservatives and Unionists saw an opportunity to attack Labour by presenting nationalization as a form of centralization, taking control of industry out of Scottish hands and placing it under bureaucrats in London. In 1946, Walter Elliot, former Scottish Secretary and Unionist MP, stood in the Scottish Universities by-election, the last election for such a seat before they were abolished. In his election address he warned, 'The legislative Union between Scotland and England was never meant to entail, and should not entail, a complete swamping of the economic identity of the Northern Kingdom such as is now being conducted in the name of nationalisation.' A resolution passed by the Scottish Unionist Party in 1947 referred to the 'increasing measure of control in Scottish administration by Whitehall and the nationalisation policy of the Socialist Government which was taking away from Scotland management of her industries'. The impact of this campaign was privately acknowledged but resisted inside the Labour government. Herbert Morrison, overall responsible for Labour's nationalization programme, opposed any inquiry into a Scottish dimension to the nationalized industries, maintaining that 'For better or for worse a framework has been set up in the various nationalisation measures and it will not be possible to do anything about that framework until there has been practical experience of its working over a number of years.' Nationalization had not been a conscious UK 'nation-building' project, though the term nationalization rather than socialization might have suggested this. But it invited criticism that what was involved was the de-nationalizing of important sections of Scottish industry. Complaints did not die down. The Unionists played the Scottish card to maximum effect, ratcheting up perceptions that Scottish interests were at stake and, of course, taking as given that there ought to be a distinctly Scottish dimension to public policy and political institutions.

At a rally at Ibrox football stadium in Glasgow in 1949, Opposition leader Winston Churchill argued that nationalization not only affected Scotland's prosperity but also the 'independence' Scotland had exerted in 'so many fields'. On the same day as Churchill's speech, Scottish Unionists agreed to hold a special meeting later that year to discuss 'Scottish Control of Scottish Affairs'. At that conference, in Churchill's presence, the party endorsed a set of proposals including establishing Royal Commission to review the financial and economic relations between Scotland and England; appointment of a Minister of State to the Scottish Office; appointment of an additional Under Secretary of State; separate authorities for industries that it proved 'impossible to denationalise'; and reverting to local or private control of tramways and buses.

Scottish Secretary Arthur Woodburn considered a range of options in response to demands for home rule in a lengthy memorandum for the Cabinet in late 1947. Amongst these was the establishment of a Scottish Economic Conference (SEC) with representatives of Scottish Office departments, nationalized industries, and other bodies with economic interests in Scotland to be charged with producing an annual review of Scottish economic affairs. The main concern his Cabinet colleagues had with this proposal was that it might provoke a demand for something similar from Wales. The SEC would deliberate in private and would not pass formal resolutions. This recognized that economic concerns were the basis of demands for home rule demands. It also involved central government acknowledging something distinctive about the Scottish economy. There was weariness in Whitehall and the Cabinet about these claims. One Cabinet Office civil servant noted that Sir Stafford Cripps, when President of the Board of Trade, was 'anxious to rid himself of some of the tiresome Scottish economic problems by pushing responsibility (but not power) on to the Secretary of State for Scotland'. In 1950, Hector McNeill, Scottish Secretary, told his Labour Cabinet colleagues that he had no doubt that the feeling that nationalization equalled centralization was strong in Scotland and noted Labour's vulnerability on the matter.

One further concession made by the Labour government was the establishment of an inquiry into financial relations between Scotland and the rest of the state. It was a return to demonstrating that the UK was generous to its peripheries. The government was initially reluctant to concede this. The Cabinet Secretary warned that it was unlikely that 'any finality on this subject could ever be achieved' but home rulers were very active at the time. The Scottish Secretary concluded that a wider body of opinion favoured more information and feared that the government was vulnerable. In May 1950, the Scottish Secretary warned that refusal to hold an inquiry was regarded as 'unreasonable' and not only by home rule supporters. He suggested that there would be merit in demonstrating that the Scottish and English economies were 'so inextricably interlocked that an exact assessment of their relative contributions to exports and imports is quite impossible'. Lord Catto, Scottish businessman and former Governor of the Bank of England, was appointed chair of an inquiry to provide evidence for this argument. By the time Catto reported in 1952, home rule agitation had subsided and interest in financial relations with it. Catto was 'hardly a best seller!', as a Treasury official noted in a letter to a Scottish Office colleague. Catto's figures did not differ markedly in relative terms from those published in 1935.

There was little government investment in roads and transport in the decade after the Second World War but a major programme was announced in 1955. Scotland benefited from this round of investment. Work began on the Clyde Tunnel in 1957 and the Forth Road Bridge was started in 1958. Major road improvement schemes were started throughout the Highlands and the major arteries serving Scotland. But as the effects of wartime investment and needs receded, Scotland continued to suffer from the decline of those industries that had ensured Scotland had been a net financial contributor to the union before the First World War. Oil was replacing coal as a source of energy with the number of miners employed in Scotland's coal fields declining from its post-war peak in 1952. Unemployment grew in the late 1950s though it was far less severe than in the inter-war slump. Nonetheless, Scottish levels were about twice those in England and the UK as a whole invariably outstripped Scotland's economic performance throughout the early post-war period. There was one key difference with the inter-war period. The government acknowledged greater responsibility for managing the economy and maintaining high levels of employment. Central government pursued a minimal regional policy for most of the 1950s but became more active in the late 1950s. In 1958, a Cabinet committee was set up to review measures the government might take to deal with unemployment and a special meeting was held to discuss the situation in Scotland.

Account had to be taken of areas suffering from high levels of unemployment when the case for a fourth steel strip mill in the UK was being considered. If a decision had been made purely on economic grounds, then the mill would likely have gone to Humberside. But in May 1958, Prime Minister Macmillan told the Cabinet that where steel mills were to be built was finely balanced and that the decision was primarily a matter of 'broad national policy' involving 'not merely economic factors but also social and political issues' and these included 'sensitive questions of Scottish and Welsh sentiment'. Initially four areas were considered: Grangemouth in Scotland, Kidwelly and Newport in Wales, and Immingham in England. The Scottish Office, assisted by the SCDI, lobbied on behalf of Grangemouth. Ravenscraig in Lanarkshire entered the frame later in the year and the Ministry of Power proposed that one-third of new capacity should be located at Colville's Ravenscraig operation and the other two-thirds at Newport in Wales. It was a classic example of post-war policy-making by consensus, taking account of a variety of interests and reaching a messy com-promise. There was no demand in Scotland at that time for Ravenscraig's manufacturing output but jobs were needed. Even after car manufacturing was established in Bathgate and Linwood, supply still outstripped demand from the local economy for Ravenscraig's strip steel meaning that transport to markets would be important. A Scottish Office note on major developments between 1951 and 1959 described Ravenscraig's potential in a way that would be repeated by Tory candidates at the 1959 election. Ravenscraig would pro-vide work for 'about 3,500 men' giving Scotland a 'significant share of crucially important sheet capacity; and will, it is hoped, serve as a powerful stimulus in attracting new light industry to Scotland, thereby reducing her dependence on older established heavy industry'. These high hopes were only partly fulfilled.

NATIONAL INSURANCE, PENSIONS, AND REDISTRIBUTION

A system of national insurance was introduced in 1911 by Lloyd George, Chancellor of the Exchequer in the Liberal government, and was then greatly expanded in 1948 with many changes made thereafter. It was based on contri-butions made by employees and employers. A Joint Commission and four sep-arate Commissions were set up to administer national insurance for Scotland, England, Wales, and Ireland. In 1912, the staff of the Joint Commission was merged with the English Commission. The Irish had led demands for 'special treatment' and were followed by similar calls from Scotland and Wales. Sir Henry Bunbury, a founding member of the Insurance Commission, thought that accepting special treatment for the component nations had 'finally wrecked the bill', splitting it up into four separate parts, but he later concluded that separate Commissions gave the work authority throughout the state. Had only one Commission operated from London it would have lacked author-ity. As he wrote in his memoirs, 'the "Celts", as we called them, were in the first critical year a powerful influence against defeatism in London ... It was, in my judgement not a necessary but a very successful experiment in applied home rule'. This view was shared by the secretary of the Scottish Commission who wrote to the Treasury in 1916 arguing that the Joint Commission was less capable of taking account of local conditions and lacked legitimacy. In addition, he argued, 'national feeling in Scotland is strong' and that 'only by a separate administration can the Scottish position be properly met'.

However, in one of the few cases of an existing Scottish dimension disappearing after having been established by UK government, the Scottish Commission was abandoned, along with those for the other components of the UK, in 1948. Uniformity had been intimated in measures passed for unemployment and poor law in the inter-war years. Poor law was effectively harmonized across Britain before being replaced with the changes brought in following the Beveridge Report of 1942. There had been unease within government during the war when the idea of a National Insurance Ministry was being discussed. Walter Elliot, a previous Scottish Secretary and Minister of Health, argued for some 'organic connection between this great Department and the other great Departments from which portions are to be torn out, to make the new Ministry'. The government's response that there was a case for some devolution of administrative responsibility to Scotland caused concern in the Scottish Office. The Scottish Office made a series of recommendations, including having a high ranking official, 'more than a mere regional officer', in charge of the new Ministry in Scotland who would make policy and not just carry out instructions; separate Scottish records with the Scottish Secretary able to access any information required; and a separate Scottish legal adviser. Complaints in the Scottish press were brought to the attention of those responsible by Scottish Secretary Tom Johnston who suggested that senior officials in the Scottish Office should be consulted throughout.

A Committee on the Machinery of Government met during the war, just as had happened towards the end of the First World War, and produced a report in 1943 setting out its thinking on social insurance:

> We consider that unified responsibility in this sphere [social insurance] is essential; we agree that careful arrangement will be necessary for local administration in Scotland...Scotland should be regarded as a special case...it is desirable that sufficient authority should be devolved to enable Scotland's position to be strong on the spot with the minimum of reference to London and that in the settlement necessary in London on large matters of principle Scottish aspects should be fully considered. For departments of either type (i.e. those which have a strong regional organisation throughout the country and those which normally have no regional organisation) the official in charge in Scotland should be carefully selected and should have sufficient standing to make his advice valuable and his voice effective in the higher councils of his department in Whitehall: he should visit London frequently in order to share in the formulation of general policy.

Officials involved in establishing the new Ministry were keen to avoid being too specific in responding to pressure from Tom Johnston and the Scottish Office, not least because similar demands had been successfully resisted when the Ministry of Labour was set up.

By the time the Royal Commission on Scottish Affairs was sitting in the early 1950s, set up by the incoming Conservative government, the situation had been resolved largely in favour of the centralized more uniform approach though a 'Scottish Controller' had been appointed. In evidence before the Commission, the Permanent Secretary to the Ministry of National Insurance maintained that he could not see how it would be politically possible to propose lower benefit rates in Scotland or that the Scottish working man should pay more for some benefits and that 'any difference in the standard benefit rate is an unreal conception so long as you adhere to the idea of a universal scheme. If you are going to start again and do something else one could look at it, but within the framework of the existing scheme I think it is an unreal proposition.'

This statement was a fair summary of the general view of benefits, pensions, and the range of redistributive direct payments made to individuals by the state. Uniformity in the universal provision of such payments was felt to be essential. The pensioner in Penzance would be paid the same as the pensioner in Perth, even if the latter's heating costs would be greater. There was no great debate on this point but it became another unstated, or at least understated, but deeply entrenched part of the ideology of union. Where differences existed such as in teachers' pensions, these arose from the separate salary system operating in Scotland.

CONCLUSION

Over the course of a century, state intervention increased and state spending escalated. Scotland shared in these developments but most importantly it did so without the eradication of Scotland as a distinct entity. The creation of an interventionist welfare state had greater impact on society and the economy than had the union and with greater potential to eradicate much that was distinctly Scottish. The transition from night-watchman state displaced or supplemented formerly distinctly Scottish civic institutions with state institutions. The developing welfare state was largely a centralized state. But it necessitated local institutions to deliver its services. Not only did the state supplant civic bodies but the central state supplanted local bodies in providing broad direction to policy while leaving delivery at the local level. Uniformity, or at least less diversity, was one possible logic of this process but the transition had been incremental, building on distinct Scottish civic institutions. Centralization did not always involve uniformity. Once more, the ideology of union was important. It was not simply that policies and institutions were established taking account of Scottish needs but a more fundamental willingness to accept that a Scottish dimension pervaded thinking and action. But it had limits. Uniformity and centralization were adopted when it came to direct transfer payments to individuals.

Given that all ministers and agencies operated under collective ministerial responsibility, there were limits to the degree to which any Scottish bodies could be autonomous. It was not as if a socialist policy would be adopted in Scotland by a Unionist Scottish Secretary.

The most common feature of Scottish public policy was the Scottish Office's ability to gain more resources from the Treasury with the consequence that the most obvious Scottish feature was extending accepted policies. The Scottish Office became the Oliver Twist of Whitehall, always asking for more. Making the case for special treatment was one of the major functions of the Scottish Office. The extent of Scottish deprivation was the major argument deployed along with citing precedent and local conditions. Essentially, the Scottish Question boiled down to a battle for extra resources through negotiation and bargaining within an overall understanding that Scotland could be treated differently—more generously.

4

Consolidating Scottish Governance

INTRODUCTION

As we have seen, the office of Scottish Secretary had few formal responsibilities when it was established and was separate from the board system. This was anomalous in an era when the executive branch of government, which included boards, was expected to be accountable to Parliament. Over time, this anomaly would be addressed but there was strong resistance to abolishing the boards which were seen as a form of Scottish control of Scottish affairs. The Scottish Office was at least a ministerial office with its political head represented in and accountable to Parliament. There was no great plan behind the establishment and development of the Scottish Office. A highly distinct system of government in Scotland emerged by the time of the First World War and had become part of the furniture of British governance. It had developed piecemeal and an effort was made to put it on a rational basis in two major reforms during the inter-war period. What existed by the outbreak of the Second World War was anomalous if viewed from a rational administrative point of view but it was accepted as an integral part of UK central government. Its evolution over the early part of the twentieth century was the answer which this generation of decision-makers gave to how Scotland should be accommodated within a changing United Kingdom and how Scotland should govern itself.

CONSOLIDATING SCOTTISH ADMINISTRATION

Between its establishment in 1885 and the First World War, the Scottish Office accumulated a number of functions. As we have seen, it started off with responsibility for local administration and education. Law and order was transferred from the Home Office within two years. Growth in responsibilities in each of these areas ensured that the Scottish Office was no sinecure by the turn of the century. When it was agreed early in the twentieth century that a new Ministry of Agriculture should be established, it was decided that a separate Board of Agriculture for Scotland should also be established. There were concerns in Whitehall about this, which would recur in later considerations of how to deal with other extensions in state intervention, and it was agreed that animal health across Britain would come under the Ministry of Health to ensure a coordinated response in the event of an outbreak of foot-and-mouth disease or some similar contagious disease.

There had long been a Scottish dimension to agriculture and land issues. Land reform had been part of the radical platform in nineteenth-century politics. There had been measures to assist the Crofting Counties, including the establishment of a Crofters Commission in 1886. Indeed, much that was distinctive about land and agriculture was concerned with the Highlands and Islands. On becoming Scottish Secretary in the Liberal government returned in 1906, John Sinclair was keen to prioritize land reform. He proposed to extend provisions made for the Crofting Counties to the whole of Scotland and to establish a Land Court and Board of Agriculture for Scotland. This met with strong opposition in the Lords where the Liberals were having difficulties on a range of matters. Two land reform bills were rejected by the Lords after being passed by the Commons. A third attempt was successful, facilitated by the Parliament Act, 1911, which removed the Lords' veto. By this time, Sinclair had moved to the Lords. As Lord Pentland, he led land reform through its parliamentary passage there. The 'Pentland Act' would be unusual in being the only Act of Parliament popularly known by the name of a Scottish Secretary. The Scottish Board of Agriculture was formally separate from the office of Scottish Secretary, in keeping with the board tradition though there was mounting criticism of the board system by this time. But it was yet another example of central government dealing with a new function on a Scottish basis.

The next significant extension of responsibilities came at the end of the First World War when the Scottish Board of Health was established. It took over the responsibilities of the Local Government Board but also gained new responsibilities. In 1918, the Haldane Report on the Machinery of Government had recommended the 'further concentration of health services under a Minister of Health' but that the new ministry should be 'established to act in England and Wales only, leaving the separate systems already in operation in Scotland and Ireland for separate treatment'. Elsewhere in the report, Haldane had criticized the board system describing it as 'less effective in securing departments where full responsibility is definitely laid upon the Minister'. The separate system involved creating a board but this anomaly was acceptable in order to meet demands for treating Scotland as a distinct entity. One novel aspect of this development was the creation of a parliamentary Under Secretary for Health for Scotland.

The Scottish Boards of Agriculture and Health existed alongside rather than as integral parts of the Scottish Office, though the Scottish Secretary was responsible to Parliament for their activities. The Scottish Secretary's remit had grown from being 'quite unnecessary', as the first office holder described it, to the point that Robert Munro, Scottish Secretary from 1916 to 1922, complained about the wide-ranging nature of his responsibilities. The Scottish Secretary, he maintained,

> must put a severe curb upon his personal predilections, and endeavour to deal with those branches of his activities, whatever they may be, that call for immediate attention. He cannot, being merely human, expand habitually to the width such a catalogue would demand. He has to live from day to day, to attend Cabinets, to think of Upper Silesia as well as, let us say, Auchtermuchty.

This suggested an office that responded to events with little time to develop policy. But transferring policy responsibilities was not an entirely one-way process. The Ministry of Transport Act, 1919, brought responsibility for roads in Scotland to the new Ministry of Transport. The Scottish Boards of Health and Agriculture lost control of railways, canals, tramways, roads and bridges, harbours and piers.

Apart from these functional responsibilities, the Scottish Secretary had a much wider remit to ensure that Scottish interests were present at the heart of government. The Scottish people's expectation that the Scottish Secretary should have Archangelic qualities, referred to by Salisbury in 1885, had no statutory basis but it had become more important than any other function. The office was also important symbolically. An attempt to appease Scottish sensibilities came in 1926 when the office was upgraded to a Secretary of State. The change from a Secretary for Scotland to a Secretary *of State* for Scotland was purely symbolic. Even the salary remained less than for other Cabinet ministers. Scottish Secretaries were members of the Cabinet continuously after 1892, with the exception of the much smaller wartime Cabinet. There was little opposition to the 1926 change in status though an MP who was also an Oxford historian objected that creating another Secretary of State would lead to a 'dissipation of its ancient dignity'. The change may have amounted to little in practice but the symbolism was played for all it was worth. It gave Scotland a status 'unknown since the '45', according to the government. The Chairman of the Convention of Royal Burghs described the change as of 'historical significance' suggesting that the office's antecedent could be dated back to the King's Secretary first mentioned in 1395. Another change brought in at the same time was to change the status and role of the parliamentary Under Secretary for Health for Scotland. It would become an Under Secretary of State and, more importantly, the remit would no longer be limited to health. The Scottish Secretary would now have a junior minister with whom he could share his growing remit of responsibilities.

More practical changes were proposed over the next few years. An attempt was made to address the board system. Reform had been restricted to England and Wales. The Royal Commission on the Civil Service (MacDonnell) reported during the First World War. It was satisfied that the Scottish Office was 'regular' but was highly critical of the Edinburgh boards. The head of the Scottish Office, appearing before the MacDonnell Commission, had defended the membership of the boards as 'university men generally of high standing of one of the Scottish universities', whereas Scottish Office staff based in Whitehall were 'not mainly men of Scotch birth'. This would be the main defence of the boards. The MacDonnell Commission described the board system as an 'anachronism' and could 'give colour to the suspicion that Governments may attach greater value to personal service to a particular Minister or to a political party than to lifelong efficient service to the State'. But the immediate post-war period was not one in which bringing Scotland into line with the rest of Britain was likely to be a priority. Providing homes for heroes clashed with the Geddes cuts in public spending when the economy faltered after a brief period of growth immediately after the war.

The boards had been given a stay of execution on the grounds that they were distinctly Scottish but this could only be a temporary reprieve. Legislation was eventually brought before Parliament in the late 1920s to replace the boards with departments run by professional civil servants. As with legislation introduced in the 1880s to set up the Scottish Office, there was disagreement as to which boards should be tackled and it took more than one attempt to start the process of change. But agreement was reached in 1928 and legislation was put to Parliament which was passed that year. In introducing the legislation in the Commons, Scottish Secretary Sir John Gilmour criticized the patronage system but insisted that there was no intention of transferring activities from Scotland to Whitehall as had been widely reported in the press. He pointed out that a clause in the bill specifically stated that the new departments, replacing boards, would remain in Scotland. He was keen to appoint a 'single advisor' at the head of a department giving him advice as Scottish Secretary rather than receiving reports from each board or even having majority and minority reports on some matters.

The views of the boards varied. The Scottish Board of Agriculture had more critics than the Scottish Board of Health. A Scottish Office civil servant would later describe the variety of relationships between the Scottish Office and the various boards and departments as a 'most curious hotpotch'. The Education Department was as 'much a separate Department as the Home Office'; the Scottish Board of Health conducted its business independently of the Scottish Office though it had direct contact with ministers; the Scottish Board of Agriculture's relationship with the Scottish Office was 'almost impossible to define' with ministerial approval of decisions usually sent to the official head of the Scottish Office who would discuss these with the Secretary of State with decisions rarely recorded by the Scottish Office—it was a 'miracle of grace that it works at all'; a number of other bodies—the Fisheries Board, Prison Commission, General Board of Control, Register House, Registrar General, National Galleries—fell into yet another category that required ministerial and sometimes Treasury authority before making decisions; and the legal departments were controlled by Legal Officers rather than the Scottish Office but dealt with the Scottish Office on matters of legislation, staffing, and finance. There was considerable variation in attitudes to reform outside Parliament. Scottish farmers were reportedly opposed to home rule but home rulers in respect to maintaining the Scottish board system. The Scottish press was largely hostile to reform.

In Parliament, the strongest defence of the boards came from those who saw the boards offering a form of Scottish control of Scottish affairs. Noel Skelton, Unionist MP for Perth, was one of the chief defenders. His father had been chairman of the Board of Supervision and the Local Government Board. He told Parliament that he knew 'intimately many of the board heads' and argued that each board 'unquestionably gives to Scotland a certain degree of administrative Home Rule'. He was concerned that the leading official at the head of the Department of Agriculture might be an 'Englishman born and bred' and argued that the Scottish Office had never attracted 'first-class civil servants'. He was joined by some of the Red Clydeside MPs, unlikely supporters of boards being controlled by Edinburgh lawyers. The Reverend James Barr, radical home ruler and Red Clydesider, warned that what was being proposed was the assimilation of 'Scottish customs and practice with those of England'. He had no objection to an Englishman as head of a Scottish department but was concerned that whoever was appointed would have no experience of 'Scottish questions'. Barr argued that what was needed was a Scottish Parliament. There was a class dimension to the Clydesiders' objections and a strong fear that Oxbridge graduates would dominate in appointments to the Scottish Office. John Wheatley was one of a number who argued that there were experts in Scotland who knew as much about agriculture as anyone 'trained at Oxford or Cambridge', a theme picked up by other speakers. Davie Kirkwood suggested that the change was designed to deprive Labour of the chance of 'putting their friends' on to the boards. The Oxbridge graduates who dominated the Civil Service were, he claimed, trained 'in the art of idleness'. Sir Archibald Sinclair, Liberal MP who became Scottish Secretary three years later, saw it as a debate in which national sentiment was in conflict with administrative efficiency and economy. The Reorganisation of Offices (Scotland) Act, 1928, was passed, half a century after similar changes in England and Wales. Advisory boards had to be conceded and assurances given that the abolition of the boards did not mean further centralization in London, a point the Scottish Secretary urged the Scottish Unionist whip to make clear to party colleagues in explaining the changes to the wider Scottish public.

However, the 1928 Act had a narrow focus and many anomalies remained. Some boards continued to exist and the departments were still formally separate from the Scottish Office. Additionally, the state continued to develop and rumblings suggested dissatisfaction with the way Scotland was governed. Home rule agitation was not immediately threatening but was part of the backdrop of Scottish politics. This was the context in which Patrick Laird, a Scottish Office civil servant, wrote two memoranda on further reform. The first was written within a month of the passage of the 1928 Act and was entitled, 'A note as to the possibility of extending devolution'. The title suggested that a lesson in presentation had been learned. The Scottish Office wanted to avoid criticism that further reforms involved removing Scottish control of Scottish affairs. Laird argued for a 'coherent system' under the Scottish Office with the Scottish Office in London dealing primarily with parliamentary business and liaising with other Whitehall departments, recognizing that the growth of state intervention required day-to-day administration to be carried out by departments in Edinburgh. There was then no Scottish Office branch in Edinburgh directly advising the Scottish Office in Dover House in Whitehall. Relations between the Edinburgh boards and departments and Dover House depended on the extent to which Edinburgh and Whitehall responsibilities dove-tailed together and whether there was an official from the Edinburgh board or department based in London. Boards which had close links with local government tended to have close relations with the Scottish Office. Without an official based in London, communication with the Scottish Office was by written submissions which were less effective than personal contacts. Laird identified possible areas for 'devolution', after applying the test of whether the 'convenience of proximity' to the Edinburgh boards and departments, Scottish local authorities, and the Scottish public was more advantageous than proximity to ministers, Parliament, and London.

In 1932, Noel Skelton, a leading critic of the 1928 reorganization but now a junior Scottish Office minister, suggested that Laird should again examine the question of how Scotland was governed in the context of debates on home rule. This was the year the National Party of Scotland was founded, attracting considerable media interest if little public support. Laird wrote a second paper and entitled it, 'Administrative Devolution'. He felt that it was best to concentrate certain services in London rather than make further devolution to Edinburgh as it was necessary to have daily contact with other departments in Whitehall. Agricultural issues, he maintained, had Imperial and foreign implications which required a London base. The question was how to reconcile the existence of boards and departments based in Scotland conducting day-to-day work with a variety of civic and other bodies with the Scottish Office based in London as part of UK central government. His solution was to unify the various bodies and departments under the Scottish Office—'to make one fold as there is one shepherd'—with a general transfer of powers and duties to the Secretary of State. Work could be conducted in Edinburgh or London depending on what was most appropriate and all correspondence and activity would be conducted in the Secretary of State's name. He accepted that legal offices, the Registrar General, and a few others might continue to have a semi-independent existence but otherwise the 'most curious hotpotch', as one of his colleagues had described the array of Scottish central government institutions, should be concentrated and consolidated.

In what sense was this 'devolution'? Laird acknowledged the danger that his proposals might be seen as an attempt to concentrate power in London, which would be 'held to be politically impossible'. Some responsibilities of other Whitehall departments might be transferred to the Scottish Office, even to Edinburgh, including the appointment of Justices of the Peace and administration of the Aliens Acts from the Home Office and Lord Chancellor; piers and harbours from the Minister of Transport, and the possibility of creating an Office of Works for Scotland. It would be another generation before some of these transfers took place. What proved more important was how the proposals were packaged and presented. They were presented as a form of devolution, involving a transfer of government from London to Edinburgh. It was one of the most successful packaging of central government activities as far as Scotland was concerned in the twentieth century.

Aware that the 1928 Act had provoked opposition, it was felt necessary to build a broad consensus. In 1935, a paper by another civil servant proposed a comprehensive review of Scottish administration preceded by an official inquiry. Treasury permission was sought and given. Sir James Rae, a Scot working as a senior Treasury official, hoped that it would 'do much to kill the idiotic "Home Rule for Scotland" movement' and found himself appointed to the committee set up to review Scottish administration. Sir John Gilmour, former Scottish Secretary and Home Secretary, was appointed chairman. The Liberal Party was represented by Sir Robert Hamilton and Tom Johnston represented Labour along with a businessman, a retired civil servant, a former Solicitor General, and Rae of the Treasury. Johnston was an important appointment as he had been a strong supporter of home rule and a critic of the 1928 Act. Godfrey Collins died before the committee's appointment was made public in late 1936 leaving it to his successor Walter Elliot to make the announcement and be given credit in many subsequent histories for initiating the process leading to what would be the first comprehensive overhaul of Scottish central administration since the time of the night-watchman state.

The Gilmour Committee report offered a general survey of Scottish administration and discussed relations between the Scottish Office and other Scottish administrative bodies, considered difficulties confronted by the system, and recommended reforms. It repeated arguments made time and again and set out proposals that were broadly predictable to anyone who had read the various papers that had been circulating within the Scottish Office for many years. It noted the peculiarly wide range of duties of the Secretary of State—Tom Johnston had previously described the office as a Pooh-bah—and how these had grown in the recent decade. According to the Gilmour Report of 1937, the Scottish Secretary was 'popularly regarded as "Scotland's Minister": and our evidence shows that there is an increasing tendency to appeal to him on all matters which have a Scottish aspect, even if on a strict view they are outside the province of his duties as statutorily defined'. The Secretary of State for Scotland was 'unique' in having his duties defined geographically rather than functionally, discharged an 'assortment of heterogeneous and disconnected functions'. He was 'expected to be the mouthpiece of Scottish opinion in the Cabinet and elsewhere'. Difficulties in liaising with Whitehall departments and between the Scottish Office in London and the various bodies in Edinburgh were acknowledged. The Committee recommended that day-to-day administration should be conducted in Edinburgh leaving the London Office as a parliamentary and liaison office. It proposed consolidating the various Edinburgh offices formally under the Scottish Secretary thus at least giving the appearance that the work of officials in Edinburgh was formally under ministerial control. Four new departments should be created directly under the Scottish Secretary—a Department of Agriculture, Scottish Education Department, Department of Health, and Scottish Home Department—operating like a mini-functionally-based Whitehall in Scotland. It further proposed that a Permanent Secretary should be appointed advising the Secretary of State, who would be separate from the heads of each of the four departments.

A committee of civil servants chaired by Sir Horace Hamilton, head of the Scottish Office, considered the proposals and Treasury approval was sought before they were presented as a draft bill to Parliament. The Hamilton Committee had little to disagree with not least as the proposals had followed the outline of debates and ideas that had been developing within the Scottish Office for some time. The committee's main job was to put flesh on the bones of Gilmour's proposals but it made one significant change. Gilmour had been hesitant in defining the role of the Permanent Secretary. Hamilton proposed a more powerful figure, more than a 'personal assistant' to the minister as Hamilton interpreted the Gilmour Report's proposals. But this was detail. The Treasury and appropriate Cabinet committee gave their approval. Debate in Parliament was perfunctory, especially as compared with the debate a decade before. Walter Elliot used the opportunity of discussing the Gilmour recommendations to raise the possibility of getting an additional junior minister for the Scottish Office, a matter raised but without recommendation by the Gilmour Committee. The Prime Minister decided that the question should be left open.

Successive Scottish Secretaries had worried about maintaining contact with Scotland. Sir Godfrey Collins, Scottish Secretary from 1932 to 1936 and a member of the Collins publishing family, was instrumental in initiating plans to consolidate the Edinburgh staff under one roof in a general headquarters in Edinburgh. Collins complained that even rapid communication could not keep him in touch with the 'spirit of Scotland, the heart of Scotland, and if the Government of Scotland is to be successfully conducted, it can only be done by those who, through personal experience, are familiar with the desires of Scotland and the atmosphere in which its people are living, and who have the opportunities of discussing with its local authorities and its citizens'. Other developments had raised the prospect of devolving functions to Edinburgh. A Committee on Local Economy for Scotland had recommended establishing a branch of the Scottish Office in Edinburgh despite the Scottish Office having no formal responsibilities for the economy.

A branch of the Scottish Office with responsibility for local government, police, and other local matters was opened at Drumsheugh Gardens in Edinburgh in 1935. It was headed by David Milne, who would become Permanent Secretary of the Scottish Office in 1946. At that time over 90 per cent of the staff of the combined Scottish departments and boards—over 1,500 people—were based in Edinburgh and fewer than 120 were based in London. The transfer of staff reduced those in London by about half resulting in about 97 per cent of the staff of the Scottish administrative bodies being based in Scotland. But the various staff were scattered in offices across the city. In 1938, Scottish Secretary Sir John Colville remarked that in the previous twelve months there had been over 1,500 meetings between Edinburgh staff of the Scottish Office and various local authorities. Over forty committees were connected with Scottish Office departments including thirty-five standing committees and five committees of inquiry, giving a sense of the expansion of government activities. These included the Advisory Council to the Scottish Education Department, various Consultative Councils on health matters, the Scottish Central Council of Juvenile Organisations, the Agricultural Advisory Council, and the Egg Laying Test Advisory Committee in the Scottish Department of Agriculture.

Consolidation of Scottish central administration in Edinburgh would not work if public officials remained spread across the city. Building a central office bringing all staff together had been mooted early in the inter-war period but cost and lack of leadership had left the idea hanging. The combination of home rule agitation, new thinking on consolidating central administration evident in Laird's papers, and awareness of the inadequacy of some of the Edinburgh accommodation, spread over some thirty buildings, brought the issue back onto the agenda. Agreement was reached to build a new headquarters in Edinburgh, a 'manifest sign of the administration of Scottish affairs in Scotland', as Godfrey Collins put it. The site of what had been Calton Jail at the east end of Princes Street was identified and an architect and design were chosen after much publicity and some controversy. There was debate as to the name for the new building with an assortment of suggestions made by members of the public: Wallace House, Scots Wha Hae House, Columba, British State, Dunedin, Government House, Caledonia, and St Andrew's House. The building which was to become St Andrew's House excited more public interest and engagement than any other part of the creation of what would be presented as 'administrative devolution'.

As war approached, preparations were made for bringing the Gilmour recommendations and the Reorganisation of Offices (Scotland) Act, 1939, into operation and for opening the newly constructed St Andrew's House. The new Edinburgh headquarters of the Scottish administration was opened in 1940, postponed because of the outbreak of war, but it never became the home to all Scottish Office civil servants in Edinburgh. The pressures that had led to reform had overtaken the Scottish Office. The building was too small to house the growing number of staff by the time the building was completed and so some remained in offices spread across Edinburgh. But the structure of the office would be the basis of Scottish government for the next half-century, though subject to change and evolution from pressures that continued to reflect the changing role of the state as well as responses to Scottish sensibilities. One of the most intriguing aspects of the 1939 reforms has been the enduring myth of administrative devolution. Civil servants were moved but within Edinburgh, not to Edinburgh. Scottish central administration was consolidated rather than transferred in 1939. The Scottish Office remained part of Whitehall where it needed to be based given that this was the seat of governmental power.

EVOLVING LOCAL ADMINISTRATION

While there was controversy surrounding the reorganization of Scottish central administration in the late 1920s and much fanfare surrounding the opening of St Andrew's House, much more attention was paid to changes in local government in the inter-war period. Industrialization and urbanization were most acutely felt at local level and the variety of ad hoc local bodies that had grown up in the nineteenth century proved inadequate in the twentieth century. As we have seen, these local bodies owed their origins to the Kirk's parochial administration and there was a keen sense of loyalty to bodies which were both distinctly local and distinctly Scottish. There were a number of pressures for reform. Larger authorities were thought to be required to have the capacity to tackle major infrastructure projects and provide education. The ad hoc nature of local administration had led to a plethora of local bodies, each focused on a specific task but with little coordination. The case for *ad omnia* authorities with wider responsibilities was repeatedly made. There was also an expectation that these bodies should be elected. None of these pressures were unique to Scotland—similar pressures were evident in England and Wales—but responses to these had to take account of Scottish geographical and demographic particularities as well as past and existing practices.

Proposals to reorganize Scottish local government were presented to Parliament in 1929 by Sir John Gilmour. Many inquiries over many years had concluded that local government was inadequate and varied considerably across Scotland. Parish councils had been established in 1845 to administer the poor law and varied in size from one with a population of 78 to Govan with 600,000. Three-quarters of Scotland's poor who required assistance lived in under 40 per cent of the largest parishes with the remainder spread throughout 830 parishes. There were over 4,300 parish councillors. There were 308 bodies responsible for highways in Scotland. The Local Government (Scotland) Act, 1929, replaced the parish councils, 27 district councils, 98 district committees, 37 education authorities, and 33 standing joint committees with 33 counties and 201 burghs. It had often been suggested that Scotland was under-governed in the nineteenth century but it appeared to be over-governed at this point in the twentieth century. Gilmour argued that this 'multiplicity of authorities caused confusion, waste, and overlapping and an unnecessary duplication'. The overlapping authorities were thought to cause confusion for the electorate. Elections were often uncontested or failed to attract enough candidates and turnout could be as low as 14 per cent. The financing of these local authorities was equally incoherent.

But there was strong opposition to the reform. In Parliament, Tom Johnston criticized the unification of authorities: 'The human child, the most delicate mechanism in the world, is to be united with sewage farms, public loans, trains, waterworks, and so on all jumbled together in this monstrosity which the right hon. Gentleman calls unification.' Larger authorities were opposed on other grounds. Cameron of Lochiel, a leading Unionist figure in local government in the Highlands, noted that many councillors would have to return to the county town of Inverness for meetings no sooner than they had arrived home from the previous one and in some cases a return home would not be possible without missing meetings. He highlighted a key feature of transport links within the United Kingdom:

> During the time that a man will come from Barra to Inverness and back, another man can go from Inverness to London, spend the whole day in the City and go to the play in the evening before the first man has got from Inverness to Barra. Is that democracy, to take the power away from the representatives of the people and put it in the hands of men with time and leisure?

But opposition also had a sentimental dimension. Tom Johnston quoted the nineteenth-century constitutional historian Cosmo Innes:

> In the homely burghs of Scotland we may find the first spring of that public spirit; the voice of the people, which in the worst of times when the Crown and the law

were powerless and the feudal aristocracy altogether selfish in its views, supported the patriot leaders, Wallace and Bruce, and sent down that tide of native feeling which animated Burns and Scott and is not yet dead...whatever of thought, of enterprise, of public feeling appears in our poor history took use in our burghs, and among the burgess class. Now, the right hon. Gentleman proposes to put an end to that old song.

There was predictably strong opposition from those affected by the legislation and key figures in local government, including many Unionists. Sir Henry Keith and Sir W. E. Whyte were outspoken critics, each viewing the changes as evidence of London's inability to understand Scotland. In 1932, both joined and became members of the executive of the Scottish Party, a small party that was one of the forerunners of the Scottish National Party.

There were criticisms that the Scottish Office was simply following plans designed for England. Sir Archibald Sinclair, Liberal MP for Caithness who would become Scottish Secretary two years later, felt it did more than this. The Bill 'out-Herods Herod in his massacre of the innocents'. Minister of Health Neville Chamberlain's reform of English local government was based on Chamberlain's long experience of and expertise in local government affairs, particularly in Birmingham, but this was felt by opponents of the Scottish Bill to be irrelevant. It was suggested that the English proposals had at least benefited from careful consideration while those for Scotland had been hastily produced. Sinclair argued that a Scottish Parliament should be created to allow those with expertise in local government to determine any reform. The sense was left that Scotland was following the English lead with little appreciation of Scottish traditions and needs. In fact, there had been debate on these matters dating back to the nineteenth century but local government reform had become embroiled in wider Scottish debates.

The measure was passed but not without political consequences beyond local government. The Scottish Unionists lost ground at the 1929 election, losing almost 5 per cent of the vote and sixteen seats. Colonel Patrick Blair, Scottish Unionist political secretary, wrote to Gilmour outlining the problems that had caused the decline in the party's fortunes. He argued that the Local Government (Scotland) Act had been deeply unpopular and warned that leaflets produced in London were often 'inappropriate and inapplicable for Scotland'.

PARLIAMENTARY PARALLELS

Having a Scottish Office headed by a minister accountable to Parliament and responsible for the passage of Scottish legislation necessitated parallel developments in parliamentary procedures and practices. These developed in the same piecemeal fashion as the Scottish Office. There were calls for more time to debate Scottish Supply, the sums of money allocated to the growing body of public bodies. In the nineteenth century, informal practices had developed whereby Scottish MPs were consulted in 'Tea Room meetings' as rudimentary concessions to the demand for separate parliamentary procedures. Scottish MPs felt that insufficient time was devoted to Scottish affairs due to parliamentary congestion, exacerbated by Irish Nationalist obstruction in the latter half of the century. This view did not disappear after the Irish Question took up less parliamentary time.

Sir Erskine May, appointed Clerk to the House of Commons in 1871, had long been an advocate of what he called 'Grand Committees'—committees that were smaller than Committees of the Whole House but larger than Select Committees. He had described these as 'little Parliaments' in an anonymous article in the *Edinburgh Review* in 1854. The term 'Grand' had entered the vocabulary of Parliament suggesting that these committees had status and deep historical roots. But May did not have Scotland in mind but imagined the establishment of committees for such matters as religion, trade, local government, and taxation. Parnell, the Irish Nationalist leader, had proposed Grand Committees for England, Scotland, and Ireland in 1878 but this had found little support. In 1882, Gladstone proposed an experiment in having two such committees—for Law and Courts of Justice and for Trade, Shipping, and Manufactures. It was suggested by Scottish Members that a Scottish Committee might be included, even one that might sit in Edinburgh. Sir George Campbell, Liberal MP for Kirkcaldy, withdrew such a proposal but argued that it 'was impossible for 650 Members sitting together in the House of Commons to do the whole details of the work of the Three Kingdoms'. There was opposition to any such committees from Members who feared that the Commons would become a 'Bill-spinning machine', as W. H. Smith, Tory MP and member of the newsagent family, suggested.

Standing Committees were established under the Commons' Standing Orders in 1888 but no Scottish committee was proposed at this stage. However, a number of Scottish Liberal MPs raised the idea over the following years but were opposed by Conservatives. In 1890, for example, Campbell urged the establishment of 'Territorial Standing committees', especially for the northern part of Britain with 'such distinctive institutions, laws, and nomenclature as are not understood by the more southern branches of the Anglian and Celtic races'. But W. H. Smith, now Leader of the House of Commons, dismissed the idea. The opportunity to establish a Scottish Grand Committee finally came when the Liberals were returned to power in 1894. Scottish Secretary Sir George Trevelyan, a Cornishman representing Glasgow Bridgeton, proposed its establishment with the support of Prime Minister Campbell-Bannerman.

Arthur Balfour opposed the establishment of a Scottish Grand Committee, arguing that it would 'revolutionise the practice' of the Commons. His comments have passed into history but are worth recalling in some detail given their continued relevance. The introduction of the 'principle of nationality into our Grand Committees', he argued, was absolutely 'subversive'. It would 'upset our immemorial traditions'. Balfour articulated his view on the role of Scottish MPs:

> Why are Scotch Members elected by their various constituencies? Are they elected simply and solely because of their views on such legislation as is described in this Resolution—'Resolution solely relating to Scotland'? They are nothing of the kind; they are elected as part of the general system. They are elected in reference to an Imperial Parliament, in which Parties have a certain balance, and in which the various Parties have a certain policy.

He challenged the very notion of Scottish interests, suggesting that when he is told that 'Scotland thinks this or that', what is really meant is that MPs support 'one or other of the great Parties in the State, that Scotland may be taken to uphold these Parties in proportion as it sends Members to support one Party or the other'. He questioned whether any bill related exclusively to Scotland; such an idea was a 'fantastic absurdity' and asked how such a 'new and revolutionary scheme for dealing with the legislation of one part of the United Kingdom' would operate in other parts of the UK. He warned that this 'insane action' might 'arouse England to a sense that she is an oppressed nationality, and compel her to use the power which she undoubtedly possesses to exclude from all share in her affairs those who do not happen to live within her borders'. What would happen if an English Grand Committee was established and the governing party did not command a majority in England?

> Give this to Scotland and refuse it to England, and you will make every Englishman and every English Member feel that he is not allowed to legislate for his own country as Scotchmen are allowed to legislate for their country. Grant it to England, and you make legislation by a responsible Government an absurdity whenever a Government happens to be in Office which does not command a majority of English votes. I have often thought of this question, and have asked myself how that dilemma is to be avoided. Never have I found anybody who could tell me a method of avoiding it, nor have I ever myself been able to devise any such method.

His comments on the implications of treating one part of the state differently would echo down the years. The West Lothian Question might equally be called the Hertford Question after Balfour's then parliamentary constituency. Unlike the case for a Scottish Office, which won all-party support in the 1880s, support for a Scottish Parliamentary Committee split opinion along party lines with Liberals supporting the idea and Liberal Unionists and Conservatives opposed. Despite Balfour's objections, the Liberals experimented with a Scottish Grand Committee in 1894 consisting of all Scottish MPs plus fifteen additional MPs and again in 1896 with twenty additional MPs. The additional

Members ensured that the Committee's composition approximated the composition of the Commons as a whole, in common with other parliamentary committees. The return of the Conservatives ended the experiment. But the Scottish Grand Committee was re-established on a permanent basis after the Liberals were back in power in 1906. The first decade of the twentieth century was a period of parliamentary reform. Almost all bills, unless ordered specifically by the Commons, were sent to standing committees. This meant that the Scottish Grand Committee became embedded within wider reform of Parliament.

Whether a bill should be debated in a Scottish Committee or by the House as a whole could be controversial. In 1911, an attempt was made to commit the Small Landholders (Scotland) Bill to a Committee of the Whole House after it had passed its committee stage in the Scottish Grand Committee in 1911. The bill was a much watered-down version of land reform favoured by Liberals but it was less the land reform proposals that created controversy in this instance. The bill also created a Scottish Board of Agriculture, a provision that had been added during committee stage. Some English Members objected that the creation of the Board meant that it was no longer an exclusively Scottish measure as the proposed Scottish Board would be responsible for the administration of contagious animal diseases with British-wide implications. Farming interests in England, particularly on the border with Scotland, saw this provision as having serious implications throughout Britain. The question was put to the House and rejected though the government backed down, as discussed above, and the Scottish Board was not given responsibility for contagious animal diseases.

DEBATING SUPPLY AND PARLIAMENTARY
TIME FOR SCOTTISH BUSINESS

Demands for more time to be spent debating Scottish Supply increased in the twentieth century. As each board and department had a separate corporate existence, there were twelve separate votes on supply at the start of the twentieth century each year in Parliament. This meant that there was insufficient time to debate every supply vote each year. In 1907, for example, there were only three short debates on the twelve votes. State spending was increasing but without increased parliamentary scrutiny. An attempt to debate the Local Government Board's spending during a debate on the Scottish Office's vote was ruled out of order. Scottish MPs argued that Scotland was treated unfairly in the sums allocated and parliamentary time devoted to Scottish affairs, especially compared with Ireland. In 1912, Prime Minister Asquith candidly admitted that Irish affairs and the lack of parliamentary time created problems: 'when the season annually comes round for compiling the King's Speech, the practical question for those concerned with its composition is what is the least instalment of that which is admittedly overdue by which England, Scotland, and Wales can be respectively for the Session be bought off'. The same applied to debates on supply. It may have been a problem afflicting other parts of Britain but this did little to remove the sense of grievance.

Nothing much changed in the inter-war period though in 1922 a problem arose as a consequence of Labour's Scottish electoral success when the Conservatives formed a government. Even with added Members representing seats outside Scotland, the Scottish Committee would still have a majority of Labour MPs. This made the Scottish Committee 'unusable', in the words of Sir Ivor Jennings, leading authority on Parliament and the constitution. Complaints continued to be made that there was insufficient time devoted to Scotland. James Henderson Stewart, National Liberal MP for East Fife, frequently criticized the lack of time devoted to Scottish business. Answers to his parliamentary questions showed that the amount of time devoted to debating supply varied considerably between 1929 and 1938, averaging 14 hours 42 minutes, from almost 23 hours in 1931 to just over 9 hours in 1933. Scotland existed as an identifiable entity in the allocation of parliamentary time but this only heightened expectations. Imperial and British affairs affected Scotland but there was a growing body of Scottish affairs that required Scottish time in Parliament. In addition, time on Scottish business other than answering questions averaged 36 hours 35 minutes. What was most significant was that it was possible to provide such information. In a debate on public spending allocated to agriculture in Scotland in 1933, Jimmy Maxton quipped that the key characteristic of the Scottish Office was the 'length of time that they take to do everything, and the shortness of time that we get to discuss what they have done'.

Tom Johnston extended parliamentary procedures as Scottish Secretary during the Second World War. The Scottish Grand Committee met in Edinburgh though this attracted few members and little interest and the experiment did not last long. There was more tolerance than enthusiasm for this initiative and even the tolerance could wear thin. Nye Bevan described the Scottish Grand Committee as a 'parochial minded body not much superior in standard to an average County Council'. But even under wartime conditions, when sensitivities might have been expected to be at a minimum, there was a willingness to respect Scottish circumstances.

By the middle of the twentieth century, Scotland was described in an article in the *Times* as enjoying 'very considerable control of its own legislation and finance within the Palace of Westminster', though this view was challenged by a 'Parliamentary correspondent' writing in *Parliamentary Affairs*. Before the war, the Scottish Grand Committee had considered the details of bills in much the same way as other standing committees. But its role widened in the immediate post-war period against the backdrop of post-war consideration of the machinery of British government and home rule agitation. There was a desire to speed up parliamentary proceedings and Sir Gilbert Campion, Clerk to the House of Commons, produced a report making a number of recommendations. Pressure for reform arose from the growth in parliamentary and government activity, common 'in almost every elective assembly in countries where modern views as to the powers and duties of the State are finding expression', as the last committee which had reviewed parliamentary procedure had acknowledged in the early 1930s. Campion noted that sessions of Parliament had hardly changed over the previous four decades and the proportion of time devoted to dealing with legislation, controlling finance, and making policy had remained broadly the same despite a significant increase in the amount of legislation. Greater use had been made of standing committees. Campion proposed that even greater use be made of standing committees, including removing report stages (following debates in committees) from the floor of the House and holding these in standing committees. In common with reports considering machinery of government, he acknowledged the special procedures for dealing with Scottish affairs. He proposed to include the Scottish Grand Committee in his general conclusions. The Committee, he suggested, should be able to divide itself into subcommittees and whether this happened or not, it should take the report stage of Scottish bills; additionally, the second readings of Scottish bills could be transferred from the House to the Committee. In responding to Campion's proposal in a memorandum in 1946, Herbert Morrison, the Lord President, warned his Cabinet colleagues that allowing the Scottish Committee to take second reading of bills might prove an 'embarrassing precedent' and noted that 'special measures' would be needed if Opposition Members were in a majority in Scotland in order to 'ensure that the Government retained control over the proceedings of the Standing committee'. Similar concerns had been expressed at the Cabinet subcommittee considering Campion's proposals. It was thought that Scottish MPs would oppose second readings of bills being taken in committee as they would be deprived the chance to speak to the bill on the floor of the House. It was also noted again that special measures would be necessary to ensure that the government retained control of proceedings.

Within a year, however, with a backdrop of home rule agitation, Scottish Secretary Arthur Woodburn proposed that Scottish bills should be referred to the Scottish Standing Committee for consideration in principle before a second reading was taken without debate on the floor of the Commons. In another memo for the Cabinet, explicitly responding to home rule agitation, Woodburn made a series of proposals including 'meeting the desire of Scotsmen for more control over their own affairs by making greater use, within the present Parliamentary system, of the Scottish Grand Committee'. Safeguards were proposed to prevent the government losing control of Scottish legislation. Scottish bills would be referred to the Scottish Grand Committee for consideration in principle on a motion from a Government minister so long as no more than ten MPs objected. After debate in the Committee, the bill would return to the Commons where it would be authorized to have been given its second reading without a debate or a vote if necessary. The Commons would in effect formally retain the power to reject any bill at second reading but normally this responsibility would be handed over to the Scottish Committee. Woodburn also proposed to accept a proposal made by Walter Elliot to allow the Scottish Grand Committee to debate Scottish Estimates for up to six days each year before formally coming before the Committee of Supply, again in effect handing over the scrutiny of Scottish public finances to the Committee. This latter proposal was not entirely novel. In 1919, the Estimates for the armed services, civil service, and revenue departments had been referred to a standing committee but that practice had operated for only one year.

These Scottish proposals formed part of the government's response to home rule agitation that appeared in a White Paper on 'Scottish Affairs' in 1948. The new responsibilities given to the Scottish Grand Committee were provided for under new Standing Orders adopted by the Commons. A contemporary commentator described the Scottish Standing Committee's 'main value as a constitutional organ' giving Scottish MPs a 'channel of self-expression on many matters peculiar to Scotland without in any way reducing or limiting their influence as members of the imperial Parliament at Westminster'. Once more, Scottish interests had insinuated themselves into a wider debate on reform. The existence of the Scottish Grand Committee meant that Scottish business was dealt with separately but it had its limitations, which were summed up well in a newspaper article following an important debate on Scottish local government in 1928: 'Scotland already enjoys at Westminster a sort of Home Rule in purely Scottish subjects, though to be sure it does not extend to the division lobbies.' Parliament as a whole would assert itself if there was any danger of government business being lost.

BALFOUR COMMISSION

Once returned to power in 1951, the Conservatives had to deliver on their promises if they were to avoid the same criticisms that they had made of Labour. Additional Scottish Office ministers were appointed including a Minister of State. A Royal Commission on Scottish Affairs was appointed, chaired by Lord Balfour. George Pottinger was appointed secretary and wrote the report which was published in 1954. 'Gorgeous George' was a young ambitious Scottish Office civil servant who went on to head the Department of Agriculture and Fisheries in Scotland. After a successful career rising through the Scottish Office, he was convicted and jailed for accepting bribes from a crooked architect in 1973. But back in the early 1950s he was a civil servant with a promising career ahead.

The Royal Commission did not consider the case for and against a Scottish Parliament but restricted its remit to considering the adequacy of the existing machinery of government. It reported in 1954 recommending the transfer of a number of responsibilities from British ministries to the Scottish Office. Roads, piers, and ferries were transferred from the Ministry of Transport; Justices of the Peace from the Lord Chancellor; animal health from the Ministry of Agriculture subject to the Agriculture Ministry remaining responsible in the case of epidemics across Britain. The respective ministers accepted these proposals. The Scottish Office would be responsible for all functions of local authorities with the transfer of roads. It is notable that many of these transfers had been proposed by Patrick Laird, the Scottish Office civil servant, when he had written his paper, 'Administrative Devolution' in 1932. Laird had then proposed a more 'coherent system' with the transfer of Justices of the Peace, the administration of the Aliens Acts, and piers and harbours. Animal health had been withheld from the Scottish Board of Agriculture on its establishment after the First World War but Scottish administration had finally shown itself to be competent and trusted.

The Royal Commission gathered considerable information on how Scotland was governed though little of this was published. It had required Whitehall departments to reflect on how they handled Scottish business and these reflections, internal to government, may have been more important than the ensuing report. A Treasury note on the machinery of government outlined the thinking behind deciding whether matters should be handled by the Scottish Secretary or a minister with UK or British responsibilities, acknowledging that these reflected trends rather following a strict logic. Scottish national sentiment was important but efficiency was the uppermost concern. The document referred to factors that favoured the 'retention of a Great Britain basis of administration' when, in fact, what it discussed was often not the retention but the adoption of a Great Britain basis as in many cases the pre-existing arrangements were local or had a Scottish dimension. But the language spoke of an underlying default assumption that a UK/British approach was appropriate unless a Scottish case was made. But it also spoke of a willingness to consider a Scottish approach. The key factors favouring a British basis were matters which concerned the 'well-being of the United Kingdom as a whole'; an acceptance that departments were best based on services or functions rather than persons or classes, as set out in the Haldane Report in 1918 on the machinery of government; and the increased capability of central departments to adapt to regional and local circumstances especially with the expansion of regional administrative arrangements that had developed during the Second World War. National finance was also thought to require central control: taxation and collection of revenues, control of expenditure, and civil establishments had to be controlled from the centre. Defence could only be organized on a UK basis though civil defence required some devolution. Pensions and national insurance required a British-wide administration. The UK economy made it difficult to separate Scotland from England as far as trade and industry were concerned and Scotland might suffer in locating factories in development areas under different arrangements but there were questions on how this general principle might operate with basic industries such as electricity. The same applied to agriculture, forestry and fisheries, transport, and the Post Office. But, it was maintained, law and order, with the exceptions of dealing with 'aliens', vivisection, and explosives, was best administered by Scottish departments. Health, local government, and town and country planning 'must in practice be identical, but differences in detail' were possible between Scotland and England.

Another official outlined five main reasons for considering devolving responsibilities: when there was value in having direct contact and a personal touch; when there was a need to adjust administration to the special needs of particular localities; avoiding delay; in the general convenience of the public; and due to the increasing weight and complexity of central government tasks. Many departments had long-established regional organizations, including taking account of Scotland as a distinct entity. The Post Office, Labour, and Transport departments had decentralized arrangements. Indeed, a 1932 report on the organization of the Post Office had given strength to the case for a decentralized approach. But not all departments shared this view. The situation across Whitehall was patchy. The reason for this was not due to a strong centralist impulse so much as lack of engagement in such concerns. While the Haldane Committee on the Machinery of Government had sat during the First World War and a similar committee did so again during the Second World War, machinery of government—at least as understood in terms of the division of functions between departments as distinct from the more general meaning of efficiency—was not something that exercised the minds of Whitehall. A Machinery of Government (MG) branch was established in 1945, headed by William Armstrong, who became head of the Home Civil Service in 1968. However, the work of the MG branch was light. Armstrong worked with a tiny staff and reportedly used his time in this post to read widely and even write a play. Machinery of Government was simply not a high priority across government but that went well beyond the implications for how Scotland was governed.

Concern was expressed that the Scottish administration was isolated. It was suggested that Scottish Office civil servants remained 'indefinitely in the narrow and parochial atmosphere of the Scottish Administration' exacerbated by a reluctance to apply for posts in Whitehall when vacancies appeared and the absence of special arrangements to give officials the chance of a period working in UK departments. This was overstated. A number of senior officials did spend time in Whitehall and the Scottish Office had its office in Dover House with officials there having daily contact with colleagues in other parts of Whitehall. A pattern had developed of high-flying Scottish Office civil servants spending some part of their career in an important UK department such as the Treasury or Cabinet Office. Preparations in Whitehall for presentations to the Royal Commission also indicated a strong view that the Scottish administration was more expensive than elsewhere in Whitehall. One Treasury official stated this categorically in correspondence with colleagues preparing briefs for the Permanent Secretary who was due to appear before the Royal Commission. On careful examination of the data, the situation proved less clear-cut.

The Ministry of National Insurance had been established only a few years before the establishment of the Royal Commission and involved the transfer of functions from Scottish departments to this new British ministry. Confidential minutes of evidence from Sir Geoffrey King, Permanent Secretary in the Ministry of National Insurance, to the Royal Commission outline the thinking which would inform post-war attitudes:

> I have always felt that politically I cannot see how any Government could possibly put forward a proposition that benefit rates in Scotland should be lower, or alternatively that the Scottish working man should pay more for some benefits. That is why I say that any difference in the standard benefit rate is an unreal conception so long as you adhere to the idea of a universal scheme. If you are going to start again and do something else one could look at it, but within the framework of the existing scheme I think it is an unreal proposition.

Universal individual benefits were expected to be uniform benefits.

The idea of a Board of Trade for Scotland was considered but dismissed. In a note prepared for internal use, Treasury officials noted that the Ministry of Commerce in Northern Ireland had 'quite real' autonomy though many matters were dealt with in London rather than Northern Ireland. Another internal Treasury note questioned the value of a Scottish Board of Trade and whether Scotland would gain any more money than the Board of Trade already spent in Scotland. It also questioned whether money would be spent more wisely by a Scottish Board. It was suggested that as most new firms in Scotland since the war had come from either the USA or from England, the Board of Trade in England might feel under less of an obligation to induce industry to set up in Scotland. However, it was conceded that there might be an advantage for Scotland in the field of tourism. The internal discussion of a Scottish Board of Trade provided evidence which went some way to confirming critics' concerns had it ever been made public. A Treasury official suggested that if a separate Board of Trade was established it would be 'necessary for the Employers and Trades Unions to set up separate organisations in the two countries', provoking another official to point out that there already was a 'separate Scottish TUC'.

Whitehall did not always show much understanding of what actually existed or happened in Scotland.

The evidence the Commission received from within Whitehall and the language used in the report spoke of a deep commitment to centralized economic management. As a Treasury official expressed it, the 'really big point is that the major economic problems of Great Britain can only be grappled with by treating the area as a single unified economic system'. The Commission referred to trade and industrial patterns which had been 'for long and inextricably interwoven with that of England and Wales and Northern Ireland'. Claims that Scotland lost out or was discriminated against were discounted for lack of evidence. It recommended against any changes in ministerial responsibilities as regards the Board of Trade or Minister of Supply. The main message from the report and from internal Whitehall discussions was that the state needed a centralized approach to economic management.

Treasury officials considered ministerial responsibilities for communication during deliberations prepared for the Commission. As communications and transport had played such an important part in uniting the state in the nineteenth century, it might seem odd that this would be considered. The Official Committee on the Machinery of Government Committee which had met during the Second World War had briefly considered transport and had offered a brief comment in late 1943: 'It seems clear...that there should be a single administration of the nation's transport system.' Within a decade, the Royal Commission was taking a different view. A briefing for the Treasury Permanent Secretary suggested that not all forms of transport required to be dealt with on a Britain-wide basis. While this was 'obviously true of railways, shipping and civil aviation' and perhaps trunk roads, it was suggested that this was not necessarily true of other roads. Many roads were administered by local authorities. Some disadvantages of transferring roads to the Scottish Office were identified. Trunk roads were part of the general transport system of the country as a whole and transferring these would require a separate road organization for Scotland, duplicating specialized technical staff. It would also be necessary to ensure that neither Scotland nor England received an unfair share of money. On the other hand, it was not thought any more difficult to reach common standards and equity in distributing money for transport than for health, housing, prisons, and any of the existing matters under the Scottish Office's responsibilities. Even within the Treasury, it was accepted that problems of determining spending as between Scotland and the rest of Britain could be avoided if the Scottish Office worked with the Ministry of Transport in determining the total amount of money to be spent on trunk and minor roads and the allocation to Scotland. The Commission accepted this view and stated that the arguments favouring a transfer were 'conclusive' but recommended that any allocation of funds should not be based on the Goschen formula but on an 'assessment of requirements'. The Commission acknowledged it had been unable to discover a formula to determine a fair proportion of expenditure on roads for Scotland but recognized that a number of factors would have to be taken into account.

The case for transferring animal health was based on the Scottish Office's existing agricultural responsibilities especially for animal husbandry. The Commission found the absence of responsibility for animal health to be anomalous especially as veterinary education and research were under the Scottish Office's jurisdiction. The Commission dismissed the old fear, articulated powerfully in the early part of the twentieth century, that epidemic diseases would not be controlled, noting that there would be a 'common appreciation of the need for interchange of information and arrangements for immediate and, when necessary, joint action'. Elsewhere in the report, the Commission had recognized the 'invaluable asset' of the Scottish Office in general terms but the proposal to transfer responsibility for animal health was a more concrete endorsement. The Commission also recommended that the appointment of Justices of the Peace should be formally handed over to the Secretary of State for Scotland from the Lord Chancellor. This largely involved formalizing an existing situation as the machinery used for selecting Scottish Justices of the Peace was already in Scotland and all advice given to the Lord Chancellor came from Scotland.

Perhaps the most significant conclusion reached by the Balfour Commission was the 'recognition by United Kingdom and Great Britain Ministers of Scotland's national status' and that much of the dissatisfaction that existed in Scotland arose from the increased intervention by government in 'everyday life'. The report noted that 'History shows that misunderstandings due to thoughtless-ness [sic], lack of tact and disregard of sentiment can be serious.' Discontent had been aggravated by 'needless English thoughtlessness and undue Scottish susceptibilities' but the 'profound change during the last forty years in the functions of government and consequently in the machinery necessary to exercise them' lay at the heart of the problem. In a passage that would be broadly repeated in the Royal Commission on the Constitution that reported in 1973, the Balfour Commission argued:

> When the State's interference with the individual was insignificant, it mattered little to the Scotsman whether this came from Edinburgh or London. But when so many domestic affairs are no longer under control of the individual and so many enterprises require some form of official authorisation, he begins to wonder why orders and instructions should come to him from London, to question whether Whitehall has taken sufficient account of local conditions and to criticise not government but what he regards, however erroneously, as the English government.

The reaction to the report was predictable. Home rulers were disappointed that home rule had been ruled out but otherwise the report's recommendations were broadly accepted. In the Commons, Arthur Woodburn for the

Labour Party described the 'subdued enthusiasm' for the report in Scotland. The Under Secretary of State who introduced the debate on the Commission's report admitted that it has 'not put forward any spectacular proposals'. Woodburn noted that while there was a parliamentary review of the nation each year it was 'only every five years or ten years or even every twenty years that we have the opportunity of reviewing the state of the Union'. The home rule agitation that had led to its establishment had subsided. This may have allowed Woodburn to quote from the 1320 Declaration of Arbroath—'For so long as there shall be one hundred of us alive we will never consent to subject ourselves to the dominium of the English. For it is not for glory, riches or honours that we fight: it is for liberty alone, which no good man relinquishes but with life'—and suggested that these words were 'as grand as the Prime Minister's declaration of defiance of Hitler and the Nazis at the beginning of the war'. Labour and Conservative politicians could be as nationalist, sometimes more so, in their rhetoric as any Nationalist when the latter were not on the rise.

The government decided against transferring operational control of epidemic animal diseases. There had been a serious outbreak of foot-and-mouth disease in 1952 that led to an inquiry under Sir Ernest Gowers, one of Whitehall's most respected civil servants and author of the classic work on the use of the English language. But otherwise, the recommendations in the Royal Commission report were implemented. One symbolically important consequence of the transfer of bridges was that the Scottish Secretary was able to announce that a bridge across the Forth would be built and that a tunnel would be constructed under the River Clyde.

CONCLUSION

Scottish central administration was consolidated in two senses over the course of the twentieth century. First, it became embedded within the system of UK central government. Second, over the course of time, it became more coherent with the different elements being managed more corporately. This meant that two divergent processes were in operation creating a distinctly Scottish sub-system of government operating within the UK system of government. Each consolidation was important but together represented a highly distinct form of government. The transition from the night-watchman state to the modern welfare state had accommodated Scotland as a distinct and relatively coherent entity. It is far from inconceivable that the more interventionist state might have removed or at least marginalized much that had made Scotland different. Sir Walter Scott's worry, discussed in the previous chapter, that 'little by little, whatever your wishes may be, you will destroy and undermine, until nothing of what makes Scotland shall remain', did not materialize because what had been distinctly Scottish was replaced by new but also distinctly Scottish institutions and practices. What might have been identified as key Scottish features of society and life in the eighteenth and nineteenth centuries may have been undermined little by little but the apparatus of the state that had emerged renewed Scottish distinctiveness within the union.

5

Pioneers

At the end of the Second World War, an Oxford historian decided to write an account of the 1945 general election. R. B. McCallum, a Scottish Liberal from Paisley, wanted to ensure that a clear record of this important election existed to avoid the controversies that surrounded interpretations of the election immediately following the First World War. *The British General Election of 1945* was to be the first in a series of authoritative Nuffield election studies. McCallum co-authored the 1945 study with Alison Readman, the Tory daughter of a colonel in the Scots Greys. McCallum later recalled that he and Readman had disagreed on only one matter. McCallum had insisted on including some pages on Scottish nationalism. She felt that the SNP was an irrelevance, better ignored. A compromise was found and some reference was made to Scottish nationalists but not much. McCallum noted that the eight SNP candidates in the election were 'vague on the constitutional side to the point of frivolity' and quoted a leaflet that demanded the 'restoration of Scottish National Sovereignty' which McCallum and Readman suggested seemed to be 'going all the way'. They also suggested that the SNP's message was 'broadly Socialist' and included the tiny SNP total share of the vote under the socialist column in their analysis.

Readman's assessment looked more accurate than McCallum's two decades on from the Second World War. The history of liberal democracies is littered with parties and movements long forgotten, many hardly even noticed when they did exist. Contemporaries often struggle to identify new political movements capable of achieving a breakthrough amongst the noise of political debate. In his 1965 study of the British political fringe, George Thayer listed a wide range of long forgotten and marginal parties, organizations, and individuals including the League of Empire Loyalists, the Social Credit Party, the Protestant Party, and a variety of far-right and far-left groups, all of which were thought by some, including sober and serious analysts, to have potential. Scottish nationalism, in Thayer's account, was described as taking a number of forms—romantic, pragmatic, and revolutionary. As late as this period, few saw the SNP as more than a fringe party though, as Thayer noted, in some cases fringe parties could set agendas, influence mainstream parties, and challenge the status quo. The origins and development of the party are often presented in terms of the continuous struggle of a small band of doughty campaigners single-handedly building a highly professional and successful electoral machine. In his study of national self-determination, Alfred Cobban had noted that in the history of ideas 'names were more permanent than things'. This is equally true of political movements and parties. There have, of course, been continuities with key individuals joining organizations at their inception and remaining within the body right through to electoral breakthrough and greater success. Some figures remained important over long periods of time, lending some degree of continuity. But influxes of new members, the impact of new contexts, challenges, and opportunities, and the need to accommodate new ideas often disrupt continuities. Even founding beliefs can change markedly while remaining formally the same.

Movements and parties resemble nations as imagined communities with members in one generation communing with previous generations. The founding members of the National Party of Scotland in 1928, possibly even those who were active in the post-1945 period, would not recognize the Scottish National Party of today and would probably struggle to understand its core beliefs, although the SNP today enjoys celebrating its origins as a party that emerged from outside the mainstream, 'built on the shoulders of giants', as its leaders frequently describe its founders and early activists. The reality is more complex, less marked by continuity, more by evolution punctuated by occasional disruptions and change of course and refinement of aims over time. That ability to change made it possible to succeed, though it did not make success certain.

CAMPAIGNING FOR IRISH HOME RULE

The Scottish Home Rule Association (SHRA) that came into existence in 1886 can only be linked tenuously with late twentieth-century demands for a Scottish Parliament. The SHRA is better understood as a response to the Irish Question. It was founded a month after Gladstone introduced his first Irish Home Rule Bill. It struggled to make an impact and was uncertain as to how to do so. Its founders were explicit in seeing Irish home rule as only possible in the context of home rule all round. Charles Waddie, an Edinburgh stationer who founded the SHRA, had published various patriotic Scottish poems prior to campaigning for home rule. He claimed to have invented the phrase 'home rule all round' and argued that any scheme of home rule for only one part of the UK would be calamitous. In 1912, days before he died and well after the SHRA had become defunct, Waddie again warned in a letter to the press that it would be a 'blunder' to consider home rule for Ireland alone. The SHRA treasurer, William Mitchell, was a Liberal in Gladstone's Midlothian constituency. He had organized a Scottish home rule meeting within a fortnight of the Irish bill being presented to Parliament. Mitchell acknowledged the link with Gladstone's Irish home rule proposals. SHRA publications emphasized home rule all round and argued that this was in keeping with contemporary developments in the Empire. As a typical early SHRA article argued, home rule all round 'points the way to the grandest ideal in modern politics, the union of the mother country with the colonies in one real United Empire, the United States of Greater Britain'. The specifically Scottish aspect drew upon a recurrent complaint. Scottish home rule would reduce parliamentary business and allow more time to focus on Scottish affairs.

The SHRA supported Keir Hardie in his historic candidacy in the Mid Lanark by-election as the first independent Labour candidate to stand for Parliament. Waddie criticized the decision after Hardie, who had been an active member of the SHRA, failed to win the seat. Hardie's response was that of the classic political pioneer: if contests were to be avoided simply because of the possibility of defeat, then no progress would ever be made. He argued that there had been no alternative candidate for home rulers to support and that the alternative candidates were 'two English barristers'.

Gladstone had wrestled with what is now referred to as the 'West Lothian Question' in considering Irish home rule, a problem articulated powerfully by A. V. Dicey, the holder of the Vinerian Chair of English Law in Oxford. Dicey's most sustained polemic against home rule, *England's Case Against Home Rule*, was published in October 1886, partly provoked by Gladstone invoking Dicey's work in the second reading debate of his first home rule bill. There was sufficient interest in the SHRA for the government to collect SHRA pamphlets and newspaper cuttings about it but it made little impact on the debate. Dicey and other opponents of Irish home rule did not even dignify the SHRA or home rule all round with any public response. Home rule all round had a similar status to that which federalism would have a century later. It operated as a rhetorical response to a complex set of problems. SHRA members appear to have been predominantly Liberal though they included land reformers, socialists, and radicals. Gladstone's second home rule bill, presented to Parliament in 1893, also failed to extend home rule to Scotland or other parts of the UK. The SHRA effectively died with this bill. At its fifth annual conference in 1892, as the campaign began to fizzle out, it was proposed that a deputation should be sent to see Gladstone in Midlothian. It was Hardie, Labour's first MP, who argued that a deputation should also be sent to Lord Salisbury, the Conservative leader. If the deputation was seen, it had little impact on the Grand Old Man or the Tory leader.

The Irish Question remained unanswered and so long as that was the case then Scottish home rule remained part of a possible response. The 1916 Easter Rising and Sinn Fein's electoral success in 1918 marked the advance of militant Irish nationalism. The Irish Question had, once more, forced a change of outlook in London. A Speaker's Conference on Devolution was set up in 1919, the result of pressure for a federal solution to the Irish Question. This was one of a number of commissions and conferences set up during Lloyd George's premiership and this one, as so many others, was a delaying tactic. Its membership included no one of significance other than the Speaker. It was divided and produced two reports, neither having much impact. Even as the Speaker's Conference met, a Cabinet committee was deliberating on how to address the Irish Question. Though this committee's brief included consideration of a federal scheme for the UK, the focus was on Ireland. It did consider whether there should be more than one subordinate Parliament but in Dublin and Belfast, not Edinburgh.

A second Scottish Home Rule Association was established in late 1918 as war was drawing to a close. It was a different body from the earlier SHRA. Ireland was still an important part of the backdrop but this new SHRA was more aligned to radical politics, drawing heavily on the labour movement, reflecting the changing nature of Scottish electoral politics. This was also the era of Woodrow Wilson, the League of Nations, and the right to self-determination. The SHRA petitioned Wilson within two months of its establishment, urging him to support Scottish self-determination. Wilson received numerous petitions, including many from groups claiming the right to self-determination, but refused to be drawn on any case other than those within the defeated powers. The Wilsonian doctrine of self-determination is often viewed as a case of naïve idealism but it was tempered by some realism, as was explicit in Wilson's 'Fourteen Points'. There was no prospect of the French or UK governments conceding a measure of self-determination and no pressure from the American president to do so.

There was, at least, some interest in Scottish home rule, measured by the responses from candidates at the election fought at the end of the war and from Scottish MPs who were returned. But these responses still indicated that Scottish home rule was of marginal interest. Only nine MPs supported home rule—three non-Coalition Liberals, two Coalition Liberals, two Labour, one ILP, and one Unionist—meaning that sixty-five Scottish MPs either opposed home rule or did not reply. The only Unionist MP to reply in favour supported 'federal devolution' and his support only lasted so long as the Irish Question remained unresolved. Four years later, only six Scottish MPs turned up to a meeting with the SHRA and two of these referred to widespread indifference to home rule in Scotland. A further meeting was called after the 1922 election when Labour became the largest party in Scotland. This was better attended: eighteen MPs attended and another ten sent apologies and good wishes but this still left fifty-six missing MPs. Another letter was sent to candidates contesting the 1924 election and forty-nine of the successful candidates replied in favour of home rule. But what did this mean? Candidates received many petitions, requests, and questionnaires in elections and even when a majority said they favoured home rule this did not necessarily translate into action and said nothing about the degree of commitment or priority attached to the issue. At each of the inter-war elections, the signs were that Scottish home rule was at best of marginal importance. The political cleavages, notably class, created around the Industrial Revolution were far more important than the centre–periphery cleavage associated with the foundation of the state. The dominant issues in Scotland, as with the rest of the UK, in the inter-war period were economic crises, industrial relations, and the looming prospect of war. In this context, Scottish home rule was irrelevant.

The problems associated with industrialization and urbanization—public health, housing, and education—were much more pressing than home rule. Unemployment was a major issue. The General Strike of 1926 and industrial relations were vastly more important than SHRA activities. The SHRA was a tiny body compared with over half a million Scots who were trade union members, about a third of the adult workforce. Teetotalism could claim to be further up the agenda than home rule. Edwin Scrymgeour, the candidate of the Scottish Prohibition Party, was returned in Dundee in 1922 and though home rule was part of his platform it was prohibition that featured in his party's name and more prominently in his parliamentary speeches. But it was unemployment that dominated his maiden speech in the Commons. Frank Bealey's classic analogy of a 'peasant's stockpot' captures the different elements of Labour ideology well, each idea flavouring the mix to a greater or lesser extent depending on when the ingredient had last been added. Home rule was part of the mix but it never strongly influenced the flavour of Labour's ideology. Socialism in its various forms was a bigger threat to those in power than Scottish nationalism. Scottish MPs operated within their party groups and did not form themselves into a 'Scottish party'. There were many moments when Labour figures would reflect on the possibilities of home rule and home rule bills were presented in Parliament. A typical example was the comment made by the chairman of the executive of the Scottish Labour Party in 1923 who maintained that had Scotland enjoyed home rule it was 'certain that a Labour Government would be in power north of the Tweed' but such sentiments never amounted to much.

This second SHRA campaigned vigorously and imaginatively but unsuccessfully. It was unable to move home rule up the political agenda. Its demise as an organization came in 1927 when an agreed home rule bill, drawn up by a constitutional convention set up by the SHRA, was rejected by Parliament. This was the fifth Labour-sponsored home rule bill in the 1920s. At the 1924 election, thirty-four of the successful candidates, overwhelmingly Labour, said they would participate in a constitutional convention but in the event very few did. Seven Labour MPs from the west of Scotland, many supported by the Irish Catholic community, were involved provoking suggestions that this would amount to Irish rather than Scottish home rule. Business interests were scarce amongst participants. Once more, deputations struggled to receive the attention of political authorities. By the end, the SHRA and its convention were reduced to discussing how they should campaign for home rule. A split occurred between those who concluded that a separate political party was required and those who felt progress could only be made through one of the existing parties making home rule its top priority. It was a debate that signalled the weakness of the home rule cause, and its failure to get the issue taken seriously.

THE CREATION OF AN INDEPENDENT PARTY

The failure to create a Scottish Parliament through the SHRA and constitutional convention led directly to the establishment of a party which placed self-government at the top of its agenda. The National Party of Scotland (NPS) was founded in 1928, growing out of that element within the SHRA who saw a separate party as the best way forward and consequently consisted predominantly of left of centre activists. Until recently, the conventional interpretation of the origins and development of the NPS drew heavily on *The Flag in the Wind*, a book written by John MacCormick, one of those involved. MacCormick's version of events exaggerates his own role in the foundation of the party while he was a Glasgow university student. The real impetus had come from within the SHRA and more particularly two other fringe pressure groups—the Scottish National Movement and Scots National League.

The party included its fair share of romantics and eccentrics, a loose collection of often highly individualistic and sometimes volatile members. The nature of the party was captured well by Oliver Brown, himself a colourful figure, who summed up the disputatious tendencies of political parties: 'I regret the day I compromised the unity of my party by admitting a second member.' MacCormick played a key role as secretary of the party and had been keen to expand the membership to include more establishment figures. His penchant for mixing with the establishment while espousing radical politics would be a recurring theme throughout his life and one he never fully resolved. MacCormick was keen to demonstrate the party's relevance by attracting and giving prominence to well-known public figures. Many within the NPS were suspicious of elites.

In 1932, another smaller party—the Scottish Self-Government Party, self-styled 'Moderates'—was established. It was an altogether different kind of party and very much on the right with more than a hint of anti-Catholicism about it. It included some more establishment figures who found the NPS's radicalism distasteful. But it also included some distinguished figures in Scottish public life, people whom MacCormick had tried unsuccessfully to attract into the NPS: Sir Henry Keith and Sir W. E. Whyte, two of the most prominent figures in Scottish local government; Sir Daniel Stevenson, former Glasgow Lord Provost and Chancellor of Glasgow University from 1934; Professor Andrew Dewar Gibb of Glasgow University; and Alexander MacEwan, Provost of Inverness. The new party's existence owed much to a split in a local Glasgow Unionist association. Some Cathcart Unionists had formed an 'Imperial Committee' in June 1932 and produced a manifesto which proposed replacing the Westminster Parliament with an Imperial Parliament with representatives from the British Empire and dominion Parliaments for Scotland, England, and Wales. Kevan McDowall, the chairman of the committee, led a breakaway amid fierce disagreements with the Unionist establishment. The Glasgow Unionist Association passed a motion accusing McDowall of disloyalty and unconstitutional practices for attempting to negotiate with the NPS. This activity attracted the attention of Lord Beaverbrook, press baron and Canadian son of a Scottish Presbyterian minister, who wrote a front page article in the *Daily Express* taking sides with McDowall against the Unionist leaders. Scottish home rule was seen as part of a wider Imperial plan. It also won the support of a range of others including some leading trade unionists though near unanimous opposition from the Unionist Party. It found little support in the NPS where there was strong opposition to Imperialism. McDowall and around thirty others resigned from the local Cathcart Unionists. While much is made of this 'breakaway' in histories of the national movement, Cathcart Unionist Association had around 2,400 members at the time. This was more like a small splinter than a breakaway and had even less impact on the Unionist Party than the establishment of the NPS had on the Labour Party. It is unlikely to have rated more than a footnote in the histories of the Scottish national movement had it not attracted the attention and support of Beaverbrook and MacCormick's highly personal account of the origins of the movement.

One of the leading figures in this new party was Andrew Dewar Gibb, who had been adjutant to Winston Churchill during the First World War, stood as a Unionist candidate for Parliament in the 1920s, and would become Regius Professor of Law at Glasgow University in 1934. Gibb's views on the Irish Catholic immigrant community in Scotland were typical of Unionist politicians and many Scots at that time. Gibb and George Malcolm Thomson, who shared Gibb's view that Scotland was being eroded by the influx of Irish Catholics, had considered what amounted to entryism with regard to the NPS but instead opted for a separate party. It also attracted Alexander MacEwan, Liberal Provost of Inverness, who was knighted the year the Scottish Party came into being, and the Duke of Montrose.

The merger of the NPS and Scottish Party made sense in that neither party was capable of making much impact on its own but together there would be internal strife. The two parties shared the mistaken belief that Scots wanted a Parliament and the absence of a party prioritizing this objective was all that stood in the way of its achievement. Each was created in response to the refusal of the established parties to put into effect what they believed were the wishes of the Scottish people. What was not appreciated was that the established parties had been responding to Scottish demands, only that home rule was not a high priority for most Scots. Labour's 1929 manifesto stated that it supported 'the creation of separate legislative assemblies in Scotland, Wales and England, with autonomous powers in matters of local concern' but this commitment appeared at the end of the manifesto, above setting up a Royal Commission on licensing laws and some vague commitments to women. The Conservative manifesto made no mention of Scotland. The NPS contested two seats in the 1929 general election and five in 1931 as well as by-elections. It did not help that its candidates were inexperienced and often naïve. Lewis Spence, who had been founder of the Scottish National Movement, a journalist and poet with a keen interest in folklore, mythology, and the occult, stood for the NPS in a by-election in Midlothian and Peebles in 1929. Spence's approach to campaigning included a lengthy speech on Burns in middle Scots, a language used between the fifteenth and eighteenth centuries. He won 4.5 per cent of the vote. Another eccentric campaigner was the novelist Eric Linklater who contested East Fife in a by-election for the SNP in 1933 where he won 3.6 per cent of the vote. Linklater based *Magnus Merriman*, one of his novels, on his experiences demonstrating a greater capacity for writing than politics.

The NPS had attracted some public figures but these were seen as 'mad and bad and dangerous' by McDowall. R. B. Cunninghame Graham, the party's first president, had been a Harrow educated Liberal Member of Parliament in the 1880s and the first socialist MP. His platform on election to Parliament in the 1880s had included Scottish home rule, abolition of the House of Lords, universal suffrage, land nationalization, an eight-hour day, and free school meals. At one point he was suspended from the Commons for swearing and on another for making disparaging comments about the Lords. He was arrested and beaten up for his part in the Trafalgar Square 'Bloody Sunday' demonstration in 1887, protesting against coercion in Ireland, and served a short prison sentence. Along with Keir Hardie, he had founded the Scottish Labour Party and subsequently stood as a Labour candidate in Glasgow. He was better known in South America, especially Argentina, where he had travelled widely and was known as *Don Roberto*. Roland Muirhead, who became party chairman, had been a member of the Young Scots' Society (YSS), a Liberal body set up in 1900 which had campaigned against the Boer War and protectionism, and for Lords reform. In 1911, the YSS had issued a manifesto in which it had suspended its support for home rule while it campaigned for Lords reform, but after the abolition of the Lords' veto it claimed to prioritize support for home rule. However, Muirhead concluded that the YSS were 'Party Liberals first, Scottish nationalists second' and drifted away to play a series of roles in home rule agitation. He remained active until the end of his long life. In 1961, at the age of 92 he marched in Glasgow against the Polaris nuclear submarines. His life had spanned meetings with Kropotkin to CND protests, seeing little success in any of the major campaigns in which he had been engaged. Muirhead had been central to the establishment of the revived SHRA in 1918, providing its funding, as well as for many other organizations including the socialist newspaper *Forward*. He was another traveller and adventurer, having spent time in South America and in an Owenite colony in Washington state. Muirhead's sister Alice had also joined and would remain with the party when her brother eventually left to set up a new organization, the Scottish National Congress, in 1951. Alice had campaigned for women's votes and was involved in the Women's International League and various bodies engaged in international cooperation. She was also involved in supporting women in medicine. Her name appears in few works on the history of the SNP but she was another of the small band of indefatigable activists who gave consistent and persistent support to the party even when the odds against success were overwhelming. Another colourful figure was the Hon. Ruaraidh Erskine of Marr, son of Lord Erskine. He was a Celtic activist who supported the 1916 Easter Rising in Dublin and campaigned for Gaelic language and culture. The poet Hugh MacDiarmid and Compton Mackenzie, novelist and Catholic convert, were also founding members.

These were not the public figures MacCormick had in mind and they were not the kind of people that McDowall and the Imperial Unionists and anti-Catholics of the Scottish Party would find palatable. MacCormick would describe MacDiarmid as 'one of the greatest handicaps with which any national movement could have been burdened', one of the 'wild men' who had put others off joining. His preference was for the kind of people who joined the Scottish Party and people such as William Power, writer and newspaper editor, whom MacCormick supported for the SNP leadership in 1942. But the more radical elements had little time for MacCormick's approach. Douglas Young, classics scholar and poet who joined the SNP in 1938, while remaining a member of the Labour Party, challenged Power for the leadership and compared MacCormick to William Wallace in a short poem entitled 'On a North British Devolutionist',

> The libbit William Wallace [libb = castrate]
> He gar'd them bleed [gar'd = made]
> They dinna libb MacFoozle.
> They dinna need.

Frustration at the lack of success led to the merger of the two parties in 1934 to form the Scottish National Party. It was an uneasy alliance and compromises were necessary. Kevan McDowall's views were summed up in the slogan, 'For Scotland, King and Empire'. He was briefly the overseas secretary of the new merged party but left in one of the first splits in the party. In 1935, a resolution proposing a change in the party's constitution precipitated McDowall's resignation. His emphasis on the Empire and that Scotland should retain membership of the Imperial Parliament put him at odds with the much larger element of the party that had come from the NPS. Over subsequent years he continued to berate the SNP for its 'Sinn Fein, Free State, separatist, disruptive propaganda'. While a number of the Scottish Party figures remained within the SNP, there was little doubt that the NPS element came out on top.

It is tempting to assume that the SNP simply consisted of such members and there is no doubt that if the public was aware of the SNP at all then it would have associated the party with these people. But a core of less well-known members kept the party afloat. By the end of the Second World War, the more colourful figures had receded in importance to be replaced by this core and a few members who had joined after the party's establishment. It was this element that provided continuity from post-war Scottish politics into the 1960s.

Unemployment remained above 14 per cent throughout the 1920s, rising to over 20 per cent in the next decade. Shipbuilding production in the early 1930s fell to about 10 per cent of what it had been at the end of the First World War. Scots were emigrating at a level unsurpassed by almost anywhere else in Europe at the time—more Scots emigrated than left Belgium, Denmark, Finland, the Netherlands, Sweden, and Switzerland combined, all states of about the same population size as Scotland—resulting in the Scottish population falling between the censuses of 1921 and 1931. The post-war promise of a 'Homes fit for heroes' led to important housing legislation, including special measures for Scotland but this failed to have much impact on the chronic shortage of quality housing. How these social and economic matters were to be addressed were Scottish questions uppermost in the minds of voters. While Cunningham Graham, Muirhead, and others had concluded that constitutional change was necessary to address these social and economic matters, others had joined for different, cultural reasons. The party loudly complained about the way Scotland was neglected, the loss through emigration of its people, and the distress caused by poor economic and social conditions, but it failed to link home rule to deep public concern about these matters.

WARTIME OPPORTUNITIES AND CHALLENGES

The SNP struggled to make an impact on Scottish politics over the following decades. It could not be claimed that the only reason Scotland did not have a

Parliament was because the established parties failed to prioritize the issue. The reason it was not prioritized was because it was not high on the public's agenda. The economic depression in the 1930s exacerbated already difficult social and economic conditions in Scotland, though preparations for war provided jobs. These were not conditions likely to make Scotland's constitutional status a high priority even had the SNP been a well-organized and politically sophisticated organization. In 1935, at the last election before the war, the SNP contested eight seats and won 1.1 per cent of the Scottish vote.

The Second World War presented an opportunity and problems for the SNP. The opportunity arose from a truce between parties represented in Parliament during the war. It was agreed that in the event of a by-election only the previous incumbent's party would contest the seat. This opened up the possibility of small, extra-parliamentary parties garnering support from voters opposed to the incumbent. The SNP was not alone in being able to take advantage of the truce. Common Wealth, a small socialist party, won seats as did Tom Driberg, a well-known gossip columnist writing under the name 'William Hickey' in the *Express*, who won a seat as an Independent. Common Wealth had close links with the SNP and supported a new 'co-fraternity' of self-government states within the UK and desisted from standing against the nationalists in Scotland and Wales. It was the only party represented in Parliament that came close to accepting the SNP's objectives. Though Common Wealth won seats during the war, it did not survive as a force much beyond the war's end. SNP support was thus inflated in a number of wartime by-elections. William Power won 37 per cent of the vote in Argyllshire in a two-candidate contest. In February 1944, Douglas Young stood in Kirkcaldy and took 42 per cent in a three-candidate contest. Though the war effort contributed to a sense of common purpose across the state as a whole, there were occasions when Scots felt aggrieved at insensitive central government behaviour. Many Scottish women were transferred to work on the war effort in England against their wishes, creating grievances exploited by the SNP.

The problems facing the SNP arose from divisions within the party over attitudes to the war and a continuing argument on how it should campaign. The party included a large number of pacifists, affected by the experience of the First World War. Allied to this was an element that convinced themselves that war could not be declared by Westminster—an early version of 'not in our name'. This had no precedent in previous conflicts that had involved Scottish armed forces. The party adopted the confusing position of supporting the war in principle with some members opposing conscription and others opposed to national service unless this was agreed by a (non-existent) Scottish authority. MacCormick and those around him were initially sympathetic to individual conscientious objections to serving in the war but opposed a campaign against the war. Douglas Young, a classics scholar in Aberdeen and chairman of the SNP branch in that city, and Arthur Donaldson, a journalist, wanted to challenge the legality of the war. Young spent some time in Saughton prison for refusing to be conscripted. Given wartime sensitivities, this element was closely monitored by the security services. At one point the homes of Young, Donaldson, Muirhead, and others were raided. Amongst those who were raided was Muriel Gibson, who went on to serve in the Women's Royal Army Corps and was mentioned in dispatches during the war, becoming a Major by the war's end. Another was Isa Hillhouse, later Fisher, who had joined the SNP in 1934 and reputedly campaigned in every election and major by-election through to the late 1980s. Her nephew, Sir Russell Hillhouse, rose through the Civil Service on his way to become Permanent Secretary at the Scottish Office in 1988. She left half her estate to the SNP and was quoted explaining why she had campaigned in the SNP's wilderness years: 'It was just a little thing. The tiniest flicker but someone had to keep it burning.' Jimmy Maxton MP, amongst others, attacked this heavy-handed security intervention which caused embarrassment for Tom Johnston, the wartime Secretary of State for Scotland, who knew Muirhead well having been editor of *Forward*, the paper bankrolled by Muirhead over many years. Files released more than fifty years later show police references to Donaldson as a 'Quisling' who 'uses the Home Rule Movement as a basis for subversive activities' but provide little evidence.

The SNP was a tiny, insignificant party with a colourful and dedicated group of members. It took heart from the slightest sign of progress, bouncing back after setback followed setback. These were people who devoted considerable time and effort to a party that made no serious progress in its first three decades. In retrospect, the results of the wartime by-elections were recalled as signs of progress but at the time the party knew that it would have had far less support without the special circumstances of the wartime electoral pact and that it had been unable to contest many other wartime by-elections. As the war was coming to an end, the death of the Labour MP for Motherwell, who had won the seat in 1935 with a majority of only 430, provided a fillip which sustained SNP activists for the next two decades. The SNP adopted Dr Robert McIntyre, a 31-year-old medical officer who had chaired Edinburgh University Labour Party as a student and had developed an interest in public health. He had been in charge of a major programme of diphtheria immunization in Paisley, visiting schools throughout the area. In 1944, McIntyre had produced a short pamphlet, 'Some Principles for Scottish Reconstruction', setting out policies that could be followed in the event of self-government. It was a broadly left of centre document with an emphasis on decentralization and participation. It offered an uneasy balance between state intervention and distrust of the state. McIntyre's background, interests, and approach were very different from most of those who had previously contested seats for the SNP. He could scarcely have been more different from Lewis Spence, the SNP's first by-election candidate. The SNP won the seat with 51.4 per cent of the votes cast. It had been fortunate in a number of respects: the wartime pact was still in place but the war was drawing to a close and, as the SNP emphasized in its literature, the 'war is not an Election issue'. Its candidate understood everyday issues better than most previous candidates and made them central to his campaign. McIntyre only served in Parliament for three months before losing the seat at the 1945 general election.

The by-election had been won despite the SNP suffering a major split in May 1942. The split occurred after Douglas Young defeated William Power for the post of party chairman. John MacCormick led a walkout from the conference to set up an alternative organization, the Scottish Convention. Different views exist as to the cause of the split, each having some validity. Personality clashes were part of the cause. John MacCormick was a talented organizer and speaker but was seen by critics as someone who preferred to focus on appealing to Scotland's 'great and good' rather than building up popular support. MacCormick recognized the importance of the special wartime conditions in his interpretation of the Argyll by-election. He saw only dangers in campaigns that might be construed as undermining the war effort and wanted to build alliances with and influence the established parties. He sought and won Labour support for a national plebiscite and cooperation on post-war reconstruction in exchange for withdrawing the SNP candidate from a by-election in Dumbartonshire in 1941. Labour's candidate accepted this but it never became party policy. This approach was viewed with suspicion by those who recalled the reasons for the foundation of the NPS and were keen to make the SNP independent of the other parties. MacCormick's candidate for leadership against Young was William Power, the Argyll candidate. Few doubted that Power, approaching 70 when he contested the leadership, would be under MacCormick's control. Young, who was also a member of the Labour Party, was in many respects much closer to MacCormick. He was less hardline on independence than many of his supporters. In a small fringe party, clashes of personalities and egos would have a significant impact. McIntyre's victory three years after the split convinced what remained of the SNP that challenging the existing parties was the way forward but the SNP remained on the fringe as became clear very soon. McIntyre became party leader in 1947 and stood down in 1956 after internal schisms.

FRUSTRATION, FUTILITY, AND MISERABLE COMPROMISE AT THE VERY MOST

In 1945, the SNP contested eight seats, saving only two deposits and winning 1.2 per cent of the vote across Scotland (averaging 9.1 per cent where it contested seats). Major H. Sleigh, an independent Scottish nationalist, also stood in Edinburgh Central winning 232 votes. He was a throwback to the kind of candidates of the past: a former cavalry officer who lived in the New Club in Edinburgh. The party ploughed on but was eclipsed by MacCormick's Scottish Convention. The Scottish Convention and the Scottish Covenant, a massive petition in favour of home rule, captured the public's imagination at a time of austerity—some rationing had become stricter at the end of the war and the severe winter of 1946–7 added to the misery. MacCormick became active in the Liberal Party, standing in Inverness in 1945. Home rule agitation brought the nearest thing to glamour to Scottish politics and attracted lots of media attention, including from overseas.

The Convention returned to the tactics of the SHRA, sending out ques-tionnaires to candidates across Scotland in the 1945 election. Of the 199 who replied, seventy-three said they favoured the creation of a Scottish Parliament including three future Labour Scottish Secretaries. But this was meaningless. Labour's 1945 manifesto outlined the party's priorities clearly: 'The nation wants food, work and homes...It wants a high and rising standard of living, security for all against a rainy day, an educational system that will give every boy and girl a chance to develop the best that is in them.' The Convention had meetings with MPs from Labour and Unionist parties and sought a meeting with the Prime Minister. Attlee's office replied suggesting that the Convention's representatives should meet Joe Westwood, Scottish Secretary, but noted that Westwood was busy. This provoked criticism from the Scottish Liberals which did little to endear MacCormick, then Scottish Liberal Vice President, to Labour members. A delegation from the Convention met Arthur Woodburn, who had succeeded Westwood as Scottish Secretary, in January 1948. The tim-ing was appalling. Only a few days before, MacCormick had been adopted as Liberal candidate to fight a by-election in Paisley, a seat Labour was defending. Making matters worse, the local Liberals had agreed a deal with the Unionists allowing the Liberals a free run against Labour. Labour won the seat with its best result in the constituency and MacCormick was criticized by fellow Liberals for agreeing a deal with the Tories. The Convention was seriously damaged. Labour was the only party likely to deliver a measure of self-government and was now less inclined to support the Convention. There was criticism within the Convention. Naomi Mitchison, writer and Labour member, and Lady Glen Coats, Liberal candidate in Paisley in 1945, resigned from the Convention's national committee in May 1948. MacCormick had to resign as Vice President of the Liberals shortly thereafter. His gamble had failed. The man who had criticized the SNP for challenging the establishment parties had succeeded in alienating the Labour Party. Many in Labour harboured a grievance against home rulers and nationalists well into the future. Though the SNP had decided against contesting the by-election, the myth became established in Labour cir-cles that the SNP had challenged Labour, with Tory support, in what was seen as an important post-war by-election. Only six years before, MacCormick had walked out of the SNP in part because it was intent on contesting elections. His inconsistency reflected frustration with the lack of progress.

The Scottish Convention held a series of 'Assemblies' drawing in broad sections of Scottish society. A scheme of home rule was drawn up but had little impact. Within months of the general election, Labour MPs were reported saying that home rule was not possible during that Parliament. Labour's position hardened over the course of the Parliament. It was clear that there was no prospect of Labour delivering home rule in the foreseeable future. By early 1949, one of the Scottish Convention's leading figures was privately informing MacCormick that there was 'very little steam in the Convention'. MacCormick's next venture was to launch the 'Covenant', a petition in favour of self-government, in an attempt to convince the main parties of the level of support for a Parliament. It was the action of a pressure group that is unable to gain direct access to those in power and must resort to indirect methods, including appeals to public opinion. The Covenant was clear but lacked a sanction:

> We, the people of Scotland who subscribe to this Engagement, declare our belief that reform in the constitution of our country is necessary to secure good government in accordance with our Scottish traditions and to promote the spiritual and economic welfare of our nation.
>
> We affirm that the desire for such reform is both deep and widespread through the whole community, transcending all political differences and sectional interests and we undertake to continue united in purpose for its achievement.
>
> With that end in view we solemnly enter into this Covenant whereby we pledge ourselves in all loyalty to the Crown and within the framework of the United Kingdom, to do everything in our power to secure for Scotland a Parliament with adequate legislative authority in Scottish affairs.

The Scottish Covenant was a pale imitation of the Ulster Covenant of 1912. The Ulster Covenant was in fact two Covenants, one signed by men and the other by women. The version signed by men included an implicit but very clear threat to 'using all means which may be found necessary to defeat the present conspiracy to set up a Home Rule Parliament in Ireland. And in the event of such a Parliament being forced upon us, we further solemnly and mutually pledge ourselves to refuse to recognize its authority.' The women's covenant expressed the 'desire to associate ourselves with the men of Ulster in their uncompromising opposition to the Home Rule Bill'. Few politically active Scots or key figures in the UK government would have been unaware of the difference between the Scottish and Ulster Covenants. It is difficult to avoid the conclusion that Scottish home rulers were less insistent than Ulster opponents of home rule.

At various intervals, the Scottish Covenant Association, as the Convention had become, announced the growing number of signatures gathered: over

100,000 Scots within a fortnight of its launch; over 400,000 by December 1949; 700,000 by January 1950; 900,000 by February 1950; and 1,700,000 by September 1950. In late 1949, an excitable MacCormick declared that the Covenant Association would not have shown that a majority of the people wanted a Parliament until 3 million signatures had been collected. This was an outlandish aim. There were only 3.37 million Scots on the electoral register in 1950 (and only 2.72 million actually voted in that year's general election). The Covenant Association was well organized with a network of active branches throughout Scotland, and a substantial membership. It organized conferences on a variety of subjects, trained its activists in canvassing and campaigning, and organized social events. It attracted considerable media attention and public imagination but this was not enough. It is unclear how many signatures were really gathered not least because there was no means of checking the validity of all signatures.

During this period MacCormick was elected rector by the students of Glasgow University but this meant little, as the election of Compton Mackenzie as rector on a similar platform in 1931 testified. A local plebiscite in Scotstoun in Glasgow that month, held during a parliamentary by-election, might have suggested overwhelming support for a Scottish Parliament but the Unionists held the seat with Labour close behind. The Liberals, MacCormick's own party, did not stand. MacCormick had explained that the Covenant was an all-party campaign and therefore could not contest the seat but had warned that the Covenant would be prepared to challenge the parties. It was all bluster. When the signatures were ignored, the Covenant invited Scottish local authorities to pass resolutions asking for a national plebiscite: twenty-seven of Scotland's burgh councils refused; eight decided to take no action; with only thirty supporting the Covenant. Support was strongest in smaller authorities—Inverness was the largest supporter—whereas those that refused to back the Covenant included Glasgow, Paisley, Dunfermline, and Kirkcaldy (all then larger than Inverness). Many more large authorities simply ignored the request. The Covenant claimed support had been strongest where party whips had been weakest but this only served to highlight the opposition or indifference of the established parties.

Signatures on a petition could not bring about change. The government did not ignore the agitation and in private was keenly aware of developments but it had no intention of making a significant concession. In December 1947, Scottish Secretary Arthur Woodburn presented a paper to Cabinet in which he outlined his interpretation of public opinion. The public, he maintained, could be divided into three broad groups: the 'extreme home-rulers (the Scottish Nationalist party)' which was 'picturesque and articulate' but with negligible support; the Scottish Convention, the less extreme wing of the home rule movement, with support which was 'difficult to estimate, as during elections its vote is not recorded because of stronger loyalty to the main political parties. It has, however, a considerable number of supporters in all parties'; and 'By far the largest group, and one which has strong emotional feeling behind it in Scotland, asks that Parliament should give more time to Scottish affairs and that, within the British constitution and the unity of the two countries, the Scots themselves should have further opportunities of administering in Scotland the business of government and of the socialised industries and other Government-appointed organisations.' The government supported Woodburn's proposals to address this third body of opinion. The home rule movement had been part of the backdrop—often distant backdrop—of Scottish politics during the inter-war period and occasional references to it would be made by those in power when considering special measures for Scottish affairs and acknowledging Scottish distinctiveness. But it was only in the immediate post-war period that home rule agitation had any direct impact on the government. The agitation alone might not have brought about changes in parliamentary procedures, administrative arrangements, or, as would happen in 1950, the establishment of a committee to consider the financial and trade statistics, but it is equally unlikely that these would have occurred without this agitation. But these concessions were not seen as advances by home rulers. Reflecting on the Covenant many years later, novelist and Covenant supporter Nigel Tranter concluded that it had been naïve not to include a 'sanction clause'. This was tried half-heartedly in a *Scottish Declaration* in 1952 which stated that a Scottish Parliament was the 'first priority in Scottish politics' with the signatory pledging to do 'everything in my power to secure the return to Parliament of Members who have promised the claims implicit in the Scottish Covenant'. But this was little different from the original Covenant and came too late. Asking people to sign a new, slightly different Covenant was an admission of failure.

An editorial in the *Glasgow Herald* in early 1950 summed up the situation, 'If and when 36 or more of the Scottish MPs were to be pledged to securing a Parliament for Scotland, then there would be unquestionable grounds for action by a Government...They must in the end either put up candidates of their own or obtain pledges from MPs of the major parties.' The SNP leadership had already reached that conclusion. The Convention/Covenant campaign carried on over the next few years with a variety of initiatives—demands for a referendum, a Royal Commission, more Assemblies, sending questionnaires to parliamentary candidates, seeking meetings with MPs, even occasionally contesting local elections and considering an electoral pact with the Liberals and SNP—but its best moment had passed. The SNP's chairman in 1946 had warned that attempting to win self-government through the established parties was pointless, involving 'wasteful, exhausting, maddening processions of deputations, prayers, appeals, protests, agitations, and so on, followed inevitably by a series of promises, assurances, safeguards, and sometimes cynical rebuffs, with frustration, futility, and miserable compromise at the very most'.

SOVEREIGNTY, MONARCHY, AND DESTINY

Yet, despite all the evidence that the national movement was moribund, there were moments of high drama, which would be looked back upon by supporters of home rule as evidence of vitality. At Christmas 1950, a group of Glasgow University students removed the Stone of Destiny, on which Scottish monarchs had reputedly been crowned from the time of the Picts, from Westminster Abbey. The Stone had been taken to London at the end of the fourteenth century. At various points in time, there had been proposals to return it to Scotland. In 1924, Clydeside Labour MP Davie Kirkwood had proposed a bill that would have resulted in it returning to Scotland. For Kirkwood, the Stone was a 'symbol of our nationhood. It is a venerable relic.' His bill was opposed by the Conservative MP for Southampton, for equally sentimental reasons. There had been previous plans to 'liberate' the Stone. On one occasion, Hugh MacDiarmid had travelled to London with this intention but had to admit to his accomplices that the money required to remove the Stone and take it to Scotland had all been spent in a pub.

In March 1950, a police guard was placed on the Coronation Stone in the Market Place in Kingston-on-Thames, believed to have been used in the coronation of Anglo-Saxon kings, fearing that it would be used as ransom for return of the Stone of Destiny. A bus-load of Scots on a trip to London were followed around London because Scotland Yard thought the trippers from Dumbarton were involved in the plot to remove the Kingston-on-Thames Coronation Stone. Telegrams had been sent to the Metropolitan Police by colleagues in Edinburgh warning them that a coach-load of nationalists were on their way to London to chalk or paint slogans on the walls of Parliament. This was a group of 'Scottish Patriots', an organization that had recently been established by Wendy Wood, an eccentric artist and writer who had been a founding member of the SNP but quickly grew impatient and left to engage in direct action. In 1932 she had led a small group who removed the Union Jack from Stirling Castle, which was an army barracks at the time, and later set up a youth organization, Scottish Watch. One Special Branch telegram in 1950 stated that it was known that Wood had been in touch with the IRA and had obtained explosives; it was unknown whether she was carrying the explosives but police in Edinburgh had 'reliable information that she will attempt to damage the King's Stone at Kingston by some means'. Whether this had indeed been the plan, the presence of a contingent of London police officers accompanying the group prevented any action. Wood was viewed with deep suspicion by leading figures in the SNP in the 1950s who thought her activities only attracted the attention of the police.

The police were less vigilant only nine months later when four Glasgow University students, led by law student Ian Hamilton, succeeded in removing the Stone, creating considerable media and police interest. Four months later they placed the Stone in Arbroath Abbey from where it was returned to Westminster Abbey. The matter was raised in Cabinet where there was discussion of whether to prosecute the perpetrators, how to handle transporting the Stone to London, and whether it might even be returned to Scotland. Hartley Shawcross, the Attorney General, warned against prosecution as it would 'do no good except perhaps to the defendants to whom it would give the opportunity of being regarded as martyrs if they were convicted or as heroes if they were acquitted…In Scotland a prosecution would produce a very adverse reaction.' Ian Hamilton, the leader of the student group, described the Stone as a 'hunk of sandstone' and would later explain his motives: 'Nobody sang in Scotland in the middle part of this century. To be more correct, those who sang did not derive their songs from Scotland.' It had been a typical, irreverent student stunt but unusual in winning public sympathy, at least in Scotland. It created a new myth or at least contributed to a sense that Scotland was different and in this at least its legacy was greater than the Covenant.

The next symbolic episode also concerned the monarch. The Royal Style and Titles Act, 1953, was passed following the death of King George VI. The new monarch was to be officially called Queen Elizabeth II, though there had never been an Elizabeth, Queen of Scots. A case was brought before the Court of Session, Scotland's top court, by John MacCormick and Ian Hamilton, the latter having graduated as a law student and from removing artefacts from abbeys. Their case was not simply that the new monarch had not been Queen of Scots but they questioned the doctrine of parliamentary sovereignty, arguing that there was a Scottish doctrine of popular sovereignty.

Just three days before the Queen's coronation, Lord Guthrie dismissed MacCormick and Hamilton's arguments on three grounds: the title was authorized by Act of Parliament and could not be subject to a legal challenge; the Treaty of Union did not prevent any numeral being used by a reigning monarch, whether historically accurate or otherwise; and the petitioners had no title to sue as the question was one of public policy not of legal right. The matter then went to appeal before three other Court of Session judges including Lord Cooper, Scotland's most senior judge as President of the Court. Cooper upheld Guthrie's judgement on the second and third points but disagreed with Guthrie's view on whether an Act of Parliament was open to legal challenge. A passage from his judgement was taken as a victory by MacCormick, Hamilton, and other home rulers and passed into nationalist folklore:

> The principle of the unlimited Sovereignty of Parliament is a distinctively English principle which has no counterpart in Scottish Constitutional law. It derives its origins from Coke and Blackstone, and was widely popularised during the eighteenth century by Bagehot and Dicey, the latter having stated the doctrine in its classic form in his Constitutional Law. Considering that the Union legislation extinguished the Parliaments of Scotland and England, and replaced them by a new Parliament, I have difficulty in seeing why it should have been supposed that

the new Parliament of Great Britain must inherit all the peculiar characteristics of the English Parliament but none of the Scottish Parliament, as if all that happened in 1707 was that Scottish representatives were admitted to the Parliament of England. That is not what was done.

It was not much of a victory but it was enough to bring cheer at a time when the home rule movement was at a low ebb. However, as had happened over the Stone of Destiny episode, there were a number of home rulers who were appalled, especially at a time when the monarch was about to be crowned. MacCormick was turning to activities that would turn away the kinds of people he had been keen to attract in the past. Dr Neville Davidson of Glasgow Cathedral and John Cameron QC, Dean of the Faculty of Advocates, had already drifted away from the Covenant Association and others followed.

Small groups operated on the fringe of the national movement during this period attracting Special Branch interest. A number of EIIR post boxes were blown up. Home Office archives include a file on 'Scottish Nationalist activities and the police' in the 1950s that provides details of meetings of the London branch of the SNP in 1954 written by Metropolitan Police Special Branch officers. It reported on a discussion in which one member 'stated very emphatically' that the Stone of Destiny was 'very important', a view not shared by all and included not only a list of those present but also names and addresses from a 'contact book' of sympathizers. The file also contained papers listing various occasions when Wendy Wood had been arrested.

The SNP had lost many of its more colourful characters and was turning into the kind of party, though without any Scottish notables, that John MacCormick had previously wanted. The problem was that its colourful characters had been what had attracted attention. It struggled to survive and frustrations spilled over into internal division. In 1955, a small group splintered away from the party complaining that there had been 'nothing but talk for twenty years' and accusing the leadership of being dictatorial. This was a time of anti-colonial activity and the new Nationalist Party of Scotland wanted to copy this activity. Robert McInytre set out the party's position, asserting that Scots were

> not good haters and we do not want to make them that. Our quarrel is not with the ordinary person in England and we do not want to build up a virulent anti-English feeling in Scotland. That sort of thing would not go down with the Scottish people. We must maintain our own standards of our own self-respect. In that way we will be successful.

McIntyre's approach was sober but he could give no guarantees that it would be successful. The new party soon faded but McIntyre concluded that criticisms had come to focus on his leadership and stood down the following year to be succeeded by Jimmy Halliday, a 29-year-old history teacher. Membership had dwindled and was well under 300. Halliday later summed up the SNP's problem with reference to Wendy Wood: 'the words and deeds of this famous lady were consistently exciting to those who had no intention of giving us their serious support, and consistently deterred many sober persons who might well have joined us had it not been that they were so well aware of Miss Wood's headlines'.

A few diehards had continued campaigning for a Scottish Parliament throughout the 1950s. The Scottish Covenant Association had been launched in 1951 but relied overwhelmingly on the activities of John MacCormick. It sought to translate the latent support it believed was evident in signatures of the Covenant into political power but was unclear how this would be done. All but four Scottish Labour MPs condemned a letter from the Covenant Association asking them to pledge support for a Royal Commission on home rule and only one, John McGovern, MP for Glasgow Shettleston, supported the Covenant pledge and even he did so hesitantly.

The Covenant Association ran out of steam and only a shell of the Association carried on through the 1950s. It was one of the most innovative and imaginative campaign organizations Scotland witnessed in the post-war period but it always drew back from directly challenging the established parties. The debates within the Covenant Association resembled those that had been held within the SHRA in the inter-war period as it became increasingly clear that the established parties would not deliver home rule. In May 1961, James Porteous, one the Covenant's leading members and who had been secretary to the Scottish Economic Committee in the 1930s, was finally conceding, as others had already done, that there was 'no use pretending we exist as an active body any longer' and suggested that the Association should adjourn *sine die*, 'like the Scottish Parliament' and let members support the SNP or Liberals. It was the 'end of another auld sang'. Labour and the Conservatives were no nearer to supporting a Scottish Parliament. Porteous felt that the SNP had changed. It was 'active and more rational' and the Covenant Association's differences with the party had lost their force. 'NATO, Customs, GATT, EFTA and perhaps the Common Market, with any other Commonwealth or international arrangements that may be made in the future', he argued, diminished differences in their objectives. An 'upsurge of national feeling' meant that getting SNP MPs elected was less remote than previously believed. A poll conducted by the Covenant Association in Peebles in June 1959 found that over 66 per cent supported a Parliament dealing with domestic Scottish affairs and a further 16 per cent supported independence. Similar polls had been held with similar results in Banff and Lanark over the previous year and were similarly dismissed or ignored. The irrepressible John MacCormick proposed to call a Scottish National Assembly after the forthcoming general election in 1959.

The obituary of the national movement was written in two articles in 1959 in the *Glasgow Herald*. The articles looked back at the ten months around

1949–50 as a period when the Scottish Convention 'shook the Union' and argued that this had been caused by the desire for excitement and drama in the dreary austerity of post-war politics. But the author, a Tory candidate in Glasgow in that year's general election, warned that administrative devolution strengthened Scottish nationalism by the enduring sense of a distinct Scottish polity. The SNP contested more seats in 1959 than it had managed four years before but failed to make meaningful electoral progress. Two months later an article in the *Observer* considered Scottish nationalism under the title, 'Best Laid Schemes Gang Aft Agley'. It noted that the SNP refused to disclose its membership figures, that the Scottish National Congress was kept afloat by the financial support of Roland Muirhead, and quoted Labour's Scottish Secretary, 'Home rule? Never heard of it'. John MacCormick died in October 1961 at the age of 56. His obituary in the *Glasgow Herald* described him as 'something of the eternal student' with a 'great deal of talent' but with 'little opportunity in politics to put it to constructive purposes'. His death marked the end of the period when the SNP competed with a non-party body as the main organization of the national movement.

The split in 1942 had reduced the SNP to a few hundred members at most. It had few resources and a dispirited and divided leadership and most of the colourful characters drifted away. The party had been eclipsed by the Scottish Convention and the Covenant Association. It struggled to find candidates to contest elections throughout the 1950s and came close to having no candidates in 1955. The party relied heavily on Robert McIntyre but he refused to stand for Parliament in 1955 unless at least one other SNP candidate came forward. It looked likely that the SNP's days were over. Jimmy Halliday, the young school teacher who would lead the party from 1956–60, came forward and agreed to stand. McIntyre would go on to contest six more general elections through to October 1974 plus another by-election in 1971. He holds the record for the number of attempts a former MP makes to get back into Parliament, aided by having won while still relatively young but also demonstrating the doggedness that was typical of many in the SNP.

The party had contested a by-election in Dundee in 1952 but was unable to stand a candidate in a by-election in Motherwell in 1954, the seat McIntyre had won nine years before, or Inverness where it had performed reasonably well in the past. It did not manage to contest any of the six Scottish by-elections in the 1955–9 Parliament including Argyll, Aberdeenshire East, and Galloway in 1958, all seats that the party would win in less than two decades. Robert McIntyre had become party chairman in 1947 and attempted to impose discipline and direction but faced dissent. A split in the party in 1955 at least brought it to the media's attention. The following year McIntyre stood down and was replaced by Jimmy Halliday as party chairman. The SNP's survival was its greatest achievement in the 1950s. Many years later in his memoirs, Halliday reflected that many people had tried to estimate the SNP's membership, 'The best informed and best qualified academics agree on a fairly low number. They all failed to understand quite how low.'

Frustrated by the lack of progress, Roland Muirhead had established the Scottish National Congress, a new body, in the early 1950s. The SNP, Scottish Covenant Association, and Scottish National Congress competed to be the main body representing the fringe that was Scottish nationalism. But which was the main organization of the national movement was only of concern to the small number of people involved in these organizations. The only party represented in Parliament that supported Scottish home rule was the Scottish Liberal Party and it returned only one Scottish MP in elections between 1951 and 1959: Jo Grimond, MP for Orkney and Shetland. Grimond's level of commitment was evident in his 1959 book, *The Liberal Future*, in which he devoted less than one of about 200 pages to the subject.

Labour abandoned any residual support it had had for a Scottish Parliament during the 1950s. In 1957, the party's Scottish conference instructed its Scottish executive to 'examine the economic and constitutional issues involved' in establishing a Scottish Parliament and make a 'more precise' declaration. The executive recommended that the party should oppose a Scottish Parliament on 'compelling economic grounds'. It noted that until 1929 the party had supported a separate Scottish Parliament but that the idea had not featured in a national statement for a quarter of a century. But Labour was critical of the handling of Scottish affairs. A special party conference in Scotland in 1958 expressed the view that Scottish affairs were being marginalized in the Commons due to increasing pressure to deal with UK and international matters and recommended a Speaker's Conference on the matter. Labour may have formally abandoned its support for home rule but continued to think in Scottish terms.

THE 1950S: A VERY BRITISH DECADE?

It is commonly asserted that the 1950s was a very British decade in Scottish politics. This claim is made with reference to Labour's abandonment of support for home rule, the electoral strength of the Scottish Unionist Party, and the marginalization of the home rule cause. But all the while the sense of Scottish identity remained strong. The Beveridge Committee on Broadcasting, set up by the government, reported in 1951 proposing the need for a distinctly Scottish approach to broadcasting to reflect what the BBC's Scottish Advisory Council described as the 'marked renascence of a Scottish national consciousness'. It referred to the Edinburgh International Festival, first held in 1947, repertory theatres, the Gaelic 'Mod', as well as industrial exhibitions as evidence of a 'remarkable recrudescence of Scottish culture'. In its evidence, the Saltire

Society, a cultural body that had been set up in 1936, noted the 'very wide influence on public tastes and opinion' exerted by broadcasting and was critical of the Scottish Advisory Council as a body that had had little effect on Scottish broadcasting. The Society argued for a BBC Scottish Board of Governors resident in Scotland with one member sitting on the 'English (or British)' Board. In its report, the Beveridge Committee proposed regional devolution and a new Broadcasting Council for Scotland was established. Home rule agitation was on the wane but there was an appreciation of Scottish cultural identity and the emerging medium would take this into account. The BBC adopted a structure that incorporated 'National Regions', a description that was fitting in its ambivalence in describing how it viewed Scotland and might have applied to other bodies, including the state itself. The first BBC television broadcast in Scotland was in March 1952. It was roundly condemned for being dull and pompous. There were stilted comments from the Secretary of State for Scotland, a prayer of dedication from the Dean of the Thistle (an office of the Scottish heraldic Order of the Thistle—the Scottish equivalent of the Garter), and a vote of thanks from Edinburgh's Lord Provost followed by ten minutes of Scottish country dancing. It was Scotland but not one familiar to most Scots, not even the few with television sets at the time. The Scottish Rugby Union refused permission to have the Scotland versus England match broadcast but a third broadcast came from Glasgow's Citizen's Theatre, a venue that had at least shown more promise of what would come later.

In 1951, the Church and Nation Committee of the Church of Scotland remarked on the growing interest in Scottish history and traditions suggesting that a 'resurgence of Scottish national sentiment' had stimulated dramatic and musical activities. The Scottish literary renaissance is normally dated from the 1920s to around the middle of the century but its impact would be felt well beyond that period. Many within the national movement feared for the existence of Scotland as a distinct nation, partly reflecting thin support for home rule. Some Nationalists devoted themselves to cultural activities. Disaffected with the SNP, Andrew Dewar Gibb, for example, drifted away and became active in the Saltire Society. Others took a different view. Billy Wolfe, who would join the SNP in 1962 and become its leader within a decade, had joined the Saltire Society in 1947 on demobilization from the army but doubted its ability to preserve Scottish identity and culture. What brought him into politics had been his belief that he and others were 'fighting a losing battle' trying to preserve Scottish identity. Similar pessimism was evident in J. M. Reid's history of Scotland, published in 1959, which warned that Scotland could disappear as a 'human entity'. Reid concluded that maintaining a sense of Scottishness was 'voluntary', requiring commitment. But this pessimism failed to take account of the constancy, indeed vibrancy, of Scottish cultural life and identity in the 1950s.

The loss of Scottish control of industry and the media was thought to diminish Scottish identity but while Scottish ownership of sections of the press, for example, was lost, the content of the Scottish press remained constant and in many cases increased. The Canadian businessman Roy Thomson (later Lord Thomson of Fleet) bought the *Scotsman* and put new life into what had become a dreary newspaper. His most important decision was the appointment of Alastair Dunnett as the new editor in 1956. Dunnett had been Secretary of State Tom Johnston's press officer during the Second World War and had served as editor of the *Daily Record*. He had been part of Johnston's inner core of advisers who had envisaged a more optimistic post-war Scottish future. Amongst the initiatives he had been engaged with was the establishment of the Scottish Tourist Board. Dunnett served as a member of the Board for over a decade. He was also Thomson's right-hand man when the Canadian ventured into the development of North Sea oil in the 1970s. Thomson's was a much more successful foray into Scottish public life that Beaverbrook's had been two decades before. In 1957, Thomson won the franchise for the new television station broadcasting to central Scotland. Scottish Television (STV) was, in Thomson's words, a 'licence to print money' but it was also an important Scottish medium. STV would prove to be more in touch with the Scottish public's tastes than BBC Scotland and along with Grampian Television, launched in 1961, these stations offered Scots a distinctly Scottish broadcasting experience though most programming would come through the network of other independent stations. Broadcasting would therefore provide a mixture of Scottish, British, and increasingly American cultural experiences. In 1960, the Independent Television Authority (ITA) invited applications for bids to broadcast in the Scottish/English borders area, a geographical area that ignored the boundaries of the UK's components. Borders Television was launched the following year as the smallest British independent channel.

The view that small communities would be subsumed within larger communities was not only feared by home rulers but was common in academic circles where modern developments were expected to lead to assimilation. Local antediluvian cultures would be swept aside by a tide of modern technology, multi-national businesses, mass communications, and progress. But the opposite occurred. There was a reaction against these developments. Mass communication had the twin effect of making people more aware of themselves, contrasted with messages coming from the metropolitan centre.

CONCLUSION

If the past and early post-war period is any guide, then Alison Readman's view, reported at the start of this chapter, was correct. Scottish nationalism did not merit attention in the first Nuffield election study in 1945 or in Nuffield studies for another two decades and more. But R. B. McCallum, her co-author, also had a point. Under the surface there was always the potential, under the right circumstances and with astute political leadership, for growth in support for home rule. This was acknowledged privately time and again by Scottish Secretaries in private communication with Cabinet colleagues, though they were not averse to exaggerating this potential in making the case for special treatment for Scotland.

Pioneers venture into the unknown, often armed only with a strong belief in the rightness of their cause and that it will eventually succeed. Supporters of a Scottish Parliament had little reason to believe they would succeed but took heart from shreds of evidence that they were making progress, often ignoring evidence to the contrary. Leading figures included many people who were not afraid to swim against the tide, including some who took pleasure in doing so, and others who were disputatious by temperament and had abundant self-confidence. These were common characteristics found amongst politically active people. What sustained the party were not the colourful characters.

By the late 1950s, it appeared that home rule agitation and potential had passed its peak. The movement was quixotic, attracted more than its fair share of eccentrics, and was prone to division. What gave it hope was not the movement itself but the underlying sense that Scotland was distinct. The movement had a capacity to turn defeats into victories. Robert McIntyre's election was taken to be proof that it was possible to get an SNP member elected to Parliament. The Covenant came to be interpreted as signifying overwhelming support for a Scottish Parliament that had been rejected by a government that was out of touch. The EIIR case came to be seen as a great success because Lord Cooper had made passing reference to a distinctly Scottish conception of sovereignty. The myths of Bannockburn and William Wallace were present but these more recent myths proved more important.

But more important than any of this was the enduring sense of Scotland as a nation. John MacCormick had argued that 'Scratch almost any Scotsman and you'll find a nationalist'. What he had identified was not necessarily widespread support for a Scottish Parliament but widespread support for the view that Scotland should be recognized as a nation. Home rulers were intent on answering how this should be done with reference to a Scottish Parliament but this was not the only answer to the Scottish Question. Nonetheless, the fact that the question might be asked at all gave heart to home rulers.

6

The Right to Be Taken Seriously

The announcement of Winnie Ewing's election to Parliament as an SNP MP completely altered the Scottish Question. It would no longer simply be a matter of how Scotland should be catered for within the United Kingdom but whether it should be part of the United Kingdom at all. The rise and fall in political salience of a Scottish Parliament would thereafter run in parallel with the for- tunes of the SNP. Having previously been only one of many home rule organiza- tions, the SNP became the dominant home rule organization over the following two decades. Scottish home rule rarely entered centre stage in British politics but it was never far out of sight, returning to view suddenly, unexpectedly, and often just when the issue was thought to have disappeared. Mrs Ewing herself would perform such feats of reincarnation in her political career before her election as a Member of the Scottish Parliament in 1999 when, as the oldest Member, she opened proceedings with the words 'I want to start with words that I have always wanted either to say or hear someone else say—the Scottish Parliament, which adjourned on March 25, 1707, is hereby reconvened.'

In 1967, she had confidently predicted that a Scottish Parliament would be established 'no later' than 1975. But she lost her Hamilton seat at the 1970 general election and though the SNP won the Western Isles, its first seat won in a general election, the consensus was that the SNP's best days were behind it. The predictions of the party's demise were confounded when it won seven seats in the February 1974 general election and a further four in October that year. Mrs Ewing won Moray in February, defeating the Secretary of State for Scotland, but lost it along with eight of her SNP colleagues at the 1979 general election. But Mrs Ewing went on to win a seat in the first direct elections to the European Parliament a few months later. This would be the pattern for the movement in which she was a prominent member.

It was tempting to dismiss the Hamilton by-election as a mid-term pro- test vote as there was much to protest against. Winnie Ewing was a highly articulate candidate and a woman in the masculine politics of west central Scotland. She linked Scotland's constitutional status to social and economic grievances as her hero Robert McIntyre had done two decades before in neigh-bouring Motherwell. 'Scotland's grievous social ills', she argued, were due to 'misgovernment, under-government'. Within a fortnight of taking up her seat, the *Financial Times* noted that she had put down a 'flood' of questions in Parliament and provoked others to do so too. Her questions were designed to gain authoritative information that would be used in campaigns but they also had the effect of forcing Whitehall to consider an array of questions in Scottish terms. Information was not always available or could not be obtained without undue cost but enough departments supplied data that contributed to the sense of Scotland as a distinct unit of government.

The SNP's fluctuating support made it difficult to sustain party discipline. Every little victory was interpreted as a sign of a major breakthrough and every defeat was followed by a period of despair and soul-searching. The SNP's inexperience when faced with onslaughts from its opponents became apparent after Hamilton. Hamilton moved the SNP and the case for a Scottish Parliament from the fringe of politics. In private, successive governments had taken full account of the 'smouldering pile that might suddenly break through the party loyalties and become a formidable national movement', as the Scottish Secretary had described the home rule movement to Cabinet col-leagues in 1947. But the gloves came off after Hamilton. Whitehall woke up to the Scottish Question as never before. When the SNP advanced in local elec-tions the following year, the *Economist* offered a typically barbed compliment. The SNP had earned the 'right to be taken as a very serious force—politically and emotionally, if not always intellectually'. The SNP's opponents mirrored the SNP in their reactions to each SNP victory. They overstated the threat posed by the SNP when it was in the ascendant and underestimated the SNP's ability to recover after defeat. Ignoring the SNP might have worked before Hamilton but it would be difficult with an MP attracting considerable media attention or for very long at any point in the future.

UNEMPLOYMENT, EMIGRATION, AND NUCLEAR WEAPONS

Though Labour had turned its back on home rule, the party continued to articulate demands and raise points on a Scottish basis. Major debates in Parliament, such as on the annual Address setting out the government's legis-lative programme, would be marked by what a London MP described in 1958 as a 'very lively Scottish interlude'. These Scottish interludes did not mean that home rule was raised. The Scottish Question was then concerned with find-ing the most effective Scottish voice within Westminster and Whitehall for a range of everyday public policy concerns. Labour held a special conference in 1958 where it was argued that Scottish affairs were neglected in Parliament due to the pressure of international and UK affairs. There was particular concern that Scotland's economic situation was receiving insufficient attention. That same year the respected Scottish Council (Development and Industry) issued a statement expressing alarm that unemployment had risen to over 70,000 and announced that it would undertake a special survey of the Scottish economy as a 'matter of urgency'. Iain MacLeod, as Minister of Labour, visited Clydeside where unemployment was particularly severe. The STUC called for immediate action including locating a steel strip mill in Grangemouth, constructing Forth and Tay road bridges, and more factory building. Work on the Forth road bridge began later that year. In 1961, a meeting in Glasgow City Chambers of MPs from all parties in Scotland—thirty-seven Labour, ten Tories, and the one Liberal—plus representatives of the trade unions resolved to seek a meeting with the Prime Minister to discuss unemployment in Scotland. The *Sunday Post* described it as the 'biggest gathering of MPs in Scotland since the Act of Union'. Unemployment had reached the symbolically significant 100,000 mark two months before. The Tory slogan in 1959, 'Life's Better with the Unionists', rang hollow in parts of Scotland, as the Scottish Unionists privately conceded. Scottish Labour may have come out against home rule but remained distinctly Scottish. It was also building up high expectations of what it would be able to do once it came to power.

Emigration continued to be a related problem. Figures given in response to a question Winnie Ewing asked in Parliament showed that 45,000 Scots had left Scotland in the year up to July 1967, a figure only slightly down on the previous year. No details existed on who these people were, or what professional or technical training they had. One change that had occurred in the previous two years was that most emigrants now left for other parts of the world beyond the UK. The SNP made much of emigration, arguing that these figures ought to be added to the number of unemployed but also argued that Scotland was losing much of its professional and technical expertise to emigration. Despite the relatively 'open door' approach to immigration that had existed between the 1948 British Nationality Act and when restrictions were introduced in the early 1960s, relatively few Commonwealth citizens came to Scotland. While immigration became an issue in elections in parts of England in the 1960s, emigration was the issue that was raised in Scottish elections, especially by the SNP.

Another development would prove important. The UK had been developing nuclear weapons. The Campaign for Nuclear Disarmament (CND) was set up in 1958 and the Labour Party voted for unilateralism at its 1960 conference though reversed the decision the following year. A deal was done with the United States to allow the UK to purchase Polaris missiles as the UK's 'independent' nuclear deterrent and permit the US to have nuclear bases in the UK.

In 1959, a number of possible options, all in Scotland, were considered and the US requested a base for its Polaris submarines. The UK government proposed Loch Linnhe, a sea loch with Fort William at its north-eastern end, which was deemed suitable by the Admiralty and the UK Atomic Energy Authority though without some logistical or amenity advantages of the River Clyde. The Minister of Defence told Cabinet that the Americans wanted the Holy Loch, 'to be within easy reach of amenities and of an airport, preferably Prestwick'. The Minister of Defence described the Holy Loch as a 'much visited part of the world near Glasgow', advised against accepting the US request, and proposed Loch Linnhe instead. However, Prime Minister Macmillan informed his Cabinet that President Eisenhower had informed him that Loch Linnhe was not satisfactory and requested a site further south 'in the Clyde area'. Cabinet minutes in July 1960 recorded the decision—'in view of the importance of preserving the special relations between the two countries and in the interests of the defensive strength of the Western Alliance, it was desirable that facilities in the Clyde area should be made available for United States POLARIS submarines'—but noted the 'considerable political difficulty in securing public support in this country for these arrangements'. The Ministry of Defence warned that it was 'important to avoid describing the facilities as an American base in Scotland'. The Scottish Office, established to represent Scottish interests in the Cabinet, played little part in these debates.

In November 1960, the decision was made public that Polaris was coming to the Clyde, provoking opposition from local authorities, trade unions, and the Kirk amongst others. Proximity to Glasgow, Scotland's largest city, was raised in debates and countered by supporters of nuclear weapons who argued that the city would be at risk as a potential Soviet target regardless of where nuclear weapons were based. In parliamentary debates, ministers were at pains to suggest that the decision on the Holy Loch had been made by the UK government and was not an American decision. There was a strong Scottish dimension to the debates. Hector Hughes, Labour MP for Aberdeen North, strongly objected to 'Scotland alone being asked to bear the burden of this unique, terrible and undiscriminating weapon'. The SNP in 1961 reaffirmed the party's support for membership of the North Atlantic Treaty Organization (NATO) but 'strenuously opposed' the UK government's decision to permit Polaris bases in Scotland without the people of Scotland having a right to choose. This was the era of marching against nuclear weapons and would see Roland Muirhead, into his 90s, marching with his small contingent of Scottish National Congress members in anti-Polaris demonstrations. Opposition to nuclear weapons on Scottish soil would be an important rallying cry for nationalists who would become amongst the most consistent opponents of nuclear weapons over subsequent decades. After Labour abandoned opposition to nuclear weapons, the SNP would attract a number of former Labour activists, disillusioned with Labour's acceptance of nuclear weapons.

SNP ADVANCES

Early signs of the SNP's potential came in by-elections. The SNP contested its first by-election in nine years in late 1961 in Glasgow Bridgeton. Ian Macdonald, an Ayrshire farmer, took under one in five votes for the SNP in the Labour-held seat and came just behind the Conservatives. Macdonald's organizational skills were thought to be behind the result. He decided to sell his farm and become a full-time organizer for the party funded by the income from the farm's sale and what little the party could afford to pay him. He played the key role in the development of a branch structure throughout Scotland and a key role in the next Scottish by-election seven months later in West Lothian. This by-election brought Tam Dalyell, Old Etonian and former Chairman of Cambridge University Conservatives, up against Billy Wolfe in what was to be the first of six electoral contests in the constituency over seventeen years, gaining the record for the number of times two candidates stood against each other in UK general elections. For the first time in forty-two years, the Tories lost their deposit in a Scottish by-election. Wolfe won 23 per cent of the vote. But it was not all progress for the SNP. Its share of the vote in a by-election in Glasgow Woodside five months later was less than half that won in West Lothian and it won only 7.3 per cent of the vote in Kinross and West Perthshire in late 1963 when Sir Alec Douglas-Home romped home as Tory Prime Minister after renouncing his seat in the Lords. Better results followed in Dundee West and Dumfriesshire before the 1964 general election.

In 1964, the SNP managed to contest fifteen seats, winning 2.4 per cent of the vote across Scotland. Two years later, it contested twenty-three seats, winning 5 per cent of the vote. It may not have come close to winning a seat but the leadership took comfort in saving thirteen deposits (at that time a party required to win one-eighth of total valid votes cast to regain a deposit of £150 submitted with nomination papers). Even if the party had members locally and a basic organization, it was sometimes unable to find the funds to pay a deposit. In Aberdeenshire East in 1959, for example, its few members failed to put together enough money and had suffered a rebuff from a local bank when it requested a loan. The seat was won by Patrick Wolrige-Gordon, an Eton-educated Cambridge undergraduate who was the son of Dame Flora MacLeod, chief of the Clan MacLeod. The SNP managed to scramble together enough money in 1964 but failed to save their deposit. Ten years later, Wolrige-Gordon lost his seat to the SNP's Douglas Henderson. A key development in the SNP in the 1960s was the fact that it was put on a firmer organizational and financial footing allowing it to contest more seats.

The 1959 general election had been the first television election and the SNP was keen to ensure it received its fair share of coverage. It argued for the right to have a party political broadcast but met strong opposition in London. Tony Benn, as Postmaster-General, proved as unreceptive to the SNP's demands as he was to calls to allow pirate radio stations to operate. While Benn's focus had been on Radio Caroline operating offshore, Scottish nationalists had launched Radio Free Scotland (RFS) in late 1956. According to Gordon Wilson, who had been involved in RFS and later became an SNP MP and leader, RFS probably attracted more media attention than the SNP during its early years. While RFS generated some excitement, the SNP in the 1960s was keen to become a mainstream party and focus shifted to campaigning to be allowed to have conventional party broadcasts.

The first official SNP broadcast was shown in September 1965. Billy Wolfe outlined the party's economic case for independence resulting in a flood of applications to join the party. Labour's problems and the SNP's opportunity were not long in coming after the 1966 general election. A seamen's strike only two months after the election undermined Wilson's government. Difficult relations with the trade unions fed into the general sense that something was wrong in the governance of the UK and damaged Labour's position as the 'natural party of government', which Wilson had hoped to establish. Industrial relations problems and economic crises did little to create an image that the UK was a successful political entity. Wilson's modernization rhetoric had played a significant part in encouraging a view that the state could deliver for its citizens. The disillusionment that set in soon after the election was felt in Scotland as much as elsewhere. The difference was that there was a channel for disillusionment.

The first dramatic sign that nationalism was on the march came from Wales where Gwynfor Evans, leader of Plaid Cymru, the Welsh Nationalists, won Carmarthen in a by-election in July 1966, overturning a Labour majority of over 9,000 votes. Winnie Ewing would later describe how the Plaid victory gave her a 'fantastic boost'. The SNP had long had close relations with Plaid and were buoyed up by the result in Wales. Ian MacDonald's work in building up a network of branches was also paying dividends. At its 1966 annual conference, the SNP claimed a ten-fold increase in its membership in four years from 2,000 to 21,000 by the end of 1965 and estimated to be nearer 30,000 six months later. Even allowing for hyperbole, the evidence of the record attendance of 600 delegates at its annual conference suggested that the party was advancing.

The following March a by-election in Pollok in Glasgow presented Labour with a challenge. The sitting Labour Member had died. Esmond Wright, one of a new breed of media-dons, a historian who had a high profile on local television, won the seat for the Tories. In his short time as MP before he was defeated at the 1970 general election, he articulated the view that the Scottish Tories needed to modernize, including supporting a measure of home rule. Wright's 1967 victory owed much to the strong SNP performance. The SNP's 28 per cent of the vote was largely drawn from Labour and allowed the Tories to take the seat. It was the last occasion when the Tories won a Westminster parliamentary by-election in Scotland. Labour's defeated candidate was Dick Douglas, who would become MP for Clackmannan and East Stirlingshire but lost that seat to the SNP before winning Dunfermline for Labour in 1979. Douglas defected to the SNP in 1990.

Hamilton had been a rock solid Labour seat. Tom Fraser had a 16,576 majority over the Tories in a two-way contest in 1966 but resigned to take up appointment as chairman of the Hydro Electric Board. Labour chose Alex Wilson, a miner with NUM support, against the wishes of many Labour supporters. The SNP candidate was Winnie Ewing who was all that Wilson was not: an articulate, charismatic young lawyer. In November 1966, the government had announced that it intended to take the UK into the European Economic Community. Polls showed opposition to EEC membership. The Nationalists had argued at their conference five months earlier that all negotiations should recognize Scotland as an independent country. The SNP message again was 'put Scotland first'. It was populist and successful. Economic crises were just around the corner. In July 1966, the government imposed a wages freeze. Controversy had surrounded the government's incomes policy and trade union dissatisfaction had undermined Wilson's government. Sterling was devalued within weeks of the by-election.

Reports circulated that a congratulatory telegram had been sent to Winnie Ewing from Dover House, the London base of the Scottish Office. Tam Dalyell raised a question in Parliament on the Dover House telegram on the morning after the by-election. Nationalist sympathizers were thought to exist under every bed. Willie Ross replied that 'no senior official would so far forget his professional code as to have any part in such a thing and I do not propose to conduct any interrogation'. Within days of the by-election, the head of the Civil Service met with a group of Permanent Secretaries in Whitehall to produce a 'quick report' on government policy affecting Scotland. As a senior Treasury official noted, the 'election of Mrs Ewing has galvanised the Scottish MPs into asking a flood of questions on this topic'. Pressure was building up for another exercise similar to the Catto Report of 1952 setting out Scotland's economic and financial position within the UK. There were few senior Labour politicians willing to support devolution. The most sympathetic was Richard Crossman, who saw rising support for Plaid Cymru and the SNP as an opportunity to raise the issue of regional devolution throughout the UK.

The Hamilton result may have come as a surprise to some but there had been ample intimations of an SNP breakthrough. Ian MacDonald had spent considerable time and effort travelling around Scotland setting up branches. What is unclear is whether the SNP had long had the potential for this growth but had failed to realize it through indiscipline, poor organization, and the absence of a network of branches or whether the growth was a result of changes in Scottish politics and society in the 1960s. In all probability, it was all of these. The SNP's vote in some of seats in 1964 was lower than in 1959 but the party managed to contest three times as many seats, perhaps dissipating its energies. There was considerable variation in the SNP's vote across Scotland from 2.5 per cent in a Borders seat to 30 per cent in West Lothian. The party had adopted the blunderbuss approach to elections. It stood candidates in as many seats as it could and where it had an organization rather than focus on building up support in a few targets.

HAMILTON AND THE CONSERVATIVES

The Scottish Unionist Party was led by a narrow social base that did at least understand the importance of playing the Scottish card. This awareness came partly from the aristocratic landowners with deep Scottish ancestral roots who continued to have considerable influence in the party in many parts of Scotland well into the second half of the twentieth century. But the party failed to appreciate the economic and social changes occurring in Scotland. The Unionist vote in 1955 is often cited as evidence of the party's electoral success. But the 1955 result was less impressive than often suggested. There has been a tendency to focus on the Unionists' achievement of winning 50.1 per cent of the vote which is often presented as the only occasion when a party in Scotland gained over 50 per cent of the vote since mass enfranchisement.

However, this ignores the composition of the vote. This Scottish Unionist vote was achieved with the support of National Liberal *and* Conservative candidates (41.5 per cent for the Unionists and 8.6 per cent for National Liberal and Conservatives). Labour won more votes and seats than the Unionists with 46.7 per cent and four more seats. Contemporary accounts were more careful in presenting the results by breaking down support in this way than many subsequent histories. Many of those elected under the Unionist banner were keen to emphasize that they were Liberal Unionists. John Maclay, for example, who became Scottish Secretary in 1957, emphasized his Liberal affiliation having been leader of the National Liberals in the Commons immediately after the end of the war. Indeed, there was some concern in Scottish Unionist Party circles when a Liberal Unionist was appointed Scottish Secretary. Nonetheless, the Scottish Unionists had performed well compared with later results. Their Labour opponents were very clear as to why this had happened. Arthur Woodburn, Labour Scottish Secretary under Attlee, would refer to speeches by Walter Elliot in which Elliot had told his local party that the emotional attachment generated in Scotland could be 'turned into the channel of getting rid of the Socialist Government'. It was, according to Woodburn, cynical. But it worked. As Labour adopted a more centralist approach, turning their back on home rule, the Conservatives were able to take advantage. But, as Norman Brook, Cabinet Secretary, told Prime Minister Attlee in late 1949, the Unionist

Party in Scotland 'will probably never support the idea of a Scottish Parliament since it could not hope to secure a majority in it'. The Scottish Unionists may have played the Scottish card to maximum effect and to the great annoyance of Labour but it drew back from supporting a Parliament for Scotland.

In 1964, after thirteen years in office, the Conservatives were on the defensive despite the Prime Minister, Alec Douglas-Home, having a Scottish seat in Parliament. A report from the Kirk's Church and Nation Committee in 1956 noted that one in every thirty-seven Scots was unemployed compared with one in 111 in England. It called for drastic measures to counter the drift south of population and industry. The Scottish Tories' grouse moor image combined with Scotland's relative economic position to erode any advantage recently held. Various voices demanded change. In 1956, the party passed a motion by a small majority asking its central council to consider a change of name to Scottish Conservative and Unionist Association. The proposers argued that the original significance of the Scottish Unionist Party had gone and that using 'Conservative' would allow the party to take advantage of literature and propaganda from the party's central office in London. But few saw the need to change. A journalist writing in the *Glasgow Herald* in late 1958 suggested that only a 'medieval theologian or an American political scientist could muster the patience necessary to complete a definitive study of the special position of the Unionist party in Scotland within the Conservative Party'. But the distinction mattered. It allowed the party to embody unionism with an emphasis on diversity within union. The frustrations that occasionally spilled over into demands for change tended to see assimilation with the party's more successful English party as the answer.

In May 1960, the Scottish Unionists met in conference after a disappointing result in the previous year's general election. The party had been organized into east and west divisions since its establishment in 1912 because, as one failed parliamentary candidate put it, 'Edinburgh and Glasgow have little truck with each other'. A Scottish central office was recommended and once more the idea of incorporating 'Conservative' into the party's name was proposed. As is often the case, there was a tendency to blame a malfunctioning organization rather than confront the message or policies that the party espoused. The party's innate conservatism made it reluctant to incorporate Conservative into its formal name.

In the wake of further setbacks at the 1964 election, the Scottish party considered reforms again. Sir John George, Scottish party chairman, put forward a series of proposals that would have replaced the two divisions with five regional groups and a beefed up Scottish central office. He revived the idea of changing the party's name to 'Scottish Conservative and Unionist Association'. He bluntly told the party's annual conference that the party was in trouble. There was, he pointed out, an alarmingly poor attendance and those who were active had a high average age with an absence of members between 25 and

40. The conference lacked fire and controversy. He wanted to see a 'clash of conflicting views' and some 'vigorous new blood'. The party in Scotland had lost thirteen seats in six years and, he warned, it could be accused of allowing Harold Wilson to become Prime Minister, 'Scotland will always mean a great deal, but in times of small majorities Scotland can mean all the difference between being in power or dwelling in the wilderness.' In broad terms, the proposed party structure followed the process of consolidation that had taken place in public administration over the earlier part of the century. By 1965, the party was ready for the changes with minimal opposition from the two divisions. The party also established a series of committees to examine its policies. One group under Sir William McEwen Younger reviewed the machinery of Scottish government. The committee only held its first meeting six weeks after the Hamilton by-election.

These developments coincided with a change of leadership in London. Sir Alec Douglas-Home was replaced by Ted Heath in August 1965. Heath was the first Tory leader elected by the party's MPs rather than emerging from a 'magic circle' of Tory grandees. His view was that a new image was required north of the border and concluded that nationalism was the 'biggest single factor in our politics today', as he told Richard Crossman, Lord President of the Council. The party's 'grouse moor image' was damaging and Heath called for imaginative and electorally appealing policies.

The Conservative vote held up reasonably well compared with the collapse in Labour support in Hamilton but the Tories could take no comfort from the result. It added to demands for change. Within weeks of the Hamilton result, a group of Edinburgh University graduates, including Michael Ancram who would become British party chairman thirty years later, launched a 'ginger group' inside the party. The 'Thistle group' published a paper calling for a revolution in the party's organization and for devolution in 'thought and policy'. They argued that housing, health, transport, and economic development policies ought to be determined 'in their Scottish context'. The following May, the group issued another pamphlet on the eve of the Scottish Tory conference arguing for a 'federal framework' for Britain and that 'fiscal independence is vital' and even proposed that there was 'no bar to a separate monetary policy for Scotland'. A future paper argued that Scottish universities should guarantee a 'certain number of places, if not a majority, to Scottish students'.

A secret meeting of senior Tories was held within a fortnight of Hamilton and it was agreed that action was necessary to combat the SNP but that any change of policy in support of a Scottish Parliament needed to come from north of the border. Sir William McEwen Younger issued his report on the machinery of Scottish government and argued in favour of a Scottish Assembly. This would provide a useful Scottish basis for Heath to make one of the most significant policy changes in twentieth-century Scottish politics at the party's 1968 annual conference. The previous week, the SNP had achieved a major breakthrough winning 30 per cent of the vote and over 100 council seats in local elections. Robert McIntyre, who had won Motherwell for the SNP in 1945, became Provost of Stirling.

This was the backdrop to Ted Heath's 'Declaration of Perth'. The leadership's management of the media was much more successful than its management of the party. Reports suggested that Heath had initially planned to propose an Assembly consisting of 'delegated' members and that he had changed this to 'elected' only thirty-six hours before delivering the speech. Heath was influenced by his main preoccupation. He wanted to secure UK membership of the European Economic Community and hoped to see a directly elected European assembly and did not want to propose anything that might serve as a precedent for an indirectly elected body. The Assembly would 'take part in legislation in conjunction with Parliament'. It came as a surprise to most delegates, including those few who supported devolution but it shook up Scottish politics. The Tories were stealing the initiative. Heath had strong backing from senior figures in the party in the south who had to overcome the reservations of Michael Noble, former Tory Scottish Secretary. Heath's proposals were expressed in very general terms and he proposed a committee to examine constitutional change in more detail under Sir Alec Douglas-Home. For a party that had been deeply hostile to home rule, it was a radical change but its grandiloquent billing stirred up opposition within the party. Sir John George's call for a clash of conflicting views was finally met as many in the party railed against Heath's 'Declaration' at the following year's conference. The Declaration was, according to one delegate, 'unimpressive, pretentious and redolent of gimmickry'. Heath was accused by an unnamed critic within the party of 'snatching a fading fashion in the Carnaby Street reach-me-downs of politics'.

Home produced a report in March 1970, a month before the general election. *Scotland's Government* proposed a 'Scottish Convention' to be directly elected with around 125 members elected on the same day as the House of Commons. It would have limited powers. But events had overtaken it. Harold Wilson had set up a Royal Commission on the Constitution the previous year and it was still sitting. Even more relevant, the SNP's electoral advance had halted. In the election that put Ted Heath into Downing Street, Winnie Ewing lost her seat and the consensus was that the SNP had performed poorly. By any measurement other than the hype generated by the SNP and media after Hamilton, the SNP had performed well. It won the Western Isles, its first seat in a general election, and increased its share of the vote to 11.4 per cent after managing to contest sixty-five seats. But objective measurements were not what counted in the immediate aftermath of the election. Heath reinterpreted the threat and decided that Scottish home rule was not a serious challenge. Industrial relations as well as the economy and his commitment to membership of the European Community would be his priorities.

HAMILTON AND LABOUR

Labour's abandonment of home rule had been a gradual process. In 1955, Arthur Woodburn, former Labour Scottish Secretary, reflected on his party's support for a Scottish Parliament in the inter-war period. He noted that in the five years up to 1937, only six of the 644 new factories built in Britain had been in Scotland and that at one point 30 per cent of the insured population had been unemployed. This was an era when the market ruled and Labour had, he claimed, supported a Scottish Parliament in order to be able to control the location of industry. Wartime intervention had demonstrated that government in London could act to direct or, as he put it, 'deflect' industries to different places. Labour's faith in the ability of the centralized state to provide jobs and welfare was at its height in the two decades after 1945. It was also a period when Labour was usually out of office and its faith in what the centralized state could do was based more on hope than experience. When the Tories had played the Scottish card to nationalization, Labour was pushed further towards a defensive centralist position. As the party expressed it in a resolution at its 1958 conference, 'Scotland's problems can best be solved by socialist planning on a UK scale.' Two years before, British party leader Hugh Gaitskell told his Scottish colleagues that economic planning needed to be done on a UK basis as were wage negotiations. The Scottish party was prohibited from discussing matters that did not come under the remit of the Scottish Office, including the emotive matter of siting Polaris on the Clyde. Class politics took priority over all else.

But there remained voices within the wider labour movement in favour of devolution. The Scottish Trade Union Congress was less hostile as were a number of unions and union leaders. The Communist Party had considerable influence in the trade union movement and its 1951 document 'The British Road to Socialism' included a commitment to Scottish home rule. Individual Labour Party members remained supporters through the 1950s including future MPs Judith Hart and John Mackintosh on the left and right of the party respectively.

Labour's election victories in 1964 and 1966 were built on a belief that modern government was able to deliver jobs and welfare. Harold Wilson appointed Willie Ross as his Scottish Secretary in 1964. Ross would serve in this role throughout Wilson's years as Prime Minister to become the longest (non-continuous) serving Scottish Secretary in the office's history. Wilson gave his Scottish Secretary considerable autonomy and Ross became one of Wilson's most loyal lieutenants in Cabinet. This autonomy irritated other Cabinet colleagues. Ross was deeply hostile to devolution and regarded himself as Scotland's guardian. He never hid his contempt for Winnie Ewing. Her presence in Parliament reminded Labour MPs of Labour's failure to address underlying social and economic problems in Scotland. Her parliamentary interventions and frequent questions seeking information on a Scottish basis added to Labour's annoyance. Labour's initial response was to attack the SNP usurper. The most frequent criticism was that she was a 'Tartan Tory' though her parliamentary contributions suggested that her sympathies lay on the liberal left.

The common interpretation of the Hamilton by-election was that the SNP victory took Labour by surprise. The situation was more complex. Labour knew that the SNP was a threat. During the by-election, a Labour MP for a neighbouring constituency sought information on government policies affecting Scotland from the Financial Secretary to the Treasury because Labour was being opposed by the SNP and 'I will be under an obligation to refer to the Scottish position.' Labour knew there was a threat but found it difficult to admit its existence. It simply did not want to take the SNP seriously.

The Scottish question was an irritant for Labour in government but some response was required. Richard Crossman, the Lord President of Council, was a keen constitutional reformer. He supported parliamentary reform as well as reform in regional and local government, both then under consideration by the Wilson government. Immediately after Hamilton, Crossman had written to Wilson warning against dismissing Plaid Cymru and SNP successes. He was attracted to Wilson's suggestion of a 'Stormont solution when you first threw it out in conversation' suggesting that Wilson had initially proposed the idea. The government had already embarked on a process of reorganization of local government in Wales, England, and Scotland but Crossman felt this should not inhibit efforts to address the Scottish and Welsh Questions. However, Cabinet Secretary Burke Trend warned Wilson to 'approach this subject with some care since the susceptibilities of other Ministers are involved—and experience shows that they can be aroused quite easily'. Trend suggested approaching the subject 'with circumspection' by appointing a committee chaired by the Home Secretary. The simplest way of launching a new examination, he suggested, might be a general and informal discussion in Cabinet with an oral introduction by the Lord President that might result in the appointment of a group of ministers to examine the implications of further devolution for Scotland and Wales before the government accept any formal or public commitment. In typical style, Wilson merged the radical and conservative advice by appointing a Ministerial Committee on Devolution to 'examine the implications of further devolution for Scotland and Wales' but chaired by Crossman. It would report its conclusions to the Home Affairs Committee of Cabinet. Crossman was disappointed that English regionalism was excluded as he envisaged major regional reforms across the state as a whole, though he emphasized that he saw this exclusion as being '*at this stage* in our proceeding'. As these discussions took place within government over the weeks after Hamilton, Crossman made public his own view that there should be separate Parliaments for Scotland and Wales in a television discussion in January 1968. This provoked parliamentary questions. Wilson was forced to dissemble, suggesting that he was not responsible for the interpretation that had been placed on the Lord President's comments. Willie Ross made clear his opposition to directly elected assemblies across the UK. It might work, he conceded, in England where central government would operate at a different geographical level but it could only work in Scotland 'on a basis of virtual fiscal and therefore economic separation, or else in a way that left central government with little power while still having to carry the main financial burden'.

Ross even raised objections to proposals from Cledwyn Hughes, his Welsh opposite number, that a Welsh Council should be established to advise the Secretary of State for Wales. Ross feared that this would create a precedent for Scotland. His preferred course of action was to concentrate on 'bashing the nationalists', a phrase that was used repeatedly in correspondence in Whitehall at this time. Wilson became concerned and urged Crossman to produce a 'more warm hearted' paper on devolution rather than focus solely on attacking the SNP and Plaid Cymru. In correspondence with the Prime Minister, Crossman noted the difficulties in reaching agreement with Ross and Hughes suggesting that the 'result of such tripartite collaboration would be the lowest common denominator and not the highest common factor of consensus'. He made a series of proposals that incorporated 'bashing the nationalists', arguing that this should be a 'central theme from now to the election'. He made clear his view that the source of SNP support was the state of the economy:

> If we can get the national economy working our way, our bashing of separatism will steadily carry more and more conviction. At present it won't win back votes because nothing will win back votes except an economic revival. But that is no reason for not starting a sustained propaganda campaign, not only in Scotland but in Wales and England as well, on the theme that Scottish and Welsh separatism would be disastrous to both.

He suggested that the Treasury should 'marshall [sic] the latest and most convincing economic arguments'. He suggested moving a 'major Whitehall office to Scotland' before the election and considering further administrative devolution including parts of the Ministry of Public Building and Works. He raised the possibility of allowing the Scottish Grand Committee to meet in Edinburgh. In essence, he argued that he favoured 'bashing separatism but I also favour balancing the purely negative character of this propaganda campaign with some positive embellishments to show the attractions of unitary UK government'. He concluded that a quasi-federal constitution that would 'roughly correspond' with the German Land system should be considered for the long term. There was a need, he maintained, to move 'away from our tradition of insular centralised administration' to conform more with the 'kind of constitutions established in many countries in the pattern laid down in the American revolution' which would meet the 'needs of our modern technocratic society' better than the 'traditional British highly centralised administration'.

While Labour deliberated in government, Ted Heath had stolen a march by making his Perth Declaration. Labour was now responding not only to the SNP's success in Hamilton but to Heath and the Conservatives. In July 1968, Crossman outlined two stages in tackling the 'problems of Scotland and Wales'. Plan A would be implemented within that Parliament and Plan B would be implemented in the next and subject to the recommendations made in the two Royal Commissions on local government (Redcliffe-Maud on England and Wheatley on Scotland). Plan A for early implementation would have three elements: the 'education of public opinion' on the advantages of the unitary system of government and extent of existing devolution, emphasizing the financial and economic dangers of separatism; further administrative devolution with the Secretary of State for Scotland assuming responsibility for ancient and historic buildings and tourism in Scotland and sharing responsibility for overseas promotion of tourism overseas with the Board of Trade; and allowing the Scottish Grand Committee to meet in Edinburgh and establishing a Scottish Affairs Select Committee. These measures, it was felt, would establish the government's *bona fides* and allow it to develop its thinking including considering a Royal Commission on Scottish Government.

There was concern that Plan B—proposals to be introduced in the next Parliament—was 'thin', as one senior official put it. While Crossman was keen on a federal type solution, roughly based on the German model, his ideas were at best sketchy. Such ideas would find little support in the Cabinet. The appointment of a Royal Commission was, in the words of Gordon Brown when still a young historian, an 'excuse to do nothing in the face of Nationalist success'. Brown's criticism that the Labour government had 'barely discussed its remit and was far from committed to changing the constitution' was wrong on this first point but correct on the second. There was considerable discussion of the remit, membership, and nature of the Commission but behind this there was little support for Crossman's bold ideas.

In July 1968, the Cabinet also considered appointing a Royal Commission. It noted that the 'situation had changed radically' since the Royal Commission on Scottish Affairs had reported in 1954. It was suggested that a Royal Commission should be established after short-term measures had been taken and that any new Commission should have wider terms of reference than that which reported over a decade before. In October, the Cabinet committee discussed future government policy and considered the matter further. Home Secretary Jim Callaghan proposed that a Constitutional Commission should be established and Ross proposed that it be called a 'Royal Commission'. Most of the committee felt that it should be called a 'Commission on the Constitution appointed by the Queen' though a number favoured a 'Royal Commission'. The symbolism of the title of the inquiry was seen as important. It was recognized that while such an inquiry would present challenges to the nationalists, it would be important to ensure that the 'Scottish and Welsh Labour Parties

[were] carefully prepared, positive and sufficiently forward-looking'. As discussions continued, it became clear that Northern Ireland would have to be included in the Commission's remit which then led to accepting the Channel Islands and Isle of Man in its remit. One of the few ministers to object to the idea of any kind of commission was Judith Hart, formerly a junior Scottish Office Minister and by now Paymaster General. She felt it would be best for the government to complete its own inquiry and announce its proposals to avoid the danger of 'stimulating a possibly declining nationalism in Scotland by appearing to shelve the issue until after 1970–71'. Crossman too had concerns but largely because Royal Commissions were then considering local government in England and Scotland. An alternative course was to set up a round table conference consisting of ministers and senior members of the government and Opposition parties, as had been done in 1955 to consider the constitution of Malta. What became very clear was that there was no obvious forum or constitutional mechanism in which to discuss these matters.

Labour became more relaxed as the 1970 election approach. The SNP were not invincible. Labour easily held South Ayrshire in a by-election only three months before the general election. The SNP came third with one-fifth of the vote. The victorious Labour candidate was Jim Sillars who won over half the votes cast. The previous year, Sillars had co-authored a pamphlet in reaction to Winnie Ewing's Hamilton victory, acerbically entitled, 'Don't butcher Scotland's future'. The SNP candidate had previously been the Labour agent in the constituency and after the announcement of Sillars's victory had warned his erstwhile party colleagues that though Labour had won the seat it would struggle to win across Britain as a whole. The message would haunt Sillars over subsequent years as a Labour MP.

THE SCOTTISH MEDIA

It is commonly and frequently asserted that demands for a Scottish Parliament and independence were the creation of sections of the Scottish media. The satirical magazine *Private Eye* once described the *Scotsman* as the 'house organ of the SNP'. There can be little doubt that the existence of a distinct and deeply embedded Scottish media contributed to the sense of Scotland as a distinct place, and the Scottish media offered a platform for advocates of a Scottish Parliament. Although, for every newspaper that supported home rule there were others that opposed it in the 1960s and 1970s. Nonetheless, the existence of a healthy Scottish media created space in which these debates could take place. As Jack Brand remarked, the Scottish press was 'at pains to identify themselves as Scottish papers' even before Hamilton. Newspaper readership in Scotland was high and that meant readership of Scottish newspapers. The *Sunday Post* entered the *Guinness Book of Records* in the 1950s for having the highest per capita readership anywhere in the world.

Hamilton made a big impact on the media. Alastair Dunnett, editor of the *Scotsman*, responded by leading the paper's strong support for a Scottish Parliament. In a series of editorials published in early February 1968, subsequently published as a pamphlet, the paper argued that Scotland should be a 'sovereign state within a federal UK framework'. Winnie Ewing herself attracted a great deal of attention. As one account expressed it, 'Television cameras and photographers' lenses gobbled her up'. The *Express* offered her a weekly column as did the *Daily Record*. She opted for the latter as it was a Labour supporting paper. Her weekly column was ghost written by Michael Grieve, journalist son of Hugh MacDiarmid. Both BBC Scotland and Scottish Television started to transmit regular political programmes in Scotland around this time. Hamilton gave Scottish journalists more opportunities to write and broadcast on Scottish politics. The SNP–media relationship was symbiotic, although it could turn sour.

However, while its opponents often suggested that the SNP was the creation of the media, privately a different view was known to exist. In 1981, Michael Ancram, Scottish Tory chairman, drew lessons from the rise of the SNP in an analysis of the challenge posed by the Social Democrats. Ancram maintained that the Tories had been mistaken in the past in attacking the SNP as a media creation when it had been a development of 'grass roots' politics. The Tories had failed to 'attack at community or branch level where from nowhere the SNP had built up a cell structure which became a branch structure based on genuinely popular support, which turned into an effective constituency fighting and fund-raising machine'. The media had played its part in maintaining a sense of Scottish national identity but the media followed rather than led the political development of the national movement. Nonetheless, the distinct Scottish media was important in the development of a Scottish political space.

CONCLUSION

A character in one of Irving Welsh's novels gains access to the bank details of Rangers Football Club supporters and attempts to access the accounts by guessing that many would use '1690' as the password. It is as likely that a high proportion of SNP activists use some mixture of 'Hamilton' and '1967' in passwords given its symbolic resonance. This date and event have been far more significant for modern Scottish nationalism than Bannockburn or

1320. Hamilton's significance can be exaggerated. It can be seen as the culmination of processes already well underway. It did not signal that Scotland
was on the verge of independence. But Hamilton was important in awakening
Scottish politics to an alternative, though deeply underdeveloped, constitutional future. Over the following three decades, the SNP was an inconsistent
but ever present threat. The Scottish Question would thereafter always include
a constitutional dimension previously only intermittently present. Its most significant impact was to entrench the existence of a Scottish political space and
encourage the sense of a Scottish economic space. The frenetic activity on the
part of the SNP's opponents, including those in Whitehall in the aftermath
of the by-election, suggests an over-reaction to what was in large measure a
protest vote. As many acknowledged at the time, the economic context had
been important.

7

Era of Planning and Social Conservatism

INTRODUCTION

Labour came close to forgetting to mention Scotland in its 1964 manifesto. Tony Benn recorded in his diary that Jim Callaghan, MP for a Cardiff constituency, woke up in the middle of the night realizing that there was 'nothing about Scotland or Wales' in the draft manifesto. It was not that Labour neglected Scotland but that senior British party figures simply devolved responsibility to the Scottish party. Harold Wilson appointed Willie Ross as his Scottish Secretary. He was Wilson's strong ally in Cabinet and was not surprised to lose office once Jim Callaghan became the new Prime Minister in 1976. He was given relative autonomy in his Scottish fiefdom. Tom Johnston's period as Scottish Secretary is often celebrated as the apogee of Scottish Office innovation and autonomy. Johnston owed this to the special wartime conditions when the Prime Minister and other senior ministers were willing to give Johnston considerable autonomy. Ross came close but had to win it through a careful relationship with the Prime Minister, and against the wishes of some senior Cabinet colleagues. The period from the early 1960s through to the late 1970s saw major developments at local and national levels in Scottish government. It was a turbulent time economically. It began with a period of optimism, especially about what government could do to improve the life of the people. This was seriously undermined, but not shattered, with a series of crises culminating in the devaluation of sterling in 1967. But far more challenging economic times lay ahead. The quadrupling of oil prices in a matter of months by Middle Eastern oil producers in reaction to Western support for Israel in the Yom Kippur war in late 1973 brought about high levels of inflation and economic stagnation. The Phillips Curve predicting an inverse relationship between unemployment and inflation proved wrong. Tory Shadow Chancellor Iain MacLeod had coined the term *stagflation* to describe this combination in 1965 when attacking Labour's then economic difficulties. But it had more resonance a decade later.

A SCOTTISH ECONOMY?

By the early 1960s, the well-rehearsed diagnoses of Scotland's economic problems were repeated in a series of reports and books. The decline of heavy industries, low growth, relatively high unemployment, high levels of emigration,
and external control of industry all affected Scotland. There had been a growth
in the number and quality of economic indicators. The Scottish economy
grew annually on average by 1.6 per cent in the decade after 1951 compared
with 4.9 per cent for the UK as a whole. That same decade, Scotland's population grew by 1.6 per cent compared with 4.9 per cent for the UK as a whole.
Unemployment was on average 1.9 times higher in Scotland than in the rest of
the UK. Divergence particularly came from the mid-1950s but increased suddenly at the end of the decade. Scotland was more susceptible to fluctuations
in the economy. An economic downturn in 1958 was more severe in Scotland
than in the UK as a whole. The consensus was that Scotland was too reliant on
heavy industries. There had been initiatives for the Highlands—a fund to foster social and economic development was opened in 1953, a modern Crofters'
Commission was established the following year.

In 1951, Alec Cairncross, one of a Lanarkshire ironmonger's eight children, returned to an academic post at Glasgow University, and founded the
first Department of Applied Economics in Britain after a period working as
a government economist. He helped revive the Scottish Economic Society,
which had not met for two decades. In 1954, he edited a collection of essays
under the title *The Scottish Economy*, the first study of its kind. What was
simultaneously emerging was a perception that there was something called
a 'Scottish economy' and that the state had responsibility for it. Cairncross
chaired a committee, set up by the SCDI, which recommended identifying
'growth points', and moving away from subsidizing areas of high unemployment to investing in areas nearby that had greater potential for growth. It
was an attempt to bridge the divide between government intervention as
social policy, designed to assist poorer people and areas, and intervention as
an economic growth policy. Government resources might be channelled into
helping areas with most need, evident in unemployment 'black spots', but it
was feared that this would do little in the long term to help generate more
jobs. Alternatively, resources might be channelled into areas with potential
for growth but this meant the government turning its back on, or at least
limiting, support for the poorer areas. The bridge in Cairncross's solution
assumed contiguity between growth points and black spots—that jobs would
conveniently be found in the growth points near to the areas with declining
industries shedding jobs.

As Gavin McCrone, later to become chief economic adviser to a succession
of Scottish Secretaries, wrote in a book published in 1965, there was a consensus that what Scotland needed was 'newer "science based" industries' instead

of the heavy investment in traditional industries. He conceded that the investment that had been made was 'necessary to save the industries from extinction' but this kind of investment did not achieve economic growth. Scottish institutions had become masters in fighting to protect ailing industries but poor in developing new growth. Businesses that were in decline were quick to look to government for assistance, creating a business dependency culture. An industry–government–trade unions nexus had emerged, institutionalized in the Scottish Council (Development and Industry) (SCDI), with no equivalent at UK level. It was described by Moore and Booth as having the 'formal trappings of a meso-corporatist tripartite organization in its structural make-up' but without the power to implement policy or control its members and thus unlike corporatist councils elsewhere in Europe. But there was another key difference. Those corporatist bodies made decisions over a broad range of subjects. Scotland's pseudo-corporatism was largely limited to holding inquiries, making recommendations, lobbying, and especially campaigning to protect declining industries. The SCDI was less 'Scotland's industrial Parliament' than Scottish industry's pressure group. There was also a Highlands and Islands equivalent. The Highland Panel was set up in 1947 and revived in 1955. Its remit was to 'encourage the exchange of ideas among Member organizations, strengthen co-ordination of activity and strategic objectives, and maximise the effectiveness and sustainability of their development policies'.

GOVERNMENT SCOTTISH ECONOMIC POLICIES

There had been little support for a Scottish Board of Trade when the Balfour Commission had considered Scottish affairs at the start of the 1950s but the additional responsibilities under the Scottish Office's remit gave impetus to a perception that a distinct Scottish economy existed. It had been commonplace to refer to Scottish economic issues but these had generally been seen as economic issues affecting a particular geography rather than requiring specifically Scottish solutions or institutions. The very existence of the Scottish Office and attendant public bodies at a time when public expectations of government allied with new responsibilities for infrastructure, especially transport, ensured that many economic issues would be viewed in Scottish terms. Crucially, they would also be thought to require Scottish solutions. But hard economic choices—classic questions of the relationship between taxing and spending—were taken at UK level. The consequence was that Scottish concerns were heavily focused on asking for more, and that almost invariably meant more money.

Any notion that the Balfour Commission's recommendations on the extension of the Scottish Office's remit would settle matters once and for all was soon dispelled. Sir David Milne, the Office's Permanent Secretary, asked the Treasury for permission to appoint an additional senior official following the transfer of responsibilities recommended by Balfour. This was turned down by Sir Norman Brook, Treasury head, who instead suggested an inquiry into the work of the Scottish Office's four departments. In a letter to Milne, Brook raised concerns:

> Are the Scottish Departments satisfied with their handling of general economic questions and of detailed economic matters like the investment programmes of the Scottish public undertakings? The impression in certain quarters is that there is little fundamental thinking on Scotland's real needs, but rather a tendency to ask for whatever seems available for England. If England has a large road programme, Scotland presses for the Forth Road Bridge. If England is to have atomic power stations, Scotland presses for one. The sum of all these investments is not necessarily the best way to spend money on capital development.

London was not averse to the Scottish Office showing some initiative on the economy. Indeed, one official a few years before had remarked that Sir Stafford Cripps, when President of the Board of Trade, had been anxious to rid himself of the 'tiresome Scottish economic problems by pushing responsibility (but not power) on to the Secretary of State for Scotland'. This had been resisted by the Scottish Office then just as Milne resisted it in the 1950s.

One of the SCDI's most important contributions in this period was the establishment, with strong Scottish Office support, of the Toothill Inquiry on the Scottish economy in 1960. J. N. Toothill was managing director of Ferranti, an electrical engineering firm specializing in defence equipment and the kind of company that the government was keen to encourage. Employment in the electronics industry in Scotland grew by 60 per cent between 1959 and 1962. But this growth was wiped out entirely by the loss of jobs in coal mining and agriculture. There was a need for even greater growth in the new sector. Toothill argued that policy should be geared more towards the promotion of growth with less emphasis on reacting to decline. This was interpreted as requiring 'planning' and some restructuring of the Scottish Office to reflect this shift. Toothill made eighty-one recommendations with around thirty-six being the responsibility of the government as a whole, including some of its most important proposals, but many were outside the exclusive competence of the Scottish Office.

There had been some consideration of a reorganization of the Scottish Office along these lines a few years before, including the idea of establishing a Development Department. Some officials thought the term 'development' might convey something too close to Labour Party thinking. The usual intra-bureaucratic politics combined with a lack of urgency led to inertia.

Toothill provided the impetus for change. The report recommended the creation of an economic planning department in the Scottish Office but rejected the idea of a Scottish Parliament. There would be no new responsibilities but a reorganization that would be symbolically significant and facilitate a shift of emphasis. In time-honoured tradition, the Scottish Office established a committee to examine the Toothill Committee's proposals. There was little appetite for an additional department within the Scottish Office and what emerged in 1962 was a reordering of offices with the creation of a Scottish Home and Health Department (SHHD) and a Scottish Development Department (SDD) in 1962. Two years later, a regional development division was established within the SDD, reporting directly to the Scottish Office Permanent Secretary.

The real test would not be in how government was organized but in the policies it would pursue. Over the following three years, White Papers were produced on Central Scotland and the Scottish Economy emphasizing the need for 'growth points', including a programme of infrastructural investment. But even if the Scottish Office focused on economic growth, other factors, including government policies, would have to be contended with. The most notable at this time was the appointment of Richard Beeching, an ICI director, as head of the newly created British Railways Board with the task of addressing heavy losses despite significant investment in rail modernization. In 1963, Beaching published his report on 'The Reshaping of British Railways', which proposed swingeing cuts in the rail network, reversing the great nineteenth-century expansion that had contributed to Scotland's economic development. There was strong opposition throughout Britain and many lines proposed for the axe were saved. In Scotland, the Highlands Panel threatened to resign *en masse* over rail closures. Key rail lines through the Highlands were saved including the Far North line from Inverness to Thurso and Wick, and the West Highland Line, from Glasgow to Mallaig and Oban. But much of the Scottish rail infrastructure was destroyed.

In November 1963, Ted Heath, as Tory Secretary of State for Industry, Trade, and Regional Development, announced the publication of a White Paper on regional development and growth in central Scotland along with one for the north-east of England. The themes of the White Paper, as described by Heath to Parliament, were growth, modernization, partnership, and continuity of development by which he meant a commitment to a sustained effort over many years to come in these regions. Heath envisaged a partnership between central and local government as well as public and private sectors, including the SCDI. Labour members did not so much question the strategy but the commitment, noting that the idea of growth points had been advocated a decade before by the Cairncross Committee. The weakness of the proposal, and that of the Cairncross Committee report a decade before, was highlighted by Judith Hart, Labour MP for Lanark who would become a junior Scottish Office Minister a year later. Hart noted that the closure of a coal mining pit in her constituency would leave 350 men without jobs and that the village was geographically some distance from the north Lanarkshire growth area. She asked whether the government was 'deliberately and unequivocally writing off parts of Scotland'. From an altogether different perspective, the *Economist* described the White Paper as 'plans for crutches, not for cures... expressions of half-worthy aspirations with remarkably little economic analysis behind them' and suggested that there was a need for much improved economic data. The underlying criticism was the absence of more than a superficial commitment to a 'regionally minded' approach.

A significant theme in post-1945 debates on the Scottish economy was the extent to which Scotland had become a branch plant economy. Toothill found that under 40 per cent of decisions on senior management appointments in branch factories in Scotland were made outside Scotland. Only 19 per cent of research and development work in such firms was conducted in Scotland and 90 per cent of investment decisions were made outside Scotland. In 1962, 67 per cent of Glasgow University science graduates and 50 per cent of its engineering graduates found employment outside Scotland.

Andrew Hargrave, Hungarian-born doyen of Scottish industrial journalists in the mid- to late twentieth century, offered an alternative critique. In a pamphlet published by the Glasgow Fabian Society in early 1964, he argued that the consensus around Toothill from SCDI and others failed to address something more fundamental. He suggested that the consensus offered little more than 'modifications, improvements extensions'. The 'senseless piece of butchery as the Beeching rail cuts *taken in isolation* [italics in original], regardless of the general transport problem or economic considerations' was an example of the lack of joined-up thinking in policy-making. While Toothill had stated its working assumption to be that 'Scotland's prosperity is tied to the prosperity of the United Kingdom and measures which would prejudice this are likely to defeat their own ends', Hargrave argued that the UK's prosperity was itself tied to the prosperity of her customers outside the UK and that Scotland was affected by protective tariffs in Canada and Australia against British cars, American tariffs against Scottish woollen goods, a failure of a sugar crop in Cuba, and wrangling over the price of Argentine beef and Pakistani jute. Scotland was, according to Hargrave, to borrow a Toothill phrase, 'inextricably interwoven' with more than the rest of Britain.

Hargrave quoted a *Scotsman* editorial from January 1964 which had asked, 'what is the inner debility in the once strong economy that has defied devoted and costly treatment?' The very idea of an 'inner debility' suggested that this 'crisis of confidence', as Hargrave described it, lay at the heart of the problem. His sympathies lay more with the Liberals than Labour on this matter. Labour was stuck in the same paradigm of what he called 'tied prosperity', concurring with an editorial in the *Financial Times*, a paper he would soon join, that argued for a 'much greater degree of devolution in our system of government' in order to carry out the necessary revolution in thinking on effective regional planning. He approvingly quoted a Liberal document that asserted that a Scottish Parliament's value would 'lie not solely in the direct action it would take, but also in the psychological advantage of having the economy shaped in terms of local genius and traditional social and population patterns, rather than as a haphazardly developing section of a larger unit' but complained that the theme was under-explored. A group of Scottish Labour MPs and trade unionists had produced a pamphlet, 'A development plan for Scotland', a few months before which had recognized a distinct Scottish 'national identity' and called for a 'regional organisation with a wide measure of autonomy' but had failed to develop the idea. There was something mystical in the Liberals' expression of the case for a Scottish Parliament that would sit uneasily with much economic analysis which was becoming increasingly 'scientific', abjuring psychological explanations of human behaviour and shrinking into the equally mythical *homo economicus*.

Hargrave argued that Scotland had some autonomy over a wide range of matters including housing, town planning, education, the law, local government, roads, electricity, agriculture, fisheries, and forestry and had distinguished universities, arts, and history, but it had 'lost out' because it lacked autonomy when it came to 'jobs, investment expansion and other such vital things'. It was not a plea for independence but, from a commentator with a deep understanding of other European countries, greater autonomy along the lines found in other parts of Europe, and more engagement with the rest of Europe. This might mean a greatly expanded Scottish Office, a Scottish Regional Council along the lines then being proposed by John Mackintosh, who would soon take up the chair in politics at Strathclyde University before becoming a Labour MP. Hargrave's own preference was a Scottish Assembly, with Scottish MPs sitting in both the UK and Scottish Assembly. It was a sharp critique and found little support. Even the chairman of Glasgow Fabian Society made plain his opposition in the foreword to the pamphlet. But the underlying thinking would have increasing resonance, linking the idea of Scotland as a distinct economic as well as political entity with expectations that government had responsibility for managing the economy, whether prioritizing economic growth or addressing the social consequences of unemployment.

WILSON'S WHITE HEAT AND LOST HOPE

Labour came to power in 1964 and would take up the idea of planning with enthusiasm. In opposition, the party had frequently accused the Conservatives' approach as not involving 'proper planning'. But economic policy was inevitably refracted through a political prism and Labour could scarcely ignore its heartlands. Machinery of government had been created and a government had been elected committed to economic planning, headed by a Prime Minister whose 'white heat of technology' rhetoric promised a shift towards new industries. Labour produced 'Signposts for Scotland', its official policy document, and Harold Wilson insisted that there would be no costly bribes to get industries to move 'here rather than there'. But it was all rather vague. There was no doubting Labour's commitment to helping the least well off in society. Labour was far less sure of how to represent the least well off beyond taking control of the levers of government power. But the levers proved less powerful than Labour ministers expected.

Andrew Hargrave's observation that the British and world economies were interdependent would haunt Wilson's government. This was the era when the balance of payments was deemed the key issue in economic policy. Britain's share in the growth in international trade after the end of the Korean War in 1953 through to the early 1970s fell proportionately compared with other developed Western states. British manufacturers lost overseas markets to competitors and foreign imported goods were sucked into the economy by British consumers. The 1950s policy of 'stop–go', alternating contraction and expansion in aggregate demand in the economy, failed to address underlying problems with imports taking a bigger share of demand after each 'stop'. Labour announced an end to 'stop–go' and a shift towards an incomes policy allied with a selective industrial policy. This 'third way', a term coined by Wilson's economic adviser Thomas Balogh, was inadequate in the face of crises in confidence in sterling especially when consumers in Britain continued to buy imported goods.

Sterling crises had occurred before Labour came to power in 1964. The Attlee government had contended with sterling crises in 1947 and 1949 leading to devaluation of the currency that spelled the beginning of the end of the sterling area—an informal international group of mainly Commonwealth states using sterling for international transactions. Labour was determined not to have to devalue the currency as it had when last in office. Within a couple of months of taking office in 1964, the Wilson government instituted its own version of 'stop–go' in managing the currency. When devaluation occurred in November 1967, within weeks of the Hamilton by-election, Harold Wilson appeared on television to reassure the public that devaluation did 'not mean that the pound here in Britain, in your pocket or purse or in your bank, has been devalued'. He blamed war in the Middle East, the closure of the Suez Canal, and dock strikes for putting a strain on the currency. The hope that this would boost exports was not realized to anything like the extent or as quickly as had been hoped for. In 1968, the government followed this up with tax rises, spending cuts, and a new phase in incomes policy. Labour had entered office with the intention of more long-term planning of the economy, including public expenditure, but lost course, buffeted by international and domestic pressures. The great hopes had been shattered, affecting how citizens saw the state.

Harold Wilson's typical response to a difficult issue was to set up an inquiry, and in 1965 the Royal Commission on Trade Unions and Employers' Associations under Lord Donovan was set up in response to a series of unofficial strikes, a fear of wage inflation, and 'restrictive practices'. Donovan concluded that Britain had a two-tier system of industrial relations. A formal system operated at industry level with negotiations taking place between trade unions and employers; and an informal level of shop floor bargaining in which managers negotiated with local trade union shop stewards. The problem in British industrial relations was that the formal level failed to take account of the reality on the shop floor. What happened in individual plants counted. However much the labour movement claimed to operate as a Britain-wide movement, refusing to contemplate divisions in the working class, the reality was that pay rates differed across the country. For the most part, pay in Scottish plants was lower than that south of the border. This was a source of industrial relations demands at the level of the plant in Scotland.

In Place of Strife, the Labour government's White Paper on industrial relations published in 1969, proposed a series of measures that would have limited trade union militancy, but proved a source of strife throughout the Labour Party. The Cabinet was divided with Jim Callaghan leading opposition to Barbara Castle's proposals. These difficulties could only undermine Labour's authority. Labour's prices and incomes policy also contributed to poor relations with the unions. Wage restraint ossified existing differentials. Lawrence Daly, leader of the Scottish miners, complained that the policy maintained differences between Scottish and English pay rates. These matters conspired to create a Scottish dimension, according to historian Jim Phillips, which contributed to a shift in Labour's attitude to devolution though the shift was difficult to discern in statements from the party. Labour's centralist certainties were slowly being undermined. Labour still had a Scottish perspective on a range of matters but this offered a critique of rather than an alternative to existing policies.

Regional policy was pursued with especial vigour by Labour. New measures were introduced so that by 1969 regional policy comprised 'an extraordinary and wide ranging array of measures', according to the leading authority on the subject at the time. Despite Wilson's promise of no costly bribes to get industries to move 'here rather than there', his government's regional policy was essentially an elaborate and complex form of just that. The Industrial Development Act, 1966, introduced new development areas which covered all of Scotland except Edinburgh and included many areas previously uncovered. Special Development Areas were designated within Development Areas. These were areas that had been particularly badly hit following pit closures and included areas in Ayrshire, Lanarkshire, and Fife. Firms planning to build new factories were put under more pressure to move to development areas. In 1965, industrial estates companies were reorganized into three large bodies with one each covering England, Scotland, and Wales. Investment grants, subsidies on labour costs, and a Selective Employment Tax (SET) that taxed the service sector to subsidize manufacturing were introduced. In 1967, a Regional Employment Premium (REP) was introduced providing manufacturing employers a weekly subsidy for every employee. It was estimated that Scotland would receive 40 per cent of REP.

Three key features of regional policy became evident. First, Scotland was increasingly being treated as a unit for purposes of regional and economic policy purposes. Second, Scotland received a significant share of regional assistance but this hardly spoke of Scottish economic vitality. The economist Gavin McCrone argued that without these special measures, Scotland's growth in the 1960s would have lagged as badly behind the UK as it had in the 1950s. This was small consolation. Regional policy was compensation for a relatively poor economic performance. Third, the more the state assumed a role in either in trying to ameliorate these disparities, especially if exaggerated claims were made of the policy, then expectations would be ratcheted up leading to disillusionment when the claims were not realized.

In the words of economic historian Alan Booth, the

> tragi-comic slide of the 1964–70 Labour government from promises of faster growth to devaluation and ultimately to major retrenchment marked a key stage in the development of postwar economic policy. Sections of both main parties and many informed public commentators concluded that managed social democracy was incapable of delivering improved economic performance. The search for fundamentally different approaches had begun.

But these radically different approaches were not Scottish solutions to Scottish problems. They primarily involved a critique of the high hopes that the 'man in Whitehall knows best', a comment attributed to Douglas Jay, President of the Board of Trade in Wilson's government until 1967 and representative of the centrist school of Labour Party thinking. But a growing body of opinion had come to see these problems in Scottish terms and sought Scottish solutions.

Many years ago, Richard Rose noted that the amount of public expenditure enjoyed by the different parts of the UK reflected a combination of the political 'muscle' of the area and the Treasury's assessment of need. Need is a highly subjective idea and each definition of need requires a champion. The Scottish Office under Willie Ross became expert in making the case that Scottish needs were paramount. While English definitions of need in each functional department provided the basis for debate, the Scottish Office could always argue that Scotland's special needs, which would change depending on the issue under discussion, had to be taken into account. The Stormont Parliament in Northern Ireland was always treated as a case apart by the Treasury but essentially played the same game as the Scottish Office in maintaining that it had its own distinct needs. Officials in Stormont and the Treasury in London created a language around notions of need: parity and leeway were fuzzy but essentially allowed Northern Ireland to make the case for more resources. Parity was the term used when officials in Belfast believed that Northern Ireland lagged behind and required to be treated the same as the rest of the UK. In practice, parity was, as the Royal Commission on the Constitution said in its report in 1973, 'a vague and flexible concept'. Leeway was an idea that acknowledged different starting points in the provision of new services. Though the Scottish Office never formalized its arguments into this language, these were the kind of slippery flexible ideas that were invoked. But such ideas required articulation and the Scottish Office was well-rehearsed in these debates and had a political head committed to increasing public spending. The establishment of the Welsh Office by the Labour government in 1964 presented a new challenge to the Scottish Office. It now had to compete with another territorial department which would also make claims based on flexible principles. While the Welsh Office lacked either the experience or scale of operations of the Scottish Office, it was headed for its first two years by Jim Griffiths, former chairman and deputy leader of the British Labour Party.

WILLIE ROSS

In a diary entry in May 1968, Richard Crossman complained that Willie Ross, the Secretary of State for Scotland, 'accuses the Scot Nats of separatism but what Willie Ross himself actually likes is to keep Scottish business absolutely privy from English business'. Ross personified the Labour Party's transition on the Scottish Question. He was avowedly Scottish and sternly unionist until late in his career when he was called upon to support a Scottish Assembly for electorally expedient reasons. He was socially conservative but progressive on matters of distribution. Few could question the commitment to Scotland of this Kirk elder and Burns enthusiast. In 1954, he had moved an amendment on the licensing of commercial television which would have banned advertising on Sundays, Good Friday, and Christmas Day. He was acutely sensitive to adverse Scottish–English/British comparisons. Nine months before the Hamilton by-election, he warned Cabinet colleagues that different treatment of Scotland and England—in pay awards to local authority workers, electricity bills, and transport costs—might give the impression that Scotland was discriminated against. It was a common enough refrain for Scottish Secretaries to play this Scottish card but Ross surpassed his predecessors in its use. He became a master in protecting and defending Scottish distinctiveness resembling a modern Scottish Manager, a latter-day Dundas.

Ross entered Parliament in a by-election in 1946 for Kilmarnock in Ayrshire. He had been a primary school teacher before the Second World War and rose to the rank of major during the war. His style of leadership is summed up in the apocryphal tale of an exchange with Frank McElhone, fellow Labour MP who was appointed to a junior ministerial position at the Scottish Office. McElhone had asked what he was to do and was told by Ross that 'Ye'll dae whit yer telt'. H. J. Hanham, in his 1969 study of Scottish nationalism, suggested that the Scottish Labour leader's attitudes 'stem largely from the inter-war period' when the party moved in opposition to home rule. Ross was part of the generation that placed high hopes on a Labour government controlling the levers of power at Westminster, including controlling the Scottish Office.

Textbooks on Scottish politics before devolution portrayed the Scottish Office as a lobbying body within government which rarely initiated policy on its own. There was some truth in this but, as Ross pointed out many years later, reflecting on his time as Scottish Secretary, Scots had high expectations of the office but power 'limped lamely behind responsibility'. There was a tendency to follow the lead but there was an expectation that the Scottish Office should be consulted. This did not always happen. Gordon Stott, Labour's Lord Advocate, referred to a 'violent argument' in a government committee discussing long sentences for prisoners. Frank Soskice, the Home Secretary, insisted on approval of a paper though the Scottish Office had not had a chance to consider its implications. Soskice thought it was 'absurd' to hold up an English reform. Stott thought this was strange as the Home Office had often wanted to hold up Scottish proposals because they might 'embarrass' the Home Secretary.

Two examples from Ross's period stand out as exceptions that prove that there were occasions when the Scottish Office managed to pursue a distinct and sometimes quite innovative policy: the reform of juvenile justice and the establishment of the Highlands and Islands Development Board. In May 1961, John Maclay, Conservative Scottish Secretary, set up a committee under Lord Kilbrandon, a senior Scottish judge who would later chair the Royal Commission on the Constitution, to consider the growing rate of juvenile delinquency in Scotland. The Kilbrandon Committee found that the vast majority of cases before Scottish juvenile courts were trivial, and considered the issue as a social as much as a law and order matter. It recommended removing those under 16 years of age from the adult criminal justice system, except in serious cases. It proposed a radical alternative, having considered Scandinavian experience, rather than simply look over the border to see what was happening in England. It proposed a system of Children's Hearings with lay members providing a more informal setting. It would be informed by the wider social context, emphasizing the role of education in assisting children and families in need. It was a more holistic early interventionist approach. The report was published in 1964 and a White Paper, *Social Work and the Community*, was issued by the Scottish Office two years later. New social work departments within local authorities were proposed which would have responsibility for the Children's Hearings. But this change was not won easily. Judith Hart, junior Scottish Office Minister, became a champion of the Kilbrandon recommendations but had to fight the Home Office, which wanted a delay until the it came up with its own proposals to tackle the problem in England. It was clear that a very different approach would be pursued by the Home Office.

The Social Work (Scotland) Act, 1968, placed a duty on local authorities to provide welfare to 'persons in need' and established the system of Children's Panels, coming into operation in 1971. There had been concern in the Cabinet Legislation Committee 'lest the extensive powers given to Scottish local authorities might encourage local authorities in England and Wales to press for similar powers', according to the committee's minutes, and there were proposals to amend the draft Bill 'so that the powers given to Scottish local authorities were, or appeared to be, more restrictive'. The fear that any Scottish innovation would result in demands for the same treatment, especially if this involved spending money, was a major impediment to independent action by the Scottish Office. But it could be done when it was backed by a strong body of opinion, especially following a report by a distinguished panel, and pursued by a minister supported by committed officials.

Another important policy innovation was the establishment of the Highlands and Islands Development Board (HIDB). In 1965, at the second reading of the bill to establish the HIDB, Willie Ross told the Commons that the Highlander had been the 'man on Scotland's conscience' for 200 years and that no part of Scotland had been given a 'shabbier deal by history from the '45 onwards'. As Ross stated, there had been many commissions, surveys, reports, and initiatives on the Highlands over the decades. The HIDB built on the work of the Highland Panel and many other similar bodies. But what was needed was an 'authority with executive powers to deal comprehensively with the problems; not to deal one at a time, but comprehensively'. It was regrettable, he maintained, that the 'powers that are in the special Scottish set-up' had not been used to 'experiment and to prove a successful way to do things, which could have been applied to other areas now suffering from exactly the same problems'. If the 'special Scottish set-up' allowed for this reform, the question arises as to why it was only used at this time in the Highlands and Islands, especially as Ross and other Labour politicians would have preferred this.

There were a number of reasons for the establishment of the HIBD. As Ross stated, it had come about after a long history of initiatives and considerable consensus on the need for action. Conservatives in Parliament were concerned that the HIDB would become a 'prototype for other areas' but willing to accept this special measure for the Highlands. As we have seen in previous chapters, the Highlands and Islands had long been treated as a special case within a special case by UK governments. Ross's comment that the Highlands were on the conscience of Scots is difficult to prove or measure but this may contain an explanation as to the willingness to provide special, and generous, support for the Highlands. In some respects, this treatment of the Highlands was a version of how, in the broadest sense, the UK saw Scotland. The Highlands and Islands were a place apart with more concentrated problems. But, despite Conservative reservations to the establishment of the HIDB, there was rarely an expectation that a concession to the Highlands would have to be made throughout Scotland or Britain.

THE CREATION OF THE SDA

Ross's desire to extend the HIDB to other parts of the UK came when Labour returned to office in 1974. Ross was back in the Scottish Office once more. In its election manifesto in October 1974, Labour had promised to establish development agencies in Scotland and Wales. It had been clear that Labour would need to make more specific promises following the election eight months before given the electoral advance of the SNP. In July, the government first made a commitment to a Scottish Development Agency (SDA) in a paper on the oil and gas industry. Ross set out a plan for an SDA in broad terms in a paper discussed within Whitehall. Senior Treasury officials could see an attraction in an SDA 'just because it might make it possible to buy off some of the pressures from Scotland without a substantial addition to expenditure there', as one official put it in July. There would be an 'element of window dressing about it' and the Treasury 'must obviously try to limit' the amount of money given to the new body.

Bruce Millan, Scottish Office Minister of State, wrote to Tony Benn, Secretary of State for Industry, setting out the rationale behind the 'SDA concept' towards the end of 1974. The SDA's 'genesis' lay in the 'necessity we all saw of demonstrating to Scottish public opinion that Scotland would receive tangible benefits from North Sea oil'. Benn was keener on a UK-wide approach provoking Ross to reply, 'I do not need to tell you that there is acute and widespread public concern about this issue in Scotland and that the need to devise some means whereby oil revenues can be brought to bear on the long-standing problems of economic rejuvenation and environmental recovery is publicly recognised.' The issue at the heart of dispute was that the Department of Industry would lose responsibilities to the Scottish Office and was not going to do so without a fight. Agreement had been reached over a series of transfers: the construction and management of government industrial estates; government purpose-built factories; and a number of functions of the National

Enterprise Board including loan finance and equity; new and joint industrial ventures; managerial and financial advice; and more generally the growth and modernization of Scottish industry. In a note to the Prime Minister, Ross also wanted substantial powers and resources for the promotion and execution of major projects of environmental regeneration. He identified areas where he and Benn could not reach agreement including grants and loans to industry. Benn feared competitive bidding for projects by different parts of the UK if the SDA had these responsibilities and the prospect of duplication of arrangements.

Tony Crosland, Secretary of State for the Environment, found himself in the unusual position of agreeing with Benn. Crosland issued a prescient warning:

> I do not think we can hope to convince anyone that these countries alone require special help. Unemployment on Merseyside and Tyneside is higher than in Glasgow; the three northern regions of England have almost twice as much derelict land to reclaim as Scotland has and possess their full share of urban squalor. Opinion in the North of England is on the watch to see that Scotland and Wales do not steal a march, and we shall be very hard pressed indeed unless we have something to offer.

As a Hull MP as well as having responsibility for local government in England, Crosland was well aware of the challenges being faced across England against the backdrop of the most serious economic crisis that afflicted the UK, and indeed global economy, as a consequence of the energy crisis. Whitehall officials had deep reservations about any measure that undermined central authority. The opening sentence of a statement in a paper produced by a committee of officials in 1974 was quoted in internal Whitehall correspondence: 'If the Government's ability to control the economy and to ensure a broadly equitable and acceptable development of the use of resources and the corresponding tax policies is to be maintained, the scope for real devolution of decision-taking seems strictly limited.'

But the momentum had been established and legislation was passed in 1975 with the SDA coming into being in December that year. The SNP argued that the SDA was inadequately resourced given the scale of the task before it and the resources that would soon be available from the North Sea. Alick Buchanan-Smith, the Conservatives' Scottish spokesman at the time, joined the SNP in this line of criticism. Teddy Taylor, Buchanan-Smith's successor, would take a very different line suggesting that the SDA was over-funded. The SDA was funded by a grant as well as by public dividend capital, i.e. the value and income for assets it would be responsible for, and the public loan fund. The SDA had two key functions reflecting the time it was established: developing the Scottish economy and improving the environment, though the latter was understood in narrower terms then than now. It came into being at a time of great economic difficulties. Henrik Halkier, the author of the most detailed study of the origins and early development of the SDA, has suggested that there was limited debate on the precise functions of the new body. He suggests that this was partly due to their uncontroversial and technical nature and because industrial investments came to 'eclipse everything else in terms of the political energy' devoted to debates. At this time, state intervention in industry of this kind was still largely uncontroversial. The political backdrop no doubt played its part. In this respect it was similar to its sponsoring department, the Scottish Office, which had, as we have seen, an important symbolic role before it had everyday functional responsibilities.

The SDA's establishment has been described in an alternative way with less emphasis on the political context. It can be seen as an extension of the kind of thinking that ran through the Clyde Valley Plan, regional policy, and the HIDB. Part of the background had been a perception that a distinct Scottish economy existed with its own problems requiring distinct solutions. The Scottish Trades Union Congress had been campaigning for a 'high powered Development Agency' since at least 1971 though organized business was slow to make the case for such a body and tended to be more reactive. The SCDI produced a paper supporting a Scottish Special Development Corporation in 1973, funded mainly by oil and gas revenues. The SNP had made the case for a Scottish Development Corporation in 1965 but this was hardly noticed. In May 1974, Ted Heath had proposed the establishment of a Scottish Development Fund and this was included in the party's October 1974 manifesto. But the most significant shift in thinking took place within the Labour Party. In 1958, it insisted that it was 'only through socialist planning on a United Kingdom scale that Scotland's many special problems can be tackled'. The Highlands and Islands were a special case and extensions of some version of this interventionist model would have to be created across Britain as a whole. In essence, while roots might be traceable back before 1967, there can be little doubt that the rise of the SNP added a political imperative to an idea in search of a political sponsor. Conservative support for the SDA had been articulated by Alick Buchanan-Smith, the party's Shadow Scottish Secretary, but he resigned from the front bench after the party signalled a hardening of its opposition to devolution. He was replaced by Teddy Taylor, a populist Tory in the mould of Norman Tebbit. Taylor and other members of the Scottish Tory front bench adopted a more critical tone. Taylor insisted that the Tories would not abolish the SDA though signalled a different role for the body if the Tories were returned to power.

There was another important backdrop to the establishment of the SDA. Ted Heath's Conservative government had come to power in 1970 on a manifesto that was caricatured by Harold Wilson as informed by free market thinking. Heath was planning, according to Wilson, a 'wanton, calculated and deliberate return to greater inequality'. Heath soon abandoned an approach that owed something to this caricature. Heath's government had a more laissez-faire approach than that of previous post-war Conservative Prime Ministers. It would involve a more market-based approach, industrial relations reform following Wilson's difficulties in this area, stricter control of public spending, and an application to join the European Economic Community (EEC). John Davies, Secretary of State for Trade and Industry, had told the Commons that the government believed that the country needed to 'gear its policies to the great majority of people, who are not lame ducks, who do not need a hand, who are quite capable of looking after their own interests and only demand to be allowed to do so'. Heath encountered major difficulties in each area but did succeed in negotiating UK membership of the EEC. The government was forced to nationalize Rolls Royce within eight months of the election after the company faced bankruptcy. Upper Clyde Shipbuilders (UCS), a company formed in 1968 from the amalgamation of five firms, was facing serious difficulties. The Heath government refused to help UCS, provoking a 'work-in', rather than a strike, by a workforce which faced the imminent prospect of being reduced from 8,300 to 2,500 or less. The shop stewards who organized the work-in became household names and the action attracted massive media interest and public sympathy aided by the novelty and disciplined organization of the work-in and Jimmy Reid's memorable phrase—'there will be no hooliganism, no vandalism and no bevvying'.

Interpretations of UCS vary and the extent to which it contributed to the sense of a Scottish 'proletarian nation' is disputed. Jimmy Reid, Jimmy Airlie, and other key figures were members of the Communist Party, a party that had long been committed to a Scottish Parliament. Support for the work-in came from across the political spectrum, from the churches and businesses and from well beyond Scotland. It appeared to unite Scotland and became part of both the British labour and national movement histories. But key figures in the labour movement, including Tony Benn and leading figures in the British trade union movement, were involved in advising and campaigning on behalf of the workforce. Each movement would tell the story of UCS in its own terms, emphasizing class or national question in its telling. Each viewed the 'enemy' to be a rapacious and alien right-wing ideology. Some understood UCS as the forging or development of the 'proletarian nation', a precursor of Scottish opposition politics in the 1980s. Selsdon Man was dead, if he had ever lived other than in the minds of his opponents, with the Heath government's U-turn and financial support for shipbuilding. At the rally in October 1972 when the workforce accepted the government deal, Jimmy Reid announced that it had been a 'victory not just for the workers but for the whole Scottish community'.

Playing the Scottish card in industrial disputes and campaigns on unemployment became a feature of the early 1970s. With only nineteen of Scotland's seventy-one seats, the Conservatives were vulnerable to the accusation that they were imposing their policies on Scotland. They were also sensitive to this criticism in a way that future Tory governments were not. The STUC saw the potential in mobilizing Scottish identity in its campaigns. It organized a Scottish assembly—the term itself was significant—in February 1972 in Edinburgh's Usher Hall. Scottish local authorities were well represented; the CBI Scotland and a number of Chambers of Commerce sent representatives and each of the political parties were present. Commentators sympathetic to home rule saw it as evidence of growing support for a Parliament. Many speeches, including some by previous opponents of home rule, suggested a link between Scottish economic development and the case for a Scottish Parliament. Sir William McEwen Younger, who as we have seen had proposed a Scottish Assembly to Ted Heath four years before, criticized Scotland's branch factory economy and gave clear support for the view that Scotland's distinct economy required distinctly Scottish solutions. James Jack, STUC general secretary, called for a 'workers' parliament'.

'OUR LAND OF CALVIN, OATCAKES AND SULPHUR'

The 1957 Wolfenden Committee Report on Homosexual Offences and Prostitution had proposed the decriminalization of homosexual relations between consenting adults. The one dissenting member of the Committee was James Adair, Scottish Kirk elder, Glasgow's Procurator Fiscal and chairman of the Scottish Council of the Young Men's Christian Association (YMCA). Adair produced a note warning that the main recommendation would corrupt youth. A subcommittee of the Church and Nation Committee considered the issue and reported in late 1957, largely endorsing Wolfenden. This was overruled by the full Church and Nation Committee. In a report endorsed by the Kirk's general assembly, the full committee expressed concern that the homosexual was 'proud of his disability' and thereby likely to 'spread' his 'perversion'. The Free Presbyterian Church managed to be even less liberal. Polls suggested that the Scottish public was overwhelmingly opposed to Wolfenden's main recommendation while opinion in England was evenly divided. The views of the churches were repeatedly reported in internal government discussions and in parliamentary debates. The Scottish press was overwhelmingly opposed to reform. The *Scotsman* carried editorials opposing legitimizing the 'bestial offence'. Parliamentarians broadly followed these opinions. The Scottish Liberals sought to avoid what was a divisive issue for them. Jean Mann, Labour MP for Coatbridge, articulated the common Labour view that the miners' lodges in her constituency would not welcome any change which might result in a homosexual couple setting up house in a mining village. Taken together, the evidence suggested that Scotland was a more illiberal place than England.

Yet, Wolfenden found that in the three years ending March 1956, there were 300 convictions for homosexual offences in England and Wales but only seven in Scotland. Peter Rawlinson, Tory MP and future English Attorney-General, explained that the Procurator Fiscal, the public prosecutor in Scotland, had discretion in determining whether to pursue a prosecution through the courts and that there were different rules governing how the police interviewed suspects. Contrary to some common interpretations, Scotland was no less immune to homosexuality than England.

The government was disinclined to legislate on Wolfenden and left it to backbenchers. When David Steel came third in the ballot for Private Members' Bills in 1967, he decided to reform the law on abortion rather than homosexuality partly because Scottish opinion seemed more receptive to the former. Steel had previously argued that there was less need for homosexual law reform in Scotland given the lack of prosecutions, a view frequently expressed by Scottish Office civil servants and ministers. Roger Davidson and Gayle Davis in *The Sexual State* note that Scottish officials and politicians continued to 'camouflage the degree of homophobia within Scottish civil society behind a constructed national identity of legal progressiveness'. A homosexual law reform bill was presented in the Commons in 1967 by Leo Abse, Welsh Labour MP, and by Lord Arran in the Lords but it covered only England and Wales. Strong opponents of the bill, including Tory MP Ray Mawby, later discovered to have been a spy for the Czech military intelligence, argued that excluding Scotland was illogical and suggested that if Scotland had been included then 'all Scottish Members would descend in their wrath and vote solidly against the Bill'. One member of the Lords quoted Sydney Smith in arguing that the Scottish public—'our land of Calvin, oatcakes and sulphur'—had been ignored.

Abse himself would later reflect that the reason for excluding Scotland was that he did not want to provoke any more trouble than was necessary to get the measure through Parliament. The role of Scottish MPs in this reform is notable, given subsequent debates on the West Lothian Question. Scottish MPs divided equally for and against the bill but what is often ignored is the proportion that did not vote. Teddy Taylor, Glasgow Tory MP who was a strong opponent of the bill, suggested that the third reading of the bill was taking place on a Monday evening to ensure that fewer Scottish MPs might be involved in the debate. Taylor and Tam Dalyell would later become vehement critics of devolution as it would result in Scottish MPs voting on matters affecting only England. But on this occasion each saw no problem in participating and voting on this matter that did not affect their constituencies.

Throughout the 1970s, efforts to liberalize the law in Scotland came up against opposition and evasion. There was a gradual shift in attitudes in sections of the press, the Kirk, and the Scottish Office but no political party, not even the Liberal Party, was willing to take a lead though individual politicians came forward. The General Assembly of the Church of Scotland supported a change in the law in 1968. Robin Cook, then Labour MP for Edinburgh Central, attempted to introduce a bill with cross-party support but without the support of parliamentary time from his own front bench it stood little chance of being passed. This was the period when devolution was on the agenda and a number of gay rights campaigners harnessed their cause to the campaign for a Scottish assembly. In the weeks before the 1979 devolution referendum, the Scottish Homosexual Rights Group urged electors to vote for an assembly, provoking predictable responses from some opponents of devolution. The breakthrough came after the Conservatives were returned to power in 1979. The key was a case taken by three gay activists to the European Court of Human Rights. The case made was not only that the existing law discriminated against them as gay citizens but also that they were discriminated against 'by reason of Scottish national minority status'. The government knew that the law would have to be changed. Robin Cook moved an amendment to the Criminal Justice Bill on the same day in 1980 that the press reported the arrest of Western journalists covering a demonstration favouring human rights for homosexuals in the Soviet Union. Scots law was in this instance, Cook argued, 'no better than that in the Soviet Union'. George Younger, Scottish Office Secretary of State, insisted that the government would remain neutral though he observed that there was no reason why the laws of Scotland and England should be the same and warned that the amendment was 'not ideal' and needed to be fully discussed. What was significant was the presumption that any change bringing Scotland into line with England required an explanation. The explanation given by many MPs was that this was an issue of 'fundamental human rights', according to Grantham Tory MP Douglas Hogg. Michael Ancram, his Scottish Conservative colleague, suggested that MPs should not 'accept English lawyers telling us what should be the law of Scotland. I hope that the House will recognise that Scotland has its own legal system. It has its principles.' The amendment was passed and the law was reformed in Scotland in 1980.

David Steel's Abortion Act, 1967, had similar origins to Leo Abse's Sexual Offences Act, 1967. It too was a Private Members' Bill that was given parliamentary time by the government. Before this Act, the law on abortion differed between Scotland and England in as much as Scots law allowed more discretion for doctors in determining whether to carry out an abortion in the health or welfare interests of a patient. Criminal intent had to be proved before a prosecution. Once more, the system of justice differed. The procurator fiscal acted as the public prosecutor rather than the police. This meant that here were fewer cases before the courts in Scotland. But in each jurisdiction there was a lack of clarity leading to different interpretations so that there were significant differences in different parts of the same jurisdiction. The greatest differences in Scotland occurred between Glasgow and Aberdeen. In 1937, Dugald Baird had been appointed to the Chair in Midwifery in Aberdeen University, having become disillusioned with working in Rottenrow, Glasgow's Royal Maternity Hospital, where the opposition of the Catholic Church and local politicians hindered his work on women's health and well-being. On moving to Aberdeen, he researched the link between social class and health, especially stillbirth and maternal health, and established the first cervical screening service resulting in a reduction in cervical cancer in the area. His wife was also a medical doctor who became a Labour councillor in the city and chair of the Regional Health Board. They established a successful multi-agency and preventative approach to public health. On the advice of colleagues in the University's Law Faculty, Baird adopted a more liberal approach to abortion on the understanding that this was possible within a reasonable interpretation of the law. When David Steel decided to amend the law he took Dugald Baird's advice to incorporate social and medical reasons in the same clause permitting termination of pregnancy. The measure was common across Britain, though excluded Northern Ireland.

REFORMING LOCAL GOVERNMENT

Throughout the twentieth century, as state intervention increased, the creaky structure of local administration and government came under pressure. Local government had been the most distinguishing feature of government in Scotland. Experience had shown that major reforms to local government, however rational in terms of providing a more effective means of providing services, could provoke strong opposition. The structure required attention by the early 1960s. A White Paper on the 'modernization' of local government was published in 1963 by the Conservative government. In 1966, the incoming Labour government established Royal Commissions to consider local government in England (chaired by Lord Redcliffe-Maud) and separately for Scotland (under Lord Wheatley). The report of the Royal Commission on Local Government in Scotland described the existing structure: 'How has the present-day structure of local government in Scotland come about? On a map the pattern of local authority areas looks like a patchwork quilt dotted liberally but unevenly with beads.'

Wheatley set out four 'broad objectives': power, effectiveness, local democracy, and local involvement. The report noted that local government discharged a 'very different range of responsibilities from those it had in 1889, when the foundations of the present structure were laid down—or even in 1929, when the structure took its definitive form'. The scale of services had changed dramatically. It acknowledged that the optimum population size for the administration of services differed depending on the service involved and that there was a case for three levels of local government—regional (for planning and associated services and the protective services), intermediate (for personal social services), and local (for environmental and amenity services and local planning)—based on what were seen as objective criteria. It confronted the meaning of 'community', recognizing its subjective meaning, and considered its relevance to the debate on structures. There were 878 parishes in Scotland, consisting largely of small villages and surrounding areas and what they referred to as 'locality' levels, 'shire' levels, and 'regional' levels. Essentially, these were concentric levels of communities. From this perspective, Scotland could be seen as on the outer ring of these communities as indeed could Britain beyond this.

The challenge was to find some means of accommodating these four broad divergent, if not opposing, objectives. Scotland's geography and demography made this more challenging. What might be appropriate in an urban area was not necessarily best in a rural part of Scotland. Social and economic challenges and opportunities differed in intensity if not in nature across Scotland. To this end, the report recommended the establishment of two tiers of local government with seven regional councils and thirty-seven districts. It aspired to create a structure that worked in a 'concerted fashion' but in which uniformity was not an end in itself. Local government, it maintained, 'must be a system, not a mere jumble of representative or consultative organs that communities happen to throw up'.

The (Kilbrandon) Royal Commission on the Constitution was established while the Wheatley Commission was deliberating on local government in Scotland. Kilbrandon had been set up to consider Scotland's constitutional status within the UK though its remit was widened to include all parts of the UK. There was an obvious overlap in the work of the two Commissions. Wheatley heard evidence, notably from John Mackintosh MP, for an 'all-Scotland solution'. Wheatley rejected this on the grounds that constitutional change was outside its remit but remarked that Scotland would 'form an unduly wide area for the administration of almost all the major local government services' which was inconsistent with the concept of local government.

Kilbrandon had been required to have 'regard to developments in local government organisation' in its remit but largely side-stepped the issue by referring to the Wheatley Report and subsequent legislation. The majority report of the Kilbrandon Commission simply described the Wheatley Commission proposals and the subsequent legislation reforming local government in Scotland. A minority report offered a more comprehensive critique of the system of government, recognizing the linkages between the different levels. In their minority report, Lord Crowther-Hunt and Professor Alan Peacock noted the weakening of local government since 1945. Local government had lost responsibility for hospitals, gas, electricity, trunk roads, public assistance, and valuation for rating though gaining responsibilities for town and country planning, social services, and child care. They noted the growing financial dependence of local government on central government. Crowther-Hunt and Peacock maintained that this 'meant that over the years the capacity of local government for initiative and independence has declined' and suggested that the failure to expand the geographical areas of local government to 'meet the needs of modern administration has accelerated the decline'. They noted the changing financial balance between central and local government. In 1870, local government was responsible for over half of total government expenditure but this had fallen to less than a third and equally striking was the decline in the proportion financed by local authorities themselves. About 80 per cent of local authorities' expenditure came from local rates, fees, and charges. By 1970, this had fallen to 45 per cent. There had been a proliferation of various ad hoc bodies, including many matters previously under local authorities but also a wide range of other matters. Crowther-Hunt and Peacock noted that these bodies were 'largely independent of democratic supervision—certainly in the day-to-day impact on the life of the community'. They concluded by emphasizing the point, underlined in the report, that the '*fundamental conse-quence of these trends has been the erosion of the extent to which we as a people govern ourselves*'.

The reorganization of local government in the 1970s followed Wheatley in broad outline but differed in important respects from what had been proposed. Instead of seven regional councils and thirty-seven districts, the Local Government (Scotland) Act, 1973, created nine regions and fifty-six districts plus three all-purpose island local authorities. This reflected local campaigns and partisan interests. Fife demanded to be a region rather than split to create two estuarial regions around the Forth and Tay. The Conservatives were keen to allow wealthier suburbs of Glasgow to escape having to subsidize Glasgow by separating them from a large city-wide authority. In addition, provision was made for the establishment of Community Councils throughout Scotland. The pattern of Community Councils varied across Scotland. The government White Paper outlining the reforms stated:

> The district authorities will not be subsidiary to the regional authorities, but will be complementary to them. Each type of authority will be independent of the other and, while consultation and co-operation between them will be essential, their statutory functions can be quite distinct, the regions dealing with the services which require management over a wide area and the districts with more local services.

Housing was to be the responsibility of the District Councils.

Debates on devolution in the 1970s generatecd considerable concerns amongst the newly established local authorities. The prospect of a Scottish Assembly taking powers from local government provoked a backlash. It is difficult to quantify the extent of opposition to devolution amongst local authorities but there is little doubt that many senior councillors feared that an all-Scotland Assembly would draw powers from local government. There was the added fear that the Assembly would be dominated by Glasgow and the west of Scotland. It was unclear how Strathclyde Region, with over half Scotland's population, would operate alongside the proposed Scottish Assembly. The new local authorities had been envisaged as playing a part in planning a more prosperous future but came into being at a time when spending was being cut. Created in anticipation of economic growth, increasing public spending, and contributing to this bright new future, the new authorities were confronted with a very difficult and more challenging world. The emphasis would be on addressing the problems associated with a downturn in the economy, high levels of inflation, rising unemployment, and cuts in public spending.

CONCLUSION

What is remarkable is the extent to which the institutions of government accommodated Scottish national identity in the apogee of the state that was evident in the period from the early 1960s through to the mid-1970s. No government until that headed by Tony Blair had attempted to present itself as the embodiment of modernization as Harold Wilson's had in the early years of his premiership. Many scholars had assumed that modernization in its various forms—government intervention, central communications, and a more homogenizing culture—would threaten identities and institutions below the central state level. Labour's ideology was then highly centrist, fuelling such expectations. But Scotland had insinuated itself into the ideology of modernist unionism. The SNP was as much the creature as the maker of the assertion of a Scottish dimension to modernization. Home rule forced its way on to the agenda built on an acceptance that Scotland was a distinct entity, albeit within a centralized state. It was simply taken for granted that much in public life required a Scottish dimension.

But a Scottish dimension was applied inconsistently. Scotland missed out on much of the liberal reforms of the 1960s. David Steel's Abortion Act was Britain-wide in scope but could hardly have been otherwise given that Steel was a Scottish MP. But Scotland was deliberately excluded from homosexual law reform. This inconsistency was entirely pragmatic. Scottish MPs were socially conservative and some of the strongest opposition to liberalization came from Scottish institutions. The Kirk could not be ignored though by the 1960s there were signs that it was no longer quite the deeply socially conservative institution it had traditionally been. But there were occasional instances of liberal thinking alongside this conservatism. These came less from the political parties or organized interests than the outcome of thinking influenced by external examples. Juvenile justice was reformed following the classic elite approach to innovative policy-making. A judge-led inquiry had taken evidence from Scandinavia. A junior Scottish Office Minister supported by officials pushed proposals for reform which would have been unlikely if left to a Scottish Parliament at the time.

8

Debating Devolution

INTRODUCTION

Commentators who thought the 1970 election marked the demise of the SNP would be shocked by what happened at the elections in 1974. The SNP's high water mark in Westminster elections came in October 1974 when it won 30 per cent of the vote and eleven of Scotland's seventy-one MPs. But what really concentrated minds were thirty-six of Labour's forty-one seats where the SNP was in second place. Within five years, the SNP had receded again and its obituary was once more being written.

In September 1971, Robert McIntyre had won 35 per cent of the vote in a by-election in Stirling and Falkirk and Gordon Wilson, later to lead the SNP, came a close second with 30 per cent of the vote in a by-election in Dundee East in March 1973. In November, Margo MacDonald won Govan for the SNP with 41.5 per cent of the vote on the same day Billy Wolfe, party chairman, won only 19 per cent of the vote behind the Conservatives and Labour in Edinburgh North. It would be MacDonald's success not Wolfe's failure that would be remembered even though she held the seat for only seventy-eight days and some of that was over the Christmas break. The Royal Commission on the Constitution had reported eight days before the by-election helping ensure that devolution was on the agenda. Judith Hart, Scottish Labour MP and government minister in the 1960s, had warned that establishing a Royal Commission carried risks. She had suggested that it might stimulate a 'possibly declining nationalism in Scotland'.

Devolution was debated against a backdrop of challenging times for the government. This was a period when there was speculation that governments might go bust. Pressure for devolution was seen in Westminster and Whitehall as just another problem to be dealt with. For many senior officials, this debate was an indulgence at a time of emergency. The one solution to the UK's economic problems was deep beneath the North Sea. That resource appeared at times to be at risk due to this Scottish debate. As far as Whitehall was concerned, there could be no prospect of this being allowed to happen. It was Whitehall's oil.

NORTH SEA OIL, THE ENERGY CRISIS, AND THE IMF LOAN

The backdrop against which these devolution debates took place was challenging. The Heath government had been forced into a U-turn in its economic policy and faced serious industrial relations difficulties. The National Union of Mineworkers (NUM) took the opportunity of the energy crisis to go on strike in late 1973. But it was not only elements of the labour movement that saw an opportunity in the energy crisis. Oil and gas had been discovered off the east coast of Scotland and to its far north. The SNP recognized the political value of oil in a world in which energy had become a scarce and valuable commodity. Donald Bain, the party's research officer, became expert in the subject and had attended a meeting of the Organization of Petroleum Exporting countries (OPEC) along with Donald Stewart, the SNP's sole MP, in 1972. The party was well prepared for the opportunities that arose when Egyptian and Syrian forces launched a surprise attack on Israel on Yom Kippur, the holiest day in Judaism. The Israeli counter-attack successfully pushed the Egyptian and Syrian forces back well behind their borders. Arab states were humiliated and turned on the United States and Western countries for supporting Israel. OPEC countries, led by Saudi Arabia, cut oil production by 5 per cent in October and then embargoed oil exports to the USA and other states. The combination of the miners' strike and cut in oil supplies forced the government to take emergency measures. Domestic and commercial consumers, essential services apart, were restricted to three days' use of electricity in any week between January and March 1974. The miners had gone on strike when the government was most vulnerable. Heath called an election in February, the first in that month since 1950, seeking a mandate to confront the miners. The SNP's professionally produced posters proclaiming 'It's Scotland's oil— with self-government' displayed black oil pouring out of the letter 'o' in oil. There was no denying the importance of oil. Labour's manifesto proposed that 'North Sea and Celtic Sea oil and gas resources' should be 'in full public ownership' and that the government should determine the 'pace of exploitation of our oil, and the use to which it is put, so as to secure maximum public advantage from our own resources'. After a week of focusing on the miners' strike, Heath shifted to attacking Labour's plans to nationalize oil. The SNP did not have to struggle to be seen to be relevant. The SNP won seven seats, including that of the Secretary of State for Scotland, the most senior Tory scalp won by any party in the election. It was in second place in a further sixteen seats.

Kilbrandon had reported four months previously but the Conservative manifesto only stated that the party was 'studying' the report which was more than Labour which studiously avoided Kilbrandon altogether in its British manifesto and dismissed devolution in its Scottish manifesto. Labour was not prepared to support a Scottish Assembly as it could see no way of reconciling an assembly with keeping the same number of Scottish MPs at Westminster. The orthodox view in the Labour Party at that time was expressed by John Smith, future party leader. He attacked the SNP for projecting itself as a new kind of party which attempted to transcend class. In another article, Smith warned that the price tag of devolution was the loss of the Scottish Secretary and some of Scotland's Westminster MPs, a price that he believed was 'too high'. He could see little value in an assembly without control of finance, trade, and industry policies which could not be conceded. In an essay in the *New Left Review*, Tom Nairn attacked Scottish Labour politicians, naming Ross and Smith as prime examples of romantic Scots in the mould of Sir Walter Scott making Labour the 'repository of this dour devotion' to the union.

Whitehall had responded to the Kilbrandon Commission in typical fashion by establishing committees, writing papers, and mustering arguments in preparation of ministerial requests. When campaigning in the February election was still going on, a Department of Energy paper set out its thinking. The scale of the discovery of oil was acknowledged. It was 'probably one of the most important events in the UK since the industrial revolution', it was of 'vital importance to the economic and strategic interests of the nation as a whole', already producing '90 per cent of our gas requirements'. All oil was imported and recent events in the Middle East demonstrated the 'importance which indigenous oil will give to the security of our energy supplies' and it was anticipated that the UK would become the 'only major oil consuming nation, except perhaps the USA' able to 'meet her own demand in 1980'. In a gross under-estimate, it was suggested that revenue from oil would be 'up to £1500 million'.

Senior officials were in no doubt as to the cause of the SNP's electoral advance. Cabinet Secretary Sir John Hunt asserted that the 'recent growth of nationalism in Scotland has been stimulated by economic and financial considerations; in particular, the discovery of oil in the North Sea' but could see no prospect of devolving responsibility in this area. Effective control of the 'nation's resources, economic strategy, levels of taxation, development of oil and so on' had to remain with Westminster. While Willie Ross berated the SNP for its use of oil in its campaigns, he used similar tactics inside Whitehall on his return to the Scottish Office. He wrote to Cabinet colleagues warning of the 'acute and widespread public concern about this issue in Scotland' and that it was 'imperative to demonstrate that Scotland will clearly benefit economically from oil'. But his Cabinet colleagues and Whitehall officials were clear. The paper acknowledged that Scottish and UK interests might 'not coincide'. The UK would want to produce enough to satisfy total demand whereas Scottish demand would be only one-tenth of the UK's and would wish to cut back production.

A confidential and undated memo written in the early 1970s noted that North Sea oil 'completely changes the picture for Scotland' from being in deficit to being massively in surplus. It accepted that there was a 'plausible case for arguing that it is Scottish' according to international conventions which had 'already been used to divide the UK continental shelf in the North Sea between Scotland and England'. It acknowledged that even conservative estimates of output and world oil prices would mean that North Sea revenues would be about £3 billion by 1980. This 'embarrassment of riches...could well exceed the likely needs of a separate Scots government' and it would be in Scotland's interests to pursue a policy similar to that in Norway where the flow of oil was restricted to make revenues last longer. However, such a policy would be 'disastrous' for the UK. Possession of oil would 'raise Scotland into another league'. It warned that arguing that 'England deserves a share in the profits' on the grounds that oil had been developed by English capital would not stand up to scrutiny as the capital had been American and European: 'Sauce for the English goose will garnish the Scottish gander as well.' The more secure argument was felt to be that as England had 'effectively subsidised the Scottish economy for many years' it was 'unjust to penalise England as the tide turned'.

The author is unknown but the arguments were similar to those made in what has become known as the McCrone Report, a report written in February 1974 by Gavin McCrone, then Chief Economic Adviser to the Secretary of State for Scotland. McCrone's paper was entitled, 'The Economics of Nationalism Re-Examined'. It started by noting that the discovery of North Sea oil and membership of the EEC were of 'major economic significance for Scotland' and that the 'whole framework' of the economic implications of nationalism had been altered. Scottish nationalism was unlike Welsh nationalism as it had been 'much more concerned with economic prosperity than nationalist movements in other countries'. McCrone argued, as he had in a book published in 1969, that the SNP case 'until recently lacked credibility'. The key issue was economic growth, something almost all agreed upon. There were, he maintained, three ways in which an independent Scotland might improve of the poor levels of growth achieved within the union. First, protectionist measures might be adopted but this would risk retaliatory measures from England and such measures would be incompatible with membership of the EEC. Second, fiscal policies might be used to encourage investment and provide tax reliefs and subsidies as the Irish Republic had successfully engaged in from the mid-1950s. However, Scotland's budgetary situation had precluded this and while it was not necessary to balance the budget, loans needed to be financed. A Scottish government would need to reduce the deficit either by raising taxes or by cutting expenditure, leaving little scope for fiscal measures designed for economic growth. Third, the Scottish currency might be devalued to stimulate economic activity, increasing demand for exports and making Scottish goods more competitive against imports in the home market. A 'good thumping 25 per cent' devaluation would have been, in McCrone's view, the 'best way of solving Scotland's economic problems of the last two decades'. The disequilibria between the components of the UK could not be dealt with through exchange rate adjustment in the context of the union. Internal regional problems simply could not be tackled in this way. Effective devaluation would have proved difficult for an independent Scotland in the past. It would have had serious inflationary consequences, given the heavy dependence on international trade as all imports would rise in price. Trade unions would resist any measure that led to a cut in real incomes. Taken together, the scope for real autonomy under independence would have been limited.

But, McCrone maintained, this analysis was redundant in the context of North Sea oil. The extent of the wealth 'still remains in large measure disguised from the Scottish public by the DTI [Department of Trade and Industry]'s failure to make provision for a proper government return' of the value of oil. The Scottish public were sceptical of SNP claims that the UK government had been poor in negotiating with the oil companies but 'authoritative support' backed SNP claims. He accepted that estimates of the value of the oil 'may be too conservative'. He doubted assertions that the oil would not belong to Scotland. In a passage that could have been written by an SNP press officer, the Scottish Office chief economic adviser stated that 'large revenues and balance of payments gains would indeed accrue to a Scottish Government in the event of independence' which would undoubtedly 'banish any anxieties the Government might have had about its budgetary position or its balance of payments'. Scotland would be in

> chronic surplus to a quite embarrassing degree and its currency would become the hardest in Europe, with the exception perhaps of the Norwegian kroner. Just as deposed monarchs and African leaders have in the past used the Swiss franc as a haven of security, so now would the Scottish pound be seen as a good hedge against inflation and devaluation and the Scottish banks could expect to find themselves inundated with a speculative inflow of foreign funds.

Surpluses would 'open up new opportunities for a nationalist Government'. Devaluation in such circumstances of a 'chronic balance of payments surplus' would be impossible.

There would be opportunities to invest its wealth and McCrone considered some of the range of options available including investment in manufacturing to allow Scotland to compete with other members of the EEC. Scotland had suffered from the 'persistence of "stop–go" in the UK economy'. Each time investment had risen, as it had in 1973, the UK government had taken strong deflationary measures just at the point when Scotland needed to see further investment. An independent Scotland would, he maintained, be able to 'break out of the "stop–go" cycle' and permit a sustained and planned rate of growth. Scotland would become more interdependent with the EEC and less tied to English markets. An active regional policy within Scotland would be necessary. McCrone had been the author of a classic work on regional policy in

Britain, giving this section of his report a strange quality. The kind of regional policy he had long advocated for Britain appeared finally to be possible in the context of an independent Scotland. Investment in construction was discussed and the section on housing suggested that he had moved beyond considering the economics of nationalism to drafting a public policy manifesto for an independent Scotland. Housing policy had been 'bedevilled in the past by the subsidisation' of poor quality public sector housing. The 'colossal public housing sector' had placed an emphasis on quantity over quality. It would be possible to subsidize housing in a different way, providing assistance to individuals regardless of the type of house they occupied or whether they were tenants or owners. These comments carried an implicit criticism of the Scottish Office. The Scottish Office was an institutionalized form of lobbying for more resources whereas a Parliament with autonomy would allow for a different type of policy, not merely an effective form of lobbying. He also acknowledged that the pace of North Sea development would differ.

The final section addressed the EEC. The EEC, he argued, guaranteed access to English and European markets. The EEC now offered the same unlimited access to markets that had led Scotland to joining the union in 1707. 'In the unlikely event of England leaving the EEC, Scottish access to the other countries could in time largely compensate for any restrictions that might arise on English trade.' The EEC was not only a bigger market but had been more buoyant than that of Britain. North Sea oil had 'far-reaching consequences' in this context. It 'tremendously increased political power' as Scotland's voting power in the EEC would be small but possession of oil gave it economic power and as a major oil producer Scotland would be in a 'key position' and 'other countries would be extremely foolish if they did not seek to do all they could to accommodate Scottish interests'. Scotland would have its own direct representatives rather than the 'indirect, and so far hardly satisfactory, form of vicarious representation through UK departments'. He concluded that for the first time since the union was passed, it could be 'credibly argued that Scotland's advantage lies in its repeal'. He warned that when this came to be appreciated, it would have a 'major impact on Scottish politics, since it is on social and political grounds alone that the case for retention of the union will in future have to be based'.

The paper was only discovered in the archives in 2005 by an SNP researcher. Had it been published thirty years before then it might well have been one of the most significant Scottish public documents of that decade. But it was circulated and read within Whitehall and key lessons were learned. North Sea oil was an asset that Whitehall simply could not afford to lose, especially in the economic and fiscal context of the time. The UK came close to bankruptcy. Harold Wilson was told by Lord Balogh, his economic adviser, in 1975, a year before the International Monetary Fund (IMF) loan, that the UK faced 'possible wholesale domestic liquidation starting with a notable liquidation' and that the 'magnitude of this threat is quite incalculable'. Inflation peaked at 25 per cent that year and averaged 13 per cent in the 1970s. Balogh warned that a 'deep constitutional crisis can no longer be treated as fanciful speculation' and he was not referring to the threat posed by the SNP. There was real concern that civil unrest might occur undermining the legitimacy of government in such trying economic conditions. Kathleen Burk and Sir Alec Cairncross later co-authored a book on the economic crisis that led to Britain seeking a loan from the IMF. They noted that the 1976 crisis was one of ideology and priorities: 'It was a watershed in postwar economic policy in which the postwar consensus on how the economy should be managed broke down, full employment ceased to be the overriding objective of policy, and control of inflation became the abiding preoccupation of government.' In July 1976, the government set a target for money supply for the first time in British history. It was simply inconceivable for Whitehall and especially the Treasury to countenance losing North Sea oil. The oil was trickling ashore in the late 1970s but it was well known that it would provide a gushing torrent of cash into the Treasury some time around the turn of the decade. No concession could be made to the SNP either in public policy terms or in arguments on oil.

The SNP ploughed on with its campaign. Its senior members understood the value of oil only too well leading them to sound obsessive about it, as if oil was the only argument in their case for independence. Margo MacDonald, victor in the Govan by-election, had lost her seat at the February 1974 election but became the party's senior vice chair, effectively deputy leader. She felt no guilt in making the case for Scotland's oil, linking it to addressing the squalor in areas such as Govan but other senior members grew embarrassed by the campaign, especially accusations that it was selfish to demand control of this vast wealth. What had started off as an outstanding electoral asset became a liability in the fullness of the 1974–9 Parliament.

The message to the public over the ensuing years was that North Sea oil would not last long, was not worth as much as the SNP claimed, would not necessarily or at least not all become Scottish oil after independence, and would create more problems than it would solve. 'It's Scottish oil' was selfish. Was it not Shetland's oil? Shetland assumed an importance in British politics as never before. It was able to exert an influence far beyond its size and its civic leaders played one side off against the other in debates on devolution and independence. In 1973, the islands' Liberal MP Jo Grimond moved the second reading of private bill legislation which gave the islands council considerably more autonomy and power than other local authorities. Its compulsory purchase powers exceeded those already in existence giving it powers over the Sullom Voe area, which would become the site of the key development for the oil industry in the islands. It gained powers to control offshore works within three miles of Shetland, powers to engage in commercial enterprises on behalf of the community, and, crucially, to establish a reserve fund out of royalties accruing from oil developments to be used for social and community support. The Council bought the land around Sullom Voe and became landlord to the oil companies that needed its use. There would be no suggestions that Shetlanders had been selfish. Its local civic leaders proved more adept than Whitehall mandarins in understanding oil's importance and in negotiating deals for the islands' communities.

LABOUR'S U-TURN ON DEVOLUTION

The precise moment when Labour changed its policy on devolution was at a special conference in Glasgow in August 1974. The conference had been preceded two months before by a meeting of the party's Scottish executive to discuss a document produced by the Labour government. It has become part of Labour folklore that a Scotland–Yugoslavia qualifying match for the football world cup that evening had a major influence on a key vote. Only eleven out of twenty-nine Executive members turned up for the meeting. Six voted against all options in the government's paper and a resolution was passed stating that 'constitutional tinkering does not make a meaningful contribution towards achieving socialist goals'. Included amongst those in the minority were Donald Dewar and George Robertson who would each later play a significant role in delivering a Scottish Parliament. The British party's national executive passed a resolution supporting an assembly and applied pressure on the party in Scotland, resented by anti-devolutionists, to hold a special conference on the subject. The special conference met in August in the Cooperative Halls in Dalintober Street in Glasgow where five resolutions were debated. One rejected an assembly as 'irrelevant to the needs and aspirations of the Scottish people' and another supported a legislative assembly within the 'context of the political and economic unity of the United Kingdom'. Another resolution opposed proportional representation (PR) in elections to the assembly and the reduction in the number of Scottish MPs as well as the abolition of the office of Scottish Secretary. The Scottish executive supported the anti-devolution position but the conference gave strong support to devolution but not at the cost of fewer MPs, no Scottish Secretary, or having PR. The trade union block votes had delivered the result. As Bob McLean, who would later lead the pro-home rule pressure group Scottish Labour Action (SLA), asked many years later, 'The Government and the pro-devolutionists had won the vote, but had they won the soul of the Party?'

There had always been residual support for home rule within the Labour Party that traced its ancestry back to Keir Hardie and the Red Clydesiders. But unity of the working class and a belief in strong central government were trump cards played by anti-devolutionists. Future Prime Minister Gordon

Brown completed his doctoral thesis, 'The Labour Party and Political Change in Scotland, 1918–1929', in 1981. The thesis explained Labour's emergence as a force in twentieth-century Scottish politics. Brown argued that the 'cauldron in which the terms of modern politics were set was the period from 1918 to 1924, with the years of 1919 and 1920 of critical significance'. In an appendix to the thesis entitled, 'Home Rule and the Labour Movement', Brown maintained that, 'If Scottish sentiment was important in determining voting behaviour in 1929, it was Labour—not the nationalists—who could mobilise it. Labour was the home rule party of the twenties.' But his most interesting comment was that

> while Labour lost much of its initial enthusiasm for home rule and concentrated attention on economic and social questions during the twenties, the real problem for Scottish Labour was that it wanted to be Scottish and British at the same time. No theorist attempted in sufficient depth to reconcile the conflicting aspirations for home rule and a British socialist advance. In particular, no one was able to show how capturing power in Britain—and legislating for minimum levels of welfare, for example—could be combined with a policy of devolution for Scotland.

Brown may have been writing about the inter-war period but had been an active and senior member of the party and would have had the party's more recent history in mind when writing these words. These were issues that his party wrestled with in the decade after 1967. Faith in the value of capturing power in Britain was diminishing. Many Labour members had become disillusioned by Labour's term in office in the 1960s, following the high hopes expressed in Wilson's rhetoric. Labour's unionism had been conditional, at least in part. This unionism was rarely assimilationist. Even hardline opponents of the SNP, including Willie Ross, were emphatically Scottish. The party in Scotland made domestic policy and often enough viewed politics through a Scottish prism. Many policies were made by Scottish institutions, including Scottish local government which had a different structure from that south of the border. Education, housing, and health—all staples of Labour policy-making—were largely made in Scotland. A number of trade unions continued to support home rule and more were moving in that direction. The party's relative strength in Scotland compared with the Tories contributed to the sense that it was Scotland's party. It would mobilize Scottish sentiment under Ross reminiscent of the 1920s referred to by Brown in his thesis though falling short of support for home rule.

Robin Cook, Brown's Scottish rival though a close colleague at this stage, was typical of many in the Labour Party in Scotland. Cook was well versed in Scottish literature and culture. He flirted with support for devolution in the mid-1970s. In a *Guardian* article in August 1976, he expressed dismay that English MPs had 'blithely bound themselves in opposition to devolution' arguing that there was now a 'specifically Scottish dimension to politics.

This is more than just a matter of the size of the vote gathered in by the SNP. The re-discovery of a national identity has permeated all walks of public life, and the Scottish media, trade union movement, and lobby groups display an assertiveness and confidence which they lacked three years ago.' He conceded that Labour's promise of an assembly had contributed to this development. He would soon change his mind and became a vocal critic of devolution only to rediscover this Scottish dimension in 1983.

The rise of the SNP added electoral expediency to the mix. Writing in 1980, Gordon Brown and co-author Henry Drucker maintained that had the decision been left to the Labour or Conservative parties in Scotland then it is 'doubtful if either would have been committed to devolution even today'. The Scottish Council of the Labour Party had been unequivocal in its opposition to devolution in its evidence to the Kilbrandon Commission. When its senior members met the Commissioners, they said they would prefer a Tory government at Westminster to a Labour-controlled Scottish Assembly. John Pollock, leader of the main Scottish teachers' union and chairman of the Scottish party, argued that devolution would take Scotland on the 'slippery slope to separatism', a phrase used repeatedly over the years. The party's Scottish Secretary denied that there was any 'such thing as a separate political culture in Scotland'. Pollock himself became an ardent supporter of devolution and eventually of independence. It is possible that over time Labour would have rediscovered its lost radicalism on home rule but the manner in which the latter adopted devolution left an impression of being hurried, imposed, and half-hearted. The electoral threat posed by the SNP concentrated minds but also created resentments. Many party members were disinclined to appease the 'tartan Tories'. The SNP was seen as a party of upstarts and opportunists. Gordon Brown wrote an essay arguing that the

> SNP's 'new politics' which 'reject class warfare' presumes the familiar priorities of wealth and power over people...their rejection of the public ownership of land, oil and basic industries and their corresponding faith in incentives, and local entrepreneurship is a familiar blend of old well worn formulas, which assumes the subservience of Scottish workers to private international controls. Their programme for a redistributive 'Scottish social justice'...not only wrongly assumes that economic growth within a mixed economy will satisfy the divergent claims of all classes for a share in that growth but...will not substantially extend social services provision.

Jim Naughtie would later describe the 'turgid style' of the *Red Paper*, as 'characteristic of leftist pamphlets of the time'. The SNP, Brown charged, was a party of the 'professional and commercial middle class', a group that had returned to Scottish political activity 'en bloc for the first time since the Liberal decline'. The SNP sounded like New Labour of the 1990s. Brown and Labour viewed politics through a class prism and had difficulty understanding devolution other than in class terms, and even that in a very crude way. If this was the view of someone who was committed to devolution, then it was unlikely others would be able to see any merit in supporting devolution. Labour would remain divided on the issue. One group remained hostile, another supported the policy loyally but unenthusiastically, and some discovered an inner home ruler and became ardent supporters of devolution.

Some had long been supporters of home rule, even a few supporters of independence including one Scottish Labour MP from this period. This element became emboldened and frustrated during the devolution years. One person who eventually found his inner home ruler was John Smith. Smith had opposed devolution. It is unclear when or how he became a convert. He became the 'Devolution Minister' when he was appointed Minister of State at the Privy Council Office with responsibility for guiding the government's devolution legislation through the Commons. Smith had come into line with the party after its U-turn and appears to have been appointed as a highly competent parliamentarian who was sufficiently loyal to the party but sceptical about devolution to manage the difficult balance of parliamentary and party management. He was part of a generation of Labour MPs who were steeped in the Scottish milieu, less ideological than many other colleagues and found the kind of writing in *The Red Paper* risible. Innately moderate, devolution came to be seen as a rejection of the extremes of 'separatists, who want to break up Britain, and diehard and blinkered unionists'. This came to dominate Labour's official message in the late 1970s but it was hardly a ringing endorsement of Scottish devolution. The party was split and Labour supporters looking for a clear lead would have been confused by divisions at all levels in the party. In January 1976, two Labour MPs broke away from the Labour Party to form the Scottish Labour Party. Jim Sillars and John Robertson had become disenchanted with Labour's lack of commitment, as they saw it, to devolution. Sillars had been particularly affected by the 1975 referendum decision to remain in the EEC and felt that the two constitutional debates were linked.

Labour was committed to holding a referendum on membership of the EEC and engaged in what turned out to be a rather phoney renegotiation of the terms of UK membership prior to the referendum. Labour was as divided on the EEC as on devolution and the referendum proved a useful way of bridging Labour's European divide. Wilson allowed ministers to abandon collective ministerial responsibility on Europe so that members of the Cabinet were openly campaigning on different sides of the EEC debate. Europe had been considered by the Kilbrandon Commission but the main report had little to say about the subject. The minority report written by Lord Crowther-Hunt and Alan Peacock was more prescient. It included a chapter on the 'Common Market Dimension' in which it argued that the EEC had 'important implications' for any scheme of devolution. Important areas of decision-making would become 'still more remote', bureaucracy would be strengthened with a greater load on UK ministers which 'greatly strengthens any case there may be made for devolution'. But few at the time foresaw the implications of EEC membership. Sillars was ahead of his time and, more importantly, of other politicians and the public. Opinion polls in early 1975 suggested that Scotland might vote against membership of the EEC while the rest of Britain voted to remain a member. The SNP campaigned for a No vote along with many Labour members in Scotland. In the event opinion shifted: while 67.2 per cent of people across the UK voted to stay in the EC, only 58.4 per cent of Scottish voters did so.

CONSERVATIVE UNIONISM REASSERTED

After their brief flirtation with devolution under Heath, the Tories returned to their more familiar and comfortable position opposing devolution. The 1970 Tory manifesto promised to bring forward proposals for a Scottish Assembly or 'Convention' as they called it. Lord Crowther, Chair of the Royal Commission on the Constitution, met Ted Heath after the election. The minute of the meeting reports Crowther telling the new Prime Minister that he had 'no illusions about the reasons for setting up' the Commission and that there would be 'no hard feelings' if the government immediately brought the Royal Commission to an end. Crowther was unsympathetic to devolution and informed Heath that devolution had 'gone about as far as was practicable, unless the Government were prepared to contemplate a "Scottish Stormont"' which Crowther did not regard as sensible. Heath decided to allow the Commission to carry on its work but shared the common view that the election signalled the end of pressure from the SNP. Devolution was off the agenda. Crowther died two years later and was replaced by Lord Kilbrandon, who was much more sympathetic to home rule and would end up sympathetic to independence. No figure of any note in the Conservative Party objected to the quiet burial of the commitment though a few would eventually look back and view the Heath years as a lost opportunity.

Heath led his party through both general elections in 1974. He attempted to revive the party's commitment to some form of devolution but he had had his opportunity. In May, the party endorsed an indirectly elected assembly consisting of councillors and included this in its manifesto. Having lost his public authority at the election, Heath soon lost it in his party. Margaret Thatcher successfully challenged Heath for the party leadership in February 1975. Her career to that point had given her little experience of the Scottish Question in any form. Her first ministerial appointment was as Parliamentary Under Secretary at the Ministry of Pensions and National Insurance, a post that would have taught her little about the territorial nature of the UK. Pensions and National Insurance, as we have seen, had become a centralized and fairly uniform policy area. In opposition in the 1960s, she held junior posts shadowing Housing and Land but with a limited territorial remit that excluded Scotland; she led attacks on Labour's prices and incomes policy while shadowing the Treasury, again with no obvious Scottish dimension; and gained little experience of the Scottish dimension as Shadow Cabinet Minister for Fuel and Power, Transport, and then Education. She became Heath's Education and Science Secretary which meant she would have had some responsibilities for Scottish universities. As the Scottish Office was responsible for education north of the border, the likelihood would have been that Mrs Thatcher would have had few dealings with her Scottish colleagues. Her career illustrated a feature of British politics that often goes unnoticed. It was possible to become Leader of the Opposition and, indeed, Prime Minister without experience or understanding of the complex territorial nature of the UK. Tory politicians would have been well aware that the party north of the border had a separate name until 1965. But the Scottish Conservatives had become more assimilated in the decade after 1965, and the old, more aristocratic, guard who would have been more conscious of their Scottish roots would prove to be less likely to support Mrs Thatcher's brand of Conservatism, which was still evolving at this time.

Mrs Thatcher inherited her predecessor's policy on devolution. The *Daily Record*, then Scotland's largest selling and diehard Labour-supporting paper, reported her first visit as leader north of the border under the headline, 'Mrs Supercool'. A woman leading a major British party was a novelty but especially a leading woman entering the profoundly male world of Scottish politics. Mrs Thatcher was on an ideological journey. It had started with a critique of the Heath government's U-turns on lame ducks and state intervention. Influenced by Keith Joseph and what came to be known as the 'new right', this market-focused ideology was largely devoid of a territorial dimension. Some key thinkers on the right who would later be described as having influenced Mrs Thatcher included a number who advocated decentralization. She was less in tune with traditionalist Conservative thinkers who valued the 'little platoon' though she was stoutly nationalist but in a way that precluded any room to share patriotism. But the key issues in her period as Leader of the Opposition that drove her critique of British government were conviction politics, British nationalism, the small state, and the free market. These elements were bound together in what became known as Thatcherism, but that took time to emerge. She had never been sympathetic to decentralization and viewed local government with suspicion so that the only elected institutions that might offer alternative sources of authority to Parliament, and might have helped her understand the Scottish Question, were ones she viewed unfavourably. It probably did not help that Ted Heath rediscovered his enthusiasm for devolution.

Devolution was the subject of his first major intervention in British domestic politics after losing the party leadership. In November 1975, he spoke strongly in favour of devolution, comparing British centralism unfavourably with German federalism. Reports around that time suggested that Mrs Thatcher was intending to adopt a harder line in opposition to devolution. His intervention failed if it was designed to prop up the Tory's already limited support for devolution. A number of Tory MPs, who would figure as key members of Mrs Thatcher's governments, were outspoken critics of devolution. Nigel Lawson complained about retaining the level of Scottish representation in the Commons after devolution as the 'oppression of England' in October 1975. John MacGregor, later a Cabinet minister under Margaret Thatcher and John Major, warned not to underestimate the 'legitimate resentment in the English regions that you [Scots] are trying to have it all ways' with devolution and 'over-representation' in Westminster. Nicholas Ridley and Leon Brittan were strong critics and made frequent parliamentary interventions. This only invigorated Heath whose contribution to a debate in Parliament in January 1976 came close to endorsing the constitutional position adopted by Jim Sillars's Scottish Labour Party. Heath argued that Scottish nationalism had arisen over the previous half-century due to economic changes, especially the decline in heavy industries and unemployment. He argued that the proposals outlined by Sir Alec Douglas-Home in 1969 would have been sufficient had they been implemented at the time but the 'time has now passed for the Home proposals'. His speech provoked critical intervention from his own side.

The IMF crisis, control of public expenditure, and labour relations were the dominant issues during Thatcher's period as Leader of the Opposition. These would lead her to see the need for strong leadership and central control and to have contempt for consensus and compromise. Devolution would have been an uncomfortable fit in this world-view. Her chief lieutenants in Parliament, including some younger members who were making a name for themselves on the back benches harrying Labour ministers, were openly hostile to devolution. The old guard was more inclined to compromise or at least obfuscate. There were no diehard devolutionists in the Conservative Party, no Tory equivalent of Jim Sillars, but plenty of diehard ultra-unionists both north and south of the border. Alick Buchanan-Smith, Thatcher's Shadow Scottish Secretary, belonged to the old Scottish patrician wing of the party and had become sympathetic to home rule. Along with Malcolm Rifkind, his junior shadowing the Scottish Office, Buchanan-Smith resigned from the front bench in December 1976 when the leadership decided that it would oppose the Labour government's devolution proposals. Teddy Taylor, a Scot who was much more in Mrs Thatcher's mould, took his place. Francis Pym, an English patrician Tory, became her devolution spokesman and tried to maintain unity by promising a constitutional convention. This committed the party to nothing specific but it became clear where the party's heart really lay. By 1979, the

Conservatives were formally committed to a constitutional convention and devolution in some vague sense. But it was clear that the party had abandoned its flirtation with devolution. What was less clear, and only became obvious in time, was that it had also abandoned old-style pluralist unionism.

KILBRANDON, SCOTLAND AND WALES BILL, SCOTLAND ACT

It took a decade from establishing the Royal Commission to passing legislation to holding a referendum. Kilbrandon's report came out in favour of a semi-federal system, though rejected federalism per se. The main report set out some general principles. First, any new proposals should preserve unity but acknowledge that unity was not synonymous with uniformity. Democracy had to be preserved and was defined as having elected representatives with real control. Reform should be acceptable to the public though 'need not be one for which the public has specifically pressed' and any break with the past should 'not be too extreme'. Good communication between government and the people was essential. An assembly was an 'appropriate means of recognising Scotland's national identity and of giving expression to its national consciousness'. Leaving aside the specific proposals, this was a reasonable summation of pluralist unionism. The report rejected separatism and federalism. It proposed an assembly, elected by single transferable vote with multi-member constituencies of about 100 members, which would assume many of the responsibilities of the Scottish Office including the 'fields of the environment, education, health, social services, home affairs, legal matters, and agriculture, fisheries and food'. The 'devolved legislative assembly should have its own separate civil service' but Scottish Office responsibilities for electricity supply, fisheries and food should not be transferred. An Exchequer board would be needed to determine spending levels. This would be independent of the Treasury and Scottish executive. This was thought preferable to the assembly raising its own revenues or having a grant from central government. The office of Secretary of State for Scotland would be abolished though a Cabinet minister in London would have responsibilities for Scotland amongst other duties. The assembly would have legislative powers and should have maximum freedom in expenditure decisions. There would be a reduction in the number of Scottish MPs at Westminster. It recommended that the scheme should be adopted in a 'more or less uniform way throughout Great Britain'.

A series of Whitehall committees dissected the report. The Treasury, the dominant Whitehall department, was hostile. A senior official outlined Treasury concerns: central government's requirements for managing the economy had to be preserved; no proposals incompatible with this should be

agreed which, he maintained, 'limits the scope very substantially'; it was necessary to have adequate central control of expenditure, including determining the degree of uniformity necessary to maintain certain services; efficiency
had to be promoted and avoid excessive staffs. According to another Treasury
official, Kilbrandon was a 'most unwelcome distraction' but, 'Horrible as the
idea is, study of legislative devolution for Scotland and Wales can hardly be
avoided.' A major theme in Whitehall discussions was the need for uniformity
in the provision of public services and a fear that devolution would generate demands for more resources. It was not the fabled 'race to the bottom'
of American federal studies but demand spiralling upwards that concerned
Whitehall. The Cabinet Secretary maintained that with the possible exception
of EEC membership, devolution would be the most important constitutional
change in half a century and warned that it was possible that the 'ultimate
consequence would be the break-up of the Union', a view repeated by others in
various Whitehall internal briefings. Cabinet Secretary John Hunt expressed
the common Whitehall view that if devolution was necessary then it should
be 'strictly limited'. The slippery slope argument was expressed in even more
dramatic terms: 'once a people with a sense of national identity acquire their
own elected assembly, they and not the central authority set the pace of further constitutional advance and there is no turning back, short of military
force'. North Sea oil had become a new dimension that had to be taken into
account. Officials and ministers veered between seeing devolution as a distraction and as boring. This was not what had brought Labour ministers into politics. They had entered politics assuming that territorial politics were settled,
if they thought about this at all. But the government believed the issue would
not go away. The task in hand was to offer something without offering much.
Whitehall Permanent Secretaries met after the October 1974 election. The
note of the meeting made it clear that a minimal approach would no longer
suffice. For a group of people appointed to keep calm in a crisis, they displayed
extraordinary excitability, fearing that a failure to act might lead to rent strikes
or blowing up pipelines. It was as if the only experience Whitehall could draw
on was Irish and colonial nationalism.

The publication of proposed legislation was held up until after the EEC referendum and a series of discussion papers were produced. A White Paper, *Our
Changing Democracy*, setting out its proposals was published in November
1975. It emphasized political unity and proposed a single chamber assembly
of 140 members elected by simple plurality every four years. There would be
no separate civil service and Westminster would be empowered to intervene
in any Assembly business. There would be a block grant based on local needs
and the desire for uniform 'standards and contributions'. The only means the
Assembly would have to raise money would be through its control of local
government taxation. In essence, the Assembly could cut the grant to local
authorities, thereby forcing local government to increase local taxation, to give

the Assembly more spending headroom. The Secretary of State would not only be retained but would have considerable powers to intervene in the operation of the devolved body. Whitehall's neuroses were on display.

The first attempt to legislate brought proposals for Scottish and Welsh devolution together in one bill. As Wales was being offered an even more modest form of devolution, the Scotland and Wales Bill was an odd concoction. As well as Whitehall concerns, the bill had to respond to pressure from Labour MPs hostile to devolution. The same device that had been used to overcome party divisions on Europe was used for devolution. The only way to get sufficient support from the Labour benches was to promise a referendum. Labour lost its overall majority in April 1976 when John Stonehouse resigned the Labour whip three weeks before his trial for fraud, theft, and other crimes. Labour was now even more vulnerable to backbench rebellions. Stonehouse had faked his death on a beach in Miami a month after the October 1974 election and was later arrested in Australia. On resigning the Labour whip he sat briefly as the first and, to date, only English National Party MP. His last contribution in the chamber was to ask Michael Foot whether he had met the 'Save England Crusade' to discuss appointing a Secretary of State for England, having asked whether Foot would make a statement on English devolution a fortnight before. Stonehouse brought no credibility to the case for an English dimension to these debates but there was little doubt that the English dimension came to play a significant part in parliamentary debates.

THE WEST LOTHIAN QUESTION

Scotland's relations with the rest of the UK would have to change significantly with devolution. The issues involved had been rehearsed in debates on the Irish Question a century before. A. V. Dicey's work was relevant especially his 1886 book, *England's Case Against Home Rule*, which was republished in 1973. Dicey conceded that Ireland was a distinct entity but maintained that home rule to only one part of the state would have unintended consequences and especially on Parliament. Members of Parliament would be unable to vote on matters devolved to Ireland's home rule Parliament though Irish MPs would be able to vote on similar matters affecting the rest of the UK. Gladstone's first home rule bill, to which Dicey's 1886 book was a direct response, failed to address this anomaly. Gladstone experimented with different responses in each subsequent home bill rule bill but failed to find a satisfactory answer. Leaving Irish representation at Westminster as it had been prior to home rule was anomalous. Removing Irish MPs altogether from Westminster either involved complete secession or would amount to taxation without representation. The In-and-Out response of preventing Irish MPs from voting on issues affecting the rest of the UK which had already been devolved would create other anomalies. It would mean that there would be different majorities on different matters. Reducing Irish representation in Westminster might limit the anomaly but would not affect the key issue. Home rule all round would have offered symmetry but there was little demand in other parts of the UK for this and would have involved a major upheaval. Considerable time in the 1970s was spent by the government examining Gladstone's experience and examining Dicey's argument. One note quoted Gladstone's submission to Queen Victoria explaining the 1893 In-and-Out proposal:

> The cabinet do not view with favour on its merits the creation of a class of Members disabled from voting on a portion of the business of Parliament; but they think the inconvenience less than that which would arise from a proposal to admit their votes as of equal authority on British questions under the new arrangement.

Labour ministers were adamant that there should be no reduction in the number of Scottish MPs. The government White Paper on devolution published in September 1974 was committed to maintaining the existing levels of Scottish MPs. Labour opposition to reducing the number of Scottish MPs had less to do with fear that it might lose an overall majority than that a reduction was bound to provoke strong opposition amongst its Scottish MPs. Scottish Labour MPs were unlikely to be willing turkeys voting for an early Christmas. In a note on the issue in late 1976, Michael Foot argued:

> Our own party interest so far as anyone can foresee, will best be served by the minimum change from the current relativities between the four countries. We can, I believe, deploy good arguments why the 1920 'scaling-down' formula [used for Northern Ireland] should not be applied to Scotland and Wales. But I believe that it is neither equitable nor politically tenable to stand rigidly on the *status quo*.

But stand rigidly on the *status quo* was exactly what Labour would do. Ministers would have preferred to have ignored the issue but it became clear that this would be one of the most contentious matters in debates in Parliament and in the media, especially in London. The party political dimension ensured that the issue would not disappear. It served the Conservatives well that it was Tam Dalyell, West Lothian's Labour MP, who became the leading critic of devolution. His persistent rendition of the question—'shall I be able to vote on many matters in relation to West Bromwich but not West Lothian, as I was under the last Bill, and will my right hon. Friend [Prime Minister Callaghan] be able to vote on many matters in relation to Carlisle but not Cardiff?'—would prove embarrassing. Had the attack been led by a Conservative politician it might have had far less impact. Enoch Powell, far right former Tory MP sitting as an Ulster Unionist, proposed that the question should be called the 'West Lothian Question' as Dalyell, MP for West Lothian, had been so persistent in asking it.

Margaret Thatcher proposed a Speaker's Conference in a letter to the Prime Minister in late 1976. She argued that the 'under-representation of England relative to both Scotland and Wales' was 'markedly greater than at any time since 1885' as a result of the greater rate of population increase in England and had nothing to do with 'special constitutional or geographical factors'. Foot believed that this was what should be done and the only issue was when this should be announced in order to gain maximum support for the bill. It was seen, in much the same way as establishing the Royal Commission on the Constitution, as a means of kicking the issue into the long grass. He proposed this to the Cabinet in January 1977 and recommended that the announcement should be timed when it was 'most helpful in relation to the progress of the Scotland and Wales Bill'. In the event, the bill fell in Parliament before the government had the chance to make the announcement. The problem Labour faced was that the announcement of a reduction in the number of Scottish MPs might have provoked a backlash against devolution amongst its Scottish MPs fearing that they might lose their seats without gaining any support. The government changed its mind by the time it introduced new legislation on devolution a year later.

Another idea considered was establishing an English or English and Welsh Grand Committee, a variant on the 'In-and-Out' idea. However, a committee consisting of only English MPs would have no overall majority for any party with the Conservatives as the largest party. An England and Wales Committee would also have no overall majority but Labour would be the largest party. In the ten general elections since 1945, the party complexion of English Members differed from that of the Commons as a whole on four occasions following elections—1950, 1964, and February and October 1974. The English and Welsh complexion of the Commons had not reflected Parliament as a whole on three occasions—1964 and February and October 1974. A note by Michael Foot suggested that any proposal that involved an 'in-and-out' solution should be rejected on technical grounds but also because of the 'very serious disadvantage it would present to our party'. Labour majorities in Parliament, he maintained, would be unaffected on foreign, defence, and economic affairs but 'our ability to pursue socialist policies in England on a wide range of social matters would be greatly impaired'.

In a comment addressing the West Lothian Question, Michael Quinlan, head of the Constitution Unit established in the Cabinet Office to deal with devolution, wrote, 'It is an implicit judgement underlying the Government's present stance that this criticism [of the West Lothian Question] can successfully be resisted, without change of policy. The present Note offers no opinion on this judgement.' But the rest of the note considered a range of options and further work showed that whatever ministers might have thought, civil servants believed this was not an issue that could be ignored. One of Quinlan's colleagues warned that a 'sensitive politician' might read the note and interpret it as suggesting that it was an implicit criticism of a lack of principle, having taken a decision to retain all of Scotland's MPs for 'narrow party political advantage'. The same official doubted Labour ministers would contemplate reducing the number of Scottish MPs and suggested that a 'nudge' in this direction would require a 'bogeyman':

> We could do this by sketching a tentative scenario (which isn't necessarily unrealistic) of the Tory party taking seats from the SNP in some areas and the SNP gaining seats at the expense of Labour in others, planting a seed of thought that in the longer term it might be to the advantage of both major parties to agree to a reduction of Scottish representation at Westminster.

but concluded that on balance it might be best not to include such 'speculation'. One idea considered was to leave the number of Scottish MPs but increase the number of English Members. Calculations suggested that England's existing 516 seats might increase to 645 to achieve the same ratio to population as Scotland resulting in a Commons of 781 Members. If Scotland retained the same number of MPs but saw a reduction in its *proportionate* share of representation along the lines of that which occurred in Northern Ireland, then there would need to be 860 English MPs creating a Parliament of 1,018 Members. There was no prospect of this happening but serious consideration was given to increasing the number of English MPs though without agreement on the actual number.

Officials studied parliamentary majorities at each election since 1945 and what the distribution would have been had there been fifty-seven, in line with a strict population basis, or no Scottish MPs. They found that contrary to 'popular misconceptions' a reduction to fifty-seven would not have altered the majority party at Westminster. The nearest, according to their calculations, would have been in February 1974 when fifty-seven Scottish MPs would have meant a Conservative–Labour tie. Even if all Scottish MPs were eliminated, the English and Welsh majority party would have been the same in all but two elections—1964 and February 1974. It would not have resulted in permanent Tory government for England. Officials read these conclusions as a 'possible nudge to Ministers in the direction of reducing Scots representation at Westminster'. It was suggested that if Labour did not reduce the number of Scottish MPs then a future Tory government might introduce an amending bill and 'carry out something much more damaging' to Labour.

Scotland's seventy-one MPs were more than Scotland would have on a population basis and the number was 'necessarily assessed on an arbitrary basis'. But, it was noted these arrangements had not met with criticism. One consequence of the devolution debates would be that Scotland's level of representation was raised onto the agenda and would become a persistent matter in debates thereafter, though never becoming of great significance. What became clear was how little attention had been paid to Scotland's representation in the Commons. One note suggested that the rationale for additional Scottish MPs was to 'ensure that their distinctive national voice was heard in the large Westminster Parliament' but another official questioned this, suggesting that the original justification had not been to 'placate nationalist sentiment' but to reflect 'dispersed population and the need to keep geographical size of constituencies in manageable bounds'.

There was a precedent which was considered in debates. The establishment of a Parliament for Northern Ireland came with a reduction in Northern Ireland's representation at Westminster. Legislation passed in 1949 gave Northern Ireland twelve seats, four fewer than it would have if the existing 635 UK seats were allocated on a strict population basis. While these debates were taking place on Scotland's representation at Westminster post-devolution, debates were occurring on Northern Ireland's representation as a consequence of Stormont being prorogued in 1972. Merlyn Rees, Northern Ireland Secretary of State, warned that what was right for Northern Ireland 'may conflict in logic with representation proposals for Scotland and Wales, where the arithmetical over-representation is to remain even after devolution'. Rees was coming under pressure from Conservatives, Ulster Unionists, the Liberal Party, the Northern Ireland Labour Party, and the Alliance Party to increase Northern Ireland representation and this was 'causing us problems'. If extra Northern Ireland seats were conceded, acknowledging that Northern Ireland had fewer MPs as the cost of having devolution, then this would raise questions about the number of Scottish MPs after devolution.

There was another side of the 'English backlash'. MPs, local politicians, and the media in the north-east of England were concerned that Scottish devolution would give Scotland an unfair advantage. Scotland already had the Scottish Office and more MPs than its population merited. In November 1974, *The Journal*, the Newcastle-based newspaper, warned that the 'North' must not become a 'poor relation' and demanded that MPs in the area should meet the government. Economic Planning Councils in the north of England complained to Tony Crosland, Environment Secretary and MP for Hull, that devolution would leave them in a relatively weak position. Scotland's share of public expenditure was of particular concern. A Scottish Assembly was expected to be a powerful voice in negotiations with the Treasury. In January 1977, Tyne and Wear County Council organized a conference in Newcastle, 'Devolution—The Case Against'. Tam Dalyell warned that a separate Scottish state would emerge within a decade of devolution. Nicholas Ridley, Tory MP for Cirencester, argued that Scottish representation in the Commons should be reduced to twenty-eight MPs and warned that devolution was a device designed to 'protect the election chances of one party at the risk of setting the English against the Scots'.

There was no 'solution' to the West Lothian Question without a radical overhaul of the constitution. But devolution was conceived as a minimal response to the Scottish Question, not an attempt to consider the constitution in its totality. Party politics inevitably played its part in proceedings. Scottish Labour MPs felt exposed as attention focused on the proportion of Scottish seats in the Commons. One of their own number ensured that this matter was uppermost in discussions of devolution in Westminster. There was little evidence that most English and Welsh MPs were deeply concerned with how Scotland was governed but became animated when they considered the anomalies inherent in an asymmetrical form of devolution and showed little interest in being part of a symmetrical home-rule-all-round solution.

THE SCOTLAND ACT, 1978

The government's first attempt to legislate for a devolved assembly was lost when the government was defeated on a motion to allocate parliamentary time for debate. The most worrying aspect for the government was that twenty-two of its own MPs had voted against the motion and caused the defeat. A further fifteen Labour MPs had abstained. Given the convention that a defeat on important government business should result in an election, Jim Callaghan faced the likelihood of a general election and defeat. However, while Labour did not want an election, the small band of thirteen Liberal MPs was even more desperate to avoid an election. Jeremy Thorpe had resigned as Liberal Party leader in May 1976 over allegations of conspiring to kill a man who had claimed to have had an affair with the MP. The Labour government struck a deal with the Liberals—the Lib-Lab Pact—which meant an election was avoided. The Liberal Party might have been expected to exert pressure on the government for home rule. But, as a study of the pact suggested, David Steel, new Liberal leader, was 'more concerned with winning access to the ante-rooms of power than with the changes which might flow from that power'. Pressure was coming from Scotland. The SNP had made substantial gains in local elections in May 1977. The government could not drop devolution without the risk of losing a large number of seats to the SNP. In late July, Michael Foot announced that separate bills for Scottish and Welsh devolution would be introduced.

The Scotland Bill was given a second reading in the Commons in November 1977. The government won with a majority of forty-four and a Conservative motion proposing a constitutional convention was defeated by forty-eight votes. Eleven Labour MPs voted against the government, fewer than had opposed it on the timetable motion that had defeated the earlier proposals. But these eleven were only a small proportion of those Labour MPs opposed to devolution. Many more voted for the bill conditionally. The main condition was that a referendum should be held before the measure was implemented.

Two days later Parliament approved a motion setting out the timetable for debate and detailed scrutiny began two days later. This was the real test of support for the government and there had been speculation that the vote would be very close. In the event, the government had a majority of twenty-six and only nine Labour MPs voted against the government with seven abstaining. The vote signalled a hardening of opposition from the Conservatives with only two Tory MPs abstaining on the motion. The government had secured a majority with the support of all eleven SNP MPs, three Plaid Cymru MPs, eleven of the thirteen Liberals, and the two Scottish Labour MPs.

As this was a major constitutional measure, the bill was debated in a Committee of the Whole House, meaning that all MPs would have an opportunity to debate the details of the proposed legislation. What became clear at the outset was that votes on the details of the bill would require skilful parliamentary handling. The bill's first clause was a declaratory statement and was struck down by a majority of fifteen against the government. The removal of the assertion that devolution did not affect the 'unity of the United Kingdom or the supreme authority of Parliament to make laws for the United Kingdom or any part of it' was embarrassing but did not affect the substance of the bill. While the declaratory first clause had been removed, this had no effect on the details of the Act which would permit Westminster considerable control over the Assembly. Westminster could repeal or amend any measure passed by the Scottish Assembly at any time. An attempt to have the additional member electoral system (AMS) used to elect the Scottish Parliament was easily defeated. The planned Assembly would be elected by first-past-the-post. An attempt to give the Assembly revenue raising powers was heavily defeated. Instead, the Assembly would be financed by a block grant from Westminster.

The Scotland Act, 1978, was a lengthy piece of legislation. It defined devolved matters in some detail and the government included a number of measures to act as controls or safeguards limiting the Assembly's autonomy. In legislating for Irish home rule or for autonomy for Commonwealth countries, Westminster had conferred general powers limited by matters that were explicitly reserved for Westminster. But the Scotland Act, 1978, worked the opposite way. There was an amendment to have the powers defined in the manner of the Government of Ireland Act but this was defeated. John Smith, minister in charge, argued that any matters accidentally not included as retained matters would be devolved by default and this was unacceptable as the government wanted to guard against 'creeping devolution'. Only matters explicitly devolved would come under the Assembly's jurisdiction. This was done by referring to existing laws creating a great degree of complexity and complicating interpretation of the Assembly's powers.

The most significant amendment to the legislation, and which some scholars have argued was the most significant backbench amendment to any legislation since 1945, was moved on Burns Night 1978. George Cunningham, a Scot representing a London constituency for Labour, moved what became known as the 40 per cent rule. It required that the government move an Order in Parliament to repeal the legislation in the event that less than 40 per cent of the eligible electorate supported devolution in the referendum, regardless of how many people actually voted. The amendment was passed by fifteen. An attempt by another anti-devolution Labour MP to extend the referendum to the whole of the UK was defeated by 184 votes to 122. An amendment which would have allowed Orkney and Shetland to opt out of devolution if a majority of the electorate in these islands voted against devolution was passed with a substantial majority of eighty-six. These votes were a more accurate reflection of attitudes towards devolution amongst Members of Parliament than the final vote on the bill at third reading. By this stage, the government had abandoned its support for a Speaker's Conference to consider the implications for Parliament as a consequence of devolution. An amendment moved by the Conservatives in the Commons was rejected.

The government suffered a further twenty-five defeats when the bill was debated in the House of Lords. A number of government defeats in the Lords were, however, reversed when the bill returned to the Commons including an amendment which would have seen the Assembly elected by AMS and another, carried by only one vote, which would have given the Assembly the power to draw up proposals for tax powers which the Secretary of State would be obliged to present to Westminster. One of the most important amendments in the Lords was one which addressed the West Lothian Question. It proposed a procedure whereby a bill passed by Scottish MPs' votes on a matter that did not relate to Scotland would require a second vote. In essence, it provided for a cooling-off period.

The Scotland Bill received Royal Assent at the end of July 1978. It had taken just over eight months of intense parliamentary debate. During its passage, John Mackintosh had warned of the danger that boredom might kill devolution. In his diary, George Younger, frontbench Scottish affairs spokesman for the Tories, referred to 'very boring' days on the Scotland Bill. If the politicians at the core of the debate felt this way, there was little hope that devolution debates would ignite excitement amongst the public.

THE SNP FALTERS

The election of seven and then eleven SNP MPs in the two elections in 1974 ensured that Scotland would play a larger part in parliamentary politics than previously. But even the rise of the SNP and perceived threat it posed to the union had to compete with an unprecedented economic crisis, a series of industrial disputes, and the politics of minority government for attention. Having eleven MPs was a new experience for what had been an extra-parliamentary party with little enthusiasm for anything to do with the House of Commons. Only two of the eleven—Winnie Ewing and Donald Stewart—had been MPs before and each had been the party's sole representative at the time. The MPs would need to work together but also work out a relationship with the party in Scotland over the following five years under intense scrutiny from their opponents—who outnumbered them in the Commons amongst Scottish MPs alone by more than six to one—as well as the media. As before, the victory was interpreted in many nationalist circles as evidence that Scotland was about to become independent and the key tension was around how the party should respond to devolution. Three fissures were evident from the start: there were significant differences over strategy, policy, and personalities in the group of eleven; there was a tension between the MPs and the party's national executive committee (NEC) in Scotland; and there was a larger tension within the party that spanned both its MPs and NEC between hardliners who supported independence and those willing to accept a measure short of independence, at least as a 'stepping stone'. So long as the party was advancing electorally these differences were manageable but tensions surfaced when the party hit a difficult patch.

Nine of the eleven SNP seats had been won from the Tories and some commentators misinterpreted this as meaning that the SNP had won 'Tory seats' by picking up Tory votes. An anti-Tory alliance had voted for the SNP in these seats. Despite contesting both 1974 elections, but especially that in October, as a moderate left of centre party, the SNP was uncertain of how it should present itself to the electorate. It advocated 'self-government' and the 'furtherance of all Scottish interests' but this did not offer a clear guide as to how SNP MPs would vote on the myriad issues that came before Parliament. Nationalization of aircraft and shipbuilding, membership of the EEC, prices and incomes policy and the social contract, and industrial relations were only some of the contentious issues debated in Parliament and across the country. Finding a particularly Scottish angle was not always easy.

The 1974–9 Parliament was a period of sharp divisions in labour relations with industrial unrest particularly difficult towards the end of the Parliament. On more than one occasion the SNP succeeded in irritating both sides of industry in an effort to avoid taking sides. The SNP initially opposed the Labour government's bill to nationalize the aircraft and shipbuilding industries. In the 1940s, opposition to nationalization had been popular in Scotland as this was seen as a defence of Scottish indigenous industries. But in the 1970s, the trade unions saw nationalization as the only way to save the shipbuilding industry. It did not help that the SNP whip in the Commons ostentatiously ripped up a telegram from shop stewards urging support for the bill at second reading.

Tensions reminiscent of when John MacCormick had been prominent in the national movement reappeared with the party unsure whether to appeal to the wider public over the heads of economic and social elites or to devote energy to appealing for elite support. Was it an alternative establishment in waiting? The Queen made a speech celebrating her Silver Jubilee stating, 'I cannot forget that I was crowned Queen of the United Kingdom of Great Britain and Northern Ireland.' This was interpreted as an attack on the SNP and independence. Donald Stewart, SNP group leader, responded by warning the monarch that her rule was based on the consent of the Scottish people but many senior figures were deeply concerned.

In 1976, the SNP annual conference debated devolution. A resolution was passed stating that the party was 'prepared to accept an assembly with limited powers as a possible stepping stone' but that 'nothing short of independence will meet the needs of the Scottish people'. An amendment to delete the passage referring to the assembly was proposed but was defeated by 594 votes to 425. Most delegates saw devolution as a Scottish solution, a base on which to build. But a substantial minority were wary of devolution as a British device to appease Scots. The SNP's internal debate mirrored what was going on inside each of the other parties. The Scottish Question had evolved a long way from being whether a distinct Scottish dimension to politics existed.

Support for the SNP remained solid in the early years of the 1974–9 Parliament, peaking when the government's first devolution proposals fell. But SNP support fell towards the end of the Parliament. There were three parliamentary by-elections in Scotland during the 1974–9 Parliament, each occurring in 1978. The first was in Glasgow Garscadden following the death of the sitting Labour MP. Despite Labour having a 7,600 vote majority at the previous general election, the SNP had high hopes of winning. Donald Dewar, former Labour MP for Aberdeen South, won the seat with reasonable ease. Dewar had been a long-standing supporter of devolution and would prove to be one of Labour's most sincere and persistent supporters of a Scottish Parliament. But his victory over the SNP signalled the demise of pressure from the SNP and would embolden opponents of devolution. Jim Sillars's SLP won only 1.6 per cent of the vote in Garscadden. The following month, Labour held the symbolically important Hamilton seat. George Robertson easily held off a challenge from Margo MacDonald, the SNP's deputy leader and best-known figure. Robertson would play a significant role in delivering devolution twenty years later but his victory confirmed the SNP's decline. The third by-election was another seat Labour was defending. The death of John Mackintosh, one of Labour's leading advocates of devolution, was a major blow to pro-home rule forces. Labour held the seat and increased its majority over the Tories in second place. The SNP managed to win under 9 per cent of the vote. Electoral setbacks provoked internal dissent and infighting creating a downward spiral for the party.

THE REFERENDUM

The Labour government conceded a referendum to get the support of anti-devolution Labour MPs. The idea of a referendum had a long pedigree. Supporters of home rule had long argued for a referendum as a means of overcoming party political opposition to a Scottish Parliament. In the late 1970s, supporters of a referendum could be found on both sides of the argument. Some advocated a referendum as a means of returning the decision to Scotland rather than have Westminster make the decision. Others felt that the best prospect—either to stop devolution or to ensure its establishment—was to remove the decision from Westminster. At various stages, a number of figures on different sides of the debate argued that independence should be included in any referendum. Ted Heath on the right and Norman Buchan on the left suggested that independence should be included on the ballot paper of the referendum. William Whitelaw, Deputy Tory leader, argued for a referendum on independence in February 1977 only to find that Francis Pym, the party's devolution spokesman, and Teddy Taylor, its Shadow Scottish Secretary, were opposed to including independence on the ballot paper a few days later. Others, including hard left Labour MP Eric Heffer, argued that the referendum should be held in all parts of the UK and not just Scotland. The parties appeared as inconsistent in their views on a referendum as they had been about devolution.

The government would have been unable to get its devolution legislation through Parliament without conceding a referendum. But when it took the decision in January 1977, it decided firmly against including a question on independence and against voters outside Scotland having a vote. Supporters of devolution had been relaxed about the demand for a referendum. There was still little anxiety after a clause was inserted to the effect that 40 per cent of eligible voters had to support devolution in the referendum. If the Scots clearly voted YES to devolution, Parliament would be bound to establish the Assembly. In retrospect, it is difficult to avoid viewing the supporters of devolution as other than complacent and unprepared. Their opponents were better organized, more coherent, and far better resourced. But amongst Tories at least, the general view was that there would be a YES vote and the aim had been to maximize the NO vote.

Hubris was the main reason for the failure of devolution in 1979 but the backdrop did not help. There had been a series of industrial disputes during the winter of 1978/9—the 'Winter of Discontent'. This damaged Labour and emboldened the Tories. The voice of business was overwhelmingly against devolution and the trade unions did little campaigning. It was an inauspicious backdrop to launching a campaign for a YES vote.

The referendum campaign can be dated from the moment a referendum was conceded. The date of the referendum was fixed for 1 March 1979. Anti-devolution campaign groups were established well before supporters managed to get organized. The government itself was busy trying to get the measure through Parliament and dealing with the various problems it confronted. There was no legal requirement then that two umbrella groups should be established or that any group should be registered. The Labour government officially supported a YES vote and it was part of the official Labour policy. The Liberals were formally in favour too, though they had few members or resources to bring to the campaign. The SNP were the most enthusiastic supporters, lending credence to the perception that devolution would be a 'slippery slope to separation'. Relations between Labour and SNP were poor, and Labour's Scottish general secretary was quoted as saying that her party would not be 'soiling our hands by joining any umbrella Yes group'. This had been the view expressed less caustically by John Smith in a private conversation with George Younger, future Tory Scottish Secretary, in late 1977. Smith and Younger then agreed that it was in neither party's interest to fight the referendum as a party campaign, as this would embarrass pro-devolutionists in the Conservative Party and anti-devolutionists in the Labour Party. Smith voiced the view that the referendum should be a fairly low-key affair. This did not augur well for a successful campaign.

The pro-devolution element in the Conservative Party was minute compared to the anti-devolution element in the Labour Party. The NO cause was simple. NO to 'more taxes', 'more politicians', 'more bureaucracy'. Anti-devolutionists portrayed a NO vote as against the measure on offer, holding out the prospect that it was possible to support devolution but vote NO. This was the official Conservative position articulated by Francis Pym, devolution spokesman, and Margaret Thatcher, though anyone listening to Teddy Taylor, the party's chief Scottish spokesman, could have been in little doubt that he was against any assembly. Having failed to win the Berwick and East Lothian by-election, the Tories were concerned that they should not come across as anti-Scottish. George Younger recorded his concerns in his diary and in meetings with senior party figures. In November 1978 as the party was preparing its campaign, he warned that 'our negative attitude to devolution & other Scottish issues undoubtedly have their effect'. Lord Home, former Prime Minister and Scottish MP, made one of the most important interventions in the referendum. Margaret Thatcher had been very keen that Home and Harold Macmillan should play a part in the referendum. Her view was that having two former Prime Ministers involved, especially with Scottish roots, was an advantage that Labour could not match. In the event, Macmillan did not intervene in the campaign but Home more than made up for his predecessor.

In a speech in Edinburgh University two weeks before polling day, Home rejected Prime Minister Callaghan's claim that the proposals before the Scottish public were a 'last chance'. Home said he would vote NO as the only way to ensure that Parliament would correct the defects of the Scotland Act. 'Parliament is sovereign and it can do anything at any point', Home argued.

He outlined five defects of the Act which required remedy. An Assembly needed to raise a proportion of its own revenue: 'Representation without the power to tax is a recipe for political irresponsibility.' Scottish MPs could vote on English bills while English MPs could not vote on comparable legislation for Scotland. This would cause confusion at best and at worst lead to frustration. The proposed Assembly was too large and there would be a serious danger of over-government. One hundred members would, he argued, be more than enough. There was no machinery by which a bill could be defined as purely Scottish before it was introduced in the Assembly and this would lead to trouble if at a later stage the measure was declared *ultra vires*. Finally, the government had refused to introduce a measure of proportional representation for elections to the Assembly, missing an opportunity to correct the swing to extremes which had been a feature of British politics in recent years. He concluded that it was important to 'get the matter right even if that means more time'. He supported the idea of a Speaker's Conference and proposed three alternatives to the existing plans. Existing MPs could form the Assembly, requiring only adjustments to Westminster's timetable. The Northern Ireland model was possible 'had it not been overlaid by religious strife'. And finally, there was a federal solution. He maintained that if Scots voted for the measure, Parliament would 'give it a pretty long run before trying to make any changes later'.

Support for devolution ebbed away in the closing weeks of the campaign, particularly amongst Conservative supporters. SNP supporters remained overwhelmingly in favour but divisions in the Labour Party sent mixed signals to Labour supporters. Commentators were focused on the turnout required to win 40 per cent of the eligible electorate and generally assumed a YES majority. The result was that 51.6 per cent voted YES on a turnout of 63.8 per cent. Six of Scotland's regional or island councils voted for the measure and six against. It was a slight numeric majority but measured against expectations it was a defeat for devolution. Opponents claimed that had the campaign been extended by a week then there would have been a NO majority. The argument gained traction in some quarters though lacked foundation. NO had campaigned vigorously in the knowledge as to when the referendum would take place. They succeeded in closing a gap which only months before seemed insurmountable. This was the second referendum in four years in which Scottish opinion had shifted dramatically over a short period of time.

The government was obliged under the terms of the legislation to move a Repeal Order in the Commons, though under no obligation to vote for repeal. Jim Callaghan knew that the Act would be repealed because a substantial part of the parliamentary Labour Party would vote for repeal. It would divide his party and raise questions about Labour's commitment to devolution and about why so much time and effort had been expended on the subject. The government simply could not afford to move the Repeal Order.

The SNP was incensed, blaming Labour for failing to show any real commitment to Labour's own Assembly plans. The Opposition parties united against Labour in a confidence motion which the government lost by one vote. The ensuing general election was the first since 1924 called as a result of a government defeat on a motion of no confidence. The Conservatives were returned at the subsequent election. The Scottish Question moved from centre-stage to the fringe.

CONCLUSION

The Royal Commission on the Constitution had been set up in response to a perceived electoral threat from the SNP. Shortly after its establishment, the threat was thought to have receded and the Commission looked for a period as if it might either be wound up or would report to a nation that had moved on from its flirtation with Scottish nationalism. It is impossible to know the extent to which the death of its original chairman, who was unsympathetic to devolution, and replacement with the more reform-minded Lord Kilbrandon made a difference to its report. But the context in which it reported was important. The SNP had not disappeared but was on the march again. The debate on Scotland's constitutional status could not be separated from the wider economic concerns of government and the prospect of vast wealth being pumped ashore from the North Sea. The energy crisis, stagflation, and poor industrial relations made it more important for Whitehall to limit the terms of the Scottish Question. Whitehall quite simply could not afford to lose control of North Sea oil and gas. It faced the dilemma of determining whether a concession would appease the Scots or feed demands. Few in Whitehall perceived the Scottish Question as other than an extension of the economic problems facing the country. The Scots were believed to be expressing disaffection with the UK's economic woes by voting for the SNP and arguing for home rule. The way the SNP articulated its case for self-government seemed to confirm this.

Devolution had few principled supporters. The SNP supported it as a stepping stone to independence. Labour had come to support it for reasons of expediency and without much conviction. The 1978 Act was almost unanimously viewed as flawed in some way. The 1979 referendum was the culmination of a long process. The result deflated home rulers but there had been a small majority in favour of the measure on offer. The perception that devolution had been denied and that Westminster's 40 per cent rule had been a deliberate device to undermine Scottish national aspirations fed into subsequent debates. But for a number of years devolution was off the political agenda. This did not mean that Scotland had been assimilated into the union. The NO campaign had insisted that Scotland was a distinct entity. It was possible to be anti-devolution while being pro-Scottish. The message may have been vague and inconsistent but the NO vote could not be portrayed as a vote to assimilate Scotland or as ignoring the Scottish dimension. Supporters of home rule had misread public opinion but opponents would misread the referendum result.

9

———

Bringing Harmony and Hope

INTRODUCTION

In reviewing general elections since 1945, David Butler, doyen of British election studies, remarked that the key events that had shaped British politics rarely included general elections. But the 1979 general election was a watershed though it was not appreciated at the time. It also marked the end of intense focus on Scotland's constitutional status. Devolution had been defeated and the SNP was reduced to a rump in Parliament. But that hardly made the election significant. Nor was it significant only because the first woman had been elected Prime Minister. Mrs Thatcher attracted much attention but even this was not what was to mark the election out as a watershed. 1979 was a watershed because of what became possible as a result of electing the Conservatives under Mrs Thatcher to power. If the Tories had a master plan to transform Britain then they hid it well.

It was tempting in the aftermath of the referendum and general election to assume that it was business as usual as far as Scotland was concerned. The problem was that the Scottish Question was constantly evolving. It was affected by changes in society, the economy, and politics. As the UK underwent significant changes in each respect, it was unwise to imagine that this would be a period of stability as far as the Scottish Question was concerned. There was continuity in important respects. The Scottish Office and Scottish Secretary would continue to play the Scottish card in negotiations with the Treasury and the rest of Whitehall, attempting to cut out a degree of differentiation from the rest of the UK. This would be done by the now familiar tactic of emphasizing ways in which Scotland differed from the rest of the UK and by using the threat of stirring up support for the SNP. Labour was the dominant party in Scotland but was not a particular concern for the Conservatives. It was SNP support and support for devolution that worried them. The Scottish dimension would insinuate itself into debates which could cause the government additional problems.

The National Coal Board announced a series of pit closures in 1981 but withdrew these in face of opposition. But in 1984, the government was ready for a confrontation with the miners. The Troubles in Northern Ireland took on a gruesome aspect during Mrs Thatcher's premiership, including hunger strikes by Irish republican prisoners and an attempt on the Prime Minister's life. The economy was the dominant persistent issue for the government. The primary focus was the control of inflation initially through the Medium Term Financial Strategy (MTFS), designed to reduce money supply in the economy. The MTFS was a disaster and was abandoned after high interest rates damaged economic competitiveness and undermined exports. Unemployment soared as manufacturing industries shed jobs. A litany of closures would be read out by Opposition politicians. The social costs of these policies were manifested in a series of inner city riots in summer 1981. The government abandoned 'monetarism' later that year, though the term continued to be used as short-hand for government economic policies. Its energies shifted to privatization. Another feature was the government's liberalization of the financial markets providing an opportunity for Scotland's traditionally staid financial sector to take advantage of what critics would refer to as 'casino capitalism'. Towards the end of Thatcher's period in office the poll tax and the European Community came to dominate politics at Westminster. Each had a significant Scottish dimension and each helped sharpen understandings of the Scottish Question.

'IT CAME WI' A LASS AND IT WILL GANG WI' A LASS'

Winnie Ewing's Hamilton victory had ushered in a period when the Scottish Question came to the fore as never before. Margaret Thatcher's election saw the end of that era. The Tories won seven seats back from the SNP and their share of the vote increased to 31.4 per cent from 24.7 per cent. It was tempting to interpret the results as a return to normality but normality did not mean that Scotland had behaved the same as the rest of Britain. As an internal Tory document noted, Scotland had recorded the Tories' poorest results with a swing of only 0.7 per cent from Labour compared with 4.6 per cent in Wales and 5.6 per cent in England. The only seat the Tories lost in the general election had been Teddy Taylor's seat in Glasgow, depriving Taylor of the chance to serve as Scottish Secretary in Mrs Thatcher's government. Three weeks after the election, George Younger reflected on the result in a letter to Sir Geoffrey Howe, Chancellor of the Exchequer, 'We remain the only political party which in the post war years has ever won a majority of the total Scottish vote, but our position in recent years has slipped very badly and, despite the set-back to the SNP, was disappointing at the last election.' His claim to have won a majority of the vote was wrong but he was otherwise correct. Six months after the general election, Conservative Central Office in London interpreted the limited data available to it as suggesting that the Tories had continued to fall.

Younger was more emollient than Taylor. He was the kind of Scottish Tory that Taylor had railed against in the past. His family had been in the brewing business for seven generations and involved at the highest level in Tory politics for years. The first Viscount Younger had been MP for Ayr from 1906 to 1922, the seat that his great-grandson would represent while serving as Margaret Thatcher's Scottish Secretary. Younger's style differed markedly from that of the Prime Minister and his more consensual approach might have been expected to create difficulties but he was a loyalist in the mould of Willie Whitelaw, Mrs Thatcher's Deputy Prime Minister until he retired in 1988. Younger adopted the traditional role of Scottish Secretary: Scotland's man in the Cabinet and the Cabinet's man in Scotland. She trusted him as her campaign manager when she was challenged for the leadership and premiership in 1990. Younger served as Scottish Secretary from 1979 until 1985, the longest continuous serving Scottish Secretary since Lord Balfour of Burleigh at the end of the nineteenth century. He was succeeded by Malcolm Rifkind, with whom Mrs Thatcher had a more difficult relationship. When John Major succeeded Mrs Thatcher he appointed Ian Lang, a close colleague, to the post before appointing Michael Forsyth in 1995.

The Tories had been in power before without a majority amongst Scottish MPs. Few Tories thought that this would be a problem after 1979. They interpreted the events of spring 1979 as showing that the Scots had never been serious about devolution. The Scots might huff and puff but would always withdraw from support for devolution. This perception would weaken the Scottish lobby immeasurably but also lead the Tories into a false sense of security. In 1978, John Mackintosh, political scientist and Labour MP, looked to the future in one of his last columns in the *Scotsman* shortly before he died:

> To put it at its simplest, the best conceivable conditions for a massive revival of the SNP would be a Conservative Government which faced, but could not handle, Britain's endemic economic problems and which clearly did not give a fig for Scottish affairs; which put a stopper on all the plans and hopes that have been built up around the prospect of a Scottish Assembly.

Nevil Johnson, Mrs Thatcher's constitutional adviser, viewed this analysis as 'apocalyptic' in the wake of the 1979 referendum. Teddy Taylor had been arguing for some time that the vote would be close while many in his party had expected a clear majority for devolution. This gave his interpretation authority.

The Conservatives had won a majority across the country and, as far as the government was concerned, it did not matter that they were a minority in Scotland. Strictly speaking that was true but it mattered politically. In 1990, Mrs Thatcher insisted that:

> We have had a socialist government in the United Kingdom which did not have
> a majority in England...We did not complain, because we believe in the United
> Kingdom and I still believe that each and every part of the United Kingdom has
> done far better by being a United Kingdom.

Given the nature of the UK constitution, the question was at what point a
political problem might become a constitutional problem. In July, the government repealed the devolution legislation in accordance with the 40 per
cent rule and kept its manifesto commitment to hold talks. These would not
be the constitutional convention that Francis Pym had made speeches about
when he was Tory devolution spokesman. Norman St John Stevas, as Leader
of the House of Commons, proposed that new Select Committees should be
established which would shadow government departments. A Scottish Select
Affairs Committee was included. As the Tories declined in Scotland, it became
difficult to find Scottish Tories to sit on the committee especially as the few
remaining backbenchers felt that the committee was being used by the opposition to attack the government. Between 1987 and 1992 the committee was
suspended only to be reconstituted in 1992 with English Tories making up the
numbers and agreement that Labour should appoint its chair.

Conservative support declined towards the end of 1979 but dramatically
so in Scotland. By the spring of 1981, research conducted for the party drew
a picture of a party with a particular Scottish problem. Phrases used by the
public to describe the Conservatives in Scotland were listed: having very few
Scots in its top ranks; not understanding the problems of Scotland; the party
of landowners; the party of the small businessman; respected abroad; not
being the traditional Scottish party; not having Scotland's interests at heart;
not caring for ordinary people; standing up to the trade unions. In April 1981,
Michael Ancram, the Scottish party chairman, wrote a note expressing concern. The Tories were polling at 17 per cent, 'our lowest level ever', and opinion
was starting to show 'real movement to the SNP'. Unemployment was seen 'by
a long way' as the most important problem facing the government in Scotland.
He warned that that the government were 'politically vulnerable in Scotland
to an economic recovery South of the Border not reflected at least in part in
the North'. Devolution could become an issue again: 'We must continue to
recognise the causes and demonstrate that Scotland is not losing out. The concept of George Younger as fighting for Scotland (almost "troublesome") within
the Government would be useful.' Devolution was still an issue though 'fairly
dormant despite considerable airing at the recent Scottish Labour conference'.
He was concerned that this issue would re-emerge at the next election and
proposed 'cosmetic moves' such as allowing the Scottish Grand Committee
to meet in Edinburgh and again stressed that it would help to portray the
Secretary of State as 'fighting Scotland's corner in Cabinet, almost how "troublesome" he is'.

One cause of relief for the Conservatives in the early years in power was that they were not always the target of criticism. In March 1981, a survey conducted for the Conservatives showed that the Scottish electorate blamed the 'Common Market' slightly more than the 'Government in London' for the economic problems facing Scotland and the 'world economic condition' just behind the government. While most Conservative voters consented to the government's view that the trade unions were primarily to blame, this was not the view of the Scottish public. It was only amongst Tory supporters that much blame was given to the previous Labour government. Those who did blame the government in London were evenly divided between those who thought this was because the government was based in London and those who thought it was due to a Conservative government. But while the EEC was blamed there was then little appetite for withdrawal. The Conservatives may have been wrong to take any comfort in these findings as they may simply have reflected Scotland's support for the Labour Party at the time. Labour had adopted its 'Alternative Economic Strategy', which had involved withdrawal from the EEC.

Even in opposition, Younger had been aware of a tendency amongst his senior colleagues to dismiss any Scottish dimension. In late 1978, Younger attended a Shadow Cabinet meeting where the dispersal of civil service jobs to Scotland was debated. Dispersal had been proposed as a means of tackling centralization over many years. The Conservatives had argued for dispersal of Ministry of Defence (MoD) workers to Glasgow and Cardiff and Overseas Development Ministry jobs to East Kilbride. Younger reported in his diary that he had to 'battle hard to avoid abandoning the dispersal altogether' and this only three months before the referendum. His colleagues were in a 'great panic about how many English marginals' would be in danger as there was no appetite for dispersal amongst staff involved. Younger reported a 'very anti-Scottish attitude' shown in the Shadow Cabinet and that no one had showed 'any sign of being sympathetic at first'. He reminded the Shadow Cabinet that the building site at St Enoch in Glasgow for the MoD was already under preparation. Mrs Thatcher's attitude was recorded: 'Mrs. T. said that if Scotland rejects the Assembly we would have to try to be as helpful as possible. But if Scotland chose an Assembly they would get nothing. That just shows the attitude of hostility we now have to counter.'

Dispersal arose again after the election. Iain Sproat, chair of the Scottish Tory Group of MPs, wrote to Mrs Thatcher's Parliamentary Private Secretary in July 1979 warning that failure to disperse jobs to Scotland would be 'absolutely ruinous for the credibility of the new Scottish Office' and that 'having beaten and all but killed off the SNP, this one decision going wrong could light the Nationalist fire all over again'. Sproat had been one of the leading opponents of devolution and came as close as any Tory MP to being an integrationist Unionist. But he recognized the need to acknowledge that policies would be viewed through a Scottish prism. Even he was not averse to playing the Scottish card and using the possible threat of the rise of the SNP.

In 1980, attempts by Standard Chartered Bank and Hong Kong Shanghai Bank (HKSB) to take over the Royal Bank of Scotland met strong opposition. Chrysler's car plant at Linwood in Renfrewshire was closed that year. Invergordon aluminium smelter in the Highlands was closed in 1981. In each case the Scottish Secretary was expected to stand up for Scottish interests. The government's view was that takeovers should only be blocked if they resulted in monopolies and the proposed mergers were referred to the Monopolies and Mergers Commission (MMC). The HKSB bid was blocked because it was not a British-based bank. The explanation in the MMC report for the rejection of Standard Chartered was the 'Scottish ring fence', that Scotland required special protection to ensure a banking sector was maintained north of the border. The Scottish Office, STUC, SCDI, the *Scotsman* and the *Glasgow Herald*, and all political parties opposed the takeover. As Geoffrey Jones noted in his history of British multi-national banking, the episode was full of ironies, amongst them being that Scots had played a significant role in international and exchange banking. On coming to power in 1979, the government had removed exchange controls which strengthened the role of the City of London in world financial markets. British nationalism had led to the rejection of the HKSB bid and Scottish nationalism had led to the rejection of Standard Chartered's bid. The government had decided against propping up failing industries but the Scottish Office, sitting in the heart of Whitehall, was playing a full part in doing what it could to protect these industries. As Scots believed that the UK government had little sympathy for campaigns to support these businesses, the Scottish Office would get little credit for its activities. But while the Scottish lobby succeeded in protecting the RBS, it was unsuccessful in saving Linwood or Invergordon.

Over 25,000 people were employed in steel in Scotland in 1974 but this had fallen to under 12,000 by 1982. In 1982, Ravenscraig steel strip mill was threatened with closure. The Scottish lobby rallied in its defence. Younger let it be known through private press briefings that he would resign if Ravenscraig was allowed to close. It was reprieved. Defending the Scottish steel industry became a measure of commitment to Scotland. Failure to pronounce in its defence was deemed anti-Scottish. But it did Younger few favours. He was expected to stand up for a Scottish interest and it was his government that was blamed for it being under threat. An added dimension arose with the miners' strike in 1984/5. The National Union of Mineworkers (NUM) wanted to maximize pressure on the government by blocking coal going into Ravenscraig. The problem was that halting the twenty-four-hour use of the blast furnaces and coke ovens would create cracks and endanger the plant. The 'Triple Alliance' of miners and railway and steel workers had been important in past industrial actions but was shattered. Mrs Thatcher would later add insult to injury, as the steel workers saw it, by thanking them in her battles with the NUM.

But while Ravenscraig was reprieved, Gartcosh finishing mill closed. Opposition politicians and trade unions portrayed the Tories as an alien force governing Scotland against the will of the majority. Sir Hector Monro, chair of the Scottish Tory backbench committee, was amongst a small number of Scottish Conservatives to oppose the closure provoking a backlash against him from right-wing Tories. Mrs Thatcher accepted that the decision to save Ravenscraig had to take the Scottish Question into account. In his revisionist history of Thatcherism in Scotland, David Torrance quotes the Prime Minister, 'There is a Scottish dimension as well as a steel dimension.' But that did not extend to Gartcosh. The final decision to close Gartcosh was taken in December 1985. A long campaign had been waged for its retention. Iain Lawson, chairman of the Scottish Conservative candidates' body, resigned from the party and joined the SNP after taking part in a march from Gartcosh to Parliament. Steel, coal, and shipbuilding had been shedding jobs. Old industrial Scotland was disappearing. The perception was that Thatcherite policies were being imposed on Scotland by a government with little and declining support. Steel was privatized in 1988. If the government hoped that this meant that it would not be implicated in any future decisions about Ravenscraig they were mistaken. Malcolm Rifkind was now Scottish Secretary and he let it be known that he opposed the decision to close Ravenscraig.

Mrs Thatcher visited Scotland frequently during her time in office. Her annual speech at the Scottish Tory conference was invariably well prepared and followed a standard pattern of praise for the Scottish Office team, hinting at how troublesome they could be, setting out the achievements of her government illustrated wherever possible with Scottish examples and outlining the dangers that the Opposition parties posed. She was keen, especially in later years, to invoke Scottish thinkers who could in any way be associated with Thatcherism. Adam Smith was a favourite, partly due to the influence of the Adam Smith Institute which had its own idiosyncratic interpretation of Adam Smith's work. But initially she was wary of some Scottish institutions, turning down invitations in her early years to attend the annual General Assembly of the Church of Scotland. In 1982, she declined an invitation from Sir John Gilmour, former Tory MP for East Fife who was Lord High Commissioner to the General Assembly, the sovereign's representative at the Assembly. She replied that with an election pending it was 'always a risk that any action of mine is presented as having a political motive, and I would not for the world want my presence at the General assembly to have any such interpretation put upon it'.

But Mrs Thatcher had no such concerns later. Over the next year she embarked on an ill-fated charm offensive following the 1987 election when the party lost half its seats in Scotland. She addressed the Scottish Tory conference arguing that Scotland had 'invented Thatcherism' long before she had been born. Scottish values of 'hard work, self-reliance, thrift, enterprise—the relishing of challenges, the seizing of opportunities' were shared in common by Scotland and the Conservatives. She made reference to four nineteenth-century entrepreneurs—Andrew Carnegie, James Watt, John McAdam, and Alexander Graham Bell. The Enlightenment philosophers Adam Ferguson, David Hume, and Adam Smith were invoked in the name of Thatcherism. Ferguson is often regarded as the 'founder of sociology', the study of society, a subject with which Mrs Thatcher had problems. Her intended meaning on the subject has subsequently been disputed, but the words she used are beyond dispute and the meaning assumed by many commentators was not in doubt at the time. Hume's *Treatise on Human Nature* included the claim that politics 'consider men as united in society, and dependent on each other'. At the very least, none of these thinkers can be unambiguously placed on the right or left, concepts that were alien to their day.

Margaret Thatcher was not the first Prime Minister to attend the Kirk's Assembly but hers was a blatant attempt to appeal to the Scots via a distinct Scottish institution. Her speech was poorly pitched, with references to scripture used to justify Thatcherism. She quoted St Paul's letter to the Thessalonians, 'If a man will not work he shall not eat', ignoring the context of Paul's letter, as theologians would later point out. Paul, they maintained, had been chastising parasitic preachers living off those who were least well off. One standard interpretation of the passage, published almost two decades before and not a response to Mrs Thatcher's interpretation, was explicit, 'It certainly does not refer to those who cannot, through incapacity, work nor those for whom no work is available.' It was crass, desperate, and ill-advised, and it backfired. The official Kirk response was to present Mrs Thatcher with two reports that had been commissioned some time before. These were unambiguous criticisms of her government's housing and social policies in Scotland. When one of the Kirk's most distinguished and respected former Moderators who had no known party affiliation criticized the speech, it was dismissed by Nicholas Fairbairn, the flamboyant Tory MP for Perth and Kinross, as from a 'socialist animal, totally uninterested in Christian duty'. Mrs Thatcher's defenders did not know when to stop digging. The Kirk had become an arch-critic of the Tories, though it was unclear whether this reflected the views of the dwindling members on the pews each week or the liberal establishment that had come to dominate Kirk decision-making at its annual General Assemblies.

Two years later, as her time as Prime Minister was drawing to an end, Margaret Thatcher was interviewed by Kirsty Wark, by then the leading Scottish broadcast political journalist in Scotland. The advice and tactics used by Mrs Thatcher were transparent as attempts to associate herself with Scotland. But frequent references to 'we in Scotland' were mocked. Robert Armstrong, her Cabinet Secretary, suggested that she possessed a 'very English Englishness'. This did not disqualify her to be Prime Minister of the UK. Stanley Baldwin, one of her Tory predecessors as Prime Minister, had not raised a Scottish eyebrow when he addressed the Royal Society of St George in 1924 stating that he was profoundly grateful that he could use the word 'England' 'without some fellow at the back of the room shouting out "Britain"'. His deep sense of being English never caused offence in Scotland, partly no doubt because it would be little remarked upon— but that in itself was a key change that occurred. Mrs Thatcher had a deep sense of being English, but her attempt to overcome this on visits to Scotland led to her over-compensating, inviting disbelief or ridicule. Her problems would be mirrored seventeen years later when Gordon Brown became Prime Minister.

A MAJOR OPPORTUNITY LOST

Mrs Thatcher's resignation as Prime Minister and leader of the Conservative Party in 1990 had little to do with her lack of support in Scotland. Public oppo- sition to the poll tax combined with disaffection amongst a growing number of senior former colleagues to encourage Michael Heseltine to challenge her for the leadership. John Major only became a member of the Cabinet in 1987 and held office as Chief Secretary to the Treasury, Foreign Secretary, and Chancellor of the Exchequer in rapid succession. He had few dealings with Scottish affairs prior to becoming Prime Minister. He had served in the Whip's office along- side Scottish Tory Ian Lang, who would form part of his campaign team for the party leadership after Mrs Thatcher stood aside. Mr Major's only minis- terial post before joining the Cabinet had been as Minister for Social Security, an office in which the Scottish Question would rarely have been encountered. He presented only one budget in his brief time as Chancellor of the Exchequer. In an attempt to address opposition to the poll tax, he announced a meas- ure designed to limit its impact. However, the announcement proposed no retrospective assistance to take account of the introduction of the poll tax in Scotland a year ahead of England, feeding the impression that the government was insensitive to Scotland. Mrs Thatcher's view was that this ought to have been noticed in Cabinet by Scottish Secretary Malcolm Rifkind.

Mr Major was still then her favourite minister, which helped him when he stood for the leadership but had little impact on how Scots saw him. Early indications were that the Scottish public were willing to give him a chance to prove he was different from his predecessor. Expectations had built up that the Conservatives would lose more seats, possibly all seats, at the 1992 election. In the event, the Tories had a minor recovery. The only seat to change hands was Aberdeen South, which the Tories regained from Labour. The Tories increased their share of the vote by 1.6 per cent of the vote across Scotland. Bob McLean of Scottish Labour Action, a strongly pro-home-rule group within the Labour Party, had coined the term 'Doomsday Scenario', referring to Scotland becom- ing a 'Tory-free zone' while the Tories won across Britain. There had been mounting speculation on the constitutional implications of the scenario. Measured against these expectations, the modest recovery in Tory fortunes was interpreted as a great breakthrough. The Prime Minister had announced that he would 'take stock' of the Scottish situation after the election. There was speculation in the media, as much in hope as in anticipation, that this would lead to a U-turn on devolution. Mr Major was happy to encourage this speculation as it gave the impression of a fresh start and an open mind. Instead the government issued a White Paper, *Scotland in the Union—A Partnership for Good*, in 1993. In its introduction, the Prime Minister stated that 'no nation could be held irrevocably in the Union against its will' and acknowledged that Scotland's place in the union had evolved over time. It was a celebration of old-style pluralist unionism, similar to the Attlee government's White Paper on Scottish Affairs and offered too little, too late. It marked a change in style if not substance. The party remained resolute in its opposition to devolution. But it required some means of demonstrating its Scottish credentials.

In July 1995, Michael Forsyth became Scottish Secretary. Forsyth was the most Thatcherite of the Scottish Secretaries but he proved loyal to John Major, even when Mrs Thatcher dropped strong hints that she was disappointed in her successor. Forsyth was a graduate of the University of St Andrews and had been a Westminster City Councillor and worked in public relations. He became MP for Stirling in 1983 and occasionally stood out as a lone Thatcher loyalist within the group of Scottish Tories. He was the only Scottish Tory MP to have argued openly for Gartcosh's closure in 1985. He showed little respect for Scottish sensibilities in his first years in Parliament but embraced John Major's efforts to engage more positively with Scotland. A kilt-wearing Forsyth attended the Scottish premiere of *Braveheart*, Hollywood's interpretation of William Wallace who had fought in the wars of Scottish independence in the thirteenth century. But his most audacious initiative was to return the Stone of Destiny to Scotland in an effort to reposition the governing party. Forsyth had become a fervent Scot. But it came over much as Mrs Thatcher had in her repetition of 'we in Scotland'. It played into the hands of home rulers and nationalists. The return of this 'hunk of sandstone', the description used by the student who led the expedition to remove it from the Coronation Throne in 1950, received the full paraphernalia of a military escort and even a handover ceremony at the Anglo-Scottish border. Various dignitaries dressed in Highland garb attended its arrival after a procession up the Royal Mile in Edinburgh. Sir Walter Scott would have been proud. But it did nothing to stem the loss of Tory support. Quite a few in the crowd in Edinburgh in July 1996 would be present three years later to witness the procession of new Members of the Scottish Parliament, which the Stone's return was supposed to stop happening.

In the run-up to the 1997 general election, there had been little speculation on the prospect of a Tory wipe-out in Scotland. This partly reflected the expectation that Labour would win but was partly because home rule hopes had been shattered in 1992 when the demise of the Tories in Scotland had not happened. But no Scottish Tory MP was left standing at the end of the count. The same happened in Wales and across Britain the Tories lost 178 seats. There had been a smaller swing from the Conservatives to Labour in Scotland than in England but there had been far fewer voters to swing away from the Tories in Scotland to start with. The election signalled the beginning of a new phase in Scottish and British politics.

LOCAL GOVERNMENT AND THATCHERISM

The Scottish Office assumed a primary function in the provision and fund-ing of services delivered by local authorities. It acted as a conduit through which money from the Treasury was spent by local authorities on such matters as education and housing. The relationship between the Scottish Office and local government needed to be close. There were tensions, as would exist in any system of inter-governmental relations. These tensions had been exacer-bated when local authorities and the Scottish Office were ideologically out of step with each other and especially when money was tight. While Labour had become the largest party at local level across Scotland there were significant authorities which were under Tory control in 1979. In local elections in 1980, the Tories lost control of Edinburgh, though they remained the largest party on the council, but retained control of six other district councils. In 1982, the Tories controlled Grampian and Tayside Regional Councils, had the same number of councillors as Labour in Lothian, and had 119 of Scotland's 440 councillors. But the party's support in local government shrank over the eight-een years the party was in government in London. The combination of few councillors, sharp policy, and ideological differences and a period of severe cuts in local authority budgets soured the relationship between central and local government.

One of the key policies in the Conservative manifesto in 1979 had been the sale of council houses to sitting tenants. Many councils had been poor landlords, paying little attention to tenants' views, creating disaffected families only too willing to buy their home. The 'right to buy' was a popular policy and Scotland's housing market was transformed over the course of her premiership. But what perplexed the Tories was that it paid no electoral dividends. Tenants became owner-occupiers against the wishes of Labour-controlled councils, many of which were as uncooperative as the law permitted in implementing the new legislative rights of tenants. Tenants were qualified to buy their house if they had lived in it for three years and were given a minimum discount of a third of its purchase price increasing by 1 per cent for each year to a maximum of half its value after twenty years. They had a right of a loan from the local authority to the value of 100 per cent of the purchase price. It was a very generous deal and the generosity was extended in subsequent years. This created tensions with local authorities but the public liked the policy, as measured by the numbers who took advantage of this new 'right'. The policy evolved over time to include different types of houses and the incentives to buy improved. As well as very generous incentives or 'bribes' as critics put it, cuts in housing support grant left local authorities with less money to service the dwindling stock of houses while retaining the debt incurred in building the houses in the first place. The local authorities were obliged to sell the houses but kept the debt. The joke would be told in housing circles in the mid-1980s that the last tenant would be living in the worst house after all others were sold and paying rent of millions of pounds to service the local government housing debt.

Until after the 1987 election, the government had a tenure rather than a housing policy in Scotland. It was social engineering in pursuit of rolling back social engineering. The consequences of the tenure policy were spelled out in the report the Church of Scotland gave to Margaret Thatcher after she addressed the General Assembly. The government knew little about the existing stock of houses as it refused to conduct a house conditional survey to get the kind of basic information necessary to develop a housing policy. Sales had 'residualized' council housing though neither side of the debate wanted to concede this. Labour local authorities insisted that council houses remained housing for a wide spectrum of society, not just the poorest and the government denied that it was pushing the poorest to the margins of society. Scotland became less distinct in its structure of housing tenure.

From 1987, the Conservatives started to develop an urban policy in Scotland that incorporated a housing policy beyond its focus on tenure. There were two motivations behind this. The first was that its tenure policy had reached its limits and there remained parts of Scotland, especially in some of the large post-1945 housing estates in Glasgow, Edinburgh, Paisley, and Dundee that required attention. There was also a British dimension. As the results of the 1987 election came in and it was clear that Mrs Thatcher was heading for another large majority, she stood on the steps of party headquarters to thank party workers and then announced, 'We must do something about those inner cities.' Many of England's inner cities had become no-go areas for the Tories, much more hostile to the party than Scotland. In 1981 and in 1985, a number had experienced serious unrest. Mrs Thatcher's attention had turned to this though other matters were to intrude and prevented her paying as much attention as she had intended. Nonetheless, in common with other Whitehall departments, the Scottish Office began to focus on a number of places which had long suffered from social and economic decline. This was done in relative harmony with the relevant local authorities. Lessons were still being learned and resources were limited when she left office but *Renewing Urban Scotland* was the beginning of a new more consensual phase.

The Scottish Special Housing Association (SSHA), established in 1937, had initially been exempt from the right to buy but was eventually included. The SSHA had been the Scottish Office's means of by-passing local authorities and building using non-traditional methods. It built houses across Scotland which proved highly popular. A network of housing associations had grown up in parts of Scotland. These were administered and partly financed through the Housing Corporation, a body set up in 1964 with Britain-wide responsibilities. A storm in January 1968 had caused massive damage to properties across Scotland and brought the state of the private rented sector to the attention of decision-makers at local and Scottish levels. It became clear that the best option in tacking problems resulting from the storm was rehabilitation and the use of housing associations. A freak of nature had given birth to a major policy innovation. The Housing Association movement offered an alternative to both municipal housing and renting from private landlords. This sector broadened its focus to include environmental and wider community improvements. After the 1987 election, the Conservatives merged the work of the SSHA and Housing Corporation in Scotland to create Scottish Homes. Resources were channelled into these community-based associations. Many housing professionals were suspicious of the move and some feared that this was all part of a Thatcherite ideological game-plan though it soon became clear that this was Thatcherism as pragmatism.

Education had long been seen as a policy area that set Scotland apart. Scottish 16–18-year-old school children studied O Grades and Highers rather than the O Levels and A Levels studied elsewhere in the UK. But some differences were more symbolic, including the language used. A 'public school' in Scotland referred to a state school whereas it referred to a fee-paying school in England. Fee-paying schools were called 'private schools', and a far lower proportion of Scots were educated in the Scottish private sector—though Edinburgh was like a little piece of England in this respect. The main divide in the Scottish system was between 'denominational' (essentially Catholic) and 'non-denominational' schools. All parties accepted this binary system. The battleground between the parties as far as education policy was concerned had long been class-based. Given Scottish educational myths, this tended to play into Labour's hands. The Thatcher government introduced an Assisted Places Scheme which provided assistance to less well-off families to send children to fee-paying schools. Opponents argued that the scheme was both socially divisive and irrelevant, or a policy designed for Edinburgh. The scheme had a limited impact. But the policy was opposed by the Educational Institute of Scotland (EIS), one of the few remaining Scottish trade unions that had not become part of a larger UK-wide union. The teachers' union was well versed in using the Scottish tradition in education in its armoury. John Pollock, EIS general secretary, had come a long way from his days when he had argued against devolution before the Royal

Commission on the Constitution, and was adept in playing the Scottish card in negotiations. EIS members voted to strike in 1984/5 in support of a pay deal and targeted ministers. An inquiry set up by the Scottish Office reported in 1986 which proposed changes in pay and conditions for Scottish teachers. However, the Treasury baulked at the costs involved, recognizing that the increase in pay would be demanded by teachers across the UK. Scottish ministers' failure to take this into account meant that they had forgotten the well-established practice of considering the potential implications for the rest of the UK of any policy initiative.

Michael Forsyth's appointment as junior Scottish Office Minister responsible for education in 1987 intensified already poor relations between the Scottish Office, local authorities, and teachers' unions. Mr Forsyth proposed to introduce a system of school boards, allowing schools to opt out of local authority control, involving greater teacher appraisal and devolved school management as well as removing further education colleges from local authority control. Taken together these amounted to a much bolder approach than hitherto which provoked accusations that this was 'Englishing of Scottish education', as described in EIS adverts placed in the Scottish press. The policies found limited support and did not have the support that the right to buy had had, leaving a strong impression that the Scottish Office was not performing its traditional role in looking after Scottish interests.

SCOTTISH PUBLIC SPENDING

The Scottish Office could not escape the public expenditure cuts imposed across Whitehall departments in the early 1980s. In November 1979, Mrs Thatcher scribbled a comment on a letter from the Scottish Office about an announcement on rate support grant, 'I didn't know Scotland had *quite* such preferential treatment.' The Scottish Secretary was coming under pressure from Cabinet colleagues and other parts of Whitehall to come into line. In the past, the Office's budget had been determined through negotiations with the Treasury on a function by function basis in which the Scottish Office had been the junior partner alongside equivalent spending departments. The Treasury would, for example, negotiate the amount to be spent on education in discussions with the English Department of Education with the Scottish Office as a bit player. Spending was largely determined by how much the Education Department could wring out of the Treasury, with the Scottish Office making claims for special treatment, i.e. more money, wherever it could. This happened across the range of Scottish Office functions. On occasion, the Scottish Office had been able to make the case for some special item of spending, such as affecting the Highlands, so long as it could convince the Treasury that this would not provoke similar demands across the state. The Scottish Office budget was the aggregate of each of these spending lines. It had autonomy to prioritize within this budget and did not have to spend money that had been allocated for education entirely on education. It had the power to vire money across budget lines. This was a power that Willie Ross had been keen to protect but also to keep relatively quiet about, to prevent provoking unwelcome inquiries.

However, that system changed in the late 1970s before the Conservatives came to office. With the backdrop of cuts in public spending that the Labour government was forced to make following the IMF loan, the government sought a means of determining Scottish Office budgets that limited lobbying and put it on a more rational decision-making basis. The prospect of devolution made it more attractive to put the determination of the Scottish Assembly's budget on such a basis. There had been occasions when new spending lines had been developed and a decision had to be made as to how much should be allocated to the different parts of the UK. A paper by a Treasury official in January 1974 explained how this was done:

> For some services, notably health and the personal social services, there are very few objectively defined standards for the provision of services, and significant differences in the levels of provision. Present policy is designed to ensure that the growth rates in England, Scotland and Wales are broadly comparable, and that additional expenditures on reduced allocations are calculated on a population basis (85 England, 10 Scotland, 5 Wales).

This arrangement was used in determining cuts across a wide range of services in spending in the late 1970s.

The formula was what would subsequently be called the Barnett formula. In 1980, Professor David Heald was the first academic to describe it. As it was the direct descendant of the Goschen formula and all formulae 'need a name', according to Heald, he had named it after Joel Barnett, the Chief Secretary of the Treasury in the late 1970s. Barnett had, in fact, played no part in its design though he was vaguely aware of it. In reply to inquiries about the formula in 1985, before it had attained the contentious status that it later had, Barnett admitted:

> I was aware of what you describe as the 'Barnett Formula' but I had not been aware that the particular formula has been thought of as my special creation. My understanding is that the allocations in the proportions of England 85 per cent, Scotland 10 per cent, and Wales 5 per cent, is a fairly long standing formula that has been used over many years before I became Chief Secretary to the Treasury. All I can tell you is that the formula was indeed used during the whole of my period in office and to the best of my knowledge and belief is still being used.

In fact, it was only used extensively in the latter part of his period as Chief Secretary.

The Barnett formula has subsequently gained totemic status and in more ways than the Goschen formula. Goschen was raised in debates in Parliament and the Scottish press, but Barnett assumed importance well beyond Scotland and was used as evidence that Scotland received more than its fair share in spending. This was done by reference to a Needs Assessment Study (NAS), conducted by the Labour government to provide a basis for understanding Scotland's relative needs when devolution looked likely. Barnett was a step towards a more rational basis for determining spending levels, especially cuts which were more troublesome than increases. It was somewhat arbitrary but it reduced the horse-trading that had previously occurred. The NAS made Barnett controversial. Whether Scottish Office spending had been determined by formula or by horse-trading was less relevant than that the outcome appeared to favour Scotland when needs were considered. The NAS provided ammunition to those who argued that Scotland was treated favourably. Other factors contributed to the controversies which subsequently surrounded Barnett. Debate on Scotland's constitutional status brought an issue that would otherwise have attracted little attention outside Scotland to the attention of politicians and media in other parts of the UK.

In private communication in 1985, Jim Ross, a senior Scottish Office civil servant in the late 1970s, outlined its key characteristics:

> The purpose of Barnett was both to simplify the Treasury's bargaining processes and to ensure that, when increases in Votes were negotiated, the total Scottish increase over all Votes should be no more than a reasonable one. The 10/85 formula was intended gradually to reduce the then existing Scottish advantage in terms of public expenditure without creating a degree of disturbance that would have created a row...In other words, the Barnett formula established a new pattern of negotiation between the Treasury and Departments, a pattern which had already been partly in operation but which was legitimated by Barnett. The Treasury settled with the main English Departments what alterations were to be made in the various functional Votes. The total Scottish Votes were then altered by the formula, and it was left to the Secretary of State to sort out the balance within the Scottish Votes.

The formula's dynamic property had been to reduce Scotland's advantage gradually. David Heald showed how this would work in his early work on the formula. But this was too gradual for the Treasury after 1979. The intention of quietly reducing Scottish advantage was made extremely difficult once Younger had announced the formula's existence. After that had happened, both defenders and critics of the Scottish Office's share of public expenditure would interpret the formula in whatever way suited their purpose.

The previous year's allocation was taken as the basis for negotiation. Negotiations then focused on increases or cuts to this base. After a decision was made on any change in English functional spending (or English and

Welsh where appropriate), Scotland would receive the equivalent proportion. If the English health budget was cut or raised by £X, then Scotland's allocation would be cut or raised by 10 per cent of £X (or 10/85 if the main change affected England and Wales). The formula was used inconsistently and, in common with public finance in general at this time, lacked transparency. It excluded agriculture, fisheries, forestry, and most of trade, industry, energy, and employment expenditure. But the inconsistency in its application meant there remained scope for further negotiations. The Scottish Office attempted to take advantage of the grey areas not covered by the formula. This created some tensions. In July 1980, the Chief Secretary to the Treasury proposed an extra reduction of £150 million a year in planned Scottish programmes on the grounds that there was evidence that the share of expenditure per head of population was higher in Scotland than in Wales and England. Only £60 million was proposed under the formula and a further £90 million cut was needed 'on account of need', according to the Treasury. According to the NAS, Scotland received £300 million more than its needs suggested. It was this £90 million that Younger objected to and he raised the issue in Cabinet. The Treasury also noted that there were parts of England, 'particularly in the North, which regarded themselves as at a marked disadvantage by comparison with the benefits now flowing to Scotland'. Younger told the Cabinet that the methodology in the NAS had been 'suspect' and even if accepted it would be 'highly damaging to announce additional cuts in Scottish programmes'. He was prepared to accept additional cuts but it was 'important that they should not be seen as discriminatory' but accepted that Scotland's share of spending per head was significantly higher than in the north of England. In October, he presented a paper to Cabinet setting out his case for avoiding deep cuts while working within the formula:

> I will of course make the formula based reductions flowing from whatever decisions we take on comparable English programmes. I see no reason why the Scottish Office should not make its full contribution to the economies we all have to make. However to go even further by discriminating against Scotland only would be to invite political disaster, and I cannot agree to it.

He warned that to make cuts

> over and above those determined by the formula would be utterly disastrous politically. Such a decision would be clearly seen in Scotland and by all Opposition parties as a deliberate act of policy directed against Scotland, and I would be hard put to explain it, let alone defend it, to our own supporters. No-one in Scotland will accept the NAS as valid evidence. I myself told the Select Committee on Scottish Affairs (with Treasury agreement) in July that the NAS could not be used for this purpose. Nor could I justify the imposition on Scottish services under my control of cuts far in excess of the level of cuts to be made on comparable services in England. Such a decision would utterly destroy cur credibility in Scotland and

would be handing the Scottish National Party precisely the issue they have been looking for.

Younger complained that the additional cuts had been made without for-mal or informal warning. He had provided cover for his defence of Scottish Office spending by gaining Treasury approval to inform the Scottish Affairs Committee of the formula that was used. Younger pointed out that the NAS had been completed in anticipation of the establishment of an Assembly and the need for an 'arm's length relationship between the UK Government and the Assembly'. He maintained that he and others had been concerned that Scotland would do less well financially and that any proposal to use the NAS in calculating Scotland's share of spending undermined what opponents of devolution had said. He anticipated cuts of 11 per cent but what was being proposed would amount to 18 per cent and this was 'impracticable' given manifesto commitments. He warned that it would be impossible to make cuts of this scale by stealth due to public knowledge of the formula and the 'close interest shown by the Scottish Select Committee and Scottish press'. Such cuts would be seen as Scotland taking 'debilitating medicine not prescribed for any other part of the UK'.

Agreement was finally reached on the Scottish Office allocation in November and was the last agreed by Cabinet. The Scottish Secretary accepted the for-mula cuts plus £10 million for 1981–2 and agreed to consider the practicality of increasing savings to £20 million in 1982–3 and £30 million in 1983–4 after he repeated his warning that abandoning the formula and seeking greater cuts 'coming only eighteen months after the referendum which led to the with-drawal of devolution proposals would destroy the Government's credibility in Scotland'. This was private acknowledgement of something the Conservatives denied in public. They had publicly maintained that they had not withdrawn devolution proposals but had offered talks. The Prime Minister was quoted in the Cabinet minutes saying that they had 'reluctantly accepted the politi-cal arguments put forward by the Secretary of State against the proposed cut of £90 million' but that further savings might be offered in health and other services.

There was little interest in relative levels of spending across the UK during periods of growth but there was much interest in relative positions in a period of public expenditure retrenchment. So long as all gained, few cared that one part of the state gained more than others. In letting it be known that a formula existed, Younger had opened a crack allowing a small degree of transparency into how spending was determined. It was enough to attract attention but too little to allow for a full understanding either of how the formula worked or whether Scotland was treated favourably.

The Scottish Office had one advantage shared with the Department of the Environment. It could pass cuts on to local government. The Scottish Office was caught between the Treasury and local authorities and found itself in conflict with both. In 1981, Leon Brittan, as Chief Secretary to the Treasury, wrote to George Younger insisting that the Scottish Office had to have an 'approach for Scottish local authorities consistent with that adopted by Michael Heseltine for English local authorities'. Brittan felt that Younger's response had been 'weaker' than expected and this would undermine what Heseltine was doing in England. Local authorities in Scotland had 'overspent' in the previous year. The Scottish Office already has considerable powers but within a few years these were increased, summarized well in a document produced by the Convention of Scottish Local Authorities (CoSLA):

> There have been rapid moves towards greater central control over local expenditure and hence policies. Prior to the passing of the 1981 Act, central government had been content to use measures aimed at influencing the aggregate level of local expenditure. The 1981 Act enabled central government to control the total level of expenditure of individual authorities. The new Bill now gives central government powers to control the detailed expenditure of individual authorities.

The Scottish Secretary referred to local government spending as being like a 'runaway train'. Scotland was seen as a 'test bed for the Government's offensive against local authority spending', according to the *Financial Times* in late 1981. The Conservatives hoped to portray their actions as protecting local government from spendthrift Labour-controlled authorities. But voters turned increasingly to Labour instead. As the Tory retreat from local government continued, the Scottish Office's authority had to be imposed.

The prospect of devolution created considerable concerns amongst the newly established local authorities in the 1970s fearing that the Scottish Assembly would take powers from local government. It was unclear how Strathclyde Region, with over half Scotland's population would operate alongside the proposed Assembly. A shift occurred in local government thinking in the 1980s. The Scottish Assembly came to be seen as a potential ally. The Assembly would likely be of the same broad political complexion as local authorities. There was an added dimension.

The most controversial measure was the Abolition of Domestic Rates Etc (Scotland) Act, 1987, which replaced domestic rates with the community charge or 'poll tax', as it became commonly known, and removed local government's power to set the level of non-domestic rates. Its opponents accused the government of imposing a regressive measure on Scotland ahead of England against the wishes of the Scottish people. The reality was more complex. Local government was financed from a mixture of sources. Government grants had become an increasingly important element, thus giving the Scottish Office considerable control of local government, but also from charges for services and domestic and non-domestic rates. Rates were a form of property tax with each property's value determining how much was paid by the householder to the local authority. As property values changed over time, properties required periodic revaluation. In Scotland these had occurred at regular intervals—in 1971, 1978, and 1985—while the most recent in England had been in 1973. George Younger felt revaluation could no longer be postponed. Prevarication would simply lead to more pain later. Michael Heseltine decided to postpone the revaluation in England as this was bound to lead to increased rates demands on properties owned by (Conservative-voting) wealthier households. The revaluation went ahead in Scotland resulting in a predictable outcry from many Tory voters especially where property values had risen relatively higher than elsewhere. Delegates at the Scottish Conservative conference in 1985 reacted with undisguised fury against the government, an unusual sight at a Tory conference. This middle-class revolt led to the decision to abolish domestic rates and introduce the poll tax in its place. Rates had never been popular, especially with Tory voters, but it was generally seen as the least bad measure and changing the system was expected to create unintended and unexpected difficulties. There had been inquiries and discussion papers on alternatives, usually enough to satisfy critics of rates, but the extent of opposition in the Tory heartlands after six years of declining support from an already low base forced the government to act. While official inquiries had ruled out alternatives to domestic rates, right-wing thinkers championed the poll tax. Michael Forsyth wrote a paper, *The Case for the Poll Tax*, for the Conservative Political Centre. George Younger abandoned his normal calm conservatism and accepted the need for radical change. He was fortunate in leaving the Scottish Office to become Defence Secretary soon after his commitment to introduce the poll tax. It was left to Malcolm Rifkind to take responsibility.

While the focus was understandably on the regressive nature of the poll tax, another important feature of the legislation was the reduction in the amount of income which local authorities could raise themselves from about 60 to 25 per cent. But there was also a focus on its introduction a year ahead of England leading to accusations that Scotland was being treated as a guinea pig. The Act to replace domestic rates with the poll tax was given Royal Assent in the dying days of the 1983–7 Parliament. The poll tax loomed large in the 1987 election in Scotland, though less so south of the border. It would contribute to the loss of half the Tories' Scottish seats. The poll tax became a by-word for unfairness and imposing policies on Scotland against its will. Opinion mobilized against the poll tax and soon spilled over into supporting a Scottish Parliament. If the poll tax had been imposed on Scotland then the imposition came from middle-class Scots concerned about rates increases. There was no evidence that Mrs Thatcher or any other member of the government outside the Scottish Office had made any effort to impose the tax on Scotland. But the change could only have occurred because the Scottish Office was headed by politicians representing a minority view in Scotland. It was the culmination of a series of measures, policies, and general tenor that were interpreted by a growing body of opinion that Scotland was governed in a manner that did not serve the majority well.

The poll tax was unpopular throughout Britain. When this became clear, English Tory MPs became fearful for their seats. Mrs Thatcher's position had been weakened by the departure of a number of key figures from her government who asserted their opposition from the backbenches. There was never much doubt that John Major would move quickly to get rid of the poll tax. The poll tax became part of Scottish political folklore. It had mobilized communities as few campaigns had done in recent times but it also meant that many Scots disappeared, opting out of society by removing themselves from the electoral register and from many other public registers that they feared might lead them to having to pay the tax. The poll tax had been imposed on Scots by Scottish Tories and was by the actions of English Tories. The abolition of the poll tax involved a further diminution of locally raised income to around 14 per cent (and below 10 per cent in some cases).

It might have been thought that this episode would have dissuaded the Conservatives from further major changes in local government. But the new council tax, another property-based tax, did not remove the persistent problems they confronted with an even lower base of support in local government. The Conservatives fell behind the SNP in the 1992 District Council elections in vote share though they gained more council seats. They won 204 of 1,158 council wards with 23.2 per cent of the vote. Labour won 468 seats with 34 per cent of the vote. Plush Bearsden and Milngavie moved from being Tory-controlled to having no party in overall control. Two years later in regional elections, the Conservatives ended up with only thirty-one councillors with 13.1 per cent of the vote with the SNP winning twice as many votes and more than twice as many councillors. Labour won around half the council seats with 41.8 per cent of the vote. Not only were the Tories losing votes and seats but they controlled no regions and were moving perilously close to losing control of the few remaining local authorities they retained. The next major innovation was the wholesale reorganization of local government.

The Local Government etc. (Scotland) Act, 1994, radically altered the structure of Scottish local government but had not been preceded by anything approaching the long debates or consensus that predated the introduction of the two-tier system two decades before. The decision was announced in 1991 by the Secretary of State for Scotland and was followed by short consultations. The consultations were described by Alan Alexander, Scotland's leading academic authority on local government at the time, as the 'Henry Ford model of consultation: you can have any model of local government so long as it is unitary'. The new system kept the three island authorities and created twenty-nine unitary authorities. The Act establishing the new authorities empowered the Secretary of State rather than the independent Local Government Boundary Commission to decide on the boundaries of the new authorities, fuelling accusations of gerrymandering. The changes also saw local government lose some functions. Control of water and sewerage was transferred to three water authorities with members appointed by the Secretary of State for Scotland. This meant that water and sewerage remained within the public sector but lost direct accountability to local elected bodies. The Children's Panel system was removed from local government and came under Scottish Office jurisdiction and responsibility for tourism was transferred to area tourist boards, again established by the Scottish Secretary. Responsibility for all but local roads was transferred to the Scottish Office. If the Tories had hoped they would fare better with new drawn boundaries then they were to be disappointed. Elections were held in April 1995 at which the Conservatives struggled to find candidates. The Conservative share of the vote fell to 11.3 per cent. Their largest vote in any authority was 29.2 per cent in East Renfrewshire. They won only 6.6 per cent in Glasgow. By contrast, Labour won over 50 per cent of the vote in twelve authorities. The Conservatives were left in control of no local authority in Scotland.

THE THATCHER REVOLUTION

The Conservative manifesto in 1979 had been a short document, especially compared with Heath's when he became Prime Minister in 1970, and contained few hints of what was to come. Scotland hardly featured in the election. The Tories included a vague commitment to 'discussions about the future government of Scotland'. Mrs Thatcher had still to establish her authority inside the party and her first Cabinet would look distinctly 'wet', to use a term not then in currency. Thatcherism was not yet fully formed and indeed proved to be highly adaptable. Mrs Thatcher faced a daunting task but she also had an opportunity that her predecessors did not have. North Sea oil would soon flow ashore and provide the Treasury with substantial revenues. Thirty years on, forty billion barrels of oil to the value of £400 billion have been extracted from the North Sea. Margaret Thatcher was a lucky Prime Minister in coming to power at the start of this bonanza. But she was also an astute politician, choosing her enemies and her battles carefully. From her perspective, she did not pick fights needlessly. She avoided a collision with the NUM in 1981 by withdrawing plans to close twenty-three pits. By 1984, she was ready to take on the miners.

If there was a Thatcher Revolution then it was an odd one. Change came incrementally, slow build-ups punctuated by interventions that were carefully planned and executed. Trade union reform moved forward step by step. The ideas found in Barbara Castle's *In Place of Strife* in 1969 were surpassed but not in one legislative action but a series of Acts of Parliament. Change was limited. There were areas of public policy that Thatcher dared not address other than in a business-as-usual manner. Some policies later marked out as evidence of a Thatcherite Revolution were stumbled upon. Privatization has been presented as evidence of an ideologically driven desire to 'roll back the state' and to increase competition. Loss-making nationalized industries were made economically viable before they went on the market. There would have been no market for loss-makers without some radical restructuring prior to sale. Privatization's roots lay in the need to raise money before the oil bonanza fuelled government spending. There was little evidence of competition in selling off public monopolies. Privatization was as emblematic of Thatcherism as any other policy or programme. It proved popular, raised revenue for the government, and contributed to a sense of purpose and direction for the government, but it lacked the ideological coherence many advocates suggested.

In essence, Mrs Thatcher was a shrewd politician. She portrayed herself as a 'conviction politician', which was in itself a shrewd choice of terms at the time. She tapped into a sense that government was drifting, failing to come to terms with British decline and offered an alternative. In substantive terms, her government placed far greater emphasis on finance capital at the expense of manufacturing industry. This was very different from the 1960s when taxes on service industries were used to subsidize manufacturing. Entering Downing Street she quoted words that would be played back over and over: 'Where there is discord, may we bring harmony. Where there is error, may we bring truth. Where there is doubt, may we bring faith. And where there is despair, may we bring hope.' These words are often offered as evidence of Mrs Thatcher's hypocrisy but are evidence of her pragmatism. This was evident in Opposition when she resisted the temptation to adopt a hardline position against devolution, as many of her supporters would have preferred, but instead argued against the devolution measure on offer by Labour while claiming to want talks and discussion, the kind of mealy-mouthed position that came to be seen as anathema to her. Her governing strategy and ideology developed as she gained confidence. Retrospective coherence was offered to her approach that was absent at the time.

Nonetheless, however the changes are packaged, the UK had changed considerably by the time she had left office. Scotland was not exempt from these changes but change was uneven. Scotland was insulated from some changes by the existence of Scottish institutions but affected more given its dependence on manufacturing industries. George Younger linked support for the party with support for regional policy. Three weeks after the 1979 election, he wrote to the Chancellor of the Exchequer:

> If we are to improve our position as I believe we must, we have to demonstrate that our policies particularly in the economic field match up to Scotland's needs. Regional policy, at least in its modern form, owes its origin to the Conservative

Government of the early 1960s and since then much can be claimed to its credit; over 100 000 additional jobs in Scotland according to the best independent estimate, greatly reduced emigration and levels of prosperity much closer to the UK average. We would do Scotland and ourselves a great damage if we were to allow that momentum to be lost.

But old-style regional policy would disappear. Sir Keith Joseph, Secretary of State for Industry, outlined the government's thinking two months after the election, indicating a shift to a more free market approach. In fact, Thatcherism was more complex and relied on a strong state and new forms of intervention. Urban policy replaced regional policy and a regulatory state arose in place of nationalized industries. There was little evidence of free market competition in privatization or the provision of welfare. The Conservatives made no moves to get rid of the Scottish Development Agency (SDA) but changed its focus. Their opponents had warned that a Thatcher-led government would get rid of the SDA, encouraged by suggestions from some senior Tories that the SDA's function might be broken up and given to other bodies. In December 1979, new guidelines were adopted for the SDA. Tackling unemployment and industrial investment were demoted in importance with state investment expected to be given only alongside private funding. It involved a more focused interventionist approach rather than the abandonment of state intervention in the economy. The SDA was, of course, a Scottish body and though Wales also had a development agency there were no similar bodies in the English regions, leading to occasional complaints in some regions of England that Scotland (and to a lesser extent Wales) was receiving preferential treatment. Mrs Thatcher praised this interventionist body on her trips to Scotland. Her first public speech as Prime Minister was at the Scottish Conservative conference. She maintained that the SDA would ease the 'transition from industries and jobs of the past, to the industries and jobs of the future' and it would 'provide temporary help for firms which have been brought low by the nation's economic ills, but which have a viable future'.

Old debates had never disappeared but resurfaced in debates on what the SDA ought to do. The government insisted that there was no future for declining industries, emphasizing the need to invest in new industries while its opponents argued for support for existing industry especially to stem unemployment. The electronics industry was the SDA's first sector-based approach, agreed following research commissioned in 1979. The term 'silicon glen' was first used in Parliament by John Mackay, junior Scottish Office Minister in 1981. The term derived from Silicon Valley in the Bay area of San Francisco which was home to some of the world's leading technology companies. Scotland had seen growth in this sector with over 100 firms employing about 40,000 people but nowhere near the scale of Silicon Valley. But Silicon Glen was as much an aspiration, a rallying idea, as a fact. There was nothing new in the idea. Cluster theory was evident in the development of heavy industries on the Clyde at the time of the Industrial Revolution. The hope was that these new high tech industries could provide growth and jobs on a scale to replace the old heavy industries. But the government was also willing to help ailing industries attempting to make the transition to a more high tech future. Ian Lang, as Scottish Office Industry Minister, had argued that the Opposition parties thought that the only jobs worth preserving were those involved in 'bashing a bit of metal and developing industrial deafness'. This was as crude a caricature of the heavy industries as Opposition descriptions of government policy as driven by a free market ideology. The government would occasionally see merit in metal bashing industries too. Weir Pumps in Glasgow was given substantial support through the SDA. Lord Weir, its chairman and leading figure in the recent campaign against devolution, had complained about the effects of high interest rates on his business. Weir Pumps survived, evolved, and prospered.

Speeches by senior Tories listed SDA achievements. The problem, as the Tories came to see it, was that the SDA was given credit for success and the government blamed for failings in the Scottish economy. This was allied with a concern that training and economic development were insufficiently integrated. In 1988, the government produced a White Paper that set out its proposals to merge the SDA with Training Agency bodies operating in Scotland. This had been an idea floated by Bill Hughes, chairman of the Confederation of British Industries in Scotland (CBIS). Hughes had taken the idea directly to the Prime Minister, by-passing the Scottish Secretary and SDA. That allowed the proposals to be presented as an imposition from outside though, like the poll tax, if it was an imposition it was an imposition by a Scotsman with Mrs Thatcher's endorsement. The idea was commended as a 'Scottish solution to respond to Scottish needs' by the Prime Minister when she addressed the CBI in Glasgow. The proposal managed to wrong-foot the Opposition with some groups supporting the idea at least in principle while others opposed it. The idea was not only to merge the two bodies but to create a two-tier structure with a central Scottish Enterprise plus a number of local enterprise trusts. It was very sketchy with little serious thought to what each level would do. Local businesses were expected to be involved which provoked most criticism as it was doubted that sufficient local business acumen existed and local government was excluded from involvement despite obvious expertise and experience. There was concern that the SDA brand was being thrown away and a belief that this was motivated by a desire to claim credit for initiatives which were denied to the government and associated with the SDA. Overall, the establishment of Scottish Enterprise and its network involved considerable continuity, an emphasis on a Scottish dimension that now extended into training. Mrs Thatcher had learned the language of Scottish politics. But as with the establishment of Scottish Homes, which involved combining an existing

Scottish public institution with the Scottish part of a British institution, the Tories failed to capitalize on what in the past they would have presented as an extension of administrative devolution and Scottish control of Scottish affairs. The Tories were coming to terms with the Scottish Question late in the day but by this stage expectations had increased and rebranding, refocusing, and extending existing institutions would be insufficient to placate Scots.

ECONOMIC TRANSFORMATION, BIG BANG, AND POOR ECONOMIC GROWTH

Mrs Thatcher might claim that her legacy in Scotland had been economic success but political failure but even the economic success was partial. Economic growth rates averaged 1.8 per cent per year (compared with 1.5 per cent under Tony Blair) but still below that for the UK as a whole though the economy was transformed. But the transformation was partial, being more successful in removing a major dilemma faced by successive governments and agencies without a clear strategy for growth. A key tension in twentieth-century Scottish economic history had been between focusing on defending declining industries and identifying potential growth. In the 1930s, this had led to a debate on whether to help existing businesses that were in trouble or trying to develop new industries. The Toothill Report in 1960 had urged that effort should shift to the promotion of growth at the expense of reacting to decline. Toothill had identified the growing electronics sector as a potential area of growth. This debate had never been resolved until the 1980s. Traditional manufacturing and extraction industries declined at the expense of service industries. This transformation might have been welcome but the manner in which it was brought about was brutal, painful, and lacked the all-important sufficient growth in new industries. Scotland lost jobs and communities were devastated in the process of removing the dilemma of defending decline vs. identifying growth without much success in providing stable alternatives for growth in the future.

If the decline was part of a strategy, it was less clear that the alternative was so well planned. Electronics had been seen as a potential growth area since the 1960s but electronics did not fare nearly so well or for anything approaching the longevity of the traditional and extraction industries. Footloose industries might take advantage of incentives to come to Scotland but could not be kept when an alternative base emerged. The fall of the Berlin Wall opened up East and Central Europe to business. The governments of these new states offered incentives that Scotland could not always compete with.

In common with the UK as a whole, Scotland saw a major growth in financial services. Mrs Thatcher's government grew concerned that the City of London might be overtaken by other financial centres and identified two key weaknesses in the financial sector: it was over-regulated and dominated by an 'old boy' network that was risk-averse. In late 1986, this led to the 'Big Bang', a major deregulation of the financial markets. The Scottish financial sector had a reputation as cautious and stable, or conservative and risk-averse from a different perspective, but changes were afoot well before deregulation. The Bank of Scotland had been taken over, though officially described as a merger, by Halifax Building Society in 2001. The most significant change occurred in the Royal Bank of Scotland (RBS). After serving as Margaret Thatcher's Scottish Secretary through to 1986, George Younger moved to the Ministry of Defence before standing down from the Cabinet in 1989. He joined the board of the Royal Bank of Scotland and became chairman in 1992. Younger's entry into the world of banking came at a time of significant change in the financial markets. Scotland's financial sector had prospered but had a reputation as staid and risk-averse. The new incentives following from deregulation created a new culture in the financial markets. Scotland was not exempt. The Scottish financial sector became more entrepreneurial and less risk-averse, as indeed did Scots—like many people across the UK—in a frenzy of consumption and low savings. The sale of council houses encouraged the view that a house was an investment and not simply a home. Scots might not have voted for Mrs Thatcher but they sure were adopting her mores and practices.

RBS was slowly transformed. In the world of corporate finance, the choice was expansion or takeover or acquiescence in a hostile bid. Many retrospective accounts of RBS's nemesis underplay the context in which the transformation of the bank occurred. Those who knighted Fred Goodwin when he was on the up were quick to scapegoat him as did the media that lauded his achievements before turning on him when the RBS world came crashing down in late 2008, ignoring their part in encouraging his rise. Fred Goodwin was a creature of his times and the regulatory regime in which he operated—the Big Bang in the City and changes in the regulatory regime when banking regulation was taken from the Bank of England and handed over to the Financial Services Authority. But for a period he and RBS were praised for their part in Scotland's economic development. What became very clear was that the old tension had not been resolved. It would be wrong to suggest that Scotland's financial community were all culpable. Asset management has proved successful both financially and in governance terms. Nonetheless, the traditional industries had gone and the basis on which a new economy had been built was deeply flawed. In the end Mrs Thatcher had been less unsuccessful in economic terms than she had been politically.

CONCLUSION

Mrs Thatcher would be taunted by her words on the steps of Downing Street on becoming Prime Minister. But where she did bring harmony, faith, and hope was to the cause of home rule. She united Scots against her and this oppositional unity eventually turned into a case for home rule. It would be a defensive understanding of home rule. Scots knew what they did not want or at least imagined that they knew what they did not want. There were many interpretations of Thatcherism. Anti-Thatcherism resembled nationalism in this sense. It created an imagined community of opponents of something that was agreed to be antithetical to Scottish interests even if its precise contours were unclear and differed from person to person. The Scottish card was increasingly played against the Conservatives by all its main opponents, contributing to the sense that being a Conservative was in some sense 'anti-Scottish'.

Thatcherism has tended to be seen as a market ideology but it was also a nationalist ideology and offered a new variant of unionism rarely seen before in British politics. This unionism was not its central component and had its origins in an interpretation of political events in 1979 combined with the more central aspects of Mrs Thatcher's world-view. Mrs Thatcher's interpretation of the events of spring 1979 informed her attitudes towards Scotland during the 1980s. The Scottish Question had been answered by Scots themselves and she need not worry too much about it. She was prepared to make obligatory references to Scottish institutions and would try to align herself with Scottish thinking and thinkers whenever possible. But it was not a priority for her. She and her advisers misunderstood the Scottish Question, viewing it in narrow constitutional terms and the need for an occasional gesture. Gestures were insufficient by the time John Major had become Prime Minister. Party politics, public policy, and issues of identity were all wrapped together along with constitutional politics in the Scottish Question. Their failure to appreciate this meant that the constitutional aspect of the Scottish Question gradually returned to the fore during the eighteen years of Conservative government.

Many Tory policies proved popular and many developed policies were already underway. But governments require legitimacy and what emerged was a problem of legitimacy in Scottish government. It was less the policies that were pursued by the Tories but the sense that they were pursued by a government that lacked support, though some appalling misjudgements such as the poll tax contributed to the sense of an alien government imposing its will on Scotland. Mrs Thatcher would look back on office and suggest that Thatcherism had been economically successful in Scotland while a political failure. There was some truth in this. Thatcherism's greatest success in terms of the relationship between the state, economy, and society was to undermine and eventually significantly alter public expectations.

This affected Scotland as much as other parts of the UK. Scotland's social and economic landscape changed considerably after 1979. The state's role changed. Scotland lost much of its manufacturing industry and new industries emerged. The extent to which government policies brought these changes about varied across sectors.

10

Here's to the Next Time

INTRODUCTION

It soon became clear that something significant had occurred when the 1997 general election results were being announced. Almost two decades before, Jim Callaghan had remarked, 'You know there are times, perhaps once every thirty years, when there is a sea-change in politics. It then does not matter what you say or what you do. There is a shift in what the public wants and what it approves of.' This time the change was against the Conservatives. Across Britain, the Tories lost seats previously thought safe as Cabinet ministers and MPs fell. In Scotland, not a single Tory MP was left when the election was over. New Labour under Tony Blair had secured an overall majority of 179. Labour was committed to a Scottish Parliament and intended to legislate for it after a referendum in which Scots would be asked whether they wanted a Parliament and separately whether it should have tax-varying powers. Within two years of the general election, elections were held to the Scottish Parliament. Plans were made to build a new iconic Scottish Parliament building. Newly elected Members met temporarily in the hall of the General Assembly of the Church of Scotland where Mrs Thatcher had delivered her 'Sermon on the Mound' just over a decade before. Mrs Thatcher had been the midwife of the Parliament. She had united Scotland to a remarkable extent but it was unity against what she stood for or, rather, what people believed she stood for. Labour had reluctantly accepted the need for devolution when last in power. But by 1997, it had embraced the idea with only a few opponents within its ranks though many, including the Prime Minister himself and other senior members of the government, had doubts. The depth of the commitment and enthusiasm for the policy on the part of the Labour Party in Scotland was such that it would have been difficult, even for a premier with Mr Blair's popularity, to have abandoned devolution. Devo-sceptics inside the Labour Party convinced themselves that devolution was part of the modernization of Britain, part of a strategy to reform Britain's creaking institutions rather than a sop to Scottish nationalism. It was as much part of 'cool Britannia' as the proposed Millennium Dome that would be built on the banks of the Thames. The Scottish Parliament would be more than a modern purpose-built Parliament; it would offer 'new politics'. But it would have unintended consequences.

When the dust had settled on the election eighteen years before Mr Blair entered Downing Street, it had been clear that devolution was dead, at least for the time being. Not for the first time, obituaries of the SNP were written. A more thoughtful piece was written by the journalist Neal Ascherson in November 1979. Ascherson had returned to Scotland to cover political developments in the 1970s. His article, 'Here's to the next time', was a farewell piece, reflecting on his 'five strange years' in Scotland. He had been a partisan as much as a journalist and declared himself impenitent in wanting Scottish self-government:

> This round of Scottish politics is over. There will be another. Too much points that way to be wrong: the irrevocable experience and preparations of the seventies; the continuing decline of the British economy and the way this Government makes the outlying parts of the UK pay most dearly for that decline; the more general decay of the British state and its unreformed institutions; the lack of purpose in the Labour movement; the relentless pressure on Scotland through the eighties of the European Community—where we have no special voice for our special interests.

He asked when change would come and concluded, 'Very much, I suspect, within our lifetimes. Until then, I and those of my mind will raise a glass and adapt the ancient Passover prayer and toast: "Next year in Edinburgh!"' There was much in this paean to a Scotland that might have been that would reverberate over the next two decades. However flawed the Scotland Act, 1978, had been it would be the basis for future support for devolution. Lessons would be learned and improvements made.

Mrs Thatcher set out to halt Britain's economic decline. She and her supporters believed this was achieved but in Scotland a different view emerged. A movement developed across the UK in favour of radical change in the country's constitution. Scottish home rule became part of that movement while simultaneously distinct. Hesitant steps towards constitutional reform, articulated as modernization, were made in opposition by Labour. In Scotland, a Scottish Parliament became the central part of this alternative vision of the UK. Labour's lack of purpose in late 1979 partly reflected exhaustion after five difficult years in government followed by defeat. Parties suffering electoral defeat, especially a heavy defeat, tend to become introspective. Labour turned in on and against itself with bruising internal battles that would only begin to be resolved after further heavier losses in 1983. The party gradually abandoned Bennite fundamentalism as it decided that power was more attractive than purity. The SNP followed the same pattern. Recoiling into the political equivalent of the foetal position, the SNP conference in autumn 1979 resolved not to 'engage in any more dealings in assemblies, devolution, or meaningful talks'. The SNP too would take time to recover its sense of proportion. Each party would find purpose again. Ascherson's observation that the European Communities would assume a greater role and some means of finding a distinctive Scottish voice would prove prescient. William McIlvaney, the novelist, had written an article a few days before the referendum in which he raised the possibility that only a 'bare majority' voted in favour of devolution, 'Would that not be a peculiarly Scottish response, leaving us still in that limbo where emotional assertion does not quite connect with the practical demands of the situation?' Scotland would be in limbo for the next two decades.

HOME RULE IN DOLDRUMS

The referendum and general election cast a long shadow over Scottish politics. Ascherson had spoken for disillusioned Scots who had seen the Scottish Assembly as the answer, partial or otherwise, to the Scottish Question. Ascherson had expressed the expectation that an assembly would be established in his lifetime and his allusion to the traditional end of the Jewish Seder suggested that the patience and commitment of home rulers would be eventually rewarded. There had been setbacks in the past and while many drifted away, some to return to campaigning in better political weather, there remained a core of supporters stretching across the parties who continued the campaign. A new body was established on the first anniversary of the referendum. The Campaign for a Scottish Assembly (CSA) brought together an impressive range of speakers at a rally that attracted 400 people in Edinburgh's Trades Council Hall. Political scientist Jack Brand chaired the CSA as a 'movement for Scotland' and not a political party. A ten-clause resolution was passed committing the CSA to set up a convention drawn from all parts of Scotland to consider detailed proposals for an assembly. This first meeting of the CSA met a week before Labour's Scottish conference. Dr Brand hoped that it would meet in a year's time and present a set of proposals to Parliament in the form of a new devolution bill. Dennis Canavan, Labour MP for West Stirlingshire, attacked the Conservative government's programme of public spending cuts but was 'drowned in a chorus of demands that he stop making political speeches and stick to devolution', according to the report in the *Scotsman*.

Jack Brand's main aim in helping found the CSA had been to encourage Labour to remain committed to devolution. He concluded that the best, if not only, prospect of establishing an assembly would be the return of a Labour government. There was little prospect of the Conservatives doing so and a danger that Labour would slide back from support. The CSA had to strike a difficult balance with members of the Labour Party and SNP. There was no agreement on the powers of an assembly and little agreement on a strategy to bring it about. Scottish home rulers were back in the 1920s. At minimum, the Assembly would be what had been proposed in the 1979 referendum. A constitutional convention representative of Scottish opinion would draw up a scheme of home rule, overcoming differences on its powers. As it became clear that the Conservatives had no intention of establishing an assembly, devolution became an important part of the alternative to the Conservatives. Dennis Canavan's attacks on the Tories at CSA meeting would later be cheered, indeed attacks on the Tory government became a standard part of CSA gatherings.

The CSA had a small membership including a number of trade union and other affiliates. In 1984, it convened a conference on local government, acknowledging that many local councillors had been hostile to devolution in the past. Under a third of Scottish local authorities sent delegates or observers and those who did urged the CSA and other bodies to support local government in its battles with the Scottish Office. Two years later, the Convention of Scottish Local Authorities (CoSLA) backed a motion by eighty-nine votes to twenty supporting the creation of a Scottish Assembly. By the late 1980s, local government was overwhelmingly in favour of an assembly and when an unofficial Constitutional Convention was set up in 1989, CoSLA provided the administrative support. The CSA itself may not have converted local government but it was a non-party body that allowed supporters of some measure of home rule to rally around it. In time, the CSA changed its name to the Campaign for a Scottish Parliament. It was a symbolic change. An assembly was thought to designate a less powerful institution than a Parliament and the name change also conveyed a deeper level of commitment. Its most important initiative was the establishment of the Scottish Constitutional Convention. This allowed campaigners to present themselves as above narrow party political advantage. The Convention was launched in 1989, nine years after the CSA's first conference at which it resolved to establish such a body. The timing of its establishment was important. It is unlikely that a Convention established in the early 1980s would have had much impact.

LABOUR'S CHANGE OF HEART

Labour underwent two major changes of direction between losing power in 1979 and regaining it in 1997. In the aftermath of defeat, the party lurched to the left. Jim Callaghan had left Downing Street believing that there was little his party could do to stop the advance of the Conservatives. Labour proposed more of the same and left the impression that they were far clearer about what they opposed than what they would do if returned to office. There was a philosophic vacuum at the heart of the party. It would be filled by ideas from those who felt Labour had betrayed its radical roots. The shift to the left involved a left-wing form of British nationalism, involving withdrawal from the EC combined with unquestioned faith in state intervention. Tony Benn, former Industry and Energy Minister in the late 1970s, led the revolt against the government in which he had served. Past behaviour as a minister had never prevented Mr Benn becoming a vehement supporter of a position or denouncing those who held his former views or doubts. At the party's 1980 conference, he announced that the next Labour government would take powers to nationalize industries, control flows of capital, and implement industrial democracy within days of coming to power. It would return power from Brussels in weeks and abolish the House of Lords by creating a thousand new peers. Tom Nairn portrayed Bennism as a form of English, rather than British, nationalism. Eric Heffer, Liverpool Walton MP, was another key figure on the Bennite left. He stood for the Labour leadership in 1983 when Benn was out of Parliament and had been vehemently opposed to devolution in the 1970s, seeing no reason to support a measure that gave Scotland an advantage over his own area.

Labour changed its method of electing its party leader at the 1980 conference. The new system would make it easier to elect a left-winger. Callaghan resigned to force the election of a new leader under the old rules resulting in Michael Foot defeating Denis Healey, former Chancellor of the Exchequer and *bête noir* of the Labour left. Healey became Foot's deputy. Foot was on the left but more pragmatic and willing to accept collective ministerial responsibility than Benn. He had been one of the few senior Cabinet ministers who had strongly supported devolution. Foot's leadership was a manifestation of Labour's troubles. He was elected because he was not Healey and it was hoped that he might unite the party. But Labour's civil war would have defeated any leader. The Tories were unpopular for most of the 1979–83 Parliament with manufacturing industry shedding jobs, creating high levels of unemployment. In 1981, Benn challenged Healey for the deputy leadership. It was a bruising contest that was narrowly won by the incumbent. Shortly afterwards, the 'gang of four'—Roy Jenkins, Shirley Williams, David Owen, and William Rodgers—left the Labour Party to form the Social Democratic Party (SDP). Twenty-eight Labour MPs eventually joined the new party though only two from Scotland—Dickson Mabon and Robert MacLennan. Scotland did not appear to be particularly fertile ground for the new party, not least because it already had a four-party system with the SNP. After failing to win a by-election in Warrington in July, Roy Jenkins stood as SDP candidate in a by-election in Glasgow Hillhead. Hillhead was the last Tory seat in the city and had been held by the party since 1918. Initially, the Liberals had been reluctant to stand aside to let the leader of this new party contest the seat but eventually Chic Brodie, who had already been nominated for the seat by the Liberals, stood aside. In 2011, Mr Brodie was elected as an SNP Member of the Scottish Parliament. In standing in a Scottish seat Mr Jenkins had been forced to give thought to his views on devolution, though far from being the dominant issue in the election. Jenkins had been unenthusiastic about devolution when he was in Harold Wilson's Cabinet. When the Scots had voted in favour of remaining in the EEC in the 1975 referendum, he had concluded that the SNP was irrelevant. In a carefully worded statement, assisted by Vernon Bogdanor of Oxford University and author of an important book on the subject, Jenkins argued the case for Scottish devolution during the by-election. The SDP included a number of members who had been hostile to devolution but the party accepted the policy with little open dissent. George Cunningham, the anti-devolution Labour MP who had moved the 40 per cent rule, would join the SDP three months after Hillhead. Jenkins was able to bring a deep historical understanding of the issues involved and would later write a prize-winning biography of Gladstone, who had attempted to tackle the Irish Question. David Owen was a strong supporter of devolution and had been the first senior UK politician to make a speech on the subject after the 1979 general election when he addressed a meeting in Robert MacLennan's Caithness and Sutherland constituency. Owen was unusual as a senior British politician in the early-mid 1980s in including references to his support for a Scottish Parliament—and used the term Parliament even before it became common in Scotland—in major speeches outside Scotland. Devolution appeared to have transcended not only Labour's internal divisions but also Labour–SDP divisions. The SDP and Liberals forged an electoral pact at the 1983 election and for a period in the lead-up to the election appeared likely to 'break the mould of British politics'.

Devolution transcended Labour's civil war. Devolution was debated at the party's first Scottish conference after the 1979 general election. Danny Crawford, representative of the Union of Construction, Allied Trades and Technicians, proclaimed that devolution was dead and argued that support had been motivated by a fear of the SNP which no longer made sense. Crawford's interpretation of Labour support for devolution had validity in the period up to 1979 but the motive would change over time. Labour's support for devolution moved away from a response to the electoral threat posed by the SNP to opposition to Thatcherism. But for the most part, anti-devolutionists saw little purpose in pursuing a change in official policy when the party looked set for a long period in opposition. Devolved government was increasingly seen less as a response to the electoral threat posed by the SNP than a form of state intervention at the British level. At the Scottish level, Labour's dominance of elections through the 1980s encouraged the view that a Scottish Assembly would pursue a very different policy agenda north of the border. A former Labour Cabinet minister was quoted in the *Scotsman* in July 1982: 'We are certain to lose the next election in England. We will return even more MPs from Scotland, but we will be out of office down here for another ten years. We will have to play the nationalist card in Scotland. We will have to go for an Assembly with substantial economic powers—short of independence, but not much short.' Labour strengthened its commitment by supporting tax-raising powers for the Assembly in 1983 and added police and universities to the Assembly's responsibilities. But the issue was still not central to the party's objectives. An interim programme issued in 1981 omitted mention of devolution. A statement on 'Scotland and Devolution' by the National Executive Committee was issued in February 1983. It insisted that Scottish devolution was not dependent on decentralization in England and Wales. Scotland was 'ready' for devolution. It already had a 'group of experienced government departments' and an array of separate institutions well 'practiced in dealing with a Scottish Administration'; Scotland has 'traditionally suffered more than the rest of the country from the present over-centralisation'; and 'consciousness of the need for devolution is greater in Scotland' due to historical and cultural reasons.

The Labour Coordinating Committee (LCC) was the faction that coordinated the left around the Bennite agenda. The Labour left had been as divided over devolution in the 1970s as the Labour right. It had been commonly asserted by the left that devolution would divide the working class and that this sop to Scottish nationalism was a distraction. There was, therefore, no reason in principle to expect that this shift to the left would further the cause of home rule. Labour in Scotland faced the same internal battles. The LCC included supporters of devolution. George Galloway, the party's full-time organizer in Dundee along with Bill Speirs of the STUC were key figures in the LCC in Scotland and strong supporters of devolution. The party leadership supported devolution but the party was suspicious of the CSA. Helen Liddell, Labour's Scottish general secretary and the person who had objected to cross-party campaigning in the 1979 referendum on the grounds that Labour should not 'soil its hands' by working with others, rejected a vote by the Scottish executive to affiliate to the CSA. In February 1982, Donald Dewar argued that Labour would work through the established party system, i.e. on its own, rather than through this 'pressure group'. Labour was focused on the next election and did not want to imply that it would need the support of any other party in delivering home rule.

Labour's devolution policy was grafted onto the alternative economic strategy as part of the party's alternative regional strategy. The alternative regional strategy was championed by Prescott who viewed devolution within a wider programme of regional government and policy. John Prescott was appointed Spokesman on Devolution and Regional Affairs by Michael Foot and produced a document, *Alternative Regional Strategy*, in September 1982. It proposed elected regional assemblies and regional planning boards for the English regions and for Wales. Regions would feed into negotiations on public expenditure, making bids based on spending levels across functions to a Minister for Expenditure Coordination. Prescott warned that there would have to be trade-offs and there would be hard bargaining between the English regions and Scotland. The key elements in the report would never be implemented as much of this would be discarded when Labour went through its second major policy change of direction that culminated in New Labour. But it represented an effort to link a highly interventionist strategy with regionalism. Though the commitment to Scottish devolution was only dealt with in an appendix, this was an effort to reconcile equity across the UK with devolution in a semi-symmetrical form. It was the left equivalent of home rule all round. There was considerable opposition to these proposals from English local authorities who feared this new regional tier would suck up powers from below and trade unions who worried that this might lead to regional wage differentials. The trade unions were also generally keener on more corporatist models rather than elected regional bodies.

A growing element in the party in Scotland was keen to prioritize its commitment to an assembly. Some members were articulating the case in nationalist language. In an article in *New Socialist* in early 1982, George Galloway who had chaired the Scottish party in 1981, maintained that the 'national question in Scotland is not dead. Scotland knows as a *nation*, that it did not vote for Mrs Thatcher; indeed, it very decisively rejected her.' He argued that it was the 'duty of all socialists to take on board the fact that *Scotland is a nation*' [his emphasis]. He warned that devolution should not 'run aground on the dry banks of Labour British nationalism'. He warned that if Mrs Thatcher was re-elected Scots would need to look again at the union. In August, he criticized those who questioned his more robust stance and warned against suggesting that Scotland should stay in the UK 'at all costs, and under any circumstances'. Some Scottish Labour MPs advocated Parnellite disruption of Parliament in the event of a Tory majority in Britain if Labour retained its majority in Scotland. John Home Robertson described George Younger as being 'like a colonial governor' rather than a minister in an elected government. In September 1982, George Foulkes wrote in the *Guardian* that 'devolution will happen one way or another' after the election. In early 1983, a series of articles were written for the press by Scotland's own 'gang of four' Labour MPs—George Foulkes, John Home Robertson, John Maxton, and David Marshall. Dennis Canavan would become part of the gang. An 'Action Plan for the Labour Movement' was drawn up and signed by the five. They claimed that a further seven or eight Labour MPs would join them in disrupting Parliament in pursuit of Scottish devolution. The Action Plan proposed parliamentary disruption, local authority and trade union pressure, as well as challenges in the courts to the Secretary of State's authority. In January, Foulkes added intrigue to the drama when he maintained that the plans were 'still shrouded in mystery and better left to word of mouth rather than cold print at present'. The plans would remain a mystery. In February 1983, even Gordon Brown, vice chair of the Scottish party, said that if Labour lost the UK election then the job of the Scottish Secretary would be made untenable in a Tory government.

Argentina invaded the Falkland Islands in April 1982. The war allowed Mrs Thatcher to appear as a strong leader and was a turning point in her premiership. This was a moment to bring the entire country together in a very British event. It was a useful backdrop to the 1983 election for the Tories. They were already ahead in the polls but the 'Falklands factor' allowed this to be consolidated. The Scots Guards and Scottish-based commandos fought in the Falklands. But support for the war was less strong in Scotland. The Scottish press may have played a part in this. Though the Scottish press supported the war, they did so less jingoistically. The *Daily Record* still easily outsold the *Sun* but, as Bill Miller noted, not with the same 'mindless belligerence'. Mrs Thatcher won the election with an overall majority of 144. Labour fell to its lowest share of the vote since 1918. It had fought on a radical manifesto, described as the 'longest suicide note in history' by one of its own front benchers. But in Scotland the Conservatives lost a seat. Labour lost seats but with forty-one of Scotland's seventy-two seats remained the largest party, with all but twice the number of seats as the Conservatives. But its share of seats hid a significant drop in its vote. With only 35.1 per cent of the vote, down 6 per cent on 1979 performance, Labour was still the largest party with forty-one of Scotland's seventy-one seats. The electoral system had once more proved kind to Labour in Scotland.

The 1983 election fuelled demands for home rule. As the results were coming in, Robin Cook, who had opposed devolution in the 1979 referendum, announced that he was reconsidering his view of the Scottish question. A month later, Cook admitted that he had never been an 'extravagant support of the Scottish dimension' but he had changed his mind: 'I don't give a bugger if Thatcher has a mandate or not. I will simply do all I can to stop her.' He argued thereafter for a federal solution, though joined other federalists in failing to put flesh on federal bones. Despite Cook's comments, there was increasing talk of the Conservatives' lack of a Scottish mandate. The idea that a governing party required separate and simultaneous mandates in the components of the UK had no constitutional foundation but became a rallying point and justification for radical action.

The Labour Party planned a post-election meeting to discuss tactics. George Foulkes prepared a paper setting out a campaign of industrial and political disruption and a nationwide plebiscite. Another paper was prepared by the party's Scottish headquarters staff which acknowledged a potential conflict between the party's duty to protect Scotland from what is saw as the worst excesses of the Tory government and its duty to recognize its 'pre-eminent potential to contribute towards the general recovery of the movement throughout Britain'. The meeting was postponed to avoid an immediate response. Not everyone in the Labour Party in Scotland was inclined to think in Scottish terms. Some anti-devolutionists were careful not to argue against devolution but questioned the tactics that gave the Scottish Question prominence. The more radical elements diluted their programme of action over the summer and were coming under pressure to abandon the 'no Scottish mandate' argument. When Dennis Canavan argued that the Prime Minister was 'decisively rejected at the general election by more than 70 per cent of Scottish voters', Mrs Thatcher retorted that on the basis of this criterion 'four out of the last five Labour Governments had no mandate to govern England'. The 'no Scottish mandate' argument was a dangerous weapon for Labour. Home rulers seemed confused on the matter. In an article on the fifth anniversary of the referendum, John Home Robertson argued that 'Sovereignty remains in the Westminster Parliament, and unfortunately the present majority there is implacably hostile to Scottish aspirations' but also argued that Labour would propose a devolution bill later that year which would be a 'sustained challenge to the spurious mandate of the Tory Administration in Scotland'. The bill never appeared that year and the inherent contradiction in his comments on sovereignty and mandate would not be confronted when Westminster rejected the bill to discover what the absence of a mandate actually meant.

Labour's leadership responded to the pressure inside the party on the Scottish Question in much the same way as they had responded to the SNP challenge in the late 1960s. They had postponed the Scottish post-election strategy meeting and Donald Dewar, who became Labour's Shadow Scottish Secretary in 1983, announced that a Green (discussion) Paper would be produced followed by a White Paper setting out proposals on devolution. It would take four years to produce the White Paper. The post-election strategy meeting was held three months after the election. Foulkes and colleagues were keen to 'provoke a constitutional crisis' but had revised the paper to remove some of its more radical elements. They no longer proposed token strikes, disruption of tax revenue, and petitioning the European Court of Human Rights and the United Nations but stuck with the 'no Scottish mandate' argument which was 'easily understood, hard to answer and politically very damaging to the Government'. But the paper was not discussed at the meeting attended by thirty-three of its forty-one Scottish MPs and forty-five trade unionists, local authority, and other party leaders. Instead, the party decided to press for a devolution debate at Westminster and to campaign for devolution which would have 'equal priority' to campaigning against job losses, local government and NHS cuts, and privatization. It would consider what action might be taken in Scottish committees in Parliament and prepare a new devolution bill within a year.

Labour did engage in some limited parliamentary disruption. In December 1983, the Labour members on the Scottish Grand Committee forced an extension of debate on the health service in Scotland. The 'usual channels' of communication between the two front benches had broken down. The government benches had understood that there was agreement that the next item of business could be discussed. Ian Lang, Scottish Tory whip, broke convention to attack Labour and Michael Ancram, junior Scottish Office Minister, accused Dewar of losing control of his backbenches. It was a sign of frustration but also that the Scottish Question was returning to politics.

There were countervailing pressures in the Labour Party. Its anti-devolutionists in Scotland had remained relatively quiet but voices in the England occasionally expressed concern that Scotland might gain an advantage with an assembly. But after 1983 there was little appetite for internal battles. Michael Foot stood down as party leader and was replaced by Neil Kinnock, Welsh Labour MP. Kinnock had come to prominence in the late 1970s as an outspoken critic of devolution. Though his focus had mainly been on Wales, on at least one occasion he had come to Scotland to speak against Scottish devolution. His aim was to make Labour electable and started the process by diluting and casting aside policy on which it had fought the 1983 election. But he dared not touch the commitment to Scottish devolution. There was no obvious Scottish dimension to his election as leader though his campaign manager had been Robin Cook. As leader, he would occasionally show irritation when asked about devolution. When asked why he had failed to mention devolution in his speech to the party's Scottish conference in 1988 he replied that neither had he talked about the weather in the Himalayas. At the following year's conference, he committed himself to legislating for devolution within a year of coming to power.

In autumn 1983, Labour's UK conference debated devolution for the first time since 1976. The conference backed a campaign for an assembly with significant economic, revenue-raising and legislative powers. There was dissent but mainly lack of interest. Devolution was rising up the Scottish political agenda but was hardly noted at UK level. A fringe meeting organized by the CSA at Labour's British conference in 1984 attracted only three people, one of whom left before discussion began and that, said Tam Dalyell, 'says it all about the current devolution case'. Labour's anti-devolutionists assumed that devolution sentiment would quietly disappear, as it had in the past.

Labour resisted efforts to create a Scottish national movement incorporating parties and organizations that were not part of the labour movement. The UK conference agreed to collaboration but only with the STUC and Cooperative Party and emphatically not with the SNP. In December 1983, a Scottish home rule bill was presented in Parliament by Liberal MP Archie Kirkwood. It proposed a federal constitution with elections by a more proportional electoral system rather than simple plurality. This provoked strong protests from Labour MPs. Donald Dewar argued that Labour MPs voted for the bill because they supported home rule in principle but attacked the other elements as calculated to put off potential support with a 'rather aggressive parade of Liberal Party obsessions with federal structures and PR'. It did not augur well for creating a Scotland-wide campaign for devolution. The CSA set up an Inter Party Forum to bring representatives of the pro-change parties together but Labour stood aloof. Labour felt that the CSA was spending too much time trying to broker a cross-party alliance.

In 1986, the CSA discussed a schools project that was launched to mark the 900th anniversary of the Domesday Book. This did not apply to Scotland but an alternative Scottish schools project was suggested. Some of those involved saw an opportunity to highlight Anglo-Scottish differences in such a project but others felt that attention should focus on the forthcoming general election. Bob McLean, one of the CSA's most active members and a Labour Party member, suggested that the main concern ought to be with the 'Doomsday Scenario' of a possible return of the Conservatives at the election rather than the Domesday Book. The term Doomsday Scenario entered Scottish political vocabulary and especially when the scenario played out in the election results the following May. The Conservatives lost eleven of their twenty-one seats with a fall of 4.4 per cent in their share of the vote. Labour increased its number of Scottish seats to fifty with a 3.9 per cent increase.

Politics was now being framed in Scottish terms as rarely before. The 'no mandate' argument was repeatedly voiced. Labour's increased support encouraged it to become more willing to cooperate with other non-Conservative parties. It could do so from a position of strength but also feared that failure to respond in some way to the Scottish dimension would undermine its support. Labour produced a draft devolution bill which was presented in Parliament and predictably voted down. It also faced considerable pressure to use unconventional methods in opposition to the poll tax which was becoming the dominant issue in Scottish politics. Labour and the SNP were now in a bidding war to claim the title of the party that hated the Tories most. Labour laid claim to the mantle by easily being Scotland's largest Opposition party. The SNP would taunt Labour's 'feeble fifty' for failing to stand up for Scotland. What each acknowledged was the importance of the Scottish dimension. In September 1988, Labour met in special conference and voted against non-payment of the poll tax though a number of individual members and trade unions favoured this course. Campbell Christie had returned to Scotland as general secretary of the STUC the previous year and was amongst those Labour members who declared that they would not pay the poll tax. Christie would play a significant part in pressing the Scottish agenda on Labour and encouraging cross-party collaboration in opposition to the Tories and in support of devolution. The poll tax was viewed in Scottish terms, portrayed as a measure imposed on Scotland against its will and evidence that Scotland was a guinea-pig.

By 1988, the Scottish question was firmly rooted in politics north of the border. The issue was not whether but how this should be made manifest. In October 1988, Donald Dewar delivered a lecture in which he suggested that 'people must decide if they are to live a little dangerously in order to achieve what they want'. This was not a call for non-payment or parliamentary disruption. Dewar's notion of 'living dangerously' was to 'negotiate and not simply to enforce the devolution package that we already have before the public'. The CSA had been developing its plans to establish a cross-party constitutional convention and this would be the means of living dangerously. Labour would put its energies and hopes into this venture for the remainder of the Parliament and into the following. Cooperation with other political parties was living dangerously in the sectarian world of Scottish politics.

In 1989, two Labour supporters in Scotland wrote an article for *Parliamentary Affairs* entitled, 'Devolution and the tartanisation of the Labour Party'. They suggested that Labour had created a Frankenstein's monster which threatened to 'run completely out of control'. Deep divisions on the 'national question' had been revealed as 'socialist nationalist or nationalist socialist' pressure groups were 'springing up almost daily'. The article offered an unsubtle caricature of what was happening but highlighted the shift in opinion inside the Labour Party in Scotland. Its anti-devolution wing had become marginalized. The party had embraced devolution. But while anti-devolutionists were dissatisfied, so too were radical home rulers. In September 1987, following a meeting of the CSA in Stirling, a number of Labour members of the CSA met and would later form Scottish Labour Action (SLA). These members were disappointed that the party had failed to press the argument that the Conservatives had 'no mandate' in Scotland. The existence of the CSA had helped create a network of supporters of devolution within the Labour Party in Scotland. SLA's main concern was to convince the party to become involved in a Constitutional Convention though it was also keen on robust opposition to the poll tax. SLA attracted the support of a number of key people who would become Members of the Scottish Parliament including Jack McConnell, later First Minister of Scotland.

SNP INSPECTS ITS NAVEL

The SNP mimicked Labour in its response to its defeats in 1979. It turned in on itself and looked within and beyond the party to find someone to blame. At the party's first conference after the election, it decided to oppose devolution, which was not on offer. Those who had argued at its Motherwell conference in 1976 against devolution felt vindicated. Those who had held leadership positions lost out in internal elections if they were too slow to redefine themselves as hardliners or stuck to the view that a pragmatic approach had been correct. Billy Wolfe had been SNP chairman for a decade and decided to stand down. Gordon Wilson, who had been one of the two SNP MPs to retain his parliamentary seat at the general election, defeated Stephen Maxwell, who had been head of the party's press office in 1973 and played a significant role in party policy-making and strategy, by 530 votes to 117. Wilson had a number of advantages over Maxwell. Maxwell was more clearly associated with the failed strategy having directed the SNP's referendum campaign. Wilson had a much longer pedigree as an SNP activist having been national secretary in the early 1960s. Wilson argued that part of the party's problem lay in tensions between the party leadership in Scotland and at Westminster. A bicephalous leadership had not worked. He had an added advantage. The '79 Group was the appropriate name for the group of which Maxwell became a leading member. It had been formed in reaction to the defeats of that year. It offered a reasonable critique of the SNP's failure though it offered a simplistic response. The party had failed to carve out a clear position on the conventional left–right spectrum, allowing its opponents to define what the SNP stood for in this respect. It identified the working class as the section of the electorate most likely to support the SNP. It therefore proposed that the party should become socialist and republican alongside its support for independence.

The '79 Group consisted mainly of students and younger members though it included a few members who later rose to prominence including Alex Salmond, future First Minister, Kenny MacAskill, Justice Minister, and Roseanna Cunningham who would also hold ministerial office in the Scottish government. The Group was reasonably united in its critique of the party but not all agreed with the details of the alternative. Republicanism had always had some support in the SNP but was generally viewed as a distraction. Even socialism was a term many were uncomfortable with given that it could be defined in a variety of ways. Salmond, for example, was never a republican and rarely used the term 'socialist' to describe himself, preferring social democrat. He would later comment that he agreed with one of the three objectives of the '79 Group, though at the time many in the party thought that independence was not the one. Critics felt that the '79 Group was attempting to dilute or even abandon independence. Salmond and others were keen to project a clearer profile of what the SNP stood for on the left–right spectrum and were reasonably relaxed about how this should be done. The key objective was to appeal to Labour voters. But in the SNP maelstrom following heavy defeats there was little prospect of a serious debate and the SNP followed Labour in turning its back on the electorate while it engaged in navel gazing.

At its 1981 conference, the '79 Group identified three resolutions that it would support, including one demanding a 'real Scottish resistance and defence of Scottish jobs' involving direct action 'up to and including political strikes and civil disobedience on a mass scale'. The second resolution argued for an 'enlarged public sector' given the 'failure of the private sector' in Scotland and the third supported a position of 'armed neutrality' including opposition to NATO membership. Jim Sillars had joined the SNP and the '79 Group and would make his first speech to an SNP conference when he spoke in favour of civil disobedience. Each resolution was passed and each reflected the context in which the conference met. The party was still coming to terms with its routing and this radicalism was a function of its frustration. The SNP was following the rhythms of British politics. British politics had become more adversarial and more sharply divided ideologically. The SNP was less inclined to align itself with the SDP in wishing to break the mould of British politics by adopting a more consensual style of politics but followed Labour in moving to the left. It held the SDP in almost as much contempt as the Labour Party though it lost few members to the new party. The only prominent defector to the SDP was Iain MacCormick, former SNP MP for Argyll. MacCormick followed his father John's path in politics in leaving the SNP for a centrist party though the younger MacCormick would eventually return to the SNP.

The SNP's flirtation with civil disobedience was a short-lived fiasco. Six party members, led by Sillars, broke into the building which had been planned to be the Scottish Assembly with the intention of reading out a declaration to an empty chamber. The break-in proved more difficult than expected and the declaration was never read out. Sillars and colleagues were arrested and charged with vandalism. Political opponents ridiculed the party and Sillars's opponents inside the party saw this as evidence that he had no understanding of its ethos and methods. The hope that the protest would attract people to a planned mass demonstration a week later was never realized when Sillars decided to abandon the demonstration. The Assembly building was an attempt to link the constitutional question to the issue of employment but succeeded in offending those SNP members who thought devolution had been a trap. Party infighting reached a climax at the following year's conference when Winnie Ewing, Jimmy Halliday, and Robert McIntyre joined others in establishing an alternative faction, the Campaign for Nationalism, forcing Gordon Wilson to propose an emergency resolution banning all internal groups. Wilson won the vote by 308 to 188. The '79 Group tried to get round the resolution by establishing the Scottish Socialist Society outside the SNP but the SNP rejected this and suspended those SNP members who had set up the new society. Amongst those suspended were Alex Salmond and Kenny MacAskill. Margo MacDonald, by-election victor in 1973 and former deputy leader, resigned from the party and avoided being suspended.

The SNP was in a sorry state as the 1983 general election drew near. The suspensions of those who had set up the Socialist Society were lifted and MacAskill was able to stand as an SNP candidate against Robin Cook. MacAskill came fourth with 13.1 per cent of the vote, slightly higher than the 11.8 per cent the SNP scored across Scotland. The SNP had lost almost a third of its vote since 1979 and fifty-three deposits in seventy-two constituencies. But it narrowly missed winning two seats in north-east Scotland. It had been pushed further to the fringe of Scottish politics. During the 1979–83 Parliament it had rarely attracted front page headlines other than when it engaged in civil disobedience or in its fratricidal battles. The 1983 election had the same effect on the SNP as it had on Labour. It provided a sharp wake-up call.

In the aftermath of the election, Gordon Wilson set out three areas where he sought changes in party policy to make it more electable. He wanted the party be more explicitly pro-EC, abandon its opposition to NATO membership, and abandon its hardline opposition to devolution including supporting a constitutional convention. Wilson had proposed an elected convention in a bill presented to Parliament in 1980. The party narrowly voted for a convention at its conference in 1984 signalling a weakening of its hardline position. It had been moving towards supporting the EC but demonstrated a major shift in 1988. The SNP launched its 'Independence in Europe' campaign provoking Donald Dewar to argue for 'Independence in the UK'. SNP attitudes towards a convention and cooperation with other parties mirrored Labour's. When one inclined to support cooperation the other backed away. Each viewed the other's motives suspiciously. Each feared that it might walk into a trap and each wanted cooperation on its own terms. Neither the Liberals nor the CSA were able to act as effective mediators. When Donald Dewar decided to 'live dangerously', the SNP decided to play safe. By the time Wilson stood down as leader, his party had become committed to European Community membership but the SNP, Wilson included, decided against participation in a convention and changing policy on NATO would wait another three decades.

The SNP sought to mirror Scottish opinion and in the early 1980s the '79 Group interpreted this as requiring a radical left message. The SNP had always been a left of centre party with a few members on the right. In the 1970s, it retained its left-wing policies but sought to portray itself as a catch-all party capable of representing all of Scotland. The consensus that emerged by the mid-1980s was that it was a 'moderate left of centre party', a term first used by Gordon Wilson. But the SNP continued to define itself in relation to the Labour Party. The '79 Group had sought to copy Labour, and even to place itself to the left of Labour. Even after a consensus had been reached it was less around a confident attempt to build an image that was distinct from other parties but was framed in terms of challenging Labour, Scotland's largest party. While Thatcherism was the Other, against which the SNP sought to define itself, it did so with Labour firmly in mind.

THE ENEMY OF MY ENEMY . . .

Mrs Thatcher had attended her first European Communities summit in December 1979 and made clear her determination to cut the UK's contribution to the EC budget. Over time, she supported greater integration of financial markets and was willing to pay the costs of losing power to EC institutions, most notably with the Single European Act. But Mrs Thatcher became increasingly concerned that the EC was adopting policies and practices that her government had rejected. Labour's policy of withdrawal from the European Communities in the early 1980s was met with stark warnings of economic catastrophe from the Conservatives. But otherwise, Mrs Thatcher's attitude to the EC shifted from pragmatism to scepticism in part because she saw powers being lost to Brussels but more because of how these powers were being used. Opinion in Scotland shifted in the opposite direction. Regional policy had been part of the deal for Britain joining the EC. Since the UK had joined, it appointed two people to serve as European Commissioners. Each of the two main parties at Westminster appointed one Commissioner. In 1973, George Thomson resigned as Labour MP for Dundee East following a career as a journalist, including a stint as editor of the *Dandy* children's comic, to take up post as the first European Commissioner for Regional Affairs. The subsequent by-election nearly caused an upset when Gordon Wilson of the SNP came within just over 1,000 votes of winning the seat. Wilson went on to take it at the subsequent general election.

The European Regional Development Fund (ERDF) grew from the time of the Thomson Report in 1973, drawn up by George Thomson, which suggested the continuous expansion set out in the Treaty of Rome had been achieved but without a 'balanced and harmonious nature'. The Conservative government had rolled back British domestic regional policy but viewed European regional policy pragmatically as a mean of securing resources for the UK. It was a side-payment to induce Britain to join and would continue to have this function in budgetary negotiations. So long as the UK government had reasonable control over how EC regional funds were spent, it was willing to ignore the policy's interventionist nature. The ERDF was increased significantly in 1986 for less favoured regions with agreement on the Single European Act. Until this point in time, neither the EC nor regions within member states had much influence on how the money was spent. Instead, central governments spent the money on predetermined policies. The accession of Greece, Spain, and Portugal to the EC and the European single market added pressure for both an increase in regional funding and a more genuinely regional policy. In 1988, the structural funds including ERDF were doubled within a new 'Cohesion policy' designed to address the objectives outlined in the Thomson Report. This new approach involved greater focus on poorer regions and a more strategic approach involving regional and local partners.

Labour proposed Bruce Millan, who had succeeded Willie Ross as Scottish Secretary in the late 1970s and had served as Shadow Scottish Secretary until 1983, when vacancies arose in 1988 for UK nominations to the European Commission. Millan's appointment caused a by-election in his Glasgow Govan constituency. The SNP fielded Jim Sillars. Sillars won the seat from Labour in a campaign that stressed his party's opposition to the poll tax and support for a non-payment campaign. The other element in his campaign was to offer a vision of an independent Scotland as a member of the European Community.

He had succeeded in winning two by-elections for different parties, eighteen years apart, each having a significant impact on Scottish politics.

Sillars entered Parliament as a conciliator, willing to cooperate with others in pursuit of a Scottish Parliament and in opposition to the Tory government. During his time as an SNP member he had been highly critical of the more uncompromising elements in the SNP. His articulation of the case for independence in Europe combined with support for a Constitutional Convention signalled a more sophisticated understanding of the Scottish Question than had often been shown by the SNP. For a brief period in the late 1980s, the SNP united around his position. But his election as MP for Govan marked a dramatic shift in Sillars's thinking. He remained a strong advocate of independence in Europe but became hostile to compromise and working with Labour. After Govan, the SNP believed it was unstoppable, encouraged by a significant shift in the opinion polls. There may have been a personal dimension as this highly sensitive politician was goaded in the Commons by former Labour colleagues. Both parties were often petty in exchanges even at the most senior levels. In late 1989, George Robertson proclaimed in Parliament that Sillars had been seen doing his Christmas shopping in Glasgow rather than performing his duties as an MP. In fact, Govan's MP had started his day early with a meeting of community activists in his constituency and had been seen buying a sandwich for his lunch by an excitable Labour activist. But the tribalism worked both ways. In April 1989, Sillars described Donald Dewar, Labour Shadow Scottish Secretary, as a 'Scottish Uncle Tom', a 'subservient colonial towards his masters, deliberately denigrating the quality and ability of his own people'.

The SNP had been edging towards support for the EC since the 1975 referendum. It had passed a resolution in favour of 'independence in Europe' at its annual conference two months before the by-election. The SNP's more Euro-friendly positioning reflected changes in Scotland. Scottish local authorities were finding that Brussels was more amenable to their requests for support than London. Trade unionists were also finding the European Community's institutions more sympathetic to their interests than London. Campbell Christie served as a member of the EC Economic and Social Committee for a decade from 1975. He brought a European perspective to debates on the Scottish Question including a more cooperative approach to campaigning. Margaret Thatcher's hostility to Jacques Delors, President of the European Commission, was matched by strong support for Delors from local authorities, trade unions, and large sections of the Labour Party and SNP. Europe had become entwined in debates on the Scottish Question. By 1992, public opinion was following elite opinion in linking these two debates. Those who tended to be most inclined to adopt a Scottish perspective on politics were also inclined to accept a European perspective. This operated on a number of levels. Though there was little evidence of an explicit European identity, there was ample evidence of a growing banal sense of being European amongst Scots. EC regional funds came with the condition that EC support was recognized and EC symbols appeared on all of the increasing number of projects across Scotland. The EC was more adept than the Conservatives in claiming credit for their policies. It was as if the SDA, local authorities, and EC were providing more support for a variety of projects in Scotland then the UK Conservative government at this time.

There was also a constitutional dimension to this. Mrs Thatcher's growing opposition to the EC had its basis in the same thinking which led her to oppose devolution. Devolution would be another challenge to UK national sovereignty. Sovereignty was perceived as absolute power and Parliament's sovereignty was thought to be one and indivisible. It was a right-wing version of the left's opposition to European integration and devolution. The left opposed any measure that inhibited the state at the centre from delivering a common, uniform policy across the state. Awareness of the existence of elected regional government across many EC member states fed into these debates. The notion of a 'Europe of Regions' became fashionable and provided a link between the Scottish and European debates though it operated at little more than a rhetorical level. Nonetheless, the rhetoric fed into constitutional understandings. But it did more than this. It fostered a keen sense of an alternative. Thatcherism in its various guises—pro-poll tax, anti-EC, anti-devolution, pro-privatization and sundry other elements identified subjectively and selectively—was becoming Scotland's Other.

CLAIM OF RIGHT AND CONSTITUTIONAL CONVENTION

The CSA produced a plan to establish a Constitutional Convention in 1984 and further proposals the following year set out roles for a convention. It would articulate and represent the demand for an assembly, draft a scheme of devolution, negotiate its implementation with Westminster, and arrange a test of support. Progress was slow until the 1987 election. Thereafter, Scotland's constitutional change moved up the political agenda. The words 'Constitutional Convention' appeared increasingly in the press over time. In 1984, the phrase appeared in under ten news stories, jumping to over eighty in 1989 when the Convention was launched and to over 350 in 1992 but falling to well under 150 in each of the following two years before rising again to over 470 in 1995 and over 500 in 1996 and 1997. A similar pattern was evident in references to devolution. These figures tell the story of the evolution of the Convention idea and wider debates on devolution over the years when the Conservatives were in power. A major impetus came after the 1987 general election. The CSA set up a Constitutional Steering Committee of 'prominent Scots' headed by Sir Robert Grieve, a distinguished former public servant who had been a central figure in the Clyde Valley Plan and Highlands and Islands Development Board. Jim Ross, retired Scottish Office civil servant who had been responsible for devolution in the late 1970s, acted as secretary and drafted the *Claim of Right for Scotland*, the report produced by the committee.

The *Claim of Right* was published in July 1988 and proposed a Convention that would have no statutory basis but would derive its legitimacy from the involvement of a wide range of representative bodies, including elected representatives and individuals. It offered a critique of the existing system of government in Scotland:

> There is a constitutional flaw in the present machinery of Scottish government: it can work only within a limited range of election results. Providing a Scottish Ministerial team, Scottish Whips and Government representation on Standing and Select Committees, requires a certain minimum number of Government party MPs from Scottish constituencies. There is no guarantee of such a number being elected. At present the governing party is below the minimum and there is no certainty that this situation will be short-lived.

It also challenged the Conservative government's constitutional legitimacy in Scotland:

> The English constitution provides for only one source of power; the Crown-in-Parliament. That one source is now mainly embodied in the Prime Minister, who has appropriated almost all the royal prerogatives…Within the United Kingdom the Scots are a minority which cannot ever feel secure under a constitution which, in effect, renders the Treaty of Union a contradiction in terms, because it makes no provision for the safeguarding of any rights or guarantees and does not even require a majority of the electorate to override such rights and guarantees as may once have been offered.

The *Claim of Right* proposed the establishment of a Convention that would consist of all Scottish MPs, representatives of local government, and representatives drawn from civil society. Its aim was to ensure that Labour would participate as this was seen as central to any prospect of success. What was proposed was designed to reassure Labour that it would not find itself in a hostile body. Three months later, Donald Dewar announced that Labour would join the Convention. However, satisfying Labour that it was safe to live dangerously came at the cost of making the SNP feel threatened. The SNP would have been a small minority in the Convention, reflecting its level of support. The SNP felt that its success in the Govan by-election in November 1988 meant that its potential support was far greater. The SNP decided against participation after a fraught meeting of a well-attended party national council. The Conservatives were never likely to agree to participate. But the Liberal Democrats, Greens, and Democratic Left (Communists) agreed to be involved. The Convention was launched in 1989. Brian Taylor, BBC Scotland's political editor, described how the Convention meetings 'frequently oscillated between politics and pomposity'. Delegates who attended the first meeting ceremoniously signed a 'Claim of Right':

> We, gathered as the Scottish Constitutional Convention, do hereby acknowledge the sovereign right of the Scottish people to determine the form of Government best suited to their needs, and do hereby declare and pledge that in all our actions and deliberations their interests shall be paramount.
>
> We further declare and pledge that our actions and deliberations shall be directed to the following ends:
>
> To agree a scheme for an Assembly or Parliament for Scotland;
>
> To mobilise Scottish opinion and ensure the approval of the Scottish people for that scheme; and
>
> To assert the right of the Scottish people to secure implementation of that scheme.

It was reminiscent of John MacCormick's Scottish Covenant but involved the assertion of popular sovereignty that had been absent in the 1950s. It was signed by all Scottish Labour and Liberal Democrat MPs who were present, including John Smith and Gordon Brown, Labour leader and future leader respectively. In total, fifty-eight of Scotland's seventy-two MPs signed the *Claim*. What this meant in practice was unclear. Kenyon Wright, a former Episcopalian clergyman, chaired the executive committee of the Convention and proved a brilliant rhetorician. He asked and provided an answer to the obvious question, 'What if that other single voice we know so well responds by saying, "We say No and we are the State". Well, we say Yes and we are the People.' This supplied the Convention with its slogan, 'We say Yes', a Scottish version of 'We the People'. The language and the underlying thinking, treating Scotland as such a distinct political unit with a right to determine its own system of government, was nationalist other than that it was envisaged that Scotland would remain in the UK. Between 1989 and the general election in 1992, the Convention had seven full public meetings. This was the Convention on public display. The Convention was at work in its committees. An Executive Committee provided leadership and a coordinating role with regular meetings from April 1989. Its membership initially consisted of ten Labour MPs or Members of the European Parliament; two Liberal Democrat MPs; five Labour local government representatives; four local government representatives representing other parties and independents; one representative from the Labour Party; three Scottish Liberal Democrats to account for Labour's dominance amongst elected representatives; representatives from two other political parties; one representative each from the churches, STUC, and other institutions; and a representative from the CSA. The Scottish Greens suspended their membership of the Convention in November 1991 when the Convention refused to agree in principle to a multi-option referendum on Scotland's constitutional status or commit itself to a clear timetable to select a voting system.

It was agreed amongst participants that the Convention should operate by consensus and that 'When a vote is proposed it shall be open to any one of the designated political groups to indicate that the matter is of such fundamental importance to that group that it could not be bound by an adverse vote. In such circumstances no vote shall be taken.' A series of working groups were set up covering the Powers of Assembly or Parliament; Financing of Assembly or Parliament; Constitutional Issues; Women's Issues; and Publicity and Public Involvement. It was a novel way to write a new constitution. The traditional method of constitutional deliberation and amendment was described by Nevil Johnson, who had been Mrs Thatcher's constitutional adviser, as 'pragmatic adaptation'. The 'customary constitution', as Johnson called the UK constitution, 'lays great store by a capacity to leave principles inexplicit, relying instead on what people feel from past experience to be appropriate in the circumstances'. Elites provided both its legitimacy and negotiated accommodations within the 'British tradition of pragmatic adaptation'. This new constitutionalism, evident in the Scottish Constitutional Convention, involved a much wider range of participants and more public deliberation. But it operated outside the formal constitution and was viewed by opponents as simply the activities of a pressure group and political parties.

This culminated in the publication of *Towards Scotland's Parliament* on St Andrew's Day 1990. It built on earlier proposals including the bill Labour had presented to Parliament after the 1987 general election and various papers produced by the CSA. It excluded broadcasting, a subject that had been included in earlier CSA proposals. A block grant based on needs from Westminster would fund the Parliament and would be reviewed regularly. It left open how 'needs' might be determined. It also proposed some assigned revenues including Scottish value added tax and limited powers to vary the income tax rate.

Some issues remained unresolved. The Liberal Democrats wanted to abolish the post of Scottish Secretary but Labour wanted it retained. Otherwise it was silent on relations between Scottish and UK governments. The Convention had spent considerable time, drawing on expert advice, on how the Parliament should be elected and how it might reach out to the Scottish public. Part of its critique of the Westminster system was that it was unrepresentative and distant from the public. Agreement was reached that an electoral system other than simple plurality should be found though it proved difficult to agree what that should be. On this issue, the most significant development was Labour's decision to abandon its commitment to simple plurality. At its 1990 Scottish conference, Labour agreed to an alternative voting system for the new Scottish Parliament. This had been pushed through by the trade union block votes. The Liberal Democrats were committed to Single Transferable Vote (STV). Labour was beginning to live dangerously. The simple plurality system worked in Labour's favour and abandoning it would likely cost Labour an overall majority but simple plurality also meant that the SNP might gain an overall majority. Labour's decision was an implicit acceptance of the potential strength of the SNP, potential that had been little in evidence for over a decade.

The Convention looked specifically at the role of women and worked to ensure that the Parliament would have a higher proportion of women than had traditionally been achieved in Scottish politics. Various women's organizations lobbied hard under the banner of 50:50 representation. The Working Group on Women's Issues made proposals concerning parliamentary hours and sittings, arguing that such matters had been impediments to women's participation in politics. Engender, a new pressure group, was established in 1992 to 'raise awareness of issues which directly affect women in Scotland'. It noted that only Greece and Northern Ireland had poorer records in women's representation in the EC than Scotland. There were then only four women MPs from Scotland out of seventy-two. There was also concern, though less effort made, to ensure improved ethnic minority representation.

Representation was the dominant issue in the Convention's deliberations. Its discussions of the powers and financing of the Parliament were more conservative and derivative of earlier proposals. In 1990 it outlined key features to guide the choice of an electoral system though it had difficulty finding a system that incorporated all of these:

(a) that it produces results in which the number of seats for various parties is broadly related to the number of votes cast for them;

(b) that it ensures, or at least takes effective positive action to bring about, equal representation of men and women, and encourages fair representation of ethnic and other minority groups;

(c) that it preserves a real link between the member and his/her constituency;

(d) that it is as simple as possible to understand;

(e) that it ensures adequate representation of less populous areas; and

(f) that the system be designed to place the greatest possible power in the hands of the electorate.

Discussions on the Parliament's powers and finances broadly followed what had been decided inside the Labour Party. The starting point, as in the Scotland Act 1978, had been the Scottish Office's responsibilities. Even the funding would follow the grant basis that was used for the Scottish Office. In large measure, this reflected the motivation behind support for a Scottish Parliament at least amongst the dominant supporters in the Convention. The problem was not the Scottish Office's responsibilities but what it did with them. The dominant view inside the Convention was that the key was to ensure the creation of a representative institution.

There was widespread expectation that the Conservatives would lose the 1992 election, whether to Labour with an overall majority or a hung Parliament, and predictions that they would lose significant support in Scotland. In the event, John Major stayed in power with a reduced overall majority and managed in Scotland to increase his party's share of the vote slightly and gain a seat from Labour. The SNP had gone into the election expecting a major breakthrough which it achieved by increasing its share of the vote by 7.1 per cent to 22.1 per cent but failed to win any additional seats compared with 1987. It lost Govan, won by Jim Sillars at the by-election, who accused Scots of being '90 minute patriots'. Sillars retired from front-line politics and would only make the occasional intervention, usually to criticize the SNP and Alex Salmond in particular with the same vituperation he had previously reserved for his erstwhile Labour colleagues. He was one of very few in the SNP who argued against supporting devolution in the 1997 referendum, warning that devolution was a trap. Mr Major had campaigned on his soapbox in 1992 and at one point had made Scotland's constitutional status a campaign issue when he insisted, 'If I could summon up all the authority of this office, I would put it into this single warning—the United Kingdom is in danger. Wake up, my fellow countrymen! Wake up now before it is too late!' He agreed to take stock of Scotland's constitutional status once the election was over.

But 1992 was not 1979. The immediate reaction from supporters of a Scottish Parliament was to organize into new campaign groups and hold protest meetings. The group Democracy for Scotland started a vigil outside the Royal High School, the building designated in the 1970s to become the Scottish Assembly. Indeed, polls suggested that the issue of Scotland's constitutional status had risen up the political agenda following the election. Mr Major's 'stock taking' exercise involved appointing Lord Fraser, former Tory MP Peter Fraser, as Scottish Office Minister of State with responsibility for the constitution and to engage in a consultation exercise. For a brief period, there was speculation that the Tories might be about to make an historic break with past opposition to devolution. Instead, they produced a White Paper, *Scotland in the Union: A Partnership for Good*, in March 1993. It was a thin document that proposed some limited changes in parliamentary procedure and administrative arrangements.

Mr Major's focus shifted to a different union. The Prime Minister had signed the Maastricht Treaty in February 1992, two months before the general election. The Treaty created the European Union (EU) including a new idea of European citizenship, giving new powers to European institutions, and paved the way for the euro, the single currency. Mr Major might have been reluctant to devolve power to Scotland but was criticized by a growing body of opinion in his party for devolving power to Brussels. A group of Tory rebels, exceeding the Tories' overall majority in Parliament follow-ing the 1992 election, opposed ratification of the Treaty in Parliament. Even more problems arose for the government in September 1992 when the UK was forced out of the European Exchange Rate Mechanism (ERM). The ERM had been introduced to reduce exchange rate variability and create monetary stability. The UK had joined in 1990 but had come under sustained pressure culminating in 'Black Wednesday' when £27 billion was spent trying to prop up sterling. The UK's relation with the EU would dominate the rest of the Parliament and be the source of deep divisions in the Conservative Party. 'Black Wednesday' would have a devastating impact on the public's percep-tion of the government's economic competence. In 1995, John Major resigned as Conservative leader to seek a new mandate from his party and was chal-lenged by John Redwood, Secretary of State for Wales. Mr Major had hoped a decisive victory would restore his authority but a third of his colleagues voted for Mr Redwood.

Scotland was sidelined at Westminster amidst these developments as Conservative support slid away across Britain. The EU offered the home rule movement an opportunity. The UK's turn to chair the European Council came in the latter half of 1992 and the Prime Minister decided soon after the 1992 election to host the meeting in Edinburgh as part of his appeal to Scots. Home rulers organized a massive demonstration—the Democracy Demonstration—to coincide with the summit. The demonstration was an important fillip after the disappointment of the general election. Home rule was not dead.

NEW LABOUR AND THE CONVENTION

One significant change followed the 1992 election. Neil Kinnock stood down as Labour leader and John Smith, former Devolution Minister, was elected in his place. Unlike Mr Kinnock, John Smith had been fully converted to the devolution cause. He had always had a strong sense of Scottish identity and would be accused of favouring fellow Scots at various points during his leadership. His support helped cement Labour's commitment to a Scottish Parliament and his comment that it was the 'settled will of the Scottish peo-ple' that a Parliament should be established became part of the mantra of the home rule movement after his death. But Mr Smith died less than two years after becoming leader. There had been indications that sections of the Conservative-supporting press might be preparing to play an 'English card' against Labour under John Smith's leadership. The prospect of a ter-ritorially polarized version of British adversarial politics seemed a real pos-sibility though it was unlikely that the leadership of either party would be entirely comfortable with this. Labour had the opposite problem from the

Conservatives. In 1987, over a fifth of the Parliamentary Labour Party (PLP) was returned from Scotland (just under a third from Scotland and Wales combined). In 1992, this proportion had fallen to 18 per cent from Scotland (28 per cent from Scotland and Wales) but still much higher than population proportions.

Devolution played little part in the election of John Smith's successor. Tony Blair's views on the subject were obscure. He had spent the early years of his parliamentary career, after entering Parliament in 1983 for Sedgefield in the north of England, in the shadow of Gordon Brown. He had had little direct experience of Scottish affairs, though he had boarded at Fettes, one of Scotland's most exclusive fee-paying schools, which would have given him an odd understanding of Scotland. He rose through Labour's ranks rapidly from his first appointment as a junior Treasury spokesman before holding a quick succession of Shadow posts at Trade, Energy, Employment, and Home Affairs. None of these would bring him into much contact with the Scottish Question. What became clear on John Smith's death was that Gordon Brown, with a solid base in Scottish Labour politics, could not rely on as much support from Scottish Labour MPs as he might have expected. A number of prominent home rulers backed Blair, though they saw Brown as more sympathetic to home rule, because they saw Blair as more likely to win a general election and were secure in the belief that Labour's commitment to devolution was irreversible. Of forty-two Scottish Labour MPs surveyed, only fifteen said they would support Gordon Brown for the leadership and six intended to support Tony Blair, while a further six said they felt an obligation to support Brown but hoped he would not stand. It was hardly an enthusiastic endorsement of Gordon Brown in what was his heartland.

Under Mr Blair's leadership, Labour embarked on a programme of reform. His decision to reform the party constitution would provide further evidence that Scottish Labour was less distinct and less left-wing than many imagined. Two days after Tony Blair announced that he would seek to change the party constitution, Labour's conference heard a delegate from Glasgow make an impassioned plea for traditional socialism—'tough on capitalism, tough on the causes of capitalism', mocking one of Mr Blair's most famous soundbites. Speculation that the new leader would run up against a problem in Scotland disappeared when the Scottish party conference agreed to Blair's proposed reform of the party's constitution. If Scotland accepted a new Clause 4, a new definition of socialism, then the rest of the party would too.

While the Constitutional Convention claimed widespread support, its real achievement was in getting the Labour Party involved. The key relationship was between Labour and the Liberal Democrats. The Convention would have collapsed had either party withdrawn and the relationship between the leadership of each was key to its deliberations. There was concern amongst other participants that the two main parties dominated proceedings. Just before the

1992 election, Bruce Black, deputy secretary of the Convention of Scottish Local Authorities (CoSLA) and also secretary to the Convention, wrote to non-party political members of the Convention's executive urging them to 'act together and speak on behalf of the Convention' complaining that the two main parties had held a press conference without involving other Convention participants and stressed that it was 'essential that steps be taken to emphasise that the Convention is not simply the two political parties but involves a range of other interests and organisations'. He insisted that the Convention was 'much broader than Labour and the Liberal Democrats' and that its 'main target of attack' should be the Conservative Party and 'not the concept of nationalism or independence'. The SNP had picked up support since 1987 and in January 1992 the Scottish edition of the *Sun* newspaper came out in favour of independence. A poll that month showed 50 per cent of Scots wanted independence. Labour and Liberal Democrats could hardly ignore what they saw as a major challenger.

But fear of the SNP was only part of their concern. The Convention had bought time. Kenyon Wright's 'We are the people' rhetoric sounded like the chant of football supporters rather than constitutional idealism. Elements within and outside the Convention were demanding action. Labour had seen off its radical home element who had called for parliamentary disruption but was now facing similar demands from the wider national movement frustrated by lack of progress. While Labour and the Liberal Democrats viewed the SNP as a threat, others in the Convention saw the SNP as potential allies. A briefing paper on strategy prepared in early 1992 noted the growing support for independence and suggested that this had 'certainly succeeded in bringing the whole question firmly to the top of the political agenda. We can only welcome this.' This was not a view shared by Labour and Lib-Dem leaders.

The Convention, including the Labour Party, agreed to support a multi-option referendum after the 1992 election as a means of providing unity across the non-Conservative parties. It would allow Labour and Liberal Democrats to support a measure of devolution, while the SNP could support independence and the Conservatives the status quo. But the Prime Minister was not going to support such a referendum and support for the idea inside the Convention was shallow. There was little prospect of local authorities across Scotland holding such a referendum even though Strathclyde Region, prior to its demise under the Conservative's reorganization of local government, had run a postal referendum on water privatization in 1994. Turnout in that referendum had been 70 per cent and 97 per cent had voted against privatization. A number of prominent Labour council leaders expressed doubts about a multi-option referendum. As any referendum would require the support of local government, this effectively killed the idea. The only alternative, without the main political parties or local authorities behind any radical strategy, was to wait until the Conservatives were defeated at a general election. A number of initiatives gave the appearance of activity but home rulers were simply waiting for a change of government at Westminster.

The Convention set up a Constitutional Commission to address matters that had remained unresolved by the Convention including the electoral system to be used in elections to the proposed Scottish Parliament. The Convention struggled to find someone to chair the Commission until Joyce MacMillan, the *Scotsman's* theatre critic, agreed to take on the job. The Commission proposed using the Additional Member System, based on the seventy-two Westminster constituencies plus a further forty Additional Members with five additional members returned from each of Scotland's eight European Parliament constituencies giving a total of 112 Members. This would make it a more proportional system than simple plurality. It sought to entrench the electoral system and the Parliament 'in order that these would be incapable of being unilaterally amended at a later date by the Westminster Parliament' but failed to explain how this would be done. It made some vague commitments to local democracy. It opposed an immediate reduction in Scottish representation at Westminster but failed to reach agreement on the future of the office of Secretary of State for Scotland. The Convention had focused on representation and paid limited attention to the Parliament's powers but it ignored how devolved government would sit within the UK system of government. There was irony in the Convention insisting that it proposed devolution within the United Kingdom, rejecting independence, while ignoring the UK-wide dimension of its proposals. Its focus had exclusively been on how Scotland should be governed *in* Scotland.

It was becoming increasingly clear that the Conservatives were likely to lose the next general election. Labour under Tony Blair was preparing for government and various reform bodies were contributing to the debate on constitutional reform. While the thrust of the debate in Scotland focused on how Scotland should be governed, others outside Scotland were considering the Scottish Question in a wider UK context. The Constitution Unit, a new think tank based at University College London, run by a former Home Office civil servant, was set up in 1995 and prepared a series of reports on constitutional change including an important report on Scottish devolution. The Unit addressed a number of issues on which the Convention and the Constitutional Commission had failed to reach agreement and stated that legislation should list powers to be retained at Westminster, leaving all other matters to be devolved, rather than the approach adopted in the 1978 Devolution Act. It also proposed that both Westminster and the Scottish Parliament should, through agreement, be able to legislate on matters not formally within their powers. It proposed that the House of Lords should be the final court of appeal in disputes on competence. It also suggested that a referendum would provide a 'strong and explicit' endorsement of devolution and provide a form of entrenchment. It addressed the funding of the

Scottish Parliament, suggesting that an independent Commission should be established to review the funding formula used to finance the Parliament and that autonomous revenue raising powers were needed to achieve fiscal responsibility and accountability. It proposed that the Parliament should have borrowing powers and it should have direct representation in Brussels with guaranteed rights to be consulted by the UK government in EU negotiations that relate to devolved matters. It was unable to provide an answer to the West Lothian Question but suggested that this might be remitted to a Speaker's conference. In terms of inter-governmental relations, the Unit proposed that the office of Secretary of State for Scotland should be abolished and that a Joint Council of UK and Scottish Governments should be established and acknowledged that the Parliament would have 'limited' scope to develop an independent economic and industrial policy.

Two Scottish Labour Party members made an important contribution to the debate. Wendy Alexander and Jim MacCormick discussed three main aspects of devolution that the Convention had failed to address: the parliamentary passage of the devolution legislation; economic and fiscal powers; and different political scenarios. They too argued for a 'reverse definition of powers', defining what would be retained at Westminster and leaving the rest to the Parliament as this would 'shift the burden of proof to Westminster, which would have to demonstrate that the Scottish Parliament had strayed into its reserved area of competence, rather than Edinburgh having to prove repeatedly that it was entitled to legislate'. They did not rule out abolishing the office of Secretary of State for Scotland. They argued that the 'more important question' was to 'directly address how to create effective inter-governmental machinery, including respected procedures to resolve inter-parliamentary disputes'. They acknowledged that 'inter-parliamentary disputes' would not be 'well served if they were to depend primarily on the position adopted by an intermediary, in the person of the Secretary of State'. A Scottish Secretary 'would provide ongoing opportunities for MPs who want to undermine devolution, question the settlement and encourage Westminster's interference in Edinburgh's affairs'. In addressing the West Lothian Question (WLQ), MacCormick and Alexander ran through the familiar list of responses and inclined to support a reduction in Scottish MPs but argued that devolution ought to be seen as part of a larger package of constitutional reform that might include electoral reform. What made this contribution most significant was that Wendy Alexander became Special Adviser to Donald Dewar on his appointment as Secretary of State for Scotland after the 1997 election and became a Member of the Scottish Parliament and Minister in 1999.

Another important contribution came from two leading authorities on legislatures. Professor Bernard Crick had been a leading advocate of the reform of the Westminster Parliament and had taken up residence in Edinburgh after retiring. David Millar had spent a career working as a parliamentary official in the House of Commons and then the European Parliament and had an encyclopaedic knowledge of European legislatures. In 1995, they produced proposals for the operation of the proposed Parliament. They were keen to ensure that the Scottish Parliament would not be as subservient to the executive as Parliament at Westminster had become. They were particularly keen that its committees should play a more important role than the equivalents at Westminster.

The hints that a referendum might be held were largely ignored. The experience of 1979 made many devolutionists wary of a referendum despite demands for a multi-option referendum. But there was one area where home rulers felt vulnerable and this had particular resonance for Labour's leadership. It had been decided that the Parliament should have tax-varying powers which were generally assumed to mean, and had been intended when initially adopted, tax-raising powers. Though these powers were meagre they had become politically significant after Michael Forsyth became Scottish Secretary in July 1995. Mr Forsyth was the only Scottish Secretary to cause devolutionists any concern. He rarely made a public statement on devolution without reference to the 'tartan tax'. 'New' Labour under Tony Blair and Gordon Brown were intent on removing Labour's image as a 'tax-and-spend' party. In 1996, Labour announced that a two-question referendum would be held in which Scots would be asked whether they wanted a Parliament and whether it should have tax-varying powers with an emphasis on *varying*. There was concern that Labour had unilaterally decided to hold a referendum and had not discussed this in the Convention. But whatever the original motives, the Constitution Unit's suggestion that a referendum would provide a degree of political entrenchment would prove correct.

CONCLUSION

The most remarkable aspect of the Scottish Question in the period during which the Conservatives were in power was the extent to which it became dominated by Scotland's constitutional status and the case for a Parliament. This happened because of the party system and the government's pursuit of unpopular policies in Scotland. The Scottish Question had, in this respect, remained an amalgam as it always had been only that it had coalesced around Scotland's constitutional status. Along the way, the commitment grew stronger. Supporters stopped talking about creating an assembly and started referring to a Scottish Parliament. Party political polarization occurred. There were those inside the Labour Party who opposed devolution but they had either fallen silent or were marginalized. The Conservative Party included a few supporters of devolution but they were even more marginalized in their party. The SNP had been highly suspicious of devolution after the election and referendum in 1979 but had hesitantly moved back to support devolution. Eighteen years of Conservative government with declining support in Scotland proved important in public perceptions of the intimate relationship between everyday public policy concerns, party politics, and Scotland's constitutional status.

11

Devolution in Action

INTRODUCTION

A referendum and general election in 1979 put an end to the prospect of a Scottish Assembly while an election and referendum created the conditions for a Parliament's creation in 1997. Supporters of a Scottish Parliament could finally move out of the shadow of 1979. Support for the Parliament had not just increased in the number of people who supported its creation but in the priority attached to its creation. This increased support was, however, largely negative. Those who supported it generally knew what they opposed. Thatcherism, however defined, had become Scotland's Other against which Scots had mobilized in favour of a Parliament. Thatcherism might have been defined variously by different people but it cohered in Scotland's public imagination as something that a Parliament would resist. It mattered little that there was no agreement on what it meant, which elements were most opposed, or that Mrs Thatcher herself had not been Prime Minister for seven years and had retired from the House of Commons. The memory and myth lived on and was the most powerful factor in mobilizing support for devolution. But what kind of Parliament would it be? What policies would it pursue? And would its establishment kill nationalism, as Labour politician George Robertson insisted, or act as a base for demanding more powers or independence? Would it finally resolve the Scottish Question?

THE 1997 REFERENDUM

There were four stages to the establishment of the Scottish Parliament after the general election held in May 1997 and each was completed efficiently. The first stage was to pass legislation to conduct a referendum in Scotland. This was completed by the end of July. The referendum was held in September 1997. The Scotland Bill was presented to Parliament in December and received Royal Assent in November 1998. Preparatory work began immediately after the referendum under an all-party Consultative Steering Group (CSG), chaired by Henry McLeish, Scottish Office Minister in charge of devolution. The first elections to the Scottish Parliament were held in May 1999. The Tory defeat and absence of any Scottish MPs in Parliament meant that parliamentary scrutiny of the legislation was minimal compared to the 1978 Act. Lessons had been learned. Having the referendum before the substantive legislation meant that debates at Westminster were based on an understanding that devolution would happen and MPs had no incentive to propose disguised wrecking amendments or use parliamentary debates as part of a referendum campaign, as had happened in the 1970s. As only a White Paper outlining what was proposed was available, the referendum was conducted on the broad principle of devolution.

The White Paper was based on the Constitutional Convention's proposals though differed in some respects. The most significant symbolic difference was that the Convention claimed to have been based on the principle of popular sovereignty while the White Paper adopted a very different stance: 'The UK Parliament is and will remain sovereign in all matters; but as part of Parliament's resolve to modernise the British constitution Westminster will be choosing to exercise that sovereignty by devolving legislative responsibilities to a Scottish Parliament without in any way diminishing its own power.' The legislation defined matters that would be reserved at Westminster and allowed other matters to come within the remit of the Scottish Parliament. This followed the approach adopted in Irish home rule legislation and reversed the approach in the Scotland Act, 1978. The tax-varying powers were cosmetic. The Parliament would be empowered to vary the rate of income tax by 3p in the pound but the main funding would come through grant. The funding formula was not defined by statute. The establishment of the Scottish Parliament was an opportunity to move beyond the 'Barnett formula' but this would have involved finding an alternative which in itself would take time, prove highly contentious, and would have required transitional arrangements. It would also have meant that devolved government would have been more of a break with the past than was desired in London. The White Paper also proposed that the number of MPs returned from Scotland would be reduced to bring it in proportion to its population. The Scottish Parliament itself would have 129 Members elected by the additional member system with seventy-two constituency members and fifty-six regional list members. Each voter would cast two votes—one for a constituency member and the other for a party on regional lists (though individuals could stand on the list). The constituency Members of the Scottish Parliament (MSPs) would be returned from the existing Scottish Commons' constituencies other than Orkney and Shetland which would each return a member to the Scottish Parliament. The regional list members would provide a greater degree of proportionality to the electoral system. The office of Scottish Secretary would continue to exist though renamed the Scotland Office.

But such details would play little part in the referendum campaign. With two questions, there might have been scope for a range of options: Yes to a Parliament and Yes to tax powers; Yes to a Parliament but No to tax powers; No to a Parliament and No to tax powers; even No to a Parliament but Yes to tax powers. The last seemed fanciful and few voters opted for this though one commentator announced this was how he would vote in opposition to devolution but feeling that if it had to happen it should be fiscally responsible for what it spent. In the event, the umbrella organizations and political parties folded the two questions into one campaign. Two umbrella campaign groups were formed. 'Scotland FORward' was distinct from the Constitutional Convention as it included the SNP after the SNP voted overwhelmingly to become involved. The political parties, especially the SNP and Labour, provided the groundwork and leadership for the campaign. Research done by Scotland FORward indicated that the main worry people had was that the Scottish Parliament would result in higher taxation though even this was not identified by more than 15 per cent of people surveyed. While elites made much of the electoral system and equal representation for women, these issues hardly resonated with the wider public. The key according to Peter Kellner, who had been commissioned to analyse the data, was that 'economic issues drive the "double no" vote, while governance issues drive the "double yes" vote' or, as Kellner put it, the 'thistle in your kilt versus pound in your sporran' divide. His advice was to stress governance issues—'Scottish pride, identity, the intrinsic values of taking its own decisions'. While the official umbrella group might have focused on this, the key activities were determined by the parties who had troops on the ground throughout Scotland. The parties largely ignored Kellner's advice and focused on what had been the reason for growth in support for a Scottish Parliament. Identity may have been the base but what mobilized opinion was opposition to the Conservatives. The memory of the Conservatives in government was still fresh. It helped that Mrs Thatcher, *bête noir* of Scottish politics, was due to address a conference of American travel agents in Glasgow in the last week of the campaign. Given the venue, Mrs Thatcher felt obliged to issue a statement opposing devolution, but otherwise kept well away from the media on her Scottish trip. The *Daily Record*, which had covered its front page with the headline 'Mrs Supercool' in 1975 on her first visit to Scotland as Tory leader, conveyed the key campaign message:

DELIGHTED she is here. Why? Because she's the best possible reason yet why Scots should vote YES YES on Thursday. Thatcher ruled Scotland from London for more than a decade and caused untold misery. We didn't vote for her. Again and again the Scottish voters rejected her cynical brand of greed and callousness.

But we could not escape her malign influence...VOTE YES YES—FOR NO MORE MAGGIES.

There was no equivalent of 'Labour Says No', as in 1979, though Tam Dalyell campaigned for a No vote despite including support for devolution in his election address at the general election only a few months before. Other Labour devo-sceptics kept their heads down. The impression created was that the anti-Tory parties were united in favour of change.

'Think Twice' struggled to be seen as anything other than a Conservative Party campaign. The Conservatives had lost all of their seats in Scotland and were left demoralized. Privately, the party was convinced it had little to gain from involvement in the campaign but could see no way of not participating. Lord Fraser, former Tory MP who lost his seat in 1987 to the SNP and became John Major's Scottish Constitutional Affairs Minister in 1992, was drafted in to head 'Think Twice'. Sections of business feared devolution but did not want to antagonize the new government and saw little point in intervening in a debate that was widely anticipated to be a foregone conclusion. This was in marked contrast to the debate in the 1970s. Sir Bruce Patullo, chairman of the Bank of Scotland, criticized the tax powers and suggested that 'Scottish business could live with a Yes, No' vote. This provoked swift responses from the parties and Patullo was put on the defensive. It was always difficult to know what business thought, not least because there could never be a single business view, given its diversity, and the vast majority of business people kept out of these debates. The Confederation of Business in Scotland (CBIS) had decided that there was little point in engaging in the referendum debate even though this intensely conservative institution was far from enthusiastic about devolution. The referendum marked an important moment in the decline of CBIS's influence. It had become associated with an anti-devolution position and was seen as too close to the Conservatives. It struggled to gain the ear of government to anything like that which it had in the 1980s when Bill Hughes, its chairman, was invited to Chequers to outline his plan for the creation of Scottish Enterprise.

Scots voted overwhelmingly for a Scottish Parliament (74.3 per cent) and emphatically for tax-varying powers (63.5 per cent) on a turnout of 60.4 per cent. There was no 40 per cent rule on this occasion but the majority for a Parliament would have exceeded this hurdle with 45.7 per cent of the total electorate voting for the Parliament. Scots came within 1.1 per cent of overcoming the 40 per cent rule for tax-varying powers. Every region of Scotland supported the Parliament ranging from 79.4 per cent in the Western Isles to 60.7 per cent in Dumfries and Galloway. All but Dumfries and Galloway and Orkney voted for tax powers (though the vote for tax powers was 48.8 per cent and 47.4 per cent in these areas respectively). Even Shetland narrowly (51.6 per cent) voted for tax powers. Research on public attitudes showed that while support for a Parliament existed across social classes, religious groups, and generations there was greater support amongst men, the working class, manual workers, younger people, council tenants, Catholics and those without a religious affiliation. Those who saw themselves as Scottish were more likely to be in favour. But social characteristics alone did not explain the results. By far the most significant characteristic of voting for a Parliament was having no identification with the Conservatives. Party political loyalties played a key part in the 1997 referendum with 88 per cent of SNP voters voting Yes/Yes; 81 per cent of Labour voters; though only 51 per cent of Liberal Democrats; and 10 per cent of Conservative voters. Scots were reasonably clear in what they were voting against if less clear in what they were voting for.

THERE SHALL BE A SCOTTISH PARLIAMENT

The referendum result meant that opposition in Parliament was limited. By convention, the Prime Minister moves the second reading of bills dealing with major constitutional change but Donald Dewar was given this task. Mr Dewar spoke of creating a 'new politics in Scotland, bringing back popular legitimacy, while creating the basis to reinvigorate Scottish life', and referred to the 'locust years' under the Tories stating that 'such madness...can certainly never happen again'. The Scottish Parliament would 'speak for the people of Scotland, is closer to their needs and concerns, and is ultimately accountable to them'. Michael Ancram, now Tory MP for Devizes in Wiltshire having briefly held Berwick and East Lothian between the two elections in 1974 and Edinburgh South from 1979 until 1987, was Opposition spokesman on the constitution. The Tories accepted the referendum result but identified four matters that required attention. The West Lothian Question had 'all the makings of a classic constitutional grievance'. Scotland would be marginalized in the Councils of the European Union as there was no statutory protection giving Scotland direct access to the EU Council of Ministers. The Parliament would undermine Scotland's financial relations with the rest of the UK as there was no statutory protection of the Barnett formula. Ancram was also critical of tax-varying powers being limited to income tax.

The Committee stage in Parliament was very different from that when the 1970s devolution legislation was passed. The government had control of the House of Commons. Amendments moved by the government passed with little or no debate. In some cases these were minor details. The power of the Scottish Parliament was extended to legislate in relation to theatres and hypnotism, largely through lobbying by Jim Wallace, leader of the Scottish Liberal Democrats. An amendment to allow the Scottish Parliament to amend the law on abortion was proposed by Liam Fox, a Tory

Scot representing an English constituency. This was opposed by the government on the grounds that the Abortion Act, 1967, had Britain-wide application. The amendment was defeated though three Scottish Labour MPs voted in favour. A similar move in the Lords, led by David Steel who had been the sponsor of the 1967 Act, was also defeated. The assumption was that the Scottish Parliament would tighten up control of abortion. While the Tories proposed that abortion should be devolved, Tory peers attempted unsuccessfully to reserve power on the law affecting euthanasia. SNP MPs moved amendments seeking to extend the powers of the Parliament but generally failed to make much impact. The one area where SNP persistence paid off was to extend the Bill's powers to legislate for land reform though the government resisted efforts to allow the Crown Estates to come under the control of the Scottish Parliament. The main prize for the Liberal Democrats was in securing an extra seat for Orkney and Shetland. An amendment in the Lords allowing the Scottish Parliament to determine its electoral system was reversed by the Commons.

Parliamentary debates highlighted how little attention had been paid to devolution's implications for the rest of the UK. The SNP had proposed that a Constitutional Court, rather than the Judicial Committee of the Privy Council, should adjudicate in disputes between the Scottish Parliament and Westminster. This was opposed at the time though a Supreme Court was established in 2009. Another amendment moved by Lord Steel proposed the establishment of a formal 'Interparliamentary Consultative Commission' to ensure cooperation and avoid damaging turf wars. In response, the government announced that it intended to establish 'standing arrangements for the devolved administrations to be involved by the UK Government at ministerial level when they consider reserved matters which impinge on devolved responsibilities' but did not intend this to be on a statutory basis. Joint Ministerial Committees consisting of ministers from UK and devolved administrations would meet but they were consultative and non-statutory, preventing any prospect of a Scottish government using the courts to challenge the UK government for failing to consult. The government also established 'concordats' between various parts of the two executives which Mr Dewar would describe as 'road maps for bureaucrats'.

While Westminster legislated, Scottish Office Minister Henry McLeish was chairing the Consultative Steering Group (CSG) charged with considering the 'operational needs and working methods of the Scottish Parliament' and developing 'proposals for the rules of procedure and Standing Orders'. The CSG set out four key principles that would guide them:

- the Scottish Parliament should embody and reflect the sharing of power between the people of Scotland, the legislators and the Scottish executive;

- the Scottish executive should be accountable to the Scottish Parliament and the Parliament and executive should be accountable to the people of Scotland;
- the Scottish Parliament should be accessible, open, responsive, and develop procedures which make possible a participative approach to the development, consideration, and scrutiny of policy and legislation;
- the Scottish Parliament in its operation and its appointments should recognize the need to promote equal opportunities for all.

The CSG attempted to develop the idea of 'new politics' but focused on the operation of the Parliament rather than the executive. The Parliament adopted the CSG principles shortly after its establishment. These four principles have subsequently been used by the Parliament and commentators to evaluate it.

The extent to which the Parliament would be different from Westminster would in large part depend on who was elected to it. Labour made a conscious effort to encourage a wider selection of candidates while ensuring that those selected would be loyal to the party. It also adopted measures to ensure that half its elected representatives would be women through having a male and female candidate standing in each set of twinned constituencies. The SNP rejected twinning but made an effort to ensure a high proportion of women were returned.

THE NARCISSISM OF SMALL DIFFERENCES

The first elections to the new Parliament were held in May 1999. Labour won fifty-six seats in the 129-Member Parliament, all but three elected in constituencies. The SNP won thirty-five but only seven were elected in constituencies. The Conservatives won eighteen seats, all returned on regional lists, and the Liberal Democrats won seventeen, twelve elected in constituencies. The Scottish Greens and Scottish Socialist Party each won a seat on a list and Dennis Canavan, former Labour MP who had not been selected to stand for his party, stood as an Independent constituency candidate and secured the highest share of the vote of any candidate in the election.

The extent to which the Scottish Parliament offered a form of 'new politics' is disputed not least because the term 'new politics' was vague. In June 1999, Scottish Tory leader David McLetchie suggested that 'new politics has been a complete sham...The truth, however blunt, is infinitely preferable to euphemisms such as consensus, co-operation and new politics.' Part of the case for the Parliament was that it would be different from Westminster. Scottish devolution's Other was based on a perception, sometimes a caricature, of Westminster. There was a tendency to exaggerate differences and ignore similarities. The similarities were often unquestioned. There had been no suggestion that the new devolved polity should be anything other than one in which the executive should be chosen from within the legislature. The politicians who designed it had experience of Westminster and consciously set out to be different or unconsciously copied it. Westminster loomed large in its creation ensuring that the Scottish Parliament would belong to the Westminster family of legislatures. As Presiding Officer, David Steel outlined twelve key differences with Westminster:

- fixed term of four years;
- no annual 'sessions' meaning that bills do not fall at a certain date in the calendar as they do at Westminster;
- elections by 'proportional representation' which results in a multi-party system;
- U-shaped chamber designed to promote consensus;
- it keeps 'civilised hours';
- much higher percentage of women;
- legislative procedure involves scrutiny before bills are debated in the chamber;
- petition system opens up the process more to the public;
- a weekly slot called 'time for reflection' led each time in public session by members of the different faith communities in Scotland (each daily session at Westminster begins with the same Anglican prayers);
- webcasting of its proceedings;
- an open and inclusive Parliament; its founders were clear that these principles must be extended to all—and that includes children and young people;
- a new Parliamentary building at Holyrood.

Lord Steel first outlined these differences during the first four-year session before changes were introduced at Westminster, under Robin Cook's period as Leader of the House of Commons, which reduced the differences. Many of Steel's 'dozen differences' were innovative at the time but the Commons subsequently adopted many of these or versions of them. 'New politics' was taken to mean a less adversarial style of politics. The electoral system was thought likely to contribute to a more consensual style of politics and the U-shaped chamber architecturally embodied consensus. It was even suggested that having more women would make the Parliament and Scottish politics gentler, ignoring the conviction politics of the former Prime Minister who did more than anyone to encourage support for the Parliament. The Parliament adopted the Question Time format, one of the key characteristics of Westminster adversarial politics.

First Minister's Questions were Prime Minister's Questions with more parties hurling abuse across a U-shaped chamber.

The dominant issue in the early years of devolution was the Holyrood building project. The old Royal High School in Edinburgh had been designated and designed to be the Scottish Assembly in the late 1970s and it had been assumed that it would house the new Scottish Parliament. The CSA had used a symbol depicting the Royal High with a key. But the Labour government decided that a new building was necessary. The decision, made in London, to site the new Parliament in a new purpose-built building opposite Holyrood Palace, the Queen's official residence in Scotland, proved highly controversial when the costs of the project escalated. Until the Holyrood building was ready, the Parliament met in the Church of Scotland's General Assembly hall. Lord Steel had argued that in the fullness of time, Holyrood would come to be seen as similar to the Sydney Opera House, an iconic building that overcame its controversial origins. An inquiry into the Holyrood project, headed by Lord Fraser who had led the anti-devolution 'Think Twice' campaign, succeeded in drawing a line under this episode.

Barry Winetrobe, former House of Commons official who played an important part advising on parliamentary procedures, offered the most trenchant critique of the Scottish Parliament in its early years. He concluded that the Parliament was 'not created by such a pure and logical process, but resulted from a complex amalgam of "bottom-up" Scottish thinking on a "new form of politics"; "top-down" adoption of existing UK constitutional and political practice, and adaptation of parliamentary procedure and practice from a variety of sources but especially from Westminster'. His comment on the four principles remain relevant:

> The first principle, 'sharing the power', is best regarded as an overarching aspiration, and the fourth principle, 'equal opportunities', should be a criterion applicable to any public institution or activity. Thus, the second and third principles, 'accountability' and 'access and participation', are the substantive, practical core of the CSG approach, with accountability being the expression of a central parliamentary function, and access and participation emphasising the 'new politics'.

Winetrobe identified tensions inherent in the design of the Parliament which were not addressed or acknowledged: notions of parliamentary and popular sovereignty; representative and participative democracy; and the roles of parties and individual MSPs. From the start, the Parliament was an executive-dominated institution. Business was generally generated at the initiative of the executive. Much attention has been drawn to the petition system but it has limitations as a form of accessible, open, responsive, and participatory politics. However, there is a consensus that the Parliament has bedded down well, is popular and has contributed significantly towards the four CSG principles. Devolution did more than create new political institutions. There are now 129 Members of the Scottish Parliament, over 400 staff working as parliamentary and party assistants or media advisers, about fifty journalists cover its work, while the Parliament itself has a staff of just under 500. It has become the centre of Scottish politics. The Holyrood village is Westminster writ small.

CHOOSING A SCOTTISH GOVERNMENT

Under the provisions of legislation, the Parliament has twenty-eight days to elect a First Minister, otherwise another election is held. This was designed to concentrate minds on agreeing an executive (to be known as the 'Scottish Executive'). There was little prospect of the first executive being anything other than a Labour/Liberal Democrat coalition given the close working relations between the two parties in the Constitutional Convention that had met from 1989. The two parties agreed a 'Programme for Government' which set out how the coalition should operate and the policies it would pursue. Sir John Elvidge, who became head civil servant in the Scottish government in 2003, later reflected on the coalition describing it as a marriage designed to secure alliances of interests between families rather than a marriage based on love. Political parties, he said, are 'Montagues and Capulets at heart'. But there was considerable agreement and trust between the two coalition parties at least at the most senior level. Donald Dewar became First Minister and Jim Wallace his deputy. The combined vote of the two parties provided an eight-seat overall majority though the election of David Steel as Presiding Officer reduced that by one. Despite the assumption that 'new politics' would allow for open debate with the Parliament asserting itself in relation to the executive, the Parliament proved to be as subservient to the executive as at Westminster if not more so, at least as measured by the number of backbench rebellions.

The Labour–Lib-Dem coalition lasted for two Parliaments. In these eight years, there were remarkably few major disagreements between the two parties. In 1999, the Liberal Democrats had promised that university tuition fees would not be charged in Scotland. The policy had the support of the opposition parties and Jim Wallace frequently pointed out that there was a parliamentary majority against tuition fees. The Labour government in Westminster had introduced a means-tested fee in 1998. The Lib-Dems also wanted local government elected by single transferable vote. Inquiries were held to consider each issue. The independent inquiry into student finance proposed a compromise. It recommended that there should be no upfront tuition fees in higher education with the Scottish Executive providing universities with the shortfall in income. Graduates would pay £3,000 into an endowment scheme when earning £25,000 per year or over with special provisions for less well-off students. The policy had some unintended, but predictable, consequences. It meant that students in Scotland would not pay tuition fees up front while students in the rest of Britain would have to pay fees. The further consequence was that governments were obliged to treat EU students in the same way as home students which meant that EU students from outside the UK would not be charged fees in Scotland while English students attending Scottish universities would have to pay fees. The inquiry on renewing local democracy under Richard Kerley, former Labour councillor, recommended that the age for standing for election should be reduced to 18 and proposed changes in the remuneration of councillors as well as a series of important managerial changes. Its main recommendation was that the single transferable vote should be used in local elections with wards of three to five members, and urged an early decision on the implementation of a new electoral system. But, while the Lib-Dems favoured implementation, Labour was divided and the reform had to wait until after the 2003 Scottish election.

Two other flagship policies associated with the early years of the Parliament were care for the elderly and land ownership. The UK government had set up a Royal Commission on Care for the Elderly under Sir Stewart Sutherland, Principal of Edinburgh University. Sutherland reported two months before the Scottish Parliament was elected and recommended that personal care for the elderly should be available according to need and paid for out of general taxation rather than being means-tested, though a minority report warned that the costs of this policy would be higher than anticipated in the main report. The UK government adopted the minority report's recommendations as did the Scottish Executive under Donald Dewar. In 1975, a Department of Health and Social Security official had written a note on devolution which warned against losing uniformity on social security, arguing that 'common sense' demanded uniform rules but warned that 'common sense may not be the most marketable of commodities in the first heady days of devolution'. That official had not taken account of the sober conservatism of Donald Dewar.

Henry McLeish became Scotland's First Minister following Donald Dewar's death in November 2000. Mr McLeish announced that his government would reconsider its position on care for the elderly and came under considerable pressure from senior colleagues in the Labour government in London to support the existing policy. The Scottish Parliament's Health and Community Care Committee issued a unanimous report supporting Sutherland's recommendations. Mr McLeish would later admit that the U-turn was 'certainly not a textbook example of government at work' but it was important in a number of respects.

Donald Dewar had been a conservative politician committed to devolution as a cultural nationalist. Few politicians in the Scottish Parliament could claim to have his breadth of knowledge of Scottish literature, culture, and history. He had supported devolution when Labour was hostile and long before it became

fashionable. The case he made for a Scottish Parliament was defensive, to prevent UK governments imposing unwanted policies on Scotland rather than to
create a Scottish institution with the capability to pursue policies that might
diverge from a Labour government in London. McLeish was developing a different understanding of devolution. Scottish solutions for Scottish problems
had been the mantra of a succession of Scottish politicians over the twentieth
century up to and including Mr Dewar but this had often simply meant that the
Scottish Office should provide a Scottish dimension, usually involving asking
for more money, to a UK or British policy. Mr McLeish took this a stage further to mean pursuing policies whether or not they diverged from elsewhere in
the UK. Care for the elderly was a policy that involved a range of institutions
including UK central government, the Scottish government, and local government. The Department of Work and Pensions (DWP) rules meant that anyone in receipt of support for care would lose Attendance Allowance. Alastair
Darling, as UK Cabinet Secretary of State at the DWP, refused to agree to the
transfer of Attendance Allowances to cover the cost of personal care made to
people on low incomes. This meant that Scottish pensioners in care homes
would lose the Allowance if free personal care was introduced in Scotland
unless the DWP changed the rules or transferred savings to the Scottish government which would otherwise accrue to this department. Mr Darling had
been a leading opponent of devolution in 1979 and was widely assumed to be
unsympathetic to devolution. There were predictions from Lord Lipsey, one
of the authors of the Royal Commission's minority report, that elderly people
would rush across the border to take advantage of the more generous policy.
But Mr McLeish would not back down and relations with London became
strained.

Care for the elderly was also significant because it showed that much
decision-making continued to involve interdependence between different
levels of government. London continued to control much welfare policy and
many of the 'wicked issues' that confronted policy-makers, including those
affecting the growing elderly population, could not be made without consideration of the role played by UK government. Many policies had spillover consequences. The Scottish policy on tuition fees and care for the elderly would,
as Mr McLeish later acknowledged in his autobiography, create demands for
similar policies in England. Care for the elderly was a test from the perspective
of those who supported devolution to mean allowing Scotland to pursue policies that diverged from the rest of the UK.

It mattered less when it came to policies that had no or only limited spillover
potential. Land ownership and control had been a major item on the radical
agenda in Scottish politics for well over a century and attempts to reform land
ownership had been blocked in the House of Lords with its significant body of
large landowners in the late nineteenth and early twentieth centuries. In 2003,
the Parliament passed legislation that its opponents warned would lead to a

'Zimbabwean land grab'. Rights of access to the countryside were extended and rural communities were able to buy land, including crofting land, even if the owner was unwilling to sell, though human rights legislation would have limited the extent to which anything approaching a Zimbabwean land grab was possible had it been a serious possibility. The policy had its origins in a committee established by Donald Dewar in 1997 when he was Secretary of State for Scotland before the Scottish Parliament was established. The measure proved less radical than the rhetoric had suggested and community ownership proved more difficult to achieve given safeguards, procedures, and timetables that had to be taken into account. Nonetheless, it was important symbolically and permitted community ownership in parts of Scotland. Assynt Crofters in Sutherland led the first major community buyout from a private owner when the Vestey family sold over 44,000 acres to the local community of 900 local residents. But a process had begun that signalled a departure from past practice in land ownership in Scotland.

Jack McConnell replaced Henry McLeish as First Minister in November 2001. Given his past record, he might have been expected to pursue a nationalist devolution strategy. Instead, Mr McConnell became the embodiment of conservative devolution. He would avoid policies that might create difficulties with his party leadership in London. A few months after becoming First Minister, he followed spending plans on health made in London with his own similar plans. His rhetoric was 'doing less, better', mimicking that of the European Commission headed by the Jacques Santer. He injected a degree of stability and ensured that relations with London improved, largely by avoiding any prospect of a dispute. The key measure his administration pursued and had greatest chance of long-term impact was changing the voting system for local government. But his administration was criticized for lacking a clear set of priorities. On the eve of the 2007 Scottish elections, John MacLaren, a former Labour special adviser who was part of McConnell's campaign team, wrote a withering attack on Jack McConnell's leadership suggesting that 'doing less, better' was 'never going to lead to great deeds' and that any initiatives such as the ban on smoking and the Fresh Talent Initiative 'stand alone rather than as part of a coherent narrative on health or on economic development'. The smoking ban was introduced in Scotland ahead of the rest of the UK but originated as a backbench proposal that was initially opposed by the coalition. Fresh Talent had been designed to address the perennial problem of a declining population. It was launched in 2004 and was agreed with the Home Office to allow overseas graduates from Scottish universities to remain in Scotland for two years after graduating to seek employment. There was opposition from English universities who saw this as potentially offering their Scottish counterparts a competitive advantage in recruiting overseas students.

Leaving aside those who wanted to extend the powers of the Scottish Parliament, there were divergent understandings of its role. A conservative understanding of devolution used the familiar language of Scottish control of Scottish affairs but meant that the Scottish Parliament should be the manifestation of diversity within the state rather than its policies. A bolder conception of devolution viewed the Scottish Parliament as creating institutions to permit Scotland to pursue policies that were appropriate for Scotland, regardless of whether they diverged from elsewhere. Conservative devolution had been the hallmark of Terence O'Neill, Northern Ireland's Prime Minister from 1963 to 1969. O'Neill explained his understanding of devolution in his autobiography. As Health Minister in the mid-1950s, he had considered removing restrictions on rent control in Northern Ireland ahead of Westminster but had been warned by Enoch Powell, Junior Housing Minister at Westminster, that pursuing a policy in Northern Ireland that might lead to demands for the same elsewhere would create difficulties for UK governments: 'If, however, you follow in our wake when we have blazed the trail, then you can justify your actions without risking your chances or possibly spoiling ours.' O'Neill took heed. A month before the 1970 general election, O'Neill argued for Scottish devolution in a speech in Edinburgh. He maintained that devolution did not mean 'spending more money than the English on a particular service, but doing it more intelligently, or in a way particularly suited to Scotland'. A question posed by a Treasury official in the 1970s summed up Whitehall concerns: 'the big question is whether public opinion in Britain would be willing to accept the growth of a marked divergence in the standards of public services as between Scotland, Wales and England, of a kind which they would not accept as between different parts of England'. Care for the elderly suggested that divergent views of devolution were emerging after its establishment.

A DECADE OF PLENTY

Stability and partnership with London were the hallmarks of devolution under Mr McConnell rather than developing new policies. He had the good fortune of being First Minister, as had his two predecessors, during a sustained period of public expenditure growth in the UK. Scotland received its share through the Barnett formula with the Scottish grant more than doubling in cash terms between 1999 and 2010, corresponding to an increase of 60 per cent in real terms or an annual growth rate of over 5 per cent. The devolved budget peaked in 2009–10 before the economic and fiscal crisis. This contributed to the institutionalization of the Scottish Parliament. There was no shortage of money to spend its way into the hearts of the Scottish people though this was true of government across the UK. As all parts of the state were experiencing unprecedented levels of public spending, there was little sense of grievance that Scotland was being favoured over other parts of the UK. At times of rising expenditure, few cared whether one part of the state benefited more than another so long as all were benefiting.

The tendency was for the Scottish spending patterns to follow those announced for the rest of the UK. In 2001, Prime Minister Blair announced a commitment to increase spending on health to match the European Union average by 2005. Given the workings of the Barnett formula, this meant that the Scottish Executive would receive a corresponding increase in spending though it need not have used it for the same purposes. But the media coverage across Britain of the Blair government's commitment made it difficult for the Scottish Executive to use the additional money for anything other than health. But it might have used health spending differently, most obviously to focus the additional resource on prevention, but would have been under pressure from Opposition parties and the media as well as health professionals to explain why the NHS in Scotland was being treated less generously than in England. There were strong pressures encouraging uniformity as well as for divergence. The theoretical ability to vire resources from one budget to another remained unchanged and the pressures to work within similar priorities as set by London also remained. That Labour was in power in both Edinburgh and London may have contributed to this but party congruence appeared to be largely irrelevant in priorities set by central and local government. In many cases, Scottish solutions for Scottish problems continued to mean using additional money to extend policies designed elsewhere. The absence of a coherent set of objectives set by its political leadership combined with inheriting an organizational structure that reflected specialization and fragmentation meant that the Scottish Executive struggled to offer that 'coherent narrative' within policy domains that had been identified by John MacLaren, far less across government as a whole.

There was no incentive to save money made available each year. To do so would have meant a cut in the following year's allocation. This would be seen as a failure. Nothing had changed in this respect with devolution. The tax-raising power was never seen as necessary given the sums flowing into the Scottish Executive from Barnett and the power to cut tax was seen as anathema in a culture that continued to measure success by sums spent and policy outputs rather than outcomes.

LIBERALIZING SCOTLAND

In 1968, Tom Nairn commented that Scotland would be free when the 'last Minister of the Kirk was strangled with the last copy of the *Sunday Post*'. He was referring as much to the social conservatism of Scotland as to its constitutional conservatism. He came to regret the comment. The increasingly

sparsely populated pews in Kirks across Scotland might still have a disproportionate number of Tory voters but the General Assembly and its committees
were advocating liberal, even social democratic solutions to Scotland's problems. In 2000, Neal Ascherson, one of Nairn's contemporaries, suggested that
the *Sunday Post* had 'done far less damage to democracy in Scotland over the
last few years than the editorials in the *Scotsman*', a paper that had once given
both Nairn and Ascherson a platform. Social conservatism had not disappeared from Scotland. The Catholic Church had replaced the Kirk as guardian
of public morals. The Catholic Church's role in Scottish society had evolved
in other ways too. The Church hierarchy continued to represent the interests
of Catholics in Scotland but the Catholic community had changed. State support for Catholic education had allowed for the creation of a Catholic middle
class to emerge. This remarkably successful example of multi-cultural public policy was rarely celebrated but was a cause for embarrassment amongst
many liberal-minded Scots who feared that separate education contributed
to sectarianism. Separate Catholic schools were generally seen as a necessary
evil rather than a good in themselves. Consequently, there was little effort to
consider whether there might be public policy lessons. By 1992, working-class
male Catholics were amongst the most likely to assert a Scottish identity of any
group in Scottish society. Cardinal Tom Winning, only the second Cardinal in
Scotland since the Reformation, grew increasingly disillusioned with Labour.
In 1998, he delivered a speech in Brussels entitled 'A New Scotland in the
New Europe' in which he described modern Scottish nationalism as 'mature,
respectful of democracy and international in outlook'. The Catholic community had lost much of its sense of alienation from Scottish society. Cardinal
Keith O'Brien followed Cardinal Winning in his views on Scottish independence. In October 2006, he made it known that he would be 'happy' if Scots
voted for independence.

    This growing self-confidence meant that the Catholic hierarchy was more
willing to speak out against social liberalism. In September 1999, the Scottish
Executive announced that legislation would be introduced to remove a clause
that had banned the promotion of homosexuality in education. Communities
Minister Wendy Alexander found herself at the centre of a socially conservative
backlash that included some of her Labour Cabinet colleagues. The Catholic
Church, large sections of the print media including the *Daily Record*, Labour's
staunchest ally, combined with Brian Souter, the SNP's largest financial backer,
in the 'Keep the Clause' campaign. Souter provided funds for a 'private referendum' in May 2000 in which 87 per cent voted to keep the clause in a poll
in which 32 per cent of the electorate participated. The Scottish Parliament
voted by ninety-nine votes to seventeen, with two abstentions, to remove the
offending clause. But it had been a bruising battle. The backlash had come as a
surprise to all parties and most commentators and undermined any sense of a
liberal ascendancy in Scottish politics. Keep the Clause had been a campaign

that defied the usual categories applied to Scottish politics. The main parties in the Parliament were united in seeking the removal of the clause against some of their own key supporters. The assertions of popular sovereignty that had been invoked in the *Claim of Right* and the battle for a Scottish Parliament had given way to the assertion of the primacy of representative democracy.

Further liberalization of the law pertaining to homosexuality occurred but using 'Sewel', or Legislative Consent Motions which allowed the Scottish Parliament to agree to allow Westminster to pass law on behalf of the Scottish Parliament. Sewel Motions, named after the Scottish Office Minister who proposed them, were used more often than had initially been expected and continued to be used by the SNP when it came to power for a variety of reasons. There were occasions when the Scottish Parliament intended to pursue the same measure as Westminster. Time was saved by consenting to allow Westminster to legislate on behalf of the Scottish Parliament. On other occasions, Scottish Parliament has agreed to allow Westminster to legislate when a measure has cut across the devolved and retained divide. While this might make sense in terms of parliamentary time and simplicity, it was used in the case of lowering the age of consent to homosexual sex to avoid another backlash similar to Keep the Clause. In such a case, a Parliament's role as the key forum for public debate, confronting difficult issues that require not only legislative change but challenging public attitudes, can be important. Scottish parliamentarians would shy away from addressing such difficult matters for some years. However, proposals to allow same-sex marriage after the 2013 election had won cross-party support in Holyrood. The *Daily Record* had abandoned its social conservatism. Holyrood's ambiguous role in leading and following public opinion would wax and wane like Parliaments in other liberal democracies.

THE SNP AND DEVOLUTION

The SNP struggled to come to terms with devolution. The party threw itself into the referendum campaign and maintained unity through to the first elections to the Scottish Parliament. Elections to the Scottish Parliament had three advantages over elections to Westminster for the SNP. The AMS electoral system would be much kinder to the SNP than simple plurality. The party had consistently had an even spread of support across Scotland which did not translate well into seats in the Commons. By contrast, Labour had a highly efficient vote in terms of its translation into seats. In 1997, the Labour Party won fifty-six seats with 45.6 per cent of the vote while the SNP won six with 22.1 per cent of the vote. The Tories won no seats with 17.5 per cent while the Lib-Dems won ten seats with 13 per cent of the vote. AMS would ensure that parties that were penalized by the simple plurality system would do better but the system would still work to Labour's advantage. The SNP had also expected to do well because this would be a Scottish election. Scottish politics would receive reasonable coverage in elections to Westminster but Scotland had less than 9 per cent of the total electorate and the proportion of seats likely to change was often lower. Voters tended to go to the polls to choose a government and very few expected the SNP would be part of any UK government. The combination of AMS, a Scottish election, and the prospect of the SNP as a potential party of government worked in the SNP's favour. But no newspaper backed the SNP and the main tabloids came out strongly against the party.

The SNP had tightened up its candidate selection processes though not to the extent that Labour had. A number of mavericks were returned for the SNP. The challenge was to forge a united group of MSPs in preparation of the next election. Its thirty-five MSPs elected in 1999 exceeded the total number of SNP parliamentarians ever elected to the House of Commons since the party's establishment. The party had had continuous, though precarious, representation in the Commons since 1967. But it was now a secure parliamentary party. Key figures who had been active and held national party office but had had to have full-time occupations outside politics became full-time politicians. Power inside the party shifted decisively to the Scottish parliamentary group though most of the key figures in the party pre-devolution remained leading figures after devolution. Alex Salmond stood down as party leader in 2000 to the surprise of many commentators though Mr Salmond had long said he had no intention of remaining leader for over a decade. John Swinney and Alex Neil contested the leadership which the former won convincingly. Mr Neil had been Labour's Scottish research officer in the early 1970s and had written that party's Scottish manifesto in October 1974 but joined Jim Sillars in the breakaway Scottish Labour Party and would follow Mr Sillars into the SNP. He had become a hardliner within the SNP. Mr Swinney had been elected as MP for North Tayside in 1997 but, along with all SNP MPs, stood for the Scottish Parliament in 1999. He had been the party's national secretary and was well known and liked throughout the party. He won the support of 67 per cent of the party's conference delegates who then determined who should lead the party.

The SNP had, however, become impatient. Many SNP activists had believed the anti-devolution rhetoric that devolution was a 'slippery slope to separatism'. The SNP had unrealistic expectations in 1999 and were disappointed to discover that there was no inevitability about independence. Debates over whether to support devolution had disappeared but many members were frustrated at the lack of progress when the SNP performed poorly at the 2001 Westminster general election. Grievances focused on the party leader. Each of the SNP's MPs had been elected to the Scottish Parliament in 1999 and all but one decided to stand down from the Commons at the 2001 election. This meant the SNP was fielding almost an entire field of new candidates. The one exception was Alex Salmond who decided to stand down from the Scottish Parliament and remain at Westminster to allow Swinney to establish himself as leader without his predecessor in the same institution.

The SNP's own constitution remained that of a largely extra-parliamentary party and not one that was expecting to form a government anytime soon. Any ordinary party member could stand for the leadership with limited support of branches. A challenge to Swinney's leadership came following further setbacks at the second Scottish elections in 2003 when the SNP share of the vote fell and it lost eight seats. Efforts to prepare for these elections had been undermined when SNP List MSPs competed amongst themselves to win high rankings. The List element of the electoral system had given the SNP twenty-eight of its thirty-five seats in 1999. Coming top of the List had been a secure way of becoming a List MSP but coming low on the List reduced the chances of being returned. Incumbent List MSPs were competing with people who had not been returned in 1999 for positions in the 2003 elections. Amongst the most prominent casualties were Margo MacDonald who was effectively deselected and Mike Russell and Andrew Wilson, two front benchers. MacDonald decided to stand as an Independent and was returned while the other two failed to get elected.

A little-known activist from Glasgow, holding no senior position in the party, stood against Mr Swinney in 2003. Though he retained the leadership with 84 per cent of the vote, the challenge undermined his position. When the SNP performed poorly in the 2005 elections, with its vote falling 7.5 per cent to 19.7 per cent, less than 2 per cent ahead of the Conservatives, he was left with little option but to resign the leadership. But he had made a major contribution to his party as leader. He had brought about reforms to the party's constitution that included electing the party leader by one member one vote, and tightening up procedures and requirements to stand as a leadership candidate. The party now explicitly endorsed a constitution that gave the leadership greater authority. It had moved from being an amateur activist party into an electoral professional party.

Roseanna Cunningham, Swinney's deputy, announced she would stand for the leadership as did Nicola Sturgeon and Mike Russell. Candidates needed the nomination of 100 members from at least twenty branches. Russell was out of Parliament but had the necessary breadth of support required to stand. Alex Salmond came under pressure from many activists to stand again and initially refused to do so. When questioned as to whether he would stand he said, 'If nominated I'll decline. If drafted I'll defer. And if elected, I'll resign.' But after further pressure he agreed to stand, announcing his decision as not only a candidacy for SNP leader but for First Minister. Nicola Sturgeon withdrew as a candidate for leader and instead stood for deputy leader. Alex Salmond was the first SNP leader elected under the new rules which gave every member a vote. He won 75.6 per cent of first preferences and Nicola Sturgeon won 53.9 per cent of first preferences for the deputy position. But Salmond was no longer a Member of the Scottish Parliament. For the remainder of the Parliament, his deputy led the SNP group in the Scottish Parliament. The return of Alex Salmond marked the end of a period of introspection. The party began to believe it could win again.

LABOUR'S DECLINE

There was nothing certain about the outcome of the 2007 Scottish Parliamentary elections. Jack McConnell had been First Minister since 2001. He attempted to take advantage of this status to question Salmond's abilities and suggested Salmond was not qualified for the job of First Minister. Raising questions of leadership was a mistake as were the tried and tested attacks on separatism with threats that businesses would leave Scotland if the SNP was returned. Lingerie entrepreneur Michelle Mone threatened to 'quit Scotland' if Alex Salmond won power, providing the *Daily Record* with a front-page headline, 'If Salmond wins next week I'll pack my bras and leave'. That paper and the *Sun* ran vehement campaigns against the SNP. On election day the *Sun* covered its front page with a picture of a noose and the headline, 'Vote SNP today and you put Scotland's head in the noose'. The *Record* warned Scots not to 'sleepwalk into independence. Do not let a protest vote break up Britain.' The press coverage was as savage as anything Michael Foot and the Labour Party had experienced in the 1983 election. The difference was the result. The SNP became the largest party by one seat. Press influence had declined and, more importantly, the SNP understood this.

Labour's support had been slipping away over many years, almost unnoticed as commentary tended to focus on the relative positions of Labour and SNP. Jack McConnell proved a liability for his party. He had become the John Major of Scottish politics, in office but not quite in power, not because he had lost control of his party in Scotland, which he commanded fairly effortlessly, but because he was seen to be under the control of his party's leadership in London and appeared not to know what to do with the undoubted authority he possessed. He had backed the UK government's replacement of the Trident missile system, leading to the resignation of one of his Cabinet ministers, and then refused to criticize the Blair government on the Iraq War. Though defence and foreign affairs were retained matters, the Scottish Parliament could debate anything and had passed a resolution critical of the Iraq War. Though neither Trident nor Iraq played a direct part in the outcome of the election, each fed into a perception that Scottish Labour had slavishly followed the bidding of the leadership in London. In earlier times, Scottish Labour had been seen as to the left of the party in Britain and Scottish party conferences had inclined to support more radical causes with many senior figures supporting unilateral nuclear disarmament, for example. Jack McConnell had been thought by many commentators to belong to this more radical leftist tendency. The trade unions had been traditional Labour bastions. But at its annual meeting during the 2003 campaign, the Scottish Trades Union Congress only very narrowly passed a motion calling on members to vote Labour. Scotland's largest trade union, Unison, opposed the motion and a number of SNP candidates were given campaign donations from trade unions.

Devolution had been having a bigger impact on Labour than had been appreciated. Even when the party had been in government in Britain in the past, its distinctiveness in Scotland had incorporated a form of oppositional politics. Labour governments had accepted nuclear weapons, failed to stand up to the United States over the Vietnam War, and cut public spending in economic and fiscal crises, but the party in Scotland developed a distance from decisions that made it uncomfortable. The Scottish party afforded members a curtain behind which they could retain their socialist purity. Scottish Labour heroes tended to be purists. Even the more right-wing elements in the Scottish Labour Party played along with the myth of radical Scotland. Gordon Brown had written a hagiography of Jimmy Maxton. *Red Clydeside* inspired party members more than Tom Johnston, the practical Scottish wartime Scottish Secretary. Willie Ross was no Labour member's hero despite bringing considerable money to the Scottish Office, the key measure of success in post-war Scottish politics.

Devolved government exposed the extent to which Scottish leftist politics was based on rhetoric. A Scottish representative institution would be able to pursue Scottish solutions to Scottish problems. Jack McConnell's career encapsulated the challenge. The young radical council leader and Scottish Labour Action founder might have been expected to have carved out a distinct Scottish policy agenda. There was no lack of money to experiment and develop a different Scotland. But when the curtain was drawn back, Labour in Scotland under Mr McConnell was exposed to be no different from the party in London. It mimicked the best and worst of the government in London. There was no alternative Scottish strategy. There was no critique of the growing income inequality that might have been expected from the Scottish party of old. Labour in government in London had offered no alternative to the emphasis on helping financial services that had been pursued by the Conservatives. Scottish Labour criticisms were muted by what was thought to be continuing growth in public spending and the 'end of boom and bust'. Stein Ringen, Oxford Professor of Sociology and Social Policy, offered a critique of New Labour in which he identified mistaken policies and the system of government as the causes of New Labour's 'failure'. What is most remarkable from a Scottish perspective is the role played by centralization in this critique. Devolved institutions operated within a centralized mindset that Labour in Scotland had failed to challenge. Labour's most thoughtful senior members were more likely to demand London's solutions to Scottish problems, though never in such terms, and to criticize the absence of 'modernization' of the party north of the border. Wendy Alexander had walked out of Jack McConnell's Cabinet in May 2002 but her problem was that the First Minister was not pursuing with enough vigour the technocratic policies that were the hallmark of government in London. Disillusion with Labour emerged earlier in Scotland than it did elsewhere. People were coming to expect more of devolution than being a bulwark against Thatcherism, which was beginning to fade in public memories. The Scottish Question was once more being transformed.

THE SNP IN GOVERNMENT

There were a number of potential options to forming a government in 2007 with forty-seven SNP MSPs, forty-six Labour MSPs, seventeen Conservatives, sixteen Lib-Dems, two Greens, and Margo MacDonald returned again as an Independent. But the Lib-Dems had made it clear they had no intention of remaining in coalition with Labour. Labour would require nineteen more votes in Parliament to have an overall majority and the SNP required eighteen. Any coalition that could command an overall majority would require at least three parties. Neither Labour nor the SNP would coalesce with the Conservatives and the Lib-Dems decided against joining a coalition. The SNP reached an agreement with the two Green MSPs and formed a minority government. There was no desire in any party for another election and Alex Salmond became First Minister. The common view in the media and amongst the SNP's opponents was that the SNP minority government would not last a full Parliament and many doubted it would last until Christmas. The SNP and Scottish civil servants had prepared for the possibility of minority government by studying the experience elsewhere, especially in Denmark. The SNP had long had to operate as a minority, manoeuvring deftly which prepared them well for the challenge of forging new parliamentary majorities anew over the course of the Parliament. Majority-building was the name of the game and Bruce Crawford, the SNP Minister for the Parliament, became an adept player.

Minority government gave the Parliament the opportunity to assert itself in relation to the executive but the Opposition parties struggled to take advantage. Labour had returned to opposition and adopted the only style of opposition it knew. The Conservatives in Scotland had long become used to being outsiders and were quicker in coming to terms with minority government. An insight into the nature of Scottish parliamentary politics came in 2009. The SNP proposed its £33 billion budget after negotiating with the other parties in the Parliament and assumed it could command a majority. Labour too assumed the budget would pass but saw no reason to lend support to the SNP. Oppositional politics demanded it vote against the budget. But what had not been accounted for was a change of heart by the two Green MSPs who voted against the budget resulting in a 64–64 division with the SNP, Tories, and Margo MacDonald voting for the budget while Labour, Liberal Democrats, and Greens voted against. Alex Ferguson, Presiding Officer, used his casting vote against the budget arguing that it was the established convention for someone in his position to vote for the status quo. It was an odd status quo as defeat on a budget would necessitate an election. A superficially revised budget was put together in days and Labour supported the government. The Greens had inadvertently highlighted the theatrical nature of much adversarial politics, another feature inherited from Westminster.

The six-member SNP Cabinet was smaller than the Cabinets during the years of coalition. The Labour–Lib-Dem Cabinet formed in 1999 had consisted of many talented individuals but they had not had the opportunity to cohere as a team in opposition. Apart from Alex Salmond, the SNP Cabinet had joined the party during a period when the party was either in decline or on the fringe of politics. This was not a Cabinet of Salmond loyalists or people unwilling to stand up to the First Minister. Civil servants were surprised to find that ministers would engage in robust but polite exchanges, challenging one another but managing to remain united. Opponents had suggested that the SNP was a 'one-man-band'. That had never been the case but as senior ministers established themselves within the government, Parliament, and the variety of policy networks, it became clear that this was a formidable team. A triumvirate of the First Minister, Nicola Sturgeon who was Deputy First Minister, and John Swinney were at the government's core. But what exactly did they bring to government and what bound them together?

Each of them was committed to independence and 'furthering Scottish interests'. But the first was more a slogan than a clearly defined constitutional objective and the latter could hardly be more vague. Beyond Winnie Ewing's call for Scotland to have a seat at the United Nations between Saudi Arabia and Senegal, independence had hardly been defined by the SNP. No two states in the world had the same relationships with the outside world. The SNP's 'independence in Europe' had provided some clarity but not a lot. But what independence gave the SNP that was increasingly absent in modern liberal democracies was a goal, however ill-defined, that could mobilize support and provide a strong sense of community amongst its members. For most of its history, independence did not need to be defined with much clarity as it was a distant hope at best. Even the election of the SNP government meant that little more clarity was needed. The party had learned from New Labour when the latter decided to hold a referendum on devolution prior to the 1997 election. By promising a referendum on its preferred constitutional option, it offered voters the chance to vote for the party without supporting that constitutional position. While its opponents argued that a vote for the SNP would result in separatism, independence expressed pejoratively, the SNP would counter that an SNP victory would only result in a referendum. The party leadership had to tread warily. It could not be seen to avoid independence for fear of antagonizing its activists whose prime motivation for campaigning for the party was to bring about independence. In 1999, independence had been listed fourteenth of fourteen priorities in its manifesto and was number ten in a list of ten key pledges.

But the party put its trust in Alex Salmond's leadership after 2004 to an extent it had never done during his first term as party leader from 1990 to 2000. Hardliners had always suspected Salmond would sell out for devolution. The enmity of his political opponents in other parties, especially evident in the 1999 election, may have convinced his party that he really was in favour of independence. The commitment to a referendum proved a useful party management tool, pushing the issue into the future. In 2007, voters elected the SNP because it was perceived as the party which would be most competent in government. Its support for independence commanded less support than the party but support for independence contributed to the sense that the SNP would stand up for Scotland in dealings with London. It was perceived to put Scotland first.

Part of its preparation for government had led the SNP to consider the structure of Scottish government. Senior officials were simultaneously reviewing how the Scottish Executive operated. Both politicians and officials reached the same conclusion. The Scottish government lacked coherence and clear priorities. Throughout its existence the Scottish Office had theoretically offered opportunities for coordination of activities but had rarely achieved this in practice. Devolved government involved more ministers which would make this more difficult. Henry McLeish had proposed to adopt 'Scottish Government' in place of 'Scottish Executive' but had met strong resistance from his party and Whitehall and was forced to back down. The SNP were keen on the change. 'Government' was a more familiar term for the public and was also thought to imply something more important than 'Executive', in much the same way that the term 'Parliament' had replaced 'Assembly' in the 1980s. But SNP ministers did not want to pursue this immediately on coming to office only to find that senior officials wanted the change immediately as this would signal wider changes in the internal structure of the government.

The key change was a focus on a small number of broad objectives and related outcomes. Five key strategic objectives in pursuit of a 'more successful country', with opportunities for all of Scotland to flourish, through increasing sustainable economic growth' were identified for Scotland: wealthier and fairer; healthier; safer and stronger; smarter; and greener. The emphasis was on the perennial issue of economic growth. The main economic powers were retained at Westminster but the SNP had concluded that economic growth could not be divorced from other matters and saw it as central to its overall strategy. The main arguments against independence could be summed up in suggestions that Scotland was too poor, small, and inadequate. Taking responsibility for the economy and confronting Scotland's historic economic weaknesses were seen as prerequisites for building support for more powers and independence. Performance would be tracked, using a method learned from Virginia, USA and reported in a highly transparent and accessible manner. Instead of a series of departments, the Scottish government was organized into directorates responsible for the five key objectives. The emphasis was on a more integrated approach. The Scottish government also recognized the importance of local government and in 2008 agreed a Concordat with local government. This loosened some of the financial controls over local government, removing much hypothecation, while reaching agreement on strategic objectives.

The SNP adopted a pragmatic, highly technocratic approach to government. It had become more like New Labour in this respect than Scottish Labour had been under Dewar, McLeish, or McConnell. It sought to work cooperatively with government in London though this was not reciprocated in London. Prime Minister Blair phoned to congratulate Rhodri Morgan on his re-election as Welsh First Minister and Ian Paisley on his election as First Minister of Northern Ireland but refused to make direct contact with Alex Salmond. Gordon Brown eventually made contact with Salmond. This sour attitude reflected the difficulty Labour had in coming to terms with a defeat after being the dominant party for half a century. Labour saw the SNP as upstart usurpers. Alex Salmond argued for a revival of formal inter-governmental machinery that had been established in 1999 but which had hardly been used but his formal request was initially ignored by London.

Labour expected that the SNP government would implode but it was Labour in London that imploded. Relations between Tony Blair and Gordon Brown had deteriorated. Mr Brown became Prime Minister in June 2007 just after Alex Salmond became First Minister. Despite his strong Scottish routes and early support for devolution, the new Prime Minister appeared uncomfortable with his Scottish identity. His discomfort did not help inter-governmental relations. Everyday relations between civil servants of the two governments were conducted professionally and amicably as were relations between many ministers. Cooperation occurred when crises necessitated at senior level as happened in the aftermath of a terrorist incident at Glasgow airport in late June 2007, an outbreak of foot-and-mouth disease two months later, and a case of swine flu in May 2009.

The most sensitive tension began within a month of the Scottish elections. The UK government signed a deal with Gaddafi's Libyan government for the return of prisoners. What made this highly sensitive was that Abdelbaset al-Megrahi was the only Libyan in a UK jail. Megrahi had been found guilty of the bombing of Pan-Am Flight 103 above Lockerbie in 1988 that had resulted in 270 deaths. He was imprisoned in Scotland. Megrahi had been diagnosed with cancer and was expected to die in prison. The UK government was keen for his release. The safety of UK citizens in Libyan in the event of Megrahi's death in a Scottish prison was a major concern. Under a Memorandum of Agreement, the UK government was supposed to have consulted the Scottish government given the latter's direct interest in this matter. The UK government had not bargained for the return of the SNP and met with strong criticism. A decision to release Megrahi on compassionate grounds was taken by Kenny MacAskill, Scottish Justice Minister, in August 2009. This proved highly controversial and was cynically exploited by the UK government which had been seeking Megrahi's release. In the words of American officials in the US Embassy in London, in papers leaked through Wikileaks, the 'UK Government has gotten everything—a chance to stick it to Salmond's Scottish National Party (SNP) and good relations with Libya' while Scotland got 'nothing'. But the cynicism backfired as public opinion swung round behind the Scottish government. However, the Megrahi affair played little part in the 2011 Scottish elections. The SNP now had the advantage of incumbency. It also helped that its opponents had predicted such outlandish consequences of an SNP victory that basic competence looked impressive. The Scottish government had few major policy achievements and nothing comparable to the flagship policies of tuition fees or care for the elderly of the early years of devolution. But Salmond's team exuded competence. Labour struggled to project an image as a government in waiting.

Until the UK elections in 2010, the SNP comfortably led in the polls but as attention shifted to who should be in 10 Downing Street, the Scottish electorate swung behind Labour. The SNP was marginalized in an election in which it looked largely irrelevant. The SNP had high hopes of making substantial gains following its 2007 performance and after winning a by-election in Glasgow East in 2008. In the event, the SNP lost Glasgow East and struggled to make an impact. The election had seen the first UK party leaders' debates but the SNP was excluded from these debates. For a brief period, the Lib-Dems looked set to make a major breakthrough after a strong debating performance by Nick Clegg, UK party leader. Scottish party leaders' debates were held but attracted far less attention. Labour succeeded in increasing its Scottish share of the vote by 2.5 per cent and held all of the forty-one seats won in 2005 against the trend across the rest of Britain. The Lib-Dems fell back in share of the vote but held their eleven seats. The SNP advanced by 2.3 per cent of the vote but failed to gain any seats and only narrowly clung on to second place in terms of share of the vote, one point ahead of the Lib-Dems and with the Tories increasing their share of the vote by less than 1 per cent and holding their only Scottish seat. Scotland had strongly backed Gordon Brown for Prime Minister but otherwise it had been a very British election.

David Cameron, who had become Tory leader in late 2005, pursued a strategy of 'detoxifying' the Tory brand, by moving the party away from its image as the 'nasty party', as one senior Tory put it. He used Labour's difficulties with devolution to portray the Conservatives as having moved on from outright hostility to a Scottish Parliament, promising a 'respect agenda' in which he would ensure good relations between Edinburgh and London.

The Conservative–Lib-Dem coalition that was formed had little Scottish support although the twelve seats and 35.6 per cent of the vote were far more than the Tories would have managed on their own. The coalition was extremely useful in Scotland for the Tories. A Lib-Dem Scottish Secretary could be appointed avoiding the difficulties that would follow from appointing a Tory to that office. For the remainder of 2010, Labour led the SNP in the polls. Just as the SNP had assumed its strong showing in the 2007 Holyrood elections would translate into strong support in Westminster elections, Labour erred by assuming its strong support in the 2010 UK elections would translate into support at the 2011 Scottish elections. It was anticipated that the Lib-Dems would suffer from entering coalition with the Tories at Westminster and most commentators assumed these disaffected Lib-Dem voters would support Labour. But as the 2011 elections drew nearer, the polls started to close as Scottish voters shifted focus from UK to Scottish elections.

The 2011 elections saw the SNP win an overall majority, something the electoral system had been designed to prevent. But electoral systems cannot overcome public opinion if expressed strongly enough. The SNP won because it was deemed highly competent as a party of government, best capable of standing up for Scotland especially as compared with the alternatives. It won despite the SNP support for independence though independence signalled that the SNP put Scotland first even if most Scots did not support the policy. Its manifesto in 2011 contained even fewer bold promises than in 2007. But there was one item that now came to the fore. The commitment to a referendum had been a means of managing party expectations by keeping alive the prospect of independence without making it a major issue in a general election. In 2007, the lack of an overall majority meant the SNP could not hold a referendum but an overall majority meant it could not be avoided.

CONCLUSION

Devolution's first decade occurred during a period of significant growth in public spending that allowed for continuity in one of the key distinguishing features of Scottish politics: spending more money on public services. This does not mean that without this growth in spending the Scottish Parliament would have struggled to establish itself. Had funding from the Treasury dried up then the Scottish Executive would have complained bitterly. The tempta-tion across the UK was to believe that 'boom and bust had ended' rather than to think more soberly about the future or address Scotland's endemic social and economic problems. These were wasted years largely because Scottish politics was defined in terms of spending and policy outputs rather than outcomes. Neither was there change in Scotland's adversarial politics. For a period with minority government, the executive branch was forced to take heed of the Parliament but even then the Parliament failed to take advantage of having an Opposition majority. Labour and Liberal Democrats behaved as Westminster-style Opposition parties allowing the SNP a remarkably easy time.

There was no inevitability to the SNP becoming the largest party. Support for independence fluctuated but remained stuck well short of a majority. What happened with devolution was that the SNP came to be perceived as more than a party supporting independence. It became a credible party of government, with everyday policies that were unrelated to the consti-tutional question. Some commentators looked for evidence that its poli-cies were designed to build the sense of Scotland as a separate entity or to pick fights with London. The SNP government was rarely unwilling to meet a challenge from London but did not go looking for fights as it knew that this would undermine the image it sought of being a responsible gov-ernment and knew that London was likely to win in any battle given the relative resources of each government. The SNP government was relaxed about passing Legislative Consent Motions which allowed Westminster to pass laws on behalf of the Scottish Parliament on matters on which there was common ground, on the understanding that these could be reversed if necessary. This confused its opponents. So long as the SNP had been in opposition, there was always some uncertainty as to what it might do in government. But after 2007, Scots had experience of an SNP government. But the SNP's success in 2011 meant that a referendum could no longer be postponed. The constitutional dimension had returned.

12

The Scottish Question: Interminable and Unanswerable

INTRODUCTION

It was suggested in Chapter 1 of this book that the Scottish Question had many dimensions and that it changed over time. It warned that there was no solution to the question but each generation had to come up with its own responses. But might the September 2014 independence referendum finally resolve the Scottish Question? If Scotland were to exit the union, would that not bring an end to the issues discussed in previous chapters? Would an emphatic vote against devolution bring an end to debate on Scotland's constitutional status? How significant is the referendum likely to be in terms of the Scottish Question? In this final chapter, an attempt is made to answer these questions, drawing on the understanding of the Scottish Question offered in the book.

AN HISTORIC EVENT?

On one matter there is near unanimity across political parties, campaign groups, and commentators. The independence referendum of September 2014 will be important. Some historians have described it as historic, even before it has occurred. There seems no doubt that it will be an important event but it is unknown as yet how important. It may take a number of years until we understand how significant it has been. It will be some time before we can ascertain its impact, if at all, on the variety of aspects of the Scottish Question: how it will affect identities, its public policy consequences, the system of government, the party system, and Scotland's relations with the rest of the United Kingdom. There is every likelihood that there will be considerable continuity regardless of the result of the referendum and many matters will remain unresolved or return as issues in the future.

The referendum question is typically British and Scottish in its Manichean choice: Should Scotland be an independent country? The Scottish government had preferred three choices: independence, the status quo, and some version of more powers. However, the UK government was clear that if there was to be a referendum then it should involve a simple binary choice. Any third alternative would only be considered after Scots voted to stay in the union. There is a lack of clarity and no guarantee that an alternative will be offered to Scots in the event of a rejection of independence. Some opponents of independence, especially those who were not keen on devolution in the first place, have argued that the rejection of independence will bring the debate to an end while other opponents of independence suggest there will be scope for additional powers. No guarantees can be given. As the experience of 1979 showed, promises can prove worthless and no government at Westminster can bind its successor even if it wanted to.

It seems almost certain that the overwhelming rejection of independence would bring an end to debate on independence for the foreseeable future. But it is difficult to see very far into the future. The issue is not whether the referendum brings an end to the debate should there be a resounding vote against independence but under what circumstances might the issue of Scotland's constitutional status return. It seems improbable that everyone who votes for independence, especially those who have committed much time and energy to the cause over many years, will simply give up altogether. Accepting the legitimacy of a vote against independence is not the same as giving up hope. Hope sustained home rulers through what appeared to be hopeless times in the past. It is likely to do so in the future. But hope alone will not bring independence back onto the political agenda. A number of additional factors are likely to determine whether and if so when the issue returns. How central government in London behaves after victory will be important and not only how it reacts to the referendum result but how sensitive it proves to be in the years ahead. It is unlikely that there will be a repeat of Margaret Thatcher's insensitivity. It is not repetition of this sort but a failure to appreciate the nature of any new context and the need to respond appropriately that will be the challenges for UK governments in the future. Understanding that the rejection of independence does not bring finality to the Scottish Question should be the easy part. The difficult part will be finding appropriate responses over time. The referendum is but one event. The union is a daily plebiscite.

Alex Salmond has said the referendum is a 'once in a generation opportunity', that there will not be another referendum for a generation. Defeat would almost certainly mean that he would be unable to call another referendum as First Minister even if he was to stay in office well into the future. There is reason to believe he would continue as First Minister. The electorate are capable of distinguishing between support for the SNP and support for independence. The electorate have shown a greater appreciation of the SNP objective of 'furthering Scottish interests' than its support for independence. SNP support in the past was impeded by the party's commitment to independence and it is conceivable that removing the prospect of independence might make the SNP a more attractive party of government. The decision on whether and when another referendum is held will not be Mr Salmond's decision. It will be decided by others coming after him and not only successors as leader of the SNP. If opinion shifts towards independence, there will be nothing to prevent demands for another referendum. Parliamentary sovereignty means that no Parliament can bind its successors. Popular sovereignty means that no generation can bind its successors. The behaviour of the UK government or, more accurately, how UK government is perceived will be important in determining whether and when independence returns following its rejection in a referendum. If Scots feel that future UK governments are taking Scotland on a journey to an unpalatable social and economic destination then the constitutional dimension of the Scottish Question will return to the fore.

If Scotland votes for independence that too will not bring finality to the Scottish Question, not even its constitutional dimension. As proponents of independence have tacitly acknowledged, independence is not as simple as stopping the world to let Scotland on, in Winnie Ewing's slogan from 1967. There are as many variations of independence as there are states in the world, indeed many more permutations are possible. Independence does not mean the same for the United States as it does for tiny Tuvalu in anything other than a formal legal sense. Nuclear weapons would be removed from Scotland. There may be uncertainty as to when this would happen but independence has come to mean having control over that decision. But in many other respects, the constitutional dimension of the Scottish Question will not be resolved with a vote for independence. Constitutional independence still involves relationships with neighbours and others which are negotiated and renegotiated over time. A vote in favour of independence would alter an important aspect of these relationships but does not end the need for constant renegotiation. Opponents of independence use the term 'separatism' or even divorce. Such terms are understandable in the adversarial heat of debate though an unhelpful analogy. It would be an odd form of separation or divorce that left a former couple living next door to each other. This debate is about relationships, how these might change over time rather than completely end.

In a debate in 1955 on the Royal Commission on Scottish Affairs in 1955, Arthur Woodburn, former Scottish Secretary, pointed out that anyone who 'thinks that this feud between Scotland and England, the sort of cold war that has gone on for hundreds of years, will be ended by the recommendations of this Royal Commission is, I think, rather optimistic'. Describing the relationship between Scotland and England or, more accurately, the rest of the UK as a feud is a gross exaggeration. Supporters of independence expect relations with the rest of the UK to improve with independence while opponents, at least in the rhetoric used in campaigns, are more likely to expect relations to be based on mutual hostility. The nature of relations between contiguous states or polities across the world and over time teaches us that such relations vary dramatically, can change, and may include a mixture of cooperation and conflict simultaneously depending on the multitude of issues that make up the relationship. The question is not whether relations will be conflictual or consensual, but what are the circumstances under which they become conflictual or consensual. A further issue is how conflict—an essential element in any political relationship and one that can be more productive than consensus—is managed.

Full answers to these questions cannot be provided not least because any relationship is defined by both or all parties to the relationship. The UK government has no reason to suggest that relations will be cordial but seeks to suggest that any relationship with Scotland after independence will be fraught with conflict. If that is to be believed, then it means that the interests of Scotland have diverged significantly from the rest of the UK or that one or both governments will seek a confrontational relationship without divergent interests. The latter seems implausible and the former suggests that the union lacks logic. A more convincing argument is that relations would be positive as Scotland and England share so much in common that union makes sense in this congress of interests. Politicians in campaigning mode behave adversarially but govern pragmatically through compromise and seeking agreement. The most likely situation is that relations will generally be cordial with episodic conflicts based on different interests that will be managed reasonably well.

Each state's independence will change over time. Independence is not an absolute nor is it immutable. Throughout most of its history, the SNP supported 'self-government' and only formally adopted independence in 2004 when it reformed its constitution though self-government had long come to be seen as synonymous with independence inside the party. Self-government had been the formulation agreed at the party's foundation permitting it to allow the predominantly left-wing supporters of independence to unite with its less radical and sometimes right-wing supporters of what would later be called devolution. Over time, the debate became one of whether devolution would offer a stepping stone to independence or inhibit progress towards that goal. But independence operated more as a slogan that mobilized its supporters than a fully worked out constitutional scheme. There were efforts, notably in the late 1970s, to draft a constitution for an independent Scotland and frequent references throughout the party's history to Scotland belonging to a community of British nations but little effort went into defining independence precisely. There was little need as it rarely looked imminent and it would have been pointless as changed circumstances would have required a redefinition.

Since devolution and especially as the SNP support rose, the party has been obliged to define independence more fully. This has forced it to confront difficult choices and adopt a pragmatic approach. It has recognized the need to appeal to public opinion and reassure potential supporters that independence is not state autarchy, isolationism, border controls, and the caricature of Scottish independence suggested by its opponents. This has led to criticisms from its opponents that what was being proposed is 'independence-lite', a diluted version of independence. Scottish independence is simply taking a more concrete form after being a slogan for decades. In the process of definition, it has become clearer that Scotland's constitutional status will not be finally resolved with independence. Scotland's relations with the rest of the UK will remain not only intimate but institutionally connected and require periodic renegotiation in key areas of the economy, including the currency and defence. There will be inherited treaty obligations, most of which will be happily accepted but some would be unacceptable. The extent to which there will be scope for renegotiation may prove limited and will depend on the resources and will on both sides of the negotiations. Scotland's scope for autonomy with independence will, like every state in the world, be limited and ever-changing.

NATIONAL IDENTITY

J. M. Reid was quoted at the start of this book. He had written that the Scottish nation was anomalous in continuing to exist without being a state. The sense of Scottish nationhood is now remarkably strong. There is no credible voice arguing for the full assimilation of Scotland into the UK. But there never was. Walker Connor famously referred to the creation of states as involving 'nation destroying', with assimilationist plans to impose a sense of belonging that required the eradication of identities that might compete with identity with the state. There was never and unlikely to be such a nation-building project by a UK government that wants to avoid resurrecting demands for independence in the aftermath of a vote against independence. There may be a temptation for UK and Scottish governments to engage in a Manichean competition in nation-building. A more relaxed attitude to national identity makes more sense. This is a battle neither has much chance of 'winning'. Neither Scottish nor British identities are likely to disappear. Attempts to undermine one identity are more likely to provoke a backlash. There is nothing natural about either identity but there is equally nothing to suggest that either is incompatible with almost any constitutional structure nor are these identities mutually incompatible. J. M. Reid's concerns were ill-founded. Constitutional status is not alone in determining national identity.

If there are threats to Scottish national identity they are more likely to come from economic and social forces rather than deliberately constructed government efforts to eradicate a sense of Scottishness or Britishness. The existence of the Scottish Parliament is only one, albeit highly important, reason to believe that Scottish identity is secure. The decline of the Scottish press means that what had once been an important transmitter of a sense of Scottish identity has declined and will likely continue to decline further. The demise of the Scottish press might have led to concerns in the past for the future of Scottish identity but few today expect that this will happen. Equally, the end of union will not end the sense of Britishness. British identity may have closer associations with the existing state than Scottish identity has ever had with any constitutional or governmental structures. But this does not mean Britishness will disappear when dissociated from the state. Both identities would be very hollow if unable to survive Scottish independence.

Identities are malleable, capable of finding life in inhospitable conditions. Even as one means of conveying the sense of identity is undermined, there is every likelihood that some alternative will emerge or become more important in transmitting national identity to future generations. Modernization failed to have the predicted impact of eradicating sub-state national and other identities. Neither the railways nor television led to the eradication of local identities. Indeed, the sense of identity can grow when threatened and in its growth it can find alternative means of becoming resilient. We have little idea of how future social and economic changes will affect identities. It may be that developments beyond social media might lead to more atomization, undermining any sense of community. The threat to Scottish and British national identities may come not from an alternative usurping identity but from any form of collective identity. So far as it is possible to imagine, and it must be stressed that our capabilities for imagining in this respect are limited, threats to national identity in the future are difficult to discern. The paradox of identity has been noted earlier in this book. An identity can become stronger even when institutions associated with it decline.

It is the sense of Britishness that has become problematic over half a century on from J. M. Reid's concerns for the survival of the Scottish nation. The identity that was so strong that it was largely unquestioned has been the focus of limited academic and political attention until relatively recently. What it means to be British is now explored and debated as had Scottishness previously, though this has less to do with the Scottish Question than the European Question. The 'Other' against which Britishness—and this applies at least equally to Englishness—is defined is Europe, 'Brussels', or some such variant. Britishness can no more be pinned down than Scottishness. Even in the event of Scottish independence, however defined, there seems every reason to believe that a sense of Britishness will endure.

SCOTTISH SELF-IMAGE AND RADICALISM

Scotland's collective self-image, at least amongst many commentators, has long been that of a radical leftist polity. This self-image was a function of an oppositional political culture. Scottish politics was defined as distinct in what it opposed rather than what it supported. In everyday public policy terms, Scotland's radicalism was more an aspiration and a mobilizing slogan than a serious set of policy prescriptions or programme. There is nothing unusual in myths informing political debate. Myths create ideals and mobilize opinion. But in Scotland, radical myths have been used to evade difficult issues. A party, movement, or indeed nation that expresses its radicalism by reference to myths and historical allusions rather than using these to mobilize opinion in favour of change is living in the past.

Radical Scotland has barely been evident under devolved government. The pragmatism and desire to win more resources for Scotland under devolution and occasionally striking out on a new route diverging from the rest of the UK owes more to Walter Elliot, Tom Johnston, and Willie Ross than to the Red Clydesiders. When Lord Acton famously commented that power corrupts he had the medieval Church in mind, not modern democracies. There is as much evidence that power granted democratically does not corrupt but matures and encourages compromise. The source of government power before devolution lay outside Scotland, though there were ample sources within Scotland in local authorities and numerous other non-state bodies but no Scotland-wide directly elected authority. This encouraged an oppositional and grievance political culture. The absence of power was corrupting in this limited sense. It encouraged a debilitating oppositional grievance culture masquerading as radicalism. Devolved government contributed to a more mature form of politics. But the nature of devolution ensured that it remained essentially oppositional. This was less evident in the early years when public finances provided increasing sums of public money. There was little to complain about in terms of the familiar claims that Scotland did not receive enough public money. The system was awash with money. That has now changed and we are likely to return to the old-fashioned grievances, regardless of which party or parties are in government in Edinburgh. While reforms to devolution brought about by the UK government, initiated by Labour and completed by the Conservative–Lib-Dem coalition, may have a solid rational foundation, reforms are unlikely to eradicate grievances within any system of inter-governmental relations. Institutional design can only play a limited part in altering perceptions.

PUBLIC POLICY CHALLENGES

Key elements of the Scottish Question have been public policy challenges. Historically poor economic growth rates, an appalling health record, and social problems that have competed with the worst in Western Europe gave rise to demands from public and private institutions in Scotland, often combining in an effective 'Scottish lobby', which tended to focus on defending ailing industries and asking for more resources to tackle the consequences of decline and social conditions. It was never difficult to make the case that Scotland's problems deserved more money. The UK Treasury was generous in response so long as a case could be made and it was unlikely to have spillover consequences in encouraging similar demands from other parts of the UK. This generosity has to be understood from two perspectives. First, there can be no doubt that Scotland has not been treated as an internal colony in which the centre stripped Scots of their assets and offered no compensation. It is legitimate to raise questions about successive UK governments' mishandling of the revenues from North Sea oil, though this mishandling goes well beyond the question of how Scotland has been treated. Leaving aside the Scottish Question, the UK has had a poor record in taking advantage of the oil wealth. Future economic historians, especially those engaged in comparative research, are likely to be highly critical of the failure of successive UK governments to establish an oil fund, whether for Scotland or for the UK. Second, it is important to consider why such generosity was necessary. In part, it has been due to the strength of the Scottish lobby and willingness of UK governments to treat Scotland differently, in this case, more generously than other parts of the UK. But it has also been because Scotland has not been a beneficiary of many mainstream policies made in London. Economic policy has been dominated by the interests of the core of the state. It should be stressed that England is not the core. Parts of England have suffered at least as much, and in some cases much more than Scotland. The Scottish lobby ensured that Scotland had a voice that has been absent or less effective in England's regions. Scotland's poor economic and social record is hardly a reason to commend UK public policy-making. Generous financial policies are compensation for the failure of mainstream policies. But such generosity has not created conditions under which the underlying problems are addressed. The 'solution' to Scottish problems has traditionally been to increase expenditure.

Devolved government improved matters to some extent. The Parliament has focused on some of Scotland's underlying problems within its limited powers. The ban on smoking will have a greater impact on long-term health than the considerable increases in expenditure on the National Health Service in Scotland over the first decade of devolution. The period of rapid growth in expenditure was a lost opportunity, second only to the wasted opportunity that the oil wealth offered. There was no strategy to focus on using this wealth to tackle underlying economic and social problems. Indeed, much of this increased resource has created more problems in encouraging expenditure on policies that have certainly allowed Scotland to diverge in public policy terms from elsewhere but not necessarily tackling underlying problems. But the most challenging aspect of these divergent policies from the early years of devolution has been that they have also created interests that previously did not exist and will now resist any attempt to reverse the policy. Scotland's care for the elderly was not 'free'. Policies create interests as often as interests create policies. In this case, a large and powerful interest has been created that will feel abandoned and object if this policy were to be reversed. The cost of this policy will grow over time as the elderly component in Scotland's population grows. Scotland's fiscal position lies at the heart of the Scottish Question, transcending public policy and constitutional dimensions.

The economic and fiscal crisis of 2007 is likely to have a greater impact on Scottish public policy than the outcome of the referendum, regardless of the outcome. The Labour–Lib-Dem Scottish coalition commissioned a report in 2005 that was made public after the SNP came to power. *Choices for a Purpose* set out the challenges both in how policy was made and in the constraints that were likely to lie ahead, even before the financial crisis. An Independent Budget Review group, set up by the SNP government at the suggestion of the Conservatives in the Scottish Parliament, issued a report in July 2010 setting out the challenges following the crisis. These documents, sponsored by all major parties in the Parliament, are sober reading. Combine these with reports from independent bodies such as the Institute for Fiscal Studies on the likely future prospects for UK public finance and there can be little doubt that some difficult decisions lie ahead if Scotland remains in the union. An independent Scotland will also face difficult decisions.

Public spending will become much tighter after the referendum. There is a fear that rejection of independence will encourage London to assert its authority and use the opportunity of a weakened Scottish government to cut Scottish spending further and faster than might otherwise have happened. It is near certain that London will be accused of this by whichever party or parties are in government in Edinburgh. The key to a stable and mature relationship would be to remove any opportunity for this to happen but this will prove difficult, if not impossible. Neither the SNP nor Labour will want to take sides with the Tories in London. Any future Labour government in London would face a very different scenario from that which operated during the first decade of devolution. Scottish Labour might find itself in the unenviable position of having to defend the cuts 'imposed' by a Labour government at Westminster reviving accusations that it is London's poodle.

But, public policy is not only about spending. The Scottish Parliament is becoming more imaginative in this respect. The smoking ban, energy and environmental targets, and efforts to shift the policy agenda to economic growth all speak of a more mature politics. The challenge has been and will increasingly come to be finding means of addressing Scotland's endemic problems using limited tools. Taxation and much welfare policy are retained at Westminster but there would be limited choice even if these matters were devolved or if Scotland became independent. There appears to be little appetite on the part of Scotland's political parties to shift the balance in tax-and-spend. Any attempt to address the maldistribution of wealth in Scotland, which the two main parties appear to agree is a major source of Scotland's problems though not a diagnosis shared with the Conservatives, requires identifying powers that would not lead to top earners fleeing Scotland. If some means could be found, there would need to be a willingness to use such powers. The extent to which this has failed to be addressed other than by a fringe amongst advocates on independence is notable.

TOWARDS PUBLIC POLICY INDEPENDENCE

A number of themes have recurred throughout this book. The Scottish Question is not one question but a series of inter-related questions and issues. Each has been important in defining what makes Scottish politics distinct. What has often made Scotland politically distinct has not always been positive nor has it always been honest. Success in Scottish politics has often been measured by how much money could be wrung out of the Treasury. The Scottish lobby became expert in defending existing institutions and industries. Scottishness often became an end in itself. An adversarial political culture, as Scottish as it is British, combined with radical rhetoric to hide a failure to confront many of Scotland's endemic social and economic problems. Devolved government combined with a period of growth in spending postponed facing up to Scotland's endemic problems. Devolution had been established as a defensive institution and the parties and participants in decision-making have taken time to articulate a positive case for devolution.

The emphasis in much post-devolution commentary has been on whether Scotland has diverged from the rest of the UK in public policy terms, an understandable and important matter. But this limiting focus ignores the much more challenging divergence that is required. Scotland needs to diverge in policy prescriptions and more importantly in social and economic outcomes from its own past whether this involves diverging, running in parallel, or even converging with policy decisions elsewhere in the UK. It is inevitable that Scottish policy-makers will constantly look over their shoulders to see what happens in England, not least because England offers important lessons, but a more independent polity would be one that is more relaxed about whether or not Scotland diverges from the rest of the

UK. In this respect, Scotland has yet to meet a key test of devolution, to abandon a high-profile policy that might currently be distinctly Scottish in favour of a policy that is more appropriate to Scottish needs, whether or not it involves convergence with the rest of the UK. This amounts to a form of non-constitutional independence that all parties and policy-makers should aspire to achieve. It is more likely to be achieved followed constitutional independence, not least given the additional tools available, but ought to be an objective within any constitutional structure. Public policy independence is conceptually distinct from constitutional independence. It involves Scottish policy-makers making decisions that go beyond the rhetoric of Scottish control of Scottish affairs.

CONCLUSION

A theme of this book has been that changes in the Scottish Question have arisen through changes that are not directly related to specifically Scottish matters. Most notable in this respect during the twentieth century have been changes in the remit and activities of the state and what citizens expect from the state. But social and economic changes, quite separate from government policies and political behaviour, are by far the most important. It is always difficult to predict what may happen in the future but the most obvious changes that are occurring are changes in welfare and the economy. It seems most likely that the sense of Scottish identity will be least affected by whatever happens in this respect. The old concern that Scotland was anomalous as a nation without being a state is now irrelevant. Nations can exist without states even though states require some sense of nationhood to survive.

The referendum is framed in strictly Manichean terms though the Scottish Question has never been posed in this way. Whatever happens in the referendum, the Question will remain unanswered definitively not least because it is more than one question but crucially because it includes a series of relationships that need to be addressed anew in each generation. These relationships are, like nations, daily plebiscites. There can be no final resolution to the Scottish Question for that reason.

Bibliographical Essay

In a bibliographical essay written over thirty years ago, Chris Allen described the study of Scottish politics and society as a bit like the nation's teeth: most notable for its gaps. That is no longer quite so true. Over the last three decades, there has been a massive growth in the output of historians, political scientists, and sociologists as well as first-hand accounts of events and developments in Scotland. There are now a number of substantial overviews of Scotland since the union or works that focus on particular periods. The most notable change has been in the output of scholars and commentators focused on the twentieth century, especially the most recent period. Many of the issues tackled can be included under the umbrella of the 'Scottish Question'. Attempting to cover the range of issues over such a period of time has only been possible by building on some of this vast output. This book has also been informed by wider literatures and debates, on the nature of national identity, the relations between nations and states, the public policy literature and wider discussions of state and society. There has been a conscious effort to avoid cramming the pages with references to literature or limiting the readership to a narrow academic audience. However, throughout the text, there are references to particular works that deserve special attention because what has been written was particularly interesting, unusual, or challenging. These have included non-academic as often as academic works. The opening paragraph of the book quotes a journalist, well known in his day though largely forgotten today, commenting on what he feared was the anomaly of a nation without a state. My intention has been to recognize contemporary work and opinions wherever possible and avoid the danger, more prevalent amongst my fellow political scientists than historians, to view the past through the lens of the present.

The work also makes use of primary sources gathered over the last three decades in archives in Scotland and England, interpretations from notes of events, meetings, and interviews attended or conducted by the author over that period of time. The National Archives and National Archives of Scotland remain under-explored as far as the issues and debates covered in this book are concerned. It is hoped that some of the archival nuggets discussed in these pages might stimulate others to go in search of more. This is not nor can it be a comprehensive account, but it aims to inform the debates on the Scottish Question in the knowledge that this Question cannot be answered definitively.

This brief bibliographical essay focuses on books rather than academic articles though articles have been hugely important in informing this work. Suffice to say that the authors cited below have in almost every case contributed to journals in short and lengthy articles that have had an influence on this book. The list of journals consulted over many years includes those from a variety of disciplines including economics, history, law, planning, politics, and sociology as well as some multi-disciplinary and many more non-academic works. Journals that have been most important in recent years and easily accessible have included the *Scottish Government Yearbooks* which became *Scottish Affairs* and the various Scottish history journals. There is no political science journal devoted to Scottish politics but articles with a Scottish focus have been published in most of the main UK journals and a number of the world's leading journals. This applies equally to sociology where, again, key articles with a Scottish focus have been published in top mainstream journals. Economics is different as there have been journals with a Scottish focus, though even where 'Scottish' appears in the title there is no guarantee that a focus on Scotland will be found in all articles. The most relevant economic works are in journals with an applied focus, *Fraser of Allander* publications being good examples. There are numerous journals which publish on regional, planning, local government, housing, and educational matters. These include some with a focus on Scotland but mostly the Scottish content finds its way into journals without any particular geographic or, at least, one which has a broader geographic focus.

General Surveys and Works of Synthesis

In recent years, a number of important books have been published that have influenced this study. Tom Devine's *The Scottish Nation* (2000) is a compendium of facts, interpretations, and rigorous research. It builds on earlier similar syntheses of Scottish historical analysis including his own path-breaking work on the Highlands and transatlantic trade. Michael Lynch's *Scotland: A New History* (1992) and T. C. Smout's *A History of the Scottish People* (1969) and *A Century of the Scottish People* (1986) remain important books that have been seminal works in understanding Scottish history. R. A. Houston and W. W. Knox's *The New Penguin History of Scotland* (2001) brings together a good range of scholarship in one volume. It is important, however, not to lose sight of other historical works that are not focused on Scotland. This book has been heavily influenced by the scholarship of historical social scientists who have sought to identify key cleavages in European society and understand the process of state-building and nation-building. The work of Stein Rokkan, Norwegian historian and political scientist, continues to be the main influence on my work, as will be evident in the framework adopted to discuss developments in Scotland, and including S. M. Lipset and S. Rokkan's classic four-fold cleavage structures in their chapter in *Party Systems and Voter Alignments*, the volume of essays they edited in 1967. Their four-fold classification—the centre–periphery and state–religion cleavages that formed around the time of state formation, and the urban–rural and class cleavages that emerged around the Industrial Revolution—is a useful framework for analysing the Scottish Question. In addition, this book has been heavily influenced by Rokkan's later work, in collaboration with Derek Urwin, on the territorial nature of state formation. At the time of his death in 1979, he had been working on classifying state formation in Europe into four types: unitary, union, mechanical, and organic federations. This resulted in a short historical overview, *Economy, Territory, Identity* (1983), completed after Rokkan's death by Derek Urwin, and *The Politics of Territorial Identity* (1982), an edited volume of essays in which Derek Urwin wrote the essay on the UK. Derek Urwin wrote a short book, *The Alchemy of Delayed Nationalism: Politics, Cultural Identity and Economic Expectations in Scotland* (1978), which was published by the University of Bergen and has not received the attention it deserved, in this author's opinion, as one of the finest works to employ the skills of historical social science in its historical breadth and social science rigour, combining an eye for detail without losing sight of the broader themes.

Much of my own work has built on Rokkan's classification of state formation and applying it to the development of the UK. The orthodox notion of the UK as a unitary state has given way to a new orthodoxy that the UK is a union state. However, with orthodoxy comes intellectual laziness. It is remarkable how few of those—political scientists, historians, and lawyers—who refer to the UK as a union state have really added anything to this idea or have given Rokkan the respect he deserves by seriously and critically engaging with his work. As argued in my *Devolution in the UK* (2009), it is difficult to apply the term to the UK as a whole, given the variety of unions that make up the UK. On reflection, it is both too glib and too parochial to simply refer to the UK as a union state. The UK is better understood today as a state of unions. Also, each of these unions, including that affecting Scotland, has been dynamic. We need to understand the dynamics of each union. This book is an attempt to build on my earlier work, which in turn owes an enormous debt to a wide range of scholars crossing a range of disciplines, including historians and political scientists but also, crucially, sociologists and economists.

Various works by Christopher Harvie remain fresh and provocative, in the very best sense, and most notable works are *Scotland and Nationalism* (1st edition 1977 but subsequently updated at irregular intervals including a 4th edition in 2004), *No Gods and Precious Few Heroes* (3rd edition 1998), and *Scotland: A Short History* (2002). *No Gods* was originally one of the New History of Scotland series published by Edinburgh University Press, which included works by Bruce Lenman and Olive and Sydney Checkland. Amongst the most provocative and important works have been a number written by Michael Fry. Michael Fry has relished and thrived intellectually in his status as an outsider amongst professional, i.e. academic, historians. It has had a healthy effect on his willingness and ability to bring fresh insights and sharp, challenging interpretations of the past and present.

Twentieth-century Scotland is now far better understood than it was two decades ago thanks to a number of complementary works. Iain Hutchison's *Scottish Politics in the Twentieth Century* (2000) is a short but packed book that takes forward the story in his *Political History of Scotland, 1832–1924* (1986). Richard Finlay's *Modern Scotland, 1914–2000* (2004) was followed by Ewen Cameron's *Impaled Upon A Thistle: Scotland since 1880* (2010) and Catriona MacDonald's *Whaur Extremes Meet* (2009). These works cover similar ground but in different ways, each bringing something fresh and new to our understanding of Scotland's past and each reflecting the particular expertise and research backgrounds of the author. These historians have set high standards.

The Union

There are many works on the Anglo-Scottish union and the bicentenary of the union in 2007 saw a number of new publications. These range from highly polemical works that use history as covers for conducting a debate on Scotland's future constitutional status to serious scholarly works. The most recent batch of books on the union include Allan Macinnes's *Union and Empire* (2007) which offers a fresh perspective and sets the union within the wider European context and the emergence of the British Empire. Douglas Watt's *The Price of Scotland: Darien, Union and the Wealth of Nations* (2007) is a fine piece of history that explores the financial consequences of the Darien disaster by an author equally qualified as an historian and expert in finance. Christopher Whatley's *The Scots and the Union* (2007) was another scholarly work published to mark the bicentenary of the union. Michael Fry set out to write a celebration of the union but ended up producing a work that led him to support independence with *The Union: England, Scotland and the Treaty of Union* (2007). There remains much yet to be written on the subject of the union, though there is little that can be written about on what happened over two centuries ago that can shed light on what should happen in the future.

Social History and Politics

Scotland's social history has been well documented by a range of historians who have interpreted Scotland's past from a variety of perspectives. The relationships between class and nation—competing, conflictual, and reinforcing— have been explored in W. W. Knox's *Industrial Nation* (1999); Keith Aitken's *Bairns o' Adam* (1997) is a history of the Scottish Trades Union Congress. Jim Phillips's *The Industrial Politics of Devolution* (2008) is an important work that draws out this relationship between the labour and national movements in the 1960s and 1970s in Scotland well. Industrialization cannot be divorced from urbanization and changes in society more generally. There are many studies of urban Scotland including books on the main urban centres. One of the most original and stimulating is Robert Crawford's *On Glasgow and Edinburgh* (2013). Crawford explores the symbiotic, competitive, and ultimately linked histories of these two cities written by a poet and professor of literature based in St Andrew's. Rural Scotland, especially the Highlands and Islands, has been well covered. The Highland Clearances remain highly controversial and provoked a classic example of Scottish 'flyting' between Tom Devine and Michael Fry. This is a subject that has attracted the attention of historians outside the academy. John Prebble's *The Highland Clearances* (1963) is probably the best-known work. Devine's works include *Clanship to Crofters' War: The Social Transformation of the Scottish Highlands (1994) and The Great Highland Famine* (1988) while Fry's controversial interpretation, *Wild Scots: Four Hundred Years of Highland History*, was published in 2005.

The role of religion in Scottish life is difficult to underestimate but that is exactly what has happened in many histories. Scotland is unusual in the relationship between religion, state, and society, partly due to the role of immigration. Parties of the right across Europe have generally drawn disproportionate support from the Catholic community whereas the Labour Party, and very recently the SNP, has been the main recipient of Catholic votes. The reason is relatively easily explained by understanding this vote as having been an immigrant and minority community vote. Callum Brown has made a major contribution here especially with his *Religion and Society in Scotland since 1707* (1997) and subsequent works. This is an area that remains shrouded in sensationalist and unsubtle commentary. Ian Budge and Derek Urwin's seminal political science book, *Scottish Political Behaviour: A Case Study in British Homogeneity* (1966) identified the relationship between religion and the vote which has been explored in many subsequent works.

Scotland's Fascination with Lost Causes and Missing Histories

The late Jim Bulpitt, Thatcherite political scientist, frequently complained that there was more work published on political failures and parties and movements of the left than on the Conservative Party. He would compare the volumes on the Independent Labour Party and Red Clydeside with those on the Primrose League, an organization that supported 'God, Queen and Country and the Conservative cause', despite the latter having vastly more members. His key point has been particularly true in Scotland where a vast literature exists on the politics of nationalism, long before the Scottish National Party became the major force in Scottish politics that it became after devolution, and on various left-wing parties and organizations. His observation could equally be made about the relative dearth of serious works on the governance of Scotland until relatively recently. As well as my own *Conservatives and the Union* (1990), there is David Seawright's important alternative perspective on the Scottish Tories in *An Important Matter of Principle* (1999) and more recently David Stewart's *The Path to Devolution and Change* (2009). David Torrance has offered a helpful revisionist view of the Thatcher years in *We in Scotland* (2009). David Torrance has also become a successful biographer of establishment figures in Scottish politics. His biography of George Younger, *George Younger: A Life Well Lived* (2008), demonstrates the importance of empathy, though not necessarily sympathy, with the subject in writing a biography. His less well-known work, *Noel Skelton and the Property-Owning Democracy* (2010) on an early twentieth-century Scottish Tory, credited with inventing the phrase 'property-owning democracy', is a fascinating read that brings ideas and personalities from the first half of the twentieth century to life.

There are now fewer works being published on Red Clydeside than in the past. This may reflect exhaustion in a debate that saw historians argue over minute details in what amounted to historical trench warfare. This debate had a lasting legacy in the myth of Radical Scotland, the idea that Scotland was particularly left-wing. This legacy is the subject of scrutiny in this book. The orthodox historical view is that Scotland's radicalism has at least been exaggerated. It has certainly been very narrowly focused. There appears little radicalism in the male-dominated, illiberal nature of Scottish politics and society. Roger Davidson and Gayle Davis's *The Sexual State: Sexuality and Scottish Governance, 1950–80* (2012) is a brilliant work of social and political history. These authors have trawled the archives and other sources to produce a study that focuses on sexual offences, reproductive issues, sexual health and education, censorship, and pornography over a thirty-year period. What is striking from today's perspective has been the speed of change in the period after that covered in this book. There have been a number of works on women in Scotland in recent times that highlight the historic under-representation of women in public offices as well as studies of the role of women in Scottish society and economy. Esther Breitenbach and Eleanor Gordon edited two volumes of essays, *The World is Ill-Divided* (1990) and *Out of Bounds* (1992). There remains much more to be studied and written about women in Scotland. A number of authors have contributed books, essays, and articles of women in contemporary Scotland over the last two decades including notable contributions by Alice Brown and Fiona Mackay.

Nationalism and National Identity

The national movement and SNP have been well served by historians and political scientists. Amongst the most notable is *Welsh and Scottish Nationalism* (1954) by Sir Reginald Coupland. Coupland died before he had completed the work, but it remains an important source, offering an unusual interpretation by a prominent historian of the British Empire. H. J. Hanham's *Scottish Nationalism* (1969) builds on Coupland and was written in the aftermath of the

Hamilton by-election but it is marred by having been written hurriedly. Keith Webb's *The Growth of Nationalism in Scotland* (1978) is a lively account and more useful than Hanham's. Much mythology surrounds the national movement and too much has been based on extremely limited engagement with sources. John MacCormick's *Flag in the Wind* (1955) is still too often treated as if it were the work of an historian rather than a highly partial account of a player keen to ensure that his version of events becomes accepted.

Richard Finlay's *Independent and Free: Scottish Politics and the Origins of the Scottish National Party, 1928–1945* (1994) brought rigour and forensic analysis to our understanding of the early years of the SNP. Paula Somerville's *Through the Maelstrom* (2013) takes that history from 1945 to 1967 with the same meticulous eye for detail and rigorous engagement with archival material. But such serious history still competes with the repetition of myths in some popular, journalistic accounts. Jack Brand's *The National Movement in Scotland* (1978) remains the best political science book on Scottish nationalism, drawing on historical sources and solid social science methods, though it was published a quarter of a century ago.

Sociologists have made a huge contribution to our understanding of national identity. Foremost amongst these has been David McCrone whose *Understanding Scotland: The Sociology of a Nation* (2001) was originally published with the subtitle, *The Sociology of a Stateless Nation* (1992). This lucid account is complemented by his study *The Sociology of Nationalism* (1998). The study of national identity in Scotland has also provided us with a mass of data and analysis but also a lot of rather superficial work. There is a tendency to use national identity as a repository for anything that cannot be explained. Serious scholars such as David McCrone have been careful to situate their research within wider debates, but too many assert the importance of national identity and 'culture' almost as givens or even as if culture is an explanatory variable rather than something demanding explanation.

Government and Public Policy

Works on the system of government have been relatively uncommon especially those explaining the operation and interactions of different 'levels' of government. Short explanatory texts were commonly published in the past when major new Acts of Parliament were passed including those reforming local administration. Key figures in local government wrote books outlining how the system worked and, in some cases, making the case for reform. Mabel Atkinson's *Local Government in Scotland* (1923) is one of the most interesting works. Sir W. E. Whyte was an important author of standard works—including books and published lectures—on the development of Scottish local government, public health, and housing in the early part of the twentieth century. In both cases, they had a keen sense of history and would set contemporary developments within a broader historical context. Town planners produced reports at various intervals, including the Clyde Valley Plan referred to in this book, that are important sources. John Percival Day's *Public Administration in the Highlands and Islands of Scotland* (1918) may have focused on the Highlands and Islands but is one of the best accounts of how public administration developed in Scotland to the start of the nineteenth century. C. de B. Murray's *How Scotland is Governed* (1938) is a short statement on the system of government on the eve of the Second World War. Works such as *A Source Book and History of Administrative Law in Scotland* edited by M. R. McLarty and G. Campbell H. Paton (1956) brought together some eminent public servants and others to reflect on past governmental arrangements. This work is legalistic but a solid basis for understanding administrative and governmental arrangements. It is less dry than Sir David Milne's *The Scottish Office* (1957), one of the new Whitehall Series, written by Whitehall Permanent Secretaries. A livelier account of the Scottish Office was produced by John Gibson, a retired Scottish Office civil servant, to mark the centenary of the Office's establishment. Gibson's *The Thistle and the Crown* (1985) drew on earlier works including George Pottinger's *The Secretaries of State for Scotland, 1926–76* (1979). Pottinger was another former (but this time disgraced) civil servant. Essays in a book edited by J. N. Wolfe, *Government and Nationalism in Scotland* (1969) remain useful on a range of government and political developments.

Ian Levitt has written extensively on Scottish government and public policy, drawing heavily on his research in the National Archives of Scotland. My own work has trodden similar archival ground. As well as his study of the poor law, *Poverty and Welfare in Scotland, 1890–1948* (1988), and many articles, he has edited two volumes of papers drawn from the archives with commentaries that are useful to anyone seeking to understand the development of the modern state in Scotland. These are *Government and Social Conditions in Scotland, 1845–1919* (1988) and *The Scottish Office: Depression and Reconstruction, 1919–1959* (1992). My own study, *Governing Scotland: The Invention of Administrative Devolution* (2003), attempts to explain the origins and early development of the Scottish Office. The reports of two Royal Commissions offered useful information, especially the evidence submitted to them, *The Royal Commission on Scottish Affairs* (1954) and the *Royal Commission on the Constitution* (1973). In each case, more valuable information can be obtained in the National Archives of debates within Whitehall and papers prepared for submission and in response to these Commissions.

Political and Social Science and the Scottish Question

There is no distinctly Scottish political science, nor should there be. But Scottish politics has been studied by political scientists as case studies, comparatively or within some broader canvas. The seminal work on Scottish politics was James Kellas's *The Scottish Political System* (first published in 1973 reaching its 4th edition in 1989). There has since been no work that has offered such a coherent overview of Scottish politics. British general elections have now been covered by Nuffield studies in each election since 1945. Each book has included at least some reference to Scotland and some include a chapter devoted to Scotland. These are invaluable guides and the coverage of the election in Scotland in each tells us much about Scotland's salience in that election. The scientific study of elections through survey research began in the early 1960s and public opinion surveys of each general election now exist from that time. Budge and Urwin's aforementioned book on Scottish political behaviour was amongst the first scientific study of Scottish public opinion. This scientific turn in the social sciences coincided with the rise of the SNP and there were many studies, usually small scale and focused, of attitudes and behaviour in Scotland. Interest in Scottish political behaviour has waxed and waned with support for the SNP. A separate Scottish election study was conducted in 1974, following the SNP's breakthrough, but interest declined after 1979 only to return with a study of the 1992 election. The 1979 referendum resulted in *The Referendum Experience*, a volume of essays co-edited by J. Bochel, D. Denver, and A. Macartney (1981). William Miller's *The End of British Politics?* (1981) seemed an odd title for a book focusing on English and Scottish political behaviour published shortly after the failure of devolution—but it proved prescient. Lynn Bennie, Jack Brand, and I conducted the first Scottish Election Study in over a decade resulting in *How Scotland Votes* (1997). Colleagues in Edinburgh University subsequently produced a series of works based on survey research that went well beyond election studies including important work on national identity and gender. Alice Brown, David McCrone, and Lindsay Paterson along with other colleagues contributed to an important time series with data that tracked changes in public opinion across a range of social and political, including constitutional, issues. The 1997 referendum was the subject of a research monograph, *Scotland Decides: The Devolution Issue and the 1997 Referendum* (2000). There have been a series of books and articles studying Scottish political behaviour and public opinion including works based on the Scottish Social Attitudes Survey by a variety of authors including Hugh Bochel, John Curtice, David Denver, Rob Johns, Charles Pattie, Chris Carman, and the aforementioned colleagues in Edinburgh University. There has been no lack of survey data and analysis in recent decades.

The study of public policy and government by political scientists has followed a similar pattern. Interest has again waxed and waned but has been reasonably consistent since devolution. Arthur Midwinter and Michael Keating made major contributions, notably with their *The Government of Scotland* (1983) and subsequent works especially by Midwinter on local government and on public policy more broadly by Keating. One of the most notable works was Chris Moore and Simon Booth's *Managing Competition* (1989). This review has focused on more general works though this book has benefited from consulting many specialized works. One highly specialized work that deserves attention is Henrik Halkier's *Institutions, Discourse and Regional Development: The Scottish Development Agency and the Politics of Regional Policy* (2006), a hefty theoretically informed tome that tracks the emergence of the idea of a special development agency for Scotland and its evolution from inception through to major reforms.

Devolution since 1999

The literature on devolution has been immense. Devolution remains a relatively recent development and it may be too early to judge its impact or trajectory. The literature on devolution has tended to focus on the extent to which devolution is different and has allowed Scotland to diverge from the rest of the UK whether in voting behaviour, policy-making, or policies pursued. Michael Keating's *The Government of Scotland* (2nd edition, 2010) is the best single-volume work on the subject. Journalism remains an important source though devolution has done little for the quality of the Scottish press. But while there may be problems with the press, Scotland still has a number of high quality political journalists who operate against a difficult backdrop of falling circulation and pressure from on high to move downmarket in their reporting. Brian Taylor and Hamish MacDonell have each produced books that offer overviews of the debate drawing on their experience of watching Scottish politics very closely. Detailed monitoring of devolution took place by a team of academics in the early years of devolution. This resulted in quarterly and annual reports that were made available on the webpage of University College London. These provide much data on the early years of devolution.

Memoirs, Biographies, and Autobiographies

Personal accounts, memoirs, autobiography, and biography often bring a subject quite literally to life and there has been a growth in this genre. The instant biographies written by journalists about a subject who is still alive, and worst of all before their retirement, are rarely interesting or offering the kind of insights of value to a serious study. But works based on empathy, placing the subject within the wider social, economic, and political context can offer perspectives otherwise absent in less humanized forms of writings. Memoirs and autobiographies have to be treated with care but nonetheless are useful sources. There has never been a biography of any major Scottish figure that comes close to Robert Caro's magisterial biographical volumes on Lyndon Johnson, but then there is no biography of any major UK political figure that comes close to it in ambition or in skill in placing its subject in the wider social, economic, and political context. We do have a number of biographies, written to grab a headline, that are as quickly forgotten as they were written. Our public figures—and this includes a much wider circle than politicians—should be encouraged to keep diaries, write memoirs, and allow access to well-preserved private papers.

The Independence Referendum

The referendum on independence has been good for business for academics and commentators writing about Scotland. Michael Keating's *The Independence of Scotland* (2009) is a balanced and thoughtful book. Gavin McCrone, retired after a career as a civil servant during which he wrote a now famous memorandum discussed in this book on the opportunities afforded to Scotland by North Sea oil in the 1970s, has written *Scottish Independence: Weighing Up the Economics* (2013), which offers a reasoned and accessible account of one dimension of the debate. A series of essay edited by Gerry Hassan and myself, *After Independence* (2013), considers a range of opportunities and challenges that independence would bring, written by leading authorities across a wide range of fields. The referendum has stimulated interest in Scotland today and in its past. It is unlikely that this interest will disappear regardless of the result.

Index

Index